Money and liberty in modern Europe

Money and liberty in modern Europe

A critique of historical understanding

WILLIAM M. REDDY

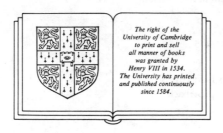

The right of the
University of Cambridge
to print and sell
all manner of books
was granted by
Henry VIII in 1534.
The University has printed
and published continuously
since 1584.

CAMBRIDGE UNIVERSITY PRESS

CAMBRIDGE
LONDON   NEW YORK   NEW ROCHELLE
MELBOURNE   SYDNEY

Published by the Press Syndicate of the University of Cambridge
The Pitt Building, Trumpington Street, Cambridge CB2 1RP
32 East 57th Street, New York, NY 10022, USA
10 Stamford Road, Oakleigh, Melbourne 3166, Australia

First published 1987

Printed in the United States of America

Library of Congress Cataloging-in-Publication Data
Reddy, William M.
Money and liberty in modern Europe.
Bibliography: p.
Includes index.
1. Money – Europe – History. 2. Social structure –
Europe – History. 3. Liberty. I. Title.
HG922.R43   1987   332.4'94   86-11709

British Library Cataloguing in Publication Data
Reddy, William M.
Money and liberty in modern Europe: a
critique of historical understanding.
1. Money – Europe – History – 18th
century 2. Money – Europe – History
– 19th century 3. Money – Social
aspects – Europe 4. Money – Economic
aspects – Europe
I. Title
332.4'94   HG220.E85

ISBN 0 521 30445 8 hard covers
ISBN 0 521 31509 3 paperback

To Donna

87-7838

J'adore la liberté. J'abhorre la gène, la peine, l'assujettissement. Tant que dure l'argent que j'ai dans ma bourse, il assure mon indépendence; il me dispense de m'intriguer pour en trouver d'autre; necessité que j'eus toujours en horreur: mais de peur de le voir finir, je le choie. L'argent qu'on possède est l'instrument de la liberté; celui qu'on pourchasse est celui de la servitude. Voilà pourquoi je serre bien et ne convoite rien.

I love liberty; I hate embarrassment, worry, and subjection. So long as the money lasts in my purse, it assures me of independence and relieves me of the need of plotting to obtain more, a need which has always appalled me. So afraid am I to see it end that I treasure it. Money in one's possession is the instrument of liberty; money one pursues is the instrument of servitude. That is why I hold fast to what I have, but covet no more.

–J.-J. Rousseau, *Confessions*

Contents

vii

Contents

Preface

THIS ESSAY IS ABOUT MONEY not in the strict sense of coinage or currency but in the much more general sense of a medium of exchange that consists of counters, whether these counters take the form of cowrie shells, money of account, credit, or specie. The question is to understand how close numerical measurement of exchanges influences social structure, and thereby has an effect on the chances for political liberty. Because the subject is the role of money in modern Europe, hardly anything will be said of the origins or development of money, and nothing will be said of the problem of defining money. Whether money necessarily begins as something that has its own use value or can serve as a store of value, what effects increases or decreases in the quantity or velocity of money have on economic activity – these and similar questions will not be considered here. By 1700 it was an integral function of any European state to issue coins and to define in law what role such coins should play in the settlement of private and public debts. That these state functions made a difference for social relationships will be assumed rather than argued here. This hardly seems controversial. The precise nature of social relationships involving money exchanges, on the other hand, and the vector of change in such relationships associated with the expansion of commerce are the subjects of widespread discussion of the highest significance, and will be dealt with in depth in this essay beginning in Chapter 2.

Before this subject can be broached, however, it is necessary to deal with the concept of class. The concept of class is a common tool for analyzing the social structure both of societies that use money and of those that do not. In modern societies where monetary exchange is the principal determinant of one's social position, analysts commonly divide people into classes defined by the kinds of monetary exchanges they engage in. This may be done either by function or by living standard. If by function, those who receive rents, dividends, interest, and other profit from the ownership of property are usually separated from those who sell their services for a wage. And the latter group is then subdivided according to kind of service. Thus one has a capitalist class (or sometimes bourgeoisie), a managerial class of wage-earning executives (often also included in the bourgeoisie), a white-collar class and a blue-collar class (proletariat, or working class). If classes are defined by living standard, then this is usually done, as in Lloyd Warner's classic Yankee City series, by establishing more or less arbitrary cutoffs between an upper, a middle, and a lower class, with each of these subdivided in turn into upper and lower segments.[1] Naturally there is considerable overlap between these two approaches – upper-class people will tend to own income-producing property, and so on – and the two approaches are often collapsed together as a result. Analysts will speak of an upper class of wealthy *rentiers;* a middle class or bourgeoisie of owners, managers, and professionals; a lower middle class of shopkeepers and clerks; and a lower class of blue-collar workers with a skilled upper and unskilled lower segment. Many other variations are possible.

Any of these schemes involves considerable abstraction from social reality, however, not only because many individuals will fit the definition of more than one class – by, for example, earning a factory wage and owning farm land at the same time – but also because individuals may change their positions drastically over a lifetime, as when the younger son of a wealthy family is excluded from inheritance or a shopkeeper accumulates real estate slowly over several decades. An individual's outlook and behavior can be as deeply influenced by future prospects as by current circumstance. How much social behavior class identity can account for and which scheme of analysis will work best are therefore controversial.

The concept of class has also been applied to nonmonetary societies and to societies that severely restrict the impact or scope of money exchanges, but such applications are themselves usually controversial, whereas few observers object to the use of class as such for modern societies. (For them class is after all a native term, as ethnographers would say.) Whether slaves or women in certain preindustrial societies, that is, persons who have no money income and no way of getting one, should be considered members of distinct classes is a subject of sometimes heated debate.

Because historians have depended heavily on the concept of class both for explaining the causes and for describing the effects of change in Europe over the last three centuries, they have not been able to escape from the difficulties that this concept presents to any analyst of social structure. On the contrary, the difficulties of this concept lie at the heart of a number of debates among historians that have continued without sign of letup for many decades. These debates have been of the highest significance both in methodological and in political terms. Nor has it been simply a question of the left versus the right. One might suppose that left-leaning historians would be in favor of a more rigorous use of the concept of class, along Marxist lines, to measure the extent of exploitation and to identify its victims, while conservative historians would attack the abstract and ad hoc character of such analysis and would prefer living standards or cultural attitudes as criteria of class membership. There has been debate of this kind, but it has hardly been the only kind of debate to occur. There has been general disagreement all around. Some conservatives have, for example, used very rigorous definitions of class in order to attack the loose usage of class labels by Marxist historians. Some Marxists have found it difficult to use the concept of class rigorously in a convincing way and have opted for bold theoretical revisions that have drawn fire from both left and right.

The first chapter of this essay provides a critical review of a number of these debates in an attempt to identify the underlying difficulty posed by the concept of class to historical explanation. The rest of the essay represents an attempt to deal with this difficulty and – in the process – to show how this difficulty has plagued not just historical debates but also the course of modern history itself. It is in this sense that the essay represents a critique of historical understanding. It is a critique in that it seeks to probe beyond current discussion to underlying presuppositions and to reconstruct understanding from scratch. All the lines of the debate over class lead back to the question of monetary exchange. There has been a strong tendency in all of modern social thought to theorize about monetary exchange as if it were uniform. The character of the monetary exchange itself is viewed as always the same, as impersonal and anonymous; class distinctions are then based either on the function or production process carried out to receive money (worker, capitalist) or else on the amounts of money received (lower, middle, upper). But social historians have found that this approach squares poorly with their evidence. Increasingly they have been forced to recognize that monetary exchange relationships are not all the same. Commerce does not homogenize. The infamous cash nexus is not impersonal or anonymous in most of its manifestations. It is this recognition that has compelled some historians to develop ever-more-sophisticated concepts of class in recent years. This is undoubtedly a reasonable response, and the present study grows out of the ongoing theoretical discussion that has resulted. But here it will be argued that a better response is to set the concept of class aside entirely, with all that it entails. Developing a new orientation to the question of monetary exchange will require, first, the elaboration of a theory of history building on interpretive method (in Chapter 2); second, the use of this theory to set out a critique of the history of liberal and Marxist economic thought (in Chapter 3); and finally, an application of a new view of monetary exchange to the interpretation of specific episodes in history (Chapters 4 and 5).

An apology is owed to the reader for the appearance of the word "Europe" in the title. Although this essay will include numerous reflections on Europe-wide and even worldwide developments, my limited expertise and considerations of length and readability strongly recommended some restriction of the scope of the inquiry. Attention has therefore been limited to the histories of England, France, and Germany; and for the pre-1867 German states, Prussia alone has received more than cursory comment. In defense of this plan it can at least be said that these three countries present striking diversity to the historian, diversity representative of the wide range of social structures and state formations that characterized Europe on the eve of the age of revolution. The issues that their separate histories have raised are sufficiently varied to ensure that any argument which seeks to encompass them all is likely to be of very general applicability.

I have incurred many debts in completing this study. It was during two brief stays in 1980 and 1982 at the Max-Planck-Institut für Geschichte in Göttingen, West Germany, that I was first given the opportunity to discover something about German history and to be fascinated by the sophistication and breadth of research currently under way in the Federal Republic. I was invited there because my work on France created common temporal and methodological interests with several members of the Institut. My attempt to come to terms with German history began in earnest only later on.

The opportunity to write this essay came during a year as Marta Sutton Weeks Fellow at the Stanford Humanities Center in 1983–84. The excellent resources and stimulating environment provided by Director Ian Watt and his staff and by colleagues at the Center and in the History Department made this a very productive period. Early versions of the first three chapters were read and commented on by Lloyd Kramer, Dena Goodman, Morton Sosna, Herrick Chapman, Drew Faust, Renato Rosaldo, William Sewell, Lynn Hunt, James Epstein, and Donna Slawson. Later chapters were presented to the Faculty Interdisciplinary Seminar on Marxism at Duke University and to the Washington, D.C., area Old Regime Study Group. Vitally useful comments on the full preliminary draft were provided by Joan Scott, Stanley Pierson, and Frank Smith. An informal seminar held in Ann Arbor, Michigan, in April 1986, provided useful stimulus for a final set of revisions. Dennis Trout gave valuable help as my research assistant in 1984–85. Erica Zweig and Dorothy Sapp prepared the manuscript. To all these persons this essay owes a good deal of whatever coherence and persuasive power it has, but none of its still uncorrected discontinuities, errors, or idiosyncracies.

I   The crisis of the class concept
in historical research

A NEW KIND OF SOCIETY emerged in Europe during the late eighteenth and early nineteenth centuries. On this there is widespread agreement; agreement also extends to characterizations of the kind of society that emerged: that it was an individualistic society, based on laissez-faire economic policies and on liberal political institutions, and that it made possible a pace of economic expansion never known before, ensuring Europe a century of unchallenged world domination. Argument has persisted, however, over three mutually interconnected issues: (1) the origins or causes of this transformation, (2) the extent to which its economic and political elements necessarily entailed one another, and (3) how broadly the benefits of this social transformation extended themselves through the social hierarchy. The peculiarities of national history have ensured that each of these points of contention has exercised a different set of national historians. The question of origins has stimulated a long and spirited debate among historians in France seeking to account for the outbreak and course of the Revolution of 1789–99. The problem of the relation between the political and economic elements of the transformation has been most keenly felt among historians of Germany in particular and of Central Europe in general, because in that region certain political institutions and entrenched power elites were able to put off liberal political reform and in the end to dilute its effects even as society around them moved toward a free-trade economy and rapid industrialization.

The question of the distribution of benefits from this transformation has been most intensely debated in England. There the old political regime survived intact because it was, in effect, already liberal in form; the onset of industrial revolution and its attendant dislocations and protests represent the events to be explained. These events have been viewed variously as the creation of a great general good attended by a few necessary evils or as an exploitative politico-economic coup carried out against the traditional way of life of the laboring poor.

Despite this rough division of labor in practice, the issues are in reality so closely connected that it is impossible to discuss one without touching on the others. Each of these issues has arisen because historians have had in the backs of their minds a single scenario that they wished either to attack or to defend, to refine or to revise. This scenario is the Marxist one, although it is in several respects not very different from non-

I

Marxist scenarios formulated both before and after Marx. (Theda Skocpol has ably demonstrated the similarities between Marxist and non-Marxist theories of bourgeois or "modernizing" social transformation.)[1] In its simplest form the scenario explains the emergence of the new society as follows: Gradual commercial development created a new social class, the bourgeoisie; this class seized power and then reformed law and society in its own interest, that is, to promote capitalist development; liberal institutions limited political power, freed the individual, and ensured the businesslike administration of government; and laissez-faire economic reform provided the individual with a competitive marketplace in which to flourish.

The problem of the origins of the French Revolution has focused on the question who. Who initiated the Revolution? Who prolonged it? Were the initiators members of a new commercial class? And it has focused on the validity of the term "class" for prerevolutionary society. Was there in fact such a thing as a bourgeoisie in the sense of a commercial class that had enough coherence in its way of life or its outlook to play a consistent political role?

The problem of Germany's "special way" through the transformation has likewise focused on the failure there of revolution from below. At first glance the scenario does not seem to apply at all. The old elites held onto power, but was this because of a peculiar weakness of the bourgeoisie – either numerical or spiritual? Or was it because of an astute compromise forced on the bourgeois class by the old elite, which ceded to the bourgeois class the economic policies it wished if not the political institutions it preferred?

And the controversy in England has tended to revolve around the question of class versus general interest. Were the interests of the commercial class sufficiently similar to those of the general populace to legitimate their energetic, laissez-faire expansionism? Or did they in fact go counter to the interest the poor had in maintaining an established way of life that expansion swept away?

All of these controversies have been going on for some time now, although not always in perfect coordination with each other. The lack of coordination is understandable, given the vast territory and lengthy time period implicated in the emergence of the new society. In view of the size of the subject and the scale of the research effort under way, no attempt at a general summing up can be anything more than tentative. Nonetheless, many recent attempts at review have signaled the necessity of significant alterations in our whole approach to the problem.[2]

In fact, the material now seems to be available for a frontal attack on the old scenario at every point where questions have previously been raised and for every country involved, even if a particular question has previously not stimulated much controversy in a given country. In other words, it now seems possible to argue that there was no such thing as a coherent commercial class acting politically to defend its interests, neither in France nor in England nor in Central Europe. Likewise, there was no necessary connection between liberal political institutions and unregulated, competitive industrialization in any of these countries. And, finally, the transformation that occurred was not in anyone's interest. In the sense in which the term "interest" has been understood by the whole historical guild, one could easily argue that this transformation violated the interests of all parties, everywhere. In other words, the notion of interest as it is normally used is nonsensical.

Challenging the old scenario in this way is not the same thing as challenging Marxism as a whole. The breadth of Marx's thinking, especially as it worked itself out late in his career, and the distance that Marxist thought has come recently in dealing with the relation between consciousness and material conditions mean that the old scenario outlined here can be jettisoned without serious threat to a great deal of the theoretical edifice that has been built up. That scenario stems from an essay written in 1848, the *Communist Manifesto;* it provided a macrohistorical framework for the further elaboration of Marx's thought. But it is also true that the detailed application of the insights of the *Grundrisse* and of *Capital* to real historical situations has been one of the continual sources of difficulty for that macrohistorical framework. (Recent investigations of specific groups' relations to the means of production, for example, have raised serious question about those groups' class identity. Examples of this are discussed later.) At the same time, Marxists have hardly been the only ones to believe in the efficacy of the idea of class interest as the underlying motive force in politics. But it is just this widely shared idea that is proving increasingly unworkable in the practice of research.

Further on in this essay (in Chapter 3) the question of the whole of Marx's theory will be dealt with at least in passing. The argument presented there will be not so much that his larger theory is wrong as that in borrowing so many of his key terms from political economy Marx also borrowed some enduring conceptual weaknesses. Not Marx's fundamental insights but his choice of technical terms and his style of using them create the constant danger of a certain kind of oversimplification. It is just this kind of oversimplification that has bedeviled the Marxist scenario of bourgeois revolution.

At the same time, this challenge to the old scenario brings liberalism into question just as much as it does Marxism. It is a well-known difficulty in the study of liberal political thought that it contained certain ambiguities from the beginning and that, thanks to its tremendous success and prestige, it was subsequently developed in numerous directions, becoming by 1850 a great tree with many branches. But it will be the contention here that all forms of political liberalism gained part of their appeal from an erroneous view of the nature of monetary exchange (and therefore of the nature of property). This critique of liberalism will shed at least some light on the strange consequences that followed from roughly 1780 on as liberal ideas were applied to the real world of social practice. And it will also suggest ways to salvage for the future what was best about liberalism, its forthright defense of freedom and equality. Too often in the past, critiques of liberalism, both from the left and from the right, have ended by throwing out the baby with the bath water. The consequences in our century have been chilling. But it is necessary to recognize that these critiques have always had a just foundation and that the horrors of the twentieth century have resulted most prominently from the fact that opponents of liberalism, whether fascist

3

or Communist, have had difficulty distinguishing aright between its faults and its virtues. Usually they were right that desperate measures were necessary to stop the evils liberalism legitimated, however true it is that their efforts misfired grotesquely.

Fundamentally this is an argument about language. Too often, in recent years, those who have come to a new understanding of language have demonstrated their discovery by creating new, private languages of their own. They have launched immediately into a heady kind of poetry that has divided their readers into the elect who understand and the frustrated, scoffing majority. But the real advantages of such an understanding of language can only come from communicating it, that is, from using the language at hand, the one that people understand and with which they have made their history and written their histories. In the following discussion, the language of a long-standing historical debate is scrutinized in order to show that the importance of language in history has not been recognized in that debate. As a consequence, the debate has been built up uncritically out of the same terms or, what is more telling, the same *kinds* of terms, as those that shaped the history under debate.

The new society of the nineteenth century was not so new after all. A very ancient form of authority and social deference was given a new set of clothes. This in itself was quite a cataclysmic occurrence, one that left no individual fate untouched. But the individual was never liberated in the way that the apostles of the new age claimed (or later its critics believed). Bourgeois freedom is slavery for the vast majority, Marx declared in 1848; in reality bourgeois freedom never came into existence. This is not to say that one should try to make it now. It was, and is, a social impossibility. But that fact demands a total reorientation of the critique of modern society.

The first step in the argument is to examine how research in social history in recent decades has led inevitably in country after country to dissatisfaction with the idea of class and class interest.

REVISIONISM IN FRANCE

In the debate over the origins of the French Revolution, the revisionists have clearly carried the day. As recently as the 1950s the bold rebellion of the delegates of the Third Estate, backed by the Paris crowd, against royal absolutism in the summer of 1789 was still seen as a class conflict in which a vigorous capitalist bourgeoisie, allied with the peasants and artisans, had overthrown the declining feudal aristocracy. Called to approve new taxes, the delegates of the Third Estate arrogated sovereignty to themselves, declaring that they constituted a National Assembly, and passed a revolutionary Declaration of Rights of Man and Citizen. This document swept away at a stroke the vestiges of the seigneurial system, noble privileges and tax exemptions, all the restrictions on trade that underpinned urban guilds, and all claims of the king to absolute power. Private property was made the cornerstone of both social and political order; absolute freedom in the enjoyment and disposal of property was made into an imprescriptible right. The result, in law at least, was to give unlimited scope in both town and country to commercial competition and capital accumulation. For a long time it seemed perfectly reasonable to suppose that this revolution was brought about by and for a class that depended on commercial and industrial wealth and stood to benefit from its free development. While it was recognized early on that the actual delegates who made the Revolution were not themselves capitalists, this was not perceived as a problem, so long as the politicians could be seen as imbued with an outlook that represented the interests of a capitalist class.[3]

But now it has become clear that such a class not only had no representatives in the revolutionary assemblies but in effect did not exist. There was no revolutionary bourgeoisie. Members of the upper strata of eighteenth-century French society were more or less homogeneous in their values and based their status on "proprietary" rather than profit-maximizing investments.[4] What few merchants or capitalists there were, insofar as they played a political role, do not appear to have favored radical solutions in 1789. They wanted the guilds reorganized; they had no desire to end the seigneurial system. Proprietary wealth was the support both of those who made the Revolution and of those who resisted it. Proprietary wealth had a rank order of prestige that had nothing to do with profitability. Land was more prestigious than commercial stocks; land with feudal rights attached was better still; property in public office gave one an elevated function, and above a certain rank, such office brought actual ennoblement to its possessor and his family. The whole of the elite, noble and commoner alike, were united, it has been repeatedly shown, in their admiration for and pursuit of such highly unproductive forms of property. They were, so the refrain now goes, a single class, a wealthy notability.[5]

But in documenting this thesis and in combating what they have seen as the blind dogmatism of their Marxist opponents, the revisionists have done more than just tear down the old Marxist scenario of bourgeois revolution for France. Inadvertently they have also undermined the whole modern notion of social class and its use in historical explanation. This becomes evident not in the work of destruction itself, as it has been brilliantly carried out by a host of researchers over the last twenty-five years, so much as in their feeble attempts to propose a plausible alternative explanation of the outbreak of the French Revolution. When it has come time to say what really did, after all, happen to bring about such a staggering crisis, there has been little agreement and even less effort expended among the revisionists, who are united only in being critical of the old view. The problem with their alternative proposals has been that they lack the great virtue of the Marxist original while sharing its great weakness.

The virtue of the idea of a revolutionary bourgeoisie was that it was at least on a scale commensurate with the events to be explained. To replace the stirring image of a proud and prosperous new capitalist class victoriously leading the attack on the feudal order, critics have proposed that the Revolution resulted merely from the frustrations of lower royal *officiers* (Alfred Cobban) or from the royal government's gradual alienation of the propertied class (Denis Richet).[6] The real seeds of revolution are now said to be found in obscure rifts and provincial hostilities between rich and poor nobles (Jean Meyer, Guy Chaussinand-Nogaret), or between the magistrates of the sovereign courts and their lesser colleagues (Lenard R. Berlanstein), or between the intellectual establishment and a "literary rabble" of ambitious but unsuccessful authors and journalists (Robert Darnton). Finally, as it were in desperation, recourse has been made to the idea of "stress zones" in the hierarchy of elite status (Colin Lucas). And some have even concluded that the Revolution had no social causes at all, only social consequences (George V. Taylor).[7] The French Revolution was an unprecedented cataclysm, marking an extraordinary break in human history, bringing a decade of bitter civil violence to France. That such a stupendous social transformation should be attributed to the stymied hopes of a few lower-level government officials or the paltry jealousy that old nobles felt for nouveau-riche *anoblis,* or to no social causes at all, is highly unsatisfying. Granted, few of the revisionists have claimed to explain the whole crisis with their discoveries. Still, there surely must be some more profound origin for the Revolution, anchored in the very course that social development had taken over the previous centuries.

The great weakness of the Marxist scenario was that it tried to attribute the Revolution to the intentional and purposive action of a specific group. This weakness has been fully exploited by its critics. They have shown that no revolutionary bourgeoisie distinct from the rest of the elite can be discerned. The critics should have known better, therefore, than to propose alternatives that were open to the same kind of attack, but that is exactly what they have done. They have broken the elite as a whole down into numerous smaller groups, each less than a distinct class but sufficiently large to be a plausible political actor. This procedure has been based on detailed empirical research into the petty details of estate management, provincial politics, professional advancement, preferment, protocol, and prestige. But obviously one can always go further with this kind of research. The documents have proved far more informative than anyone could have imagined in the beginning; there is no reason to suppose that they will not continue to yield even more. Hence there is nothing to stop further efforts to challenge the distinctness, coherence, and self-consciousness of each new, smaller social group that is proposed as a political actor. Surely lesser royal officials, provincial nobles, lawyers, magistrates, pamphleteers, and merchants can be broken down into even smaller groups with distinct attitudes and grievances. Chaussinand-Nogaret, for example, insists that "the traditional nobility, often engaged side by side with the young *noblesse commensale,* was involved in all the most important mining and metallurgical enterprises, those which broke through the traditional forms of family exploitation." At the same time he admits that only a tiny minority of old nobles were connected with such novel ventures.[8] But how is it that a large subgroup, the traditional nobility, can be said to be involved in something merely by virtue of the fact that a few of its members are involved? To talk this way merely replicates the worst conceptual sins of the Marxists who are under attack.

The revisionists have put French society under a microscope and shown that no group can be found that fits the old stereotype of revolutionary bourgeoisie. But what is to stop later revisionists from raising the microscope to a higher level of magnification, to reveal that the currently proposed alternative groups have in their turn only a spurious unity? Eventually one gets down to the individual, whose unity is at least ensured by the existence of his body. But, then, why stop here? Individuals are often utterly incoherent, after all. Why be taken in by the illusion that the individual actor was necessarily coherent and consistent, especially in the midst of a political and economic crisis that must have shaken the roots of every man's and woman's identity? As Darnton's deft portraits have shown, many major actors in the drama did not act consistently.[9] Why should the faces in the crowds be any different? They are anonymous to us but were not so to themselves.

This is the knotty problem that the attack on the revolutionary bourgeoisie has brought to the fore. The enchanting coherence of the old approach is gone. How simple it was for Georges Lefebvre, the grand practitioner of Marxist revolutionary history in our century. In 1957 it was still possible to write sentences like the following: ". . . News that an Estates-General was to be convened sent a tremor of excitement through the bourgeoisie."[10] Or, speaking of the aftermath of the October Days:

> Along with the aristocracy a group of bourgeois were indignant that violence had been done to the king. . . . The nobility was now struck in its material possessions and not only in its pride by suppression of orders and privileges. . . . At the same time the Third Estate split: the petty bourgeoisie, if not the proletariat, would be excluded from political life only with strong protest. . . . As Mirabeau told the bourgeois, they needed an energetic government to consolidate their accession.[11]

A story of phantoms, or so it would appear now. But the only replacements so far offered with which to rewrite the story have been equally suspect phantom groups, as well as new cleavages and rivalries whose only advantage has been that they are too small and too numerous to be worth attacking singly.

Aware of the problem but unable to come up with a solution, revisionists have taken to talking about social groupings in a most confusing way, as in the conclusion to Chaussinand-Nogaret's work on the nobility, where he remarks, "Introducing class struggle into a society of orders simply distorts one's whole perspective. The orders themselves were nothing more than the transparent envelope of a multitude of *corps* which crumble on contact; from one order to another *corps* were united by a community of interests but isolated by juridical frontiers."[12] Even defenders of the old Marxist scenario have been reduced to this kind of confusing language, as in the following comment from Michel Vovelle:

> Second order behind the clergy in law, the nobility was the first in fact, and perhaps the only order that had a real homogeneity. It corresponded to an economico-social definition without genuine ambiguity, forming the *core* of the rentier class and being the *major* beneficiary of feudal appropriation. A whole assemblage of privileges – political, fiscal, juridical – sanctioned their de facto preeminence; class and order, here, reveal a real *convergence* [emphasis added].[13]

One may legitimately object that the italicized words in this passage do, after all, introduce an element of genuine ambiguity, especially the concluding term, "convergence" (*complicité* in the original). Vovelle goes on to explain that the bourgeoisie was dominated by a "mixed" group, not really capitalist, not really feudal, and that France was, as a result, a society in transition.[14] But if the bourgeoisie is basically mixed, with most of its wealth taking on the same form as that of the nobility, then how can the nobility be characterized as a genuinely distinct class? And if it is not, then against whom was the Revolution waged?

The question that is raised is whether it is possible to continue to speak of socially distinct sets of individuals, united by some identifiable trait or traits, as having shared intentions. But without this convention, the social origins of political conflict and change will have to be totally reconceived. To judge from the most recent research, the ruling elite of France, formerly as homogeneous and unified as one could desire, suddenly and inexplicably divided into two hostile groups in the fall of 1788 along a previously invisible fissure that cut down through the elite from top to bottom following no reasonable line of demarcation.[15] Hence Lucas's desire to speak of "stress zones"; but even the inventor of this term hesitated to attribute to these minor stresses the whole force of the split. As a result, there is currently no acceptable theory of the social origins of the French Revolution.

But how significant is this dilemma? Can the conclusions of the revisionists about the irrelevance of class to the outbreak of the French Revolution be exported to other countries on the eve of their respective transformations at the end of the eighteenth century?

At first glance, it would seem not. None of the disturbing ambiguities of French wealth and rank seem relevant to the situation in either of two other key countries, England and Prussia. Here are some of the reasons why. In England property in land had already been stripped of many of its seigneurial and judicial elements. Titles of nobility were restricted to such a tiny minority of the population that they were not a realistic target of ambition. Government offices were therefore bought and sold more with a cold eye on what income they would bring than with a concern for the honorifics and exemptions associated with them. Profit-maximizing investment seems to have been the rule in every realm of society. Nothing could be more dramatic than the process of enclosure in agriculture carried out on a vast scale with the aid of Parliament and with the sole aim of simplifying the production of cash crops. The eighteenth century was the golden age in England of the gentleman agronomist, draining fens and fencing wastes, introducing new crop rotations and new breeds of cattle, not averse to investing in a canal or a turnpike road if it might add to his net worth. The landowning aristocracy was itself a capitalist class. At the same time the burgeoning manufactures of the towns were under the control of an apparently quite distinct group, outsiders, religious dissenters who had no hope of political influence or acceptance in polite society, who ran their businesses not in order to retire as soon as possible to the countryside (as was the rule in France) but as ends in themselves, family patrimonies to be nourished and passed on. A readily identifiable manufacturing class was taking shape with its own distinct interests and outlook, prepared to mount sizable political movements when it seemed to be necessary for the good of business, as the successes of the Great Reform Bill (1832) and of Corn Law Repeal

The crisis of the class concept

(1846) demonstrate. Not only was English government already liberal in form, but English society was already capitalist. The dramatic transformation of the period was more an economic one, a reorganization of commercial relationships that followed on the discovery of dramatic new means of production.[16]

Prussia, at first glance, lay at the opposite extreme. There an exclusive and self-conscious aristocracy, the Junkers, totally dominated society. Service in the officer corps and the upper bureaucracy was reserved to them and provided the legitimation of their preeminent rank. They operated their landholdings with the aid of direct labor services from bound serfs over whom they exercised extensive police and judicial power. Ownership of these lands, like government office and military rank, was reserved to those of noble birth exclusively. Heavy dependence on an export economy had stunted the growth of towns, so that persons of intermediate rank were numerically few and politically powerless. Only destruction of the Prussian army by Napoleon in 1806 forced upon this society a recognition of the need for change. Even then reforms were haphazard and piecemeal because so strongly resisted by certain factions among the Junkers, and their application in the end did not really challenge the powerful hold of this class on state and society.[17]

It is not surprising, therefore, that the issue of class has stimulated far less debate in the historiography of these two countries than it has for France. But closer inspection raises problems: As in France, once the microscope is brought into focus, neat class boundaries dissolve; larger homogeneity becomes apparent; and smaller groupings suggest themselves as the important factors in political struggle. The whole notion of class as an explanatory principle in history is again brought into question.

In England the characters of classes have too often been extrapolated from the biographies of famous men in a misleading way. It is true that improving landlords, for example, were far more common in England in the eighteenth century than they were in France, but it may be that they remained exceptional even so. G. E. Mingay concluded from his study of eighteenth-century estate records that "although large owners did much to improve estate administration, to consolidate holdings, and bring waste land into cultivation, they did not, in general, do very much towards new discoveries; nor it appears did they greatly extend the use of improved techniques by means of progressive leases or home farms, long supposed to be the great instruments of technical advance." Elsewhere Mingay estimates that the borrowings of the gentry for dowries and for refurnishings and redecorations of their country homes and parks were far larger than their productive commercial investments.[18] Profit was shunned in favor of a form of prestige far less tangible but apparently quite desirable. There can be no doubt that enclosure ran its course, virtually wiping out the open-field village and reducing common land to a negligible residue over a great portion of the English countryside. But how frequently such enclosures resulted in higher yields of marketable produce per acre of arable land—as opposed to the mere exploitation of short-term market scarcities or the formation of convenient country seats for the enhancement of status—is no longer clear. Cases have been found of old open-field villages adopting the new crop rotations and breeding techniques of the agricul-

9

tural revolution with great success.[19] On the whole, yields per acre may have increased more rapidly in France than in England in the eighteenth century.[20] In England some of the more prestigious forms of wealth were every bit as unprofitable and therefore "noncapitalist" as in France, with the difference that they were not so intimately connected with state functions and exemptions. Even this difference is only one of degree, when one recalls the role of landownership in the control of parliamentary seats through rotten boroughs and electoral bribery.

Moreover, the manufacturing and landowning classes were not so distinct as was once supposed. For every Richard Arkwright or Robert Owen who worked himself up from obscurity to ownership of a great enterprise there were two others whose connections or background lay with the established gentry. This became even more true as time went on, and it meant that the attitudes and outlook of many English industrialists were deeply influenced by the old landed elite.[21] Still others resisted utilitarian doctrines on religious grounds.[22] It is no longer possible to attribute the appeal of parliamentary reform or of the Anti-Corn-Law League to the existence of a manufacturing class with interests distinct from those of the old elite, utterly committed to a Ricardian outlook.[23] The neat, one-to-one correspondence between ideology and class interest that was once believed to account for the French Revolution turns out in England, as well, to be fraught with problems.

As for Prussia, it must be remembered that Junker domination of this society was founded on grain exports through the Baltic to the Netherlands, England, and beyond. The recrudescence of serfdom in this region was made possible by the same developing commercial links as are deemed to have broken down feudal relations elsewhere.[24] The irony of this has by now been repeatedly underscored. Grain was for Prussia what cotton was for the American South or sugar for the West Indies, a commodity produced for world trade by bound labor under the control of a harsh landowning elite.[25] All three regions directly benefited from the quickening of international trade associated with the onset of industrial revolution in England in the second half of the eighteenth century. England's new factories needed raw material and their work force needed food; after 1765 England no longer supplied enough grain for its own consumption.[26] "Noncapitalist" because utterly backward technically, Prussian agriculture shared in the boom begun in Lancashire, and the impact of the resulting prosperity in the final decades of the century was already blurring old social distinctions, and pushing the state toward reform, well before Napoleon arrived on the scene.

The heavy demand and continually rising prices for grain stimulated a speculative real estate boom in Prussia after 1786 that resulted in the doubling, tripling, and even quintupling of land prices. Since 1769 state credit and mortgage guarantees had been available to protect nobles from foreclosure, and now these financed the feverish price rise. The pressure to keep the boom going forced the king to issue numerous dispensations for the purchase of noble land by commoners, so that by 1800, roughly 10 percent of *Rittergütter* (noble estates) were held by commoners with peasant or urban backgrounds. Rapid turnover favored concentration of holdings in the hands of great magnates; smaller noble landowners found their relative social rank eroding. The old paternalistic bonds between lord and serf were undermined by rapid turnover.[27] Both results call to mind the similar consequences of enclosure in England. Even before 1806 a few Junkers began to invest in improved techniques of cultivation; certain others insisted that bound labor was inefficient because it was lazy and poorly motivated, and to prove the point they formally freed their serfs.[28] Neither of these trends became significant before 1806, but it is indicative of the direction of things that such changes had begun and were being avidly defended in print by otherwise perfectly conservative aristocrats. In 1806, with defeat and the cutoff of normal trade with England, the speculative boom fell in like a house of cards.[29] One of the first emergency measures taken following the surrender to Napoleon was a moratorium on debt payments and foreclosures that saved many Junker landowners, preventing a disaster for the Prussian elite that could have been worse than the collapse of the army.

In view of these developments a debate has arisen whether eighteenth-century Prussian agriculture ought to be viewed as a feudal throwback or as part of the general European advance toward capitalism. Some Marxist historians have held for the former, for obvious reasons: Otherwise, the Prussian nobles would have to be seen as progressive capitalists instead of as part of the aristocratic order that had to be (but was never) overthrown by the German bourgeoisie. Against this view, however, Hanna Schissler cites the comments of J. Nichtweiss that the recrudescence of serfdom must be seen as part of "the adjustment of estate management to new economic conditions, to the development of capitalism in Western Europe and certain regions of Germany . . . which . . . led directly to the breaking down of the rigid forms of exploitation of the old agriculture." Schissler herself says of the Junker stratum, in language reminiscent of Vovelle and Chaussinand-Nogaret, "If its political and social status was defined in terms of the idea of a social estate, and in reality was affected by this idea, the land-owning nobility developed the ever sharper features of an economic class as a result of the process of commercialization."[30] Viewed in this way, the Prussian Junker becomes one of those ambiguous phenomena, one of those confusing intermediate forms that the revisionists in France have made so much of. Like the "businesslike" noble estate owners of Toulouse uncovered by Robert Forster or the upwardly mobile entrants into the *noblesse de la robe,* they are neither bourgeois nor aristocrat.[31] The old class categories break down. Reform in Prussia can therefore be seen as a response to an internal dynamic of social development paralleling changes in France, instead of as an imitative reaction to defeat by Napoleon. By living off a booming export trade, by speculating in land with borrowed money, the Prussian nobility proved itself to be anything but backward or feudal in nature. By destroying noble land values the defeat of 1806 wreaked havoc on a profitable business; reform was the only way to put it back on its feet.

And the reforms that were carried out did exactly this. Serfdom was not abolished outright. Labor dues were made redeemable at the cost of a third to a half of the peasants' subsistence plots or an equivalent in cash. A great deal of peasant land was reintegrated into noble demesnes, and thousands of peasants were forced to seek work as wage laborers from their former lords, either because their plots had become too small to support them or because they could not meet the heavy annual redemption payments through sale of their own produce. The restrictions on access to estate ownership, to the officer corps, and to the government bureaucracy were swept away, but noble families were protected with strict laws of entail and inheritance similar to the forms of protection used by English gentry. And state-financed credit continued to favor the large landowner.[32] From 1807 on, furthermore, the pattern of investment changed. No longer did Junkers run up debts merely to enlarge the surface of their holdings. Instead they invested in the new agricultural techniques, adapting output to demand, increasing yield per acre, minimizing labor costs. Agricultural productivity rose 122 percent in Prussia between 1800 and 1849, by one estimate.[33] All it had taken was one quick lesson, the shock of defeat, for the Prussian nobility to get the message. From 1807 on they fit the definition of capitalists as satisfactorily as any other landowning group in Europe. Yet old attitudes remained vital; noble status did not become meaningless overnight. The close relationship between large landowners and Prussian military and governmental service remained. Their heavy influence on Prussian politics, their prestige and authority in every realm of social life, continued with little abatement.[34] Was this an "old" class or a "new" one?

Judged by the rigorous standards that have grown up in the debate over the French Revolution, Prussian Junkers cannot be ascribed to either category, nor can the landowners and manufacturers of industrializing England. Viewed from a European perspective, all were subgroups – each with its own peculiar variations on a common set of themes – of a single continentwide elite. Moreover, this elite was learning in a single uneven yet massive movement, between about 1780 and 1820, to invest money in a thoroughly capitalist manner: "capitalist" in the strict sense of seeking to maximize return through the transformation of production methods. At the same time, this was an elite that held tightly to many age-old notions of prestige, honor, authority, and – for lack of a better term – highly unprofitable "conspicuous consumption." Capitalism was more of a new trick that they added to their bag than the special skill of a new class struggling to find its place in the sun.

This elite in most areas shaded off toward the bottom in imperceptible degrees, so that it would be impossible (or highly arbitrary) to draw a line and to say that above this line is the elite and below it are the poor. In Western Europe there were plenty of members of what Lefebvre once called the "rural bourgeoisie," substantial and ambitious peasants; there were innumerable literate scribblers, young lawyers, impoverished aristocrats, small-scale merchant-manufacturers, landowning masons, and wig-sporting glassworkers who lived on the fringes between elite and poor. Without them the character of the elite would have been entirely different; its values, ambitions, fashions, cultivation, and privileges would have been meaningless. Where would the power of the Paris Parlement have been without the *basoche,* the rabble of law clerks and pamphleteers who haunted the lower floors of its meeting hall, and who mobilized the Parisian crowd in its defense?[35] Where would the country gentry of England have gained their self-confidence and snobbery if there had been no respectable but poor widows and younger sons – Jane Austen's heroes and heroines – to honor and envy them and to eat gratefully at their tables? Even in Prussia there were numerous government officials, tenant farmers, and smallholders who filled the space between serf and lord in the eighteenth century, as well as many noble families reduced to their level. Besides, Prussia would not have existed without the merchants and growing urban masses of the western seacoast who were rich enough to buy imported grain but not rich enough to own their own farms.

The idea of seeing the political crisis that spread across Europe at the dawn of the nineteenth century as a consequence of class conflict in any simple sense becomes completely untenable. The relationship to the means of production of this Europe-wide elite was extremely varied and complicated; and all levels of this broad elite shared access to the same diverse and complicated range of methods for getting money. Government service, landownership, tax exemptions, and market restrictions, as well as new agricultural and industrial technologies, provided income for people at every level of the elite in quite diverse mixes that had characteristic (but constantly changing) patterns in different regions. All one can say for certain is that accompanying the French Revolution and the onset of industrialization in England was a relative rise in importance everywhere of those forms of investment that were strictly capitalist.

It also remains certain that the transformation was associated with widespread social conflict of every imaginable form: factional infighting, riot and insurrection, forcible takeovers of power, civil war, terror, repression. Mobilizations of large segments of society for specific political ends occurred on an unprecedented scale. It is equally certain that in those transactions that mark a person's rank and identity (that is, access to advantageous marriage alliances, to property, office, craft membership, and so on) highly restrictive and prejudicial arrangements remained routine (however much their specific character or justification may have shifted), and distribution of goods and resources remained sharply unequal. If there were no identifiable classes, there was certainly a steep hierarchy. But there is no neat relationship between these stark social inequalities and the battle lines that were constantly being drawn in the political arena. Even among the sans-culottes of the Year 2, the most characteristically artisanal political movement of the period – at least by reputation – it is possible to find important industrialists whose leading role in the movement was a direct result of their economic stature as large employers within poor Parisian neighborhoods.[36] Even among the Prussian Junkers, where the transition to a reformed social order appears to have occurred almost painlessly, a closer look shows that every step of the way reforming bureaucrats met strong resistance both from within the government and at the local and provincial levels, resistance that forced them to scale back, and delay implementation of, their already modest plans. Even the Prussian solution, in other words, was the outcome of a fierce internal conflict within the elite.[37]

The crisis that is emerging for historical explanation out of the debate over the French Revolution might be characterized as one of emplotment. What kind of narrative can be constructed that deals adequately with the obviously deep social roots of conflict in this period without merely identifying various political factions with specific social groupings – whether classes or orders or professions – whose interest that faction is said to represent? At present there is no answer to this question.

The old solution to this problem was in fact a product of the age under examination. It was during the French Revolution that political factions began to identify themselves and their opponents by social epithets. The "sans-culottes," the virtuous poor workers, confronted an "aristocratic" plot of continentwide proportions, according to a way of talking that became prevalent in Paris by 1792. From there it quickly spread, and countervocabularies were as quickly formulated by the Revolution's enemies, who saw the drama as one pitting civilization against the mob. Already in 1788 the word "class" had begun its fateful new career under the pen of Sieyès as a politically charged means of referring to functionally defined subgroups within society.[38] However much the passionate epithets of the time have been superseded by a calmer and more precise terminology among historians, the basic strategy has remained unchanged. Conflict is still seen as arising from the mutual hostility of socially distinct groups with distinct interests. This is the problem that now confronts historical explanation: Research shows that the facts cannot be squeezed into such boxes. Something other than the collective self-interest of classes or orders, however defined, will have to be found to account for the motivations that underlay political conflict and social change in this pivotal period.

LIBERALISM AND THE GERMAN WAY

The catastrophes of the twentieth century have turned German historiography into a work of diagnosis. The excesses of the Nazis and their terrible defeat have been turned into a lesson. Germany became a powerful industrial state and developed advanced forms of political participation by 1914 without ever becoming a genuine liberal democracy. Germany was therefore the one exception to a rule that seemed to apply to all other great industrial powers by that time. But the price of this exceptionalism was pathology; the exception proved the rule. Where modernization and liberalism do not advance hand in hand, disaster follows. This is the lesson that had repeatedly been drawn from the study of German history since 1945. It was drawn first and most forcefully by English-speaking historians with a strong liberal outlook that they did not hesitate to advertise. Since 1960 this lesson has increasingly been accepted and elaborated by liberal West German historians as well.[39]

As applied to the course of nineteenth-century German history, however, this lesson has taken on the form of an implicit acceptance of the Marxist scenario of revolution, the very one that revisionists have so successfully challenged for France in the last thirty years. Nowhere is this more apparent than in accepted views of the "failed" German revolution of 1848, as Geoff Eley has recently argued.[40] A standard interpretation of 1848 sees the failure as a question of class alliances. In 1848 Germany like the rest of Europe was shaken by popular uprisings that forced every existing government to make sweeping concessions. Liberals and democrats who had long been languishing under the neglect and censorship of Restoration-era regimes were welcomed into the corridors of power. At Frankfurt an all-German Parliament was assembled, its members hastily elected by a broad new electorate that, if not fully democratic, was wider than anything in previous experience. This Parliament set about its work with a will; it wrote a Declaration of Rights and a Constitution, just as liberals had done in America and France before them. In the process, however, it made a fatal error; instead of avidly courting the support of the revolutionary masses and keeping their fervor for change alive, German liberals everywhere turned to existing executive and military institutions (that is, to the surviving Restoration regimes themselves) to keep order in the streets. They would have none of the rabble's excesses interrupting the important work of reform; in their folly they undercut the one political force that had ensured their rise to power. As a result, within twelve months of the outbreak of the revolution the popular movement had been broken; the old monarchs and their ruling circles were once again in the saddle, and they dismissed the liberals they had so fearfully welcomed into government a year before. The Prussian king disdainfully refused to accept the crown offered by the Frankfurt assembly, who wished him to be first ruler of its new constitutional monarchy. Soon after, the Parliament's members were in their turn dispersed like so many fishwives gathered in the street, as were the members of every other liberal assembly created during the revolution. The victory of reaction could not have been more complete, and the way was open for Bismarck later to unify Germany by military conquest, thwarting all hope for a popular and democratic revolution.[41] The first step had been taken on the road to Nazism.

This standard interpretation depends on the Marxist scenario by implication; the revolution of 1848 "failed" in that it did not fit the Marxist scenario. The German bourgeoisie failed to take over when they should have; as a result the normal form of bourgeois class rule, liberal democracy, never developed in Germany.

The first thing to notice about this interpretation is that, like the standard scenario of the French Revolution, it stems ultimately from the participants themselves. Just as those who made the French Revolution were the first to identify social strata with specific political factions, so the reigning explanation of why the German revolution of 1848 failed was first proposed, in its aftermath, by the German liberals who had led it. Leonard Krieger's analysis of the revolution's impact on German liberalism shows how little has changed in the diagnoses of failure since the end of 1848. The revolution's failure was interpreted at that time in terms of an odd dichotomy between "ideal" and "real" that cut across the existing social realm in peculiar ways, but it has retained great persuasive power to this day.

Krieger cites, for example, the painful reflections of Eduard Lasker, looking back from the perspective of the early 1860s:

> I grant for myself that the core of my life will always be the spirit which the year 1848 called forth. . . . Yet I grant that it was a grave mistake, to a certain extent an excess of idealism to have dwelt so long on fundamental rights and dur-

ing this labor not to have brought the other, material, elements into equal consideration.[42]

In reaction to the subsequent course of events, Lasker had retreated from a demand for representative government to a more cautious insistence on rule of law as the true key to liberty. Having retreated this far he "raised this compromise to an absolute dogma," in Krieger's words. Lasker wrote:

> Rule of law and rule of police are two different ways to which history points, two methods of development between which peoples must choose and have chosen. . . . The true man is the independent citizen. . . . He has no other claim on the state than protection from injurious force; for this he has to sacrifice nothing to the state but his desire to attack the rights of others. . . . In the *Rechtstaat* [rule of law] the violation of law is the worst evil; it may be suffered at no time from any side.[43]

Absolute obedience to the law: Here was a principle that, unlike the heady idealism of 1848, at least brought the other "material" elements – the Prussian state and its bureaucracy – into consideration. But it did so in a way that also has a fateful, even a tragic, ring to it now, after the holocaust a century later.

Ten years earlier another disillusioned liberal, August Ludwig von Rochau, had already published a work entitled *Principles of Practical Politics {Realpolitik}*, in which he argued that

> the discussion of the question, what *should* rule, whether justice (*Recht*), wisdom, virtue, whether an individual, many, or few – This question belongs in the realm of philosophical speculation; practical politics has to do first of all with the simple fact that it is power alone that can rule. To rule means to exercise power and only he who possesses power can exercise power. This direct connection of power and rule forms the fundamental truth of all politics and the key to all history. . . . *Recht* is related to power as the idea is to fact.[44]

This opposition between idea and fact was strange for the simple reason that existing power relations are themselves always infused with and maintained through communicative, ideational, symbolic elements. No society is ruled by violence alone, just as none has ever dispensed with violence. The Prussian state of mid-century, with its dreamy and erratic kings, and the confused political balance in *Mitteleuropa* of which it was a part are strange things to refer to as merely "material" conditions. So, for that matter, were the revolutionary masses, whose hardships and aspirations had led them first to support and then to abandon German liberals. The phrase "material elements" in the context of the thinking of Lasker, Rochau, or other German liberals in the 1850s and 1860s appears to have meant forces whose principles or ideals they did not understand or refused to recognize as intellectually legitimate. The idea that "only he who possesses power can exercise power" begs the essential question what brings power – which has always been some combination of an ideal or principle of legitimacy and a threat of violence.

Post-1848 German liberals now insisted on reform only when it seemed called for by existing real conditions, as they understood them. This was the hard lesson of 1848. Hence, Rochau felt constitutional regimes to be legitimate only because the "younger social forces" of the age – in effect, the rising bourgeoisie – demanded this form of political rule.[45] Rudolf Haym likewise insisted on "the most thorough-going possible liberalism in Prussia . . . not for its sake alone" but to help Prussia in the task of achieving German unity.[46] Long before Bismarck appeared on the scene to bully the liberal opposition in the Prussian assembly in 1862, his infamous policy of *Realpolitik* had already been laid out by the liberals themselves. His blustering 1862 speech before the liberal majority in the Prussian assembly reads like a passage from one of their own works: "Not through speeches and majority votes will the great questions of the age be decided – that was the great mistake of 1848 – but through iron and blood."[47] Theodore S. Hamerow quotes the following opinion from one of Bismarck's rare supporters in the press at the time of his appointment as Prussian prime minister in 1862:

> People are breathing a deep sigh of relief at the prospect of once again seeing a man act and confound a hundred thousand chatterboxes. Whatever may come, it cannot be worse than the epidemic of petty-mindedness which is presently raging and from which our poor Germany must ultimately dissolve in a solution of notes, articles, and speeches. If Herr von Bismarck cuts this process of decay short one way or another, then we will honor him as our personal benefactor. And we believe that he will do it because he must.[48]

A peculiar dichotomy between ideas and forces, developed to explain the failure of the revolution of 1848, had by 1860 become a commonplace of German political discourse. Bismarck's opportunistic wars of 1864, 1866, and 1870–71 seemed to fulfill his own prophecy of 1862. And his constitutional concessions of 1867 were highly reminiscent of compromises the liberals had already long advocated. The new Imperial Parliament (the Reichstag), after 1871 reduced almost to an advisory role with no control over ministries or power to introduce legislation, represented a frank recognition by Bismarck that the liberalism of many Germans in his enlarged state could not be totally ignored. But they got only as much as he deemed it in their power to demand. His highly successful policies appear then to have been founded on the liberals' explanation of their own failure. His stunning political achievements sank home the lesson that principles and power were strangers to one another – a fateful principle.

But history seemed to prove it right, and many historians have echoed German liberalism's own self-diagnosis. Krieger attributed the failure of 1848 to the "withdrawal of real social supports from the political liberals," and the result was that "within the liberal movement as outside it the recognition of the power of the amoral existent fact reduced the ideal of individual freedom to the status of a formal political doctrine."[49] Michael Stürmer concluded likewise that the liberal majority in Frankfurt was "victim of its own interests" because as property owners and members of the educated classes, the men who made up that majority hesitated to call upon the artisans and journeymen in the streets for political support. The real facts of interest overcame the "naive" belief in the "unity of liberalism and democracy."[50] According to Reinhart Koselleck, "Fear of a mass uprising threw the bourgeoisie back upon the state," ensuring that the force which brought the constitutional movement to the fore also brought it down. This force was the "social crisis" that had caused the revolution.[51] Real forces, factors, and interests wreaked havoc on liberal ideals; historians have consistently agreed with the breast-beating conclusions that the liberals painfully worked out in the aftermath of the debacle. Now, however, to the consequences of the liberal failure have been added the greater disasters of the twentieth century.

The real forces, factors, and interests that the liberals are said to have neglected were, it is worth noting, those represented by social classes, by the old ruling elites of the all-too-numerous German states on the one hand and by the troubled artisanal and peasant masses on the other. In other words, the German liberals are said to have failed to calculate in terms of a political struggle between upper and lower social strata, a form of calculation that was supposedly central to the ideology of the (by comparison) successful French Revolution.

The second thing to notice about the standard interpretation of 1848 in Germany is that the liberals' failure is often explained as resulting either from comparative weakness or immaturity of the German bourgeoisie or else from its complete absence from German society. This approach has been shared by a wide range of historians of both Marxist and liberal persuasions because, in contrast to France, with its successful Revolution, in Germany the failure of the revolution has not stimulated a search for the revolutionary bourgeoisie. Many Marxists have seen the bourgeoisie of that time as failing to be revolutionary, as engaging in "an alliance with the nobility and a common front against the mass of the people," as Helmut Bleiber puts it.[52] Their opponents have gone a step further, insisting that the term "bourgeoisie" in the Marxist sense is not really appropriate to the Germany of the pre-March era.[53] What most historians have had to say about the social origins of the German liberals of 1848, in fact, resembles very closely what the revisionists in France have maintained about the social origins of the Revolution of 1789. The resemblance is so close that it makes one pause. After all, if the social origins of the two events were so similar, then origins alone explain nothing about the failure of 1848 in Germany.

According to Krieger, the most important source of support for German liberalism in the pre-March era came from "those members of the older middle classes who grew with the quantitative development of the German economy until they reached the point of feeling hemmed in by aspects of a system to which they were still committed." By "older middle classes" Krieger means port merchants, prosperous peasants, urban artisans, and above all members of the "intellectual estate" – that is, professors, writers, lawyers, and reform-minded bureaucrats who felt both a "desire for modern liberal reforms" and a "continuing attachment" to existing institutions.[54] James Sheehan remarks in summary that "it is misleading to consider the social basis of liberalism as some kind of embryonic 'bourgeoisie' that dimly reflects analogous groups in England, France, or Belgium. Instead we must see them as vividly reflecting the diverse and fluid realities of the German Vormärz."[55] Wolfram Fischer has provided a careful investigation of the social underpinnings of liberalism in Baden, the most liberal of German states before 1848, showing that it was high-level bureaucrats in charge of the administration who, elected to the Landrat (the new constitutional Parliament), led the opposition after 1819. Economically Baden was particularly backward; its small towns and numerous independent peasants provided few candidates for political leadership; but liberal officials won easy popularity and dominated the Landrat.[56] From the least likely of social origins in the least likely of states arose the most successful liberal movement of the period. Likewise it has been shown that in Prussia's Rhineland territories, reform bureaucrats, ranking nobles, and rich urban merchants, bankers, and manufacturers mingled on equal footing in social clubs and arranged legal and administrative reforms through intimate and informal consultation. When the leading intellectual of the region, David Hansemann, urged in the early 1830s that Prussia should have a constitution, he was careful to praise the existing system and received a warm letter of thanks from the king for his thoughtful proposals.[57] Michael Stürmer has remarked in general of 1848 that "the large-scale merchants, manufacturers, bankers, lawyers, and professors neither in 1847 nor afterwards became the spearhead of revolution" because they were too closely connected to the landed interests of the eastern nobility and too habituated to the idea of reform from above.[58] They entered the revolutionary assemblies and ministries of 1848 only halfheartedly.

More recent research has further undermined the idea that German liberalism before 1848 was a bourgeois phenomenon in any sense of the term. The enthusiastic support of a wide spectrum of master craftsmen, shopkeepers, and even journeymen for (often vague) liberal goals – brought to light in some recent studies – has made it impossible to speak of liberalism as a middle-class ideology.[59] Or, as Wolfgang Schieder notes, "in Germany, in contrast to England and France, up until 1848 the concept of a middle class [*Mittelstand* – literally, middle estate] continued to include the whole unbroken *bürgerlichen* spectrum" – that is, the whole spectrum of town dwellers or citizens.[60] The contrast with England and France in 1848 is valid, but it must be remembered that the support of shopkeepers and journeymen for liberal ideas in both France and England in the 1790s was equally conspicuous.

Koselleck reflects on the origins of revolution within urban Prussia this way:

> The estate of towndwellers [*stadtbürger* – literally, *bourgeois* in the old French legal sense of the term], as it developed economically, pressed to become full citizens of the state [*Staatbürgertum*], a status from which they saw themselves closed out by the very bureaucratic estate [*Beamtenstand*] which had set them free economically and had given them full internal self-government. As soon as the leaders of the bourgeoisie [*Bürgertum*] gained sufficient strength from the social grievances – the reverse side of economic freedom – to put pressure on the

whole constitution of the state, they were able to force the transition from town dweller to citizen. In a certain way, they drew those political conclusions from the management of reform that it was not possible to draw.[61]

Obviously, in their efforts to account for the causes of the German revolution of 1848 and its rapid failure, historians have been led into the same kind of linguistic difficulties as have the revisionists in France. By subtle redefinitions and intricate interweaving of incommensurate terms they have sought to convey a sense of the growing incongruity of the existing system of social stratification in Germany in the pre-March era. Krieger's notion that the "old middle classes" were feeling "hemmed in" is highly reminiscent of Colin Lucas's conclusion that commercial prosperity had created "stress zones" within the French ruling elite by 1789. Koselleck's masterful juxtaposition of old and new social vocabulary conveys a sense of confusion and transition not unlike Chaussinand-Nogaret's talk of the "communities of interest"—a very modern notion of how society groups itself—that cut across the old *corps* within the "transparent envelopes" of the orders.

By their very convergence these two lines of development within European historiography threaten to undercut each other. If there was no revolutionary bourgeoisie in France and yet the Revolution was successful, then the absence of a revolutionary bourgeoisie in Germany is no explanation for its failure. Moreover, the inability of the revisionists in France to come up with a viable alternative explanation of the causes of the Revolution means that there is no new point of comparison with which to develop new explanations of Germany's failure. The alternatives proposed by revisionists could easily be found in Germany. There were plenty of frustrated lower-level officials in both countries. Marx and Engels are only the best known of a whole host of German literary rabble, embittered by censorship and exclusion, who rushed to take advantage of the new situation in 1848. There was certainly plenty of new money looking anxiously for landed estates, government positions, and titles of nobility in Germany. The old nobility had indisputably gone a long way down the road of *embourgeoisement,* probably farther in Germany by 1848 than in France a half-century earlier; and in both cases the inclination to close ranks and draw artificial distinctions more sharply was growing. One is inclined to conclude that there is currently no satisfactory social explanation for the profound contrast between these two revolutions, just as there is currently no accepted social explanation of the first one.

Of course, not every author cited here attributes the failure of 1848 directly and explicitly to the absence of a revolutionary bourgeoisie. Recent interpretations have muted—without neglecting—the role of this factor. Both Stürmer and Sheehan, for example, take pains to explore the impact of German disunity and the European balance of power on the course of the revolution.[62] Political disunity has more recently been conceived of as having social as well as political consequences. As Mack Walker has argued, the existence of numerous small, independent states created the conditions necessary for the eventual rift between "hometownsmen" and the "General Estate" – that is, between artisans and shopkeepers and the liberal elite.[63] (Note, again, the playing with social vocabulary.) Sheehan has shown how the diversity of German states impeded national organization among liberals, pushing them to view their movement as a community of the spirit rather than a concrete political interest group.[64] But then, the party of Enlightenment and reform was equally devoid of formal organization in France up until the spring of 1789 and equally believed itself naively to have no need of such things. Furthermore, there was plenty of particularist sentiment among French "hometownsmen" on the eve of the Revolution. The *cahiers de doléance* are full of complaints about local matters, denunciations of machinery and economic progress, and demands to shore up the guilds. The Vendée uprising and the federalist revolts of the summer of 1793 demonstrate strong local loyalties and an abysmal lack of understanding of national-level politics among provincial populations.[65] The only difference that remains secure between the German and the French cases is that Germany had no political focal point, no capital city, no single governmental structure for the revolutionaries to seize and hold onto. But if this is all that distinguishes the two cases, then it would seem to follow that there is no relationship between the structure of German society in 1848 and the peculiar unfolding of the revolutionary crisis there – a highly unsatisfactory idea. Perhaps a question ought to be raised about the conventional distinction between state and society.

The identification of classes and interests in late nineteenth-century Germany is a field equally filled with confusion and paradox. As Germany's rapid industrialization proceeded and the institutional forms of Bismarck's unified state were consolidated and accepted after 1871, there was an accompanying social transformation of the ruling elite that makes the identification of "aristocratic" and "bourgeois" elements increasingly arbitrary. Yet historians have insisted on making such identifications and on asserting that the aristocratic element remained tragically preeminent in Germany in contrast to the other industrializing nations. Closer scrutiny of the specifics of such arguments, especially in a comparative context, raises serious difficulties. The German bourgeoisie, for example, is said to have become "feudalized," to have adopted, that is, feudal, nonliberal values in emulation of the preeminent Prussian Junkers who continued to dominate the government in Bismarck's new empire. Usually cited in this context is the increasingly conservative outlook of the bureaucracy at all levels, the rush of businessmen for titles of nobility and landed estates, the influence of the reserve officer corps, the aristocratic code of honor propagated by student brotherhoods.[66] The search for evidence of feudalizing elements in bourgeois life has sometimes been pushed to extremes. One historian has argued that the growth of middle-class suburbs after 1870 represented a search for the prestige of rural estates. Heidi Rosenbaum, recognizing that suburbs appeared everywhere in the Western world about this time, denies the significance of this factor but points nonetheless to the prevailing taste for building "little castles" or imitation palaces as a sign of bourgeois "aristocratization."[67] But obviously this was also a very general pattern, as true of late nineteenth-century Chicago as of Berlin.

In reality all of these facets of "feudalization" can be found in abundance in other European countries, a fact that has led two recent comparative studies to quite opposite conclusions. Arno Mayer in his *Persistence of the Old Regime* has extended the feudalization idea to the whole of European society; it was not difficult for him to find evidence of the middle-class pursuit of titles, of noble marriage partners, of landed property, and of military honor in every country he looked at.[68] Almost simultaneously David Blackbourn turned the argument on its head.[69] If Germany was similar to other countries, in his view, it merely shows that the bourgeoisie actually did dominate German politics and social life by the end of the nineteenth century. Where others have insisted that only real parliamentary sovereignty represents the proper form of bourgeois domination, Blackbourn sees such domination in the creation of a public realm, of *Oeffentlichkeit* in Habermas's sense, the existence of which does not depend on true parliamentary sovereignty. The spread of zoos, museums, and opera, the flourishing of the press, the organization of parties and of a parliamentary forum, even a debilitated one, in Germany after 1870 prove that this was indeed a bourgeois society. Evidence of "feudalization" Blackbourn dismisses as merely signs that the bourgeoisie was now able to take over for itself the old symbols of aristocratic domination; in other words, the apparent "feudalization" was only the final step in the bourgeoisie's rise to power.

This kind of interpretive game can be played endlessly. What Mayer sees as signs of aristocratic "flexibility" and "adaptability" – for example, the adoption of capitalist management and open sale of East Prussian estates – Blackbourn triumphantly points to as indicators of *embourgeoisement*. One is soon reduced to speaking, not of classes and their interests, but of the complex interplay of values, the subtle transformation of social symbols. It is just in this sense that Michael Stürmer has recently characterized German society of the late nineteenth century from the kaiser down as fundamentally bourgeois in its values. On the same tack Pat Thane and José Harris have recently, half in jest, coined the term "aristocratic bourgeoisie" to refer to European bankers in the period after 1880. The condition of using these terms meaningfully appears increasingly to be that one detach them from any exact socioeconomic definition. Soon the identification of any one person or thing as strictly bourgeois or strictly aristocratic begins to appear gratuitous. Whether the elaborate paternalism of the Krupp enterprise, for example, was a sign of feudal backwardness or a facet of advanced capitalist rationality is not a question to be resolved by looking at evidence.[70] Out of such material one may construct a history of the German catastrophe to fit any taste; it can be laid to the domination of the bourgeoisie or else to its defeat, to the abstractness and lack of realism of German liberalism or to its overly realistic assessment of power relations, to the backward or to the progressive character of German capitalism. Indeed, all of these characteristics are cited together in some cases without any sense of contradiction.

The idea of class has been a central one in European politics ever since Sieyès wrote his pamphlet "What Is the Third Estate?" For a long time the idea of class interest has provided a hardheaded, apparently realistic underpinning to narratives of European social history in the nineteenth century used both by actors like Bismarck and Lasker and by observers. For long it guided innumerable historians through the confusing maze of evidence that always arises when the details of social life are under investigation. But it has reached a point of diminishing returns, not just for the understanding of revolution but also for the understanding of normal times. Enough of the maze has been plotted out to show that too many paths crisscross class boundaries in countless directions both inside and outside politics.

Some may feel no discomfort with this state of affairs and may even view it as normal. Human reality is complex; the power of language is limited. One cannot expect the term "class" when used with theoretical rigor to yield neat results. It is really superior practice, some will insist, for historians like Chaussinand-Nogaret, Koselleck, or Walker to mix the social vocabularies of different periods and theories or to invent expressions of their own in the search to convey to the reader a sense of the delicate balance of perception and practice that characterized a particular period. "Class" is simply one additional less-than-adequate social term available to historians, with its own advantages and drawbacks. There is much to be said for this view. Nonetheless, even its supporters must recognize that this approach to historical explanation requires the greatest attentiveness to vocabulary. The concept of class has a long historical association with rigorous theorizing about society. No one can afford to be indifferent to the implications that the term carries with it as a result of its history. A critique of rigorous usage of the term may show that all usage of it is dangerously misleading.

STANDARD OF LIVING AND WAY OF LIFE IN ENGLAND

The question of the revolutionary bourgeoisie has stimulated little discussion among historians of nineteenth-century England, not only because there was no revolution but also because the existence of a numerous and growing business class has never been challenged. Instead, the search for a bourgeois revolution has been extended backward into the seventeenth century, and controversy over class and class interest in the nineteenth century has focused on the formation and political behavior of an industrial working class.

Early on, the attempt to interpret the Puritan rebellion of 1640–49 as a bourgeois revolution raised difficulties of exactly the same character as those encountered in the case of the French Revolution. Just like France in 1789 or Germany in 1848, England in 1640 had no numerous group of industrial capitalists organized to defend its interests or grasp for power. Since the ruling elite was made up almost exclusively of substantial landowners, controversy has arisen over whether some segment or stratum of this elite had emerged to form a new "gentry" class, capitalist landowners, in sum, with a businesslike outlook and the ability to prosper in a harsh, inflationary economy. It is not possible to follow this long argument through all of its steps here; in the end, just as in the French case, the discussion seems to have mired itself in an inconclusive and unsatisfactory lack of clarity about social relations, prestige, values,

23

and standards. The principal antagonists, instead of talking about identifiable classes, have fallen to discussing "status inconsistency" ("stress zones"), to questioning the existence of a social crisis, or to disputing whether the Puritan defenders of parliamentary power had ulterior motives (especially, fear of the lower orders) or were in actuality sincerely concerned with liberty and salvation.[71] A large measure of agreement exists about the nature of social change in the period by now, but not about its causes or the proper social vocabulary for discussing the shifting subtleties of rank and influence. Said Lawrence Stone in 1972, "The rise of the gentry, interpreted as something a good deal more profound and complicated than merely a redistribution of economic resources, is politically the single most important social development of the age."[72] But, it may be objected, the issue from the very beginning of this controversy has been the question whether a metaphor such as "the rise of the gentry," with all its familiar narrative implications, is really a useful way to think about the "profound and complicated" shifts and reversals that occurred. Stone, like Vovelle, belies himself.

The most recent shift in the direction of the debate over the Puritan rebellion was signaled by the appearance in 1979 of Conrad Russell's *Parliaments and English Politics, 1621–1629,* an immensely detailed narrative of parliamentary proceedings during the troubled 1620s.[73] It is noteworthy that this narrative allows Russell to document in abundance the thesis that members of Parliaments were ambivalent, that they had no one clearly focused desire or interest, but were torn between the conflicting pulls of county loyalties, crown demands, and court patronage. By implication, notions of class or class interest can offer no help in understanding this complex motivational web. There is in fact a parallel argument about the French Revolution recently propounded by Patrice Higonnet. In his view 1789 was a moment of flux; despite the emerging overall unity of the elite, the old distinction between nobleman and commoner retained just enough persuasive power to polarize the political arena in a way that was not strictly in accord with social fact. People were ambivalent, and social epithets helped them resolve their ambivalence, albeit in ways that were not very fruitful over the long run. It is remarkable that, with reference to both revolutions, historiography is now penetrating the shell of the individual to find there, not desires or interests, but collectively significant uncertainties, imposed from the outside by prevailing vocabulary or by institutional contexts.[74]

The period of the industrial revolution proper in England, roughly from about 1770 to 1850, according to a traditional interpretation, gave rise to a full-blown market system. The establishment of this system required the mobilization of all the basic factors of production – land, labor, and capital – so that they could be put up for sale at competitive prices to industrial entrepreneurs. Enclosure transformed the land, banking institutions created a capital market, population growth and economic dislocation threw up a propertyless laboring class ready to sell its services for wages. The principal change in social structure, therefore, was long considered to have been not within the elite so much as among the poor: the creation of the working class. The most remarkable fact about the historiography of this question is that the greatest Marxist historian to deal with it and its principal revisionist are one and the same person, E. P. Thompson.

Before the publication of E. P. Thompson's *The Making of the English Working Class* in 1963, historians had assumed that the development of industry had directly created a new class of wage laborers who were directly responsible for the disruptive protest movements of Luddism, Owenism, and Chartism.[75] A new class meant a new contender for power. This idea could be traced back to Marx and Engels (or even further), but, like so many other features of the revolutionary scenario, it was not actively disputed by non-Marxists.[76] Controversy arose instead over whether this new class's protests were justified, whether the pioneers of industrialism or its enemies deserved the greater sympathy of posterity, whether industrialization as carried out in England was or was not in the general interest.

Central to this controversy was the question of standards of living. Defenders of industrialism hoped to disarm its critics if they could show that its benefits were early and widely distributed. The Luddites and Chartists could then be viewed as misguided, or at best as exceptional victims of an essentially benign process. Critics of industrialism saw the danger of such a strategy, and they responded in two ways. First, they successfully disputed the optimistic figures on standards of living put forward by their opponents. Further rounds of research followed; the obvious documentary resources were in time exhausted. All general answers, it became apparent, were bound to be inconclusive. Nonetheless, agreement gradually emerged that the standard of living of the English poor may have actually tended slightly downward during the early decades of the industrial revolution as the demands of investment in plant and infrastructure weighed heavily on the growing national product. But by 1850 or thereabouts, all concurred, things definitely began to get better.[77] Secondly, those who sympathized with the working class and its protests sought to shift the ground of argument away from the standard of living narrowly conceived to larger and more diffuse questions of morality, environmental deterioration, and political oppression. Even if members of the new working class suffered on the average only slight reversals in their living standards, they nonetheless saw a general deterioration in the quality of their relationships, their surroundings, and their political voice.[78]

Thompson concentrated on the latter strategy, but in the process of gathering an extensive and detailed documentation for such an argument he also became aware of an extraordinary diversity of economic standing, social prestige, relations to the means of production, political participation, and self-consciousness among the laboring poor at the very time the factory system was supposed to have been homogenizing them into a single working class. Rather than being dismayed, he welcomed this discovery: After all, it undercut the relevance of the standard-of-living debate even more effectively than he at first, perhaps, hoped. At the same time, he put forward an avowedly Marxist interpretation of all the diverse protests against change in different trades and regions that he carefully catalogued. They were, he said, the actions of a class making itself. Across all this diversity a single pattern was discernible, "exploitation"—at once a political and an economic attack on established modes of production and the ways of life they supported. Exploitation was the stimulus of working-class formation, defined as the laboring poor's coming to awareness of their unity of interests against the propertied entrepreneurial elite. The working class consciously made itself out of the diverse ingredients that had entered the maw of commencing industrialization and laissez-faire reform.[79]

Apart from the problems that this thesis generated within English working-class history, for both the early nineteenth century and after, its bold sweep and its capacity to encompass inexhaustible empirical details were alone sufficiently stunning to require time before its implications were all digested.[80] Thompson had in effect openly embraced revisionism of the very kind that Marxists were resisting in the debate over the French Revolution or the Puritan rebellion. From his own evidence it was all too easy to see that there was no uniform class of wage laborers behind the stormy protest movements of the period. Any facile link between social structure and political conflict seemed definitively ruled out. On Thompson's evidence alone his thesis has been disputed.[81] The majority of those who engaged in protest or resistance were clearly from artisanal trades, often independent craftsmen, whose traditions went deep into the past but whose future was doomed. Wheelwrights, stockingers, saddlers, shoemakers, and tailors were condemned to skill dilution and gradual disappearance; they were not the working class but its preindustrial predecessors. Yet Thompson insisted that they be included in the ranks of the new class on the grounds that that is how they came to see the matter (a difficult contention to disprove with evidence alone). By shifting the definition of the notion of class onto the terrain of consciousness he saved the old scenario even as he undermined it. This feat has been the admiration and frustration of labor historians ever since. In the end it has been necessary to question whether Thompson's solution can remain the definitive one. In the meantime, in the sphere of working-class history at least, he has forced Marxists and non-Marxists alike to confront the issue of class consciousness in its own right — and therefore also the issues of social vocabulary, ritual, tradition, collective action, and so on. These can no longer be considered ancillary matters to be dealt with after the basic facts of economy and social structure are known. In the end the status of such basic facts and their relation to consciousness has become unclear since consciousness has a way of creating its own basic facts and its own interests. The differences between Marxist and non-Marxist in the face of such difficulties have lost their sharpness of definition.

A good example is the debate over the "labor-aristocracy" question in late nineteenth-century England. Labor aristocracy is one of those peculiar, paradoxical notions like the feudalization of the bourgeoisie in imperial Germany. It goes back to Lenin, who wanted to explain the absence of a revolutionary socialist movement in England. Again it is a question of something that did not happen, of a class that did not defend its interests or grasp for power in proper form. Lenin claimed that English industry had bought off the most highly skilled and self-conscious members of the working class by giving them a share in the superprofits of colonial exploitation.[82] Under the impact of Thompson-inspired historical investigation, however, the diversity and complexity of the so-called labor aristocracy have been fully explored. Lenin's thesis in its simplest form has fared rather poorly, not because the issue of England's privileged economic position in the world at that time is deemed irrelevant, but because it has been impossible to draw a simple causal link between that privileged world position and the political and social outlook of the English working class. Some of the labor aristocrats, it turns out, worked in unskilled jobs at tasks assigned in other countries to women and children.[83] Even the wages of the most skilled were lower than those of equivalent U.S. workers.[84] The strength and persistence of deference have been explained as arising, not from high wages or conspicuous privilege, but from the experience of workplace authority, from a particular fit between familial and workplace social needs, or from a widening split between subversive thought and accommodative action made possible by the "essentially incoherent and fragmented character of ideology."[85] Not money but a host of finely articulated social ties and a negotiated cultural leadership allowed many mid-Victorian industrialists even to count on the votes of their employees for Tory candidates. Merely to support the Liberal Party was, for many, an act of bold independence.[86] For others it meant deference not to employer but to an intermediate class.[87] Even in this truly liberal social order, it appears, political allegiance was determined by sentiments of loyalty, deference, and admiration for social betters in which considerations of class interest, strictly defined, played only a negligible role.

Those who were not labor aristocrats, the unskilled casual laborers and outworkers, did not follow the moderate lead of their better-off class brethren in any case. Instead, Gareth Stedman Jones has argued, they retreated into a reserved and sullen rejection of society as a whole, finding an outlet for their social and political alienation in the corner pub and the Victorian music hall. This "remaking" of the working class transformed even those who shared least in the superprofits of empire into a conservative element in the social order.[88]

Even before Thompson's work appeared, similar research was already under way in France and there were glimmerings in Germany as well. By 1963 Michelle Perrot, Maurice Agulhon, Remi Gossez, and Rolande Trempé, for example, were already at work in France on large projects of a kindred nature.[89] All sought to characterize the elusive unity that held together variegated groupings of shopkeepers, artisans, peasants, laborers, and their middle-class leaders in nineteenth-century protest movements. Perrot's vast study, organized as an almost platonic picture of the typical Third Republic strike, generalizes across the whole diverse range of working-class experience; Agulhon's notion of an archaic peasant communalism as the mobilizing element behind the uprising of 1851 closely parallels Thompson's views on the transitional nature of, for example, the Luddites. In the last decade numerous studies have appeared on both France and Germany, directly inspired by Thompson, all seeking to achieve a similar balance between the exploration of diversity and the identification of unifying conscious experiences among the laboring poor of the nineteenth century. Numerous variations on Thompson's solution have been tried out. Skilled artisans and industrial workers have been seen as brought by ephemeral trade crises into

27

momentary political alliances.[90] Members of certain trade groups – miners, mule spinners, seamstresses – once considered to be archetypical industrial workers have been shown to be more like artisans in pay, skill level, or habitual outlook.[91] No one speaks of the "proletariat" anymore but of "proletarianization" – a term that can be used to cover a disturbingly wide variety of specific alterations in status, skill, pay, or political consciousness.[92] By an act of faith implicit in the word, all such changes are deemed to be tending toward a single, if still distant, end point.

Even the notion of the self-conscious artisan has now come under attack in its turn as an oversimplification, a myth, propagated in part by literate, militant artisans of the past who, in reality, hated their work and would have preferred to be middle class.[93] The revisionism implicit in Thompson's approach, despite his brilliant last-ditch defense of the idea of the working class, has triggered a constantly widening awareness of the extraordinary range of statuses, experiences, and political aspirations that characterized those who worked with their hands in the nineteenth century. As in the case of the nonexistent revolutionary bourgeoisie, whether in France or Germany, as in the case of the "flexible" aristocracies of England and Prussia or the "feudalized" middle classes of Bismarck's empire, so in the case of the European working class, social historians over the last two decades have been brought to a point where no characterization of a group's identity or unity seems immune from challenge. Whenever it becomes a question of linking political comportment with social or economic status, endless subtleties and the constant discovery of new exceptions and subgroups have taken the place of the simple schemas of class conflict. It has become difficult to dispute any one historian's thesis for the simple reason that all are equally disputable and the critique itself seldom immune from challenge.

THE PROBLEM OF COLLECTIVE INTERESTS

Should the concept of class be dispensed with entirely? Some insist that it should. They point out that prerevolutionary French society, for example, was a society of "orders" or "estates." These were the words used then, and therefore they are the only words historians should use.[94] But this is an unacceptable alternative. The social vocabulary of a particular society at a particular moment is not the same thing as its social structure. The way relationships are spoken about or thought about is not the same thing as the way they are. Whether class or some other concept is used, it is necessary for historians to have a social vocabulary of their own with which to distinguish and discuss different forms of human relationships. Social terms and concepts are an important element of human relationships but are not identical to them. It is precisely when the terms fail that social change becomes likely. Explaining change is impossible without an independent vantage point. At the same time the use of any social vocabulary by the historian is going to be itself a highly political act, implying preferences and principles not shared by all.

Part of the originality of Thompson's contribution is that he redefined the term "class" to apply simultaneously to an economic and political predicament and to the consciousness of that predicament that emerged in response among its victims. Thompson insisted repeatedly that exploitation, as he called it, was no more structural or unconscious than the opposition it provoked. Each was one side of a human relationship. But he has never fully spelled out the implications of this view.

Lawrence Stone, with his usual lucidity, has commented on the search for origins of the Puritan rebellion in a manner applicable to the whole current status of social history:

> If the historian is to reduce his evidence to intelligible order he is obliged to use abstract concepts and collective nouns. In discussing society he deals in groups labelled peasants, yeomen, gentry and aristocracy; or tenants and landlords, wage-labourers and capitalists; or lower class, middle class and upper class; or Court and Country; or bourgeois and feudal. . . . Every individual can be classified in many different ways. . . . In assessing the motives of the single individual, the precise admixture of calculation and emotion, the effects of heredity and environment, are difficult enough to determine even when the evidence is available in unusual quantities. How much more complicated it all becomes when it is a question of handling these abstract nouns, of dissecting them and of perceiving the precise relevance of the various threads which make up the pattern not of individual but of collective behavior.[95]

This represents a cogent statement of at least a part of the problem. Social historians have been struggling for a long time to identify with some security a social dimension to the motives of political actors. This has been the principal means of linking political conflict to underlying social causes. But both common sense and long experience of research show that it is at best a slippery road on a foggy night that leads from social status to political motive. Motive in the best of circumstances is not observable and difficult to pin down. Any human action is influenced by as great a multitude of subjective factors as of objective ones. This is so obvious that, on reflection, one must wonder why it has taken so much work to establish that social history is not immune from the general uncertainty that characterizes our knowledge of the motives of others.

The underlying assumption about human motives that went along with the old scenario of class conflict and bourgeois revolution was, however, a simple and quite compelling one. It still commands the allegiance of a great many. This assumption is that on the whole, and especially in their social and political dealings with one another, most people want money and power. This is not true of everyone, but it is true of enough people that the traces of such desires should be unmistakable in history, especially if one looks at large-scale events like the French Revolution or the process of industrialization in England or the unification of Germany. Here large numbers of human beings were involved in contending for money and power in the high-stakes arenas of politics, war, and capital investment. Social change was an inevitable side effect of their contention. The problem of motives has usually been considered to be easier when we look at the patterns of collective behavior. The complexities of individual perception and calculation have been assumed to be washed out by the simplicity of the average person's, and therefore of any large-enough group's, desires. But a long struggle over the evidence has got to the point where Lawrence Stone can plausibly turn this assumption on its head. Collective motives are not easier to understand, but harder. The progress of research on a number of fronts points inevitably in this direction.

CLASS BY ANOTHER NAME

Is the concept of class, then, undergoing a crisis? It is only fair to say that many of those involved in the areas of research reviewed in this chapter would not agree. Social historians have in fact widely hailed recent developments in research as signs of the concept's vitality rather than of its decrepitude.[96] That simple pairings of social classes with political factions can no longer provide plausible explanations of conflict or revolution, that the class identity of specific individuals or groups can no longer be considered a straightforward issue – these are causes not for concern, many believe, but for celebration. At last the conditions have been realized for a definitive reworking of the concept of class along Marxist lines; the challenge is variously seen as involving a new conception of the relationships among consciousness, ideology, and daily experience; or as requiring that class structures and class struggle be seen as operating at a deeper, longer-term level of social reality, one that is not directly apparent on the surface at any given moment. The concern with rethinking the relation between ideology and experience shows up in recent works by William Sewell, Raymond Williams, Rainer Wirtz, Sean Wilentz, and Jacques Rancière. Concern with the underlying structure of classes and their conflicting interests is evident in the work of Geoff Eley, Ronald Aminzade, David Abraham, and Hanna Schissler. These approaches have been combined in E. P. Thompson's controversial 1978 essay "Class Struggle without Class?" and in the work of David Blackbourn.[97]

At least two things may be said in favor of the view that class is undergoing not a final crisis but a healthy period of reformulation. First, the general sense of class as a dividing line, however fuzzy its edges, between empowerment and impotence, authority and deference, security and fear, is in no way challenged by the findings of the new research that has been reviewed here. No one has suggested that modern society is not characterized by stark differentials in access to subsistence goods, to education, to physical comforts, to authority, or to political influence. Insofar as "class" is the term used to refer to such differentials, it has obvious validity. Questions have been raised only about two related notions deeply embedded in the concept of class that informed the old Marxist scenario of revolution: (1) the notion of relation to the means of production as an unambiguous marker of class identity and (2) the notion that individual political factions ought to be seen as representing the interests of specific classes defined in terms of this unambiguous marker.

Second, new thinking about class among social historians has been paralleled by a general shift in the treatment of class and class conflict within the Marxist tradition as a whole since World War II. This shift is evident in the rediscovery of Gramsci, as well as in the writings of figures like Ralf Dahrendorf, Nicos Poulantzas, Lucio Colletti, Pierre Bourdieu, or more recently, Erik Wright and Michael Burawoy.[98]

Constantly at issue in the writings of these and other recent Marxist thinkers are the two linked difficulties mentioned in the previous paragraph. These two problems have emerged as central not only in historical research but in any attempt to give a Marxist account of the rise of the new middle class in the twentieth century, of the failure of the old working class to retain a revolutionary stance vis-à-vis the established order, or of the spread of revolution in peripheral peasant and plantation-dominated countries. Solutions of considerable variety have by now been proposed to these difficulties; some resemble each other closely, but each one has quite distinct implications. Two recent and very influential proposals illustrate the nature of the problem: Pierre Bourdieu has insisted that there is a kind of "cultural" capital circulating in modern societies that shapes elite access to power and to surplus appropriation in ways quite different from fixed productive capital.[99] Erik Wright, in his search to account for the complexity of class structure in present-day industrial societies, has proposed two whole new mechanisms of exploitation – in addition to the traditional ones of feudal coerced labor and wage labor. He calls them skill-based and organization-based exploitation. (Wright adds that none of these four mechanisms apply to exploitative relations within families or households.)[100] One can see a close resemblance between Bourdieu's notion of cultural capital and Wright's concepts of skill-based and organization-based exploitation; but one must also recognize that in the Wright scheme, a whole new theory of history results, with two completely new stages of revolution, while in Bourdieu's nothing of the sort is expressed or implied.

The profusion of such inventions in recent years testifies to the vitality of the Marxist tradition and to the creative energies unleashed by the effort to bring refractory new evidence into the scope of the theory's basic categories. But one may legitimately question whether all these new theoretical departures do not add up to a fundamental alteration in the status of the theory itself. Will it not be necessary to conclude in the end that Marxist theory represents not a discovery, not a form of knowledge or a "science," but instead an interpretive framework that consists of categories built on underlying metaphors and that is infinitely manipulable? If so, then the crisis of the class concept for the Marxist tradition consists not of the fact that there is no way to rework class to fit new findings or to answer revisionist objections but of the fact that there are too many ways to rework it, all of which are equally successful, none of which is evidently superior to any of the others. One can speak of classes as distinguished by their access to cultural capital, or to organizational capital, or to sexual capital. Do advertisers engage in symbol-based exploitation? One can speak, as Burawoy does, of class relationships that "manufacture consent" or of what he calls "the politics of production," or for that matter of the "production of politics" or the "politics of reproduction."[101] Following Bourdieu, one can speak of the "mode of production of opinion." One can discover class conflict in the design of a bathroom or in the Nicene Creed. One can measure the extraction of surplus value from the "labor" of Hollywood movie extras. This is all to the good. The claim being made here is not that such novel manipulations serve no purpose. On the contrary, nothing is more important than the continued elaboration of such penetrating juxtapositions of terms. The claim is that much current discussion of new notions of class is based on metaphorical extensions or inversions of received Marxist categories that are thereby revealed to be no more than metaphors themselves.

Marx took many of his basic terms from Ricardian political economy, a theoretical language whose metaphorical origins were already lost in the past before Marx came across it. Ricardo by 1817 could assume, for example, that his readers were habituated to thinking of society as a vast marketplace; so deeply had this metaphor taken root by then that the original insight encoded into it had been lost from view. Metaphors give insight, after all, only so long as one remembers that they are metaphors – that is, constructs, human artifacts. By 1817 the idea that prices were measurements akin to experimental findings in chemistry or observations of stars and planets in astronomy also had a long history. Had it been otherwise no one would have accepted, to say nothing of understanding, Ricardo's highly schematic, breathlessly abstract theory of wages and rents, which resembled nothing so much as a Newtonian model of the solar system or Carnot's laws of thermodynamics. For Ricardo, not only was society a great marketplace but this marketplace operated by laws not of human making whose discovery was the legitimate object of scientific inquiry. No figure of speech for him, but self-evident truth, was embodied in the idea that society was "like" a market or a market "like" the solar system. Marx subjected Ricardo's highly technical language to a dialectical critique. In Marx's hands, not just Ricardian theory but the whole language of the liberal tradition – including key words like "class," "labor," "commodity," or "value" – was shown to be an instrument of mystification in its everyday meanings. Yet he never jettisoned the terms that he unmasked. Once he was fully aware of their limits and their dangers, he saw no reason to replace them.

More will be said of this in Chapter 3. It is enough to note here that the concept of class in both the liberal and the Marxist traditions always refers back to relationships of exchange. Where money is involved in these relationships, the precise quantities exchanged remain central, in both traditions, to one's estimation of the character of the relationship. If the money is deemed to be an insufficient retribution for the quantity of commodity or service delivered, then the class relationship in question is an exploitative one. The principal bone of contention between the two traditions has been and continues to be how one decides what represents sufficient retribution. In the Marxist tradition, one accepts that money is an instrument of measurement and contends only that prices are always inaccurate reflections of true value.

The aim of this study, however, will be to shift the whole controversy onto entirely new grounds, to replace the underlying metaphorical structure of the language in common usage in both traditions. A given quantity of money, it will be argued, means utterly different things to different people. In the end, modern society is less like a marketplace than like a royal court in which belief in the validity of prices is like the profound respect once accorded to titles and degrees of nobility, with all the finely calculated — and utterly illusory — distinctions of personal worth they make possible. And, as at court, those who do not believe, or do not act as though they believe, receive no invitation to the banquet.

But before these issues can be pursued further, some consideration of recent attempts by social historians to employ new interpretive methods is in order. That will be the task of the next chapter. From a critique of these attempts will emerge a very simple theory of history, a bare-bones schematism that says very little about what the future will bring and that lays the groundwork for a new approach to monetary exchange.

2 Meaning and its material base

THE SIMPLICITY OF THE NOTIONS of money and power has bewitched historians and others for a long time. One can interpret almost any action as arising from a
desire for money and power and end up with a quite plausible result. Who is to say
that money and power do not motivate the pope in making a trip to Guatemala or
the young poet as he publishes his first volume of verse? Obviously, if either actor is
successful he or she will have more money and power, among other things. The idea
that this is the basic or underlying motive of human action links all realms of endeavor – religion, metaphysical speculation, politics, amateur astronomy, tulip growing – into an apparently neat, single skein of power relations. But seeking money and
power by writing a poem is a very different thing from doing so by selling short on
the New York Stock Exchange. The idea that both are merely different means to the
same end explains nothing about why individuals might choose such radically different means or why some might succeed in gaining money and power by these diverse
means. This is exactly the problem that confronts social historical research today. It
is impossible to say why some provincial lawyers in France supported the Revolution
of 1789 and others did not or why, among those who did, some became Feuillants,
others Girondins, and others Montagnards.[1] For a long time it seemed plausible that
the collective interests of large groups – that is, of classes – were so self-evident that
organization and leadership were easily achieved around such interests. But there is a
crushing weight of evidence, painfully built up, that now rules out this idea. Yet to
suppose that there is no systematic social dimension to the complex motives that
urge people forward is clearly unacceptable, is tantamount to saying that there is no
such thing as society, that groups have no influence over individuals, that we are all
droplets in a gaseous cloud tossed about in Brownian motion by the random impact
of loose motivational molecules.

MOTIVES IN PRACTICE

In the face of the dilemma just outlined, it is not surprising that social historians began turning to cultural anthropology, literary theory, and structuralist philosophy

for assistance, nor that one of the first results was a forthright declaration of independence for the realm of the cultural from the blunt facts of mere material interests.

Natalie Davis in 1973, for example, in an influential essay entitled "Rites of Violence," asserted that previous historical explanations of religious violence in sixteenth-century France attributed too much importance to underlying economic motives.[2] The rhythm of religious violence did not correlate with grain scarcities or price fluctuations, nor did the social composition of violent crowds allow one to discern economic conflicts of interest between perpetrators and victims. Instead, Davis argued, these occurrences must be taken at face value. Much as an ethnographer works in the field, the historian must search for deep regularities of meaning in the words and actions of religious communities. She demonstrated, moreover, that there were numerous and striking regularities to be found in the religious riots. Violent action was usually an extension of some more common social activity; it served to demonstrate theological doctrine, to purify the community of religious contamination, to supplement the function of the magistrate. Davis developed a whole taxonomy of violent acts revealing a profound spiritual, political, and social rift between the Catholic and Reformed churches in sixteenth-century French towns.

In another article that appeared at the same time, "The Moral Economy of the English Crowd in the Eighteenth Century," E. P. Thompson rejected in terms even more definite than Davis's what he called "the spasmodic view of popular history" by which collective actions are treated as "compulsive, rather than self-conscious or self-activating," as if they were "simple responses to economic stimuli." For historians of the spasmodic school, "it is sufficient to mention a bad harvest or a down-turn in trade, and all requirements of historical explanation are satisfied."[3] Thompson, like Davis, had his eye on the interpretive methods of cultural anthropology as an alternative approach. He demanded that the popular masses of eighteenth-century England be credited at a minimum with the human capacities that make possible "the delicate tissue of social norms and reciprocities which regulates the life of Trobriand islanders and the psychic energies involved in the cargo cults of Melanesia."[4]

At about the same time historians were becoming aware of the work of Michel Foucault, a philosopher who, drawing on his familiarity with French psychoanalysis and structuralist anthropology, began in the 1960s to interpret French social institutions and intellectual traditions of the eighteenth and nineteenth centuries. He employed what he called an "archaeological" method; that is, he in effect assumed the existence of the most radical discontinuities over time in the way human beings used language, with thoroughgoing effects on every realm of social and institutional activity. He argued that the linguistic, biological, and social "knowledge" of specific periods in the past differed in the same fundamental ways as did their asylums, economies, prisons, and schools from those of subsequent periods.[5] Foucault made the past look suddenly, uncannily strange to historians whose stock-in-trade was continuity, development, and connection. Foucault's unfamiliar past required the same kinds of interpretive care as Davis's rioters or Thompson's crowds. Clifford Geertz's important collection of essays *The Interpretation of Cultures* also appeared in 1973, providing the example of an interpretive method that drew heavily on literary criticism and phenomenology and whose potential for use in historical research was clear.[6] A great many social historians saw these and other works as representing an important and timely challenge, offering a possible way out of the dilemma that Lawrence Stone so nicely summarized in 1972. Obviously interest could no longer be taken as something given, and the existence of class could no longer be taken as self-evident. What unites people in the first instance is not common economic or political goals, but what Davis calls "perception," Foucault "the order of discourse," Geertz "meaning." This dimension of social reality in the past had to be unearthed and reconstructed with the loving care that an archaeologist employs when piecing together potsherds.

Application of these new methods (for there were significant variations among them) of cultural interpretation and attempts to solve the problems that arise from their application have been a major preoccupation of social historians working on all three countries under consideration over the last decade. It is difficult to sum up the results of these efforts because they are still largely confined to specialized studies dealing with small fragments of the national pasts that do not quite add up to a whole, revised vision. There has been a significant amount of work done, in English history, on the development of political economy, revealing its intimate links to social conditions and political outlooks in that country from the seventeenth through the early nineteenth centuries.[7] The general project of the History Workshop group in England, and the methodological debates over that project, have focused on immensely detailed knowledge of day-to-day working-class life and struggle in the industrial era.[8] Thomas Laqueur and Gareth Stedman Jones have reexamined the period of reform agitation and Chartism between 1815 and 1848, seeking to come to terms with the "language" of working-class political action in a formative period.[9] In Germany "Alltagsgeschichte," that is, careful reconstruction of the shape of everyday life, has come into vogue and stirred debate.[10] In addition, the exercise of power by bureaucratic elites has begun to receive close scrutiny, revealing the complex conceptions of honor and of social well-being that moved government officials in Prussia and elsewhere to discipline social life so much more minutely than did English or French administrators. German peasants and workers have been shown as well to have been capable of subtle yet pervasive forms of resistance to the omnipotent reach of elite authority. In the work of David Sabean and Alf Lüdtke, popular culture no longer appears as an autonomous, unchanging sphere untouched by the developing power of the state.[11]

Rather than trying to review all of this work in detail, however, which would be quite difficult, I will concentrate on the Davis essay just mentioned and on a few recent works on the origin and course of the French Revolution. As always, attitudes toward the great French Revolution of 1789–99 remain divided; but the interest of this decisive episode has become, if anything, greater as new methods have arisen that promise to put it in an entirely new light. As a result, recent work on this one subject can offer a convenient means of reviewing the strengths and weaknesses of new interpretive approaches to European history as a whole. What historians of the

French Revolution have attempted to deal with, in particular, is a weakness inherent in the works of Davis, Foucault, and Geertz and in the method of cultural interpretation in general, that is, the difficulty of depicting (not to mention accounting for) change, which has always been, after all, the historian's primary concern. The discussion that follows will identify drawbacks in all these efforts and then attempt to get beyond these drawbacks by outlining a new theory of history.

The picture Davis paints is static and monolithic. Because all evidence is used to build up a picture of a single array of symbolic relationships, it is difficult to see how this array developed, whether it varied from place to place, whether individuals varied in their commitment to it, or why it declined later. Davis depicts communities wholly given over to their particular religious world view, innocent of any second thoughts or doubts, ignorant of any notion of a neutral, secular, nonreligious realm. This view is difficult to square with other well-known facts about the period, with the cynical maneuverings of the great families, the scheming of Catherine de Medici, the guarded skepticism of Montaigne, or the blithe (and very popular) apostasy of Henry IV.[12] Cultural anthropology as currently practiced is a poor tool for understanding diversity, personal calculation, crisis, or change.

Of course, under normal circumstances individual doubts, fears, and ambivalences raise few difficulties. Many areas of social action are so highly routinized and rule-governed that the attitudes of the individual have little observable effect on their operation. In such cases the motives of social actors are in effect prescribed. Individuals must either accept the prescribed motives and make them their own or else cease to engage in that form of activity. This point requires illustration. Eighteenth-century France was full of these kinds of routinized activity right up to the eve of the Revolution and provides a convenient source of examples of how they worked.

It is not necessary to ask, for example, why a merchant partnership of La Rochelle outfitted a ship in the 1730s. Only one motive was possible for engaging in such activities: profit. Nor is it necessary to wonder why the partnership sent that ship to West Africa in search of slaves to resell in Saint-Domingue in the Caribbean, where indigo was loaded for transport back to La Rochelle. The Atlantic triangular trade was well established by then and could be quite profitable, if the ship met with no mishaps and if the Saint-Domingue planters' letters of credit were good. Today, we may deplore this fact. We are shocked that a successful slave rebellion on board the La Rochelle-based *Galatée* while off the African coast in 1737 appears in a merchant's journal as no more than an austere notice of unavoidable financial losses.[13] It is repugnant that slave deaths on board ship were calculated as a normal part of operating costs.[14]

But it is not necessary to question the immediate motive of the individual merchant. To be a merchant was to embrace the search for profit as it was then practiced. By the eighteenth century international trade, from the individual participant's point of view, was a tightly organized cultural construct with rules as strict and outcomes as clearly defined as in the game of chess. One either played to win or else one did not play. What one did with one's earnings was another matter. One was perfectly free to continue plowing them back into trading ventures, but in actuality almost no one in La Rochelle or elsewhere did this indefinitely. Sooner or later most successful merchant families began investing in land, a far less remunerative but more secure form of wealth. Not to have done so would have marked any particular merchant as an oddity, without necessarily endangering his reputation or that of his family, however. The rules of profitable trade were rigorous and unambiguous. But eighteenth-century French communities also had another set of rules for an ancillary, less carefully laid-out game, that of family advancement. Profits from the first game served as a ticket of entry into the second. Within this second game, by following the prescribed course, with careful planning and a little luck, it was possible to manage a gradual social assent, slowly transferring the family's wealth out of trade into land and ennobling office. Robert Forster's research has led him to argue that merchants may have played the game of family advancement with less self-consciousness than historians usually assume.[15] But there is no doubt that the game's existence and the rules that governed it were known to all.

Over the long run there were many families that did not achieve this transition. The problem may have been in part motivational. One may scrutinize individual lives and account for such failures by discovering weaknesses of will, indifference, troubles of conscience, dissipation of energy in unproductive channels, even outright rebellion against the prescribed merchant way of life, with its distant and often illusory goals, with its petty jealousies and invidious distinctions. Doubtless there were hundreds of people in the merchant communities of La Rochelle or Bordeaux who did not really want this way of life and turned away from its rigors wholly or partially, ceding the advantage to those with greater sureness of purpose. Nonetheless, such private doubts and disillusionments did nothing to change the game itself or to alter the motive of family advancement that it prescribed. Of course, in 1789, the whole applecart was upset; people possessed by other kinds of longings had a chance to shine. Later, after 1799, when the old game of routine social advancement was finally reconstituted in France, it had new rules and prescribed an altered, but very similar, set of motives.

The same could be said for every sphere of social life. It is not necessary to ask what a journeyman windowmaker wanted when he left home on his *tour de France* in 1759.[16] To go on the tour was to accept the desires that went along with it. The tour offered an escape from home and, beyond it, the possibility of mastership, free from the petty commands and oppressions of journeyman status. It was a chance to see the world, to collect stories of exploits and defeats, to prove one's prowess and skill, to make some money and spend it with a free hand, to enjoy the pageantry, gallantry, and violence of the journeyman life. To do the tour without making one's own the desire for some of these things would have been very difficult. Unlike the rules of international trade, but like the rules of family advancement, the code of the journeyman tour left room for much flexibility and variation; but there were nonetheless limits on the range of personal desires that could be accommodated within it.

To understand the rules of this kind of established practice, there is nothing to match the methods pioneered by cultural anthropology. What drinking or violence means within the whole range of journeyman practice, what the purchase of a rural *seigneurie* means within the merchant circles of La Rochelle – these are not matters that can be summed up under the term "interest." Instead, they require a literary evocation based on the careful analysis of texts such as records of rituals, family letters, autobiographies, laws and charters, treatises on social rank, or political speeches on the virtues of specific reforms.[17]

The only problem with the method of cultural interpretation is that it threatens to leave the individual out of account in a manner different from, but not altogether more convincing than, the old notion of class interest. He is dissolved into typicality, treated as a bundle of symbolically significant conventions, as a member of a symbolically defined, rather than a socioeconomic, class. This is exactly what Natalie Davis intended to accomplish in her essay on religious riot, as she said in her own defense two years after its publication:

> We find we must imagine a multidimensional model of social structure, one
> that incorporates and goes beyond the standard one of socio-economic classes.
> We must stretch our definition of "social tensions" well beyond the issue of
> wealth and poverty. And rather than being "covered by a religious cloak" [as Da-
> vis's critic, Janine Estèbe, contended], the social face of the Reformation is as
> real as its obverse, the spiritual face, different sides of the same coin.[18]

Instead of being dissolved in socioeconomic typicality, the individual is lost in cultural convention; his impulses and tastes are nothing more than the integrated components of a larger sociosymbolic coherence.

Such a method can always yield satisfying results in the study of a steady state. At most moments of history, after all, there is almost nothing that the individual could do that is not, in effect, anticipated by the established practices of society. Even if one refuses to accept the prescribed motives of one's milieu, in most societies this is also a kind of routine, and there are both practical structures and ideas ready to be applied to it. Conversion to Calvinism was by 1560 in France an act surrounded by a well-ordered array of contending conventional interpretations. Such conversion was no longer a common means of rebellion by the eighteenth century. But one need only read a few of the novels of that time – *Manon Lescaut* or *Le paysan perverti* – or a few of the sermons of Bossuet or the *Tableau* of Mercier to realize that a halfhearted commitment to a way of life or an outright rebellion against it was a normal occurrence. Deviance was anticipated by moral thought, legal principle, the geography of urban space, the current taxonomy of social forms, and the available furniture of the imaginary.[19] Any individual aberration could be classified and yield an administrative file as well as predictable private reactions. The interpretation of culture provides a means of piecing together the world views that inspire the multifarious and polyvalent routines that can make deviance, crime, and ennobling office look like parts of the same coherent order.

But interpretation of this kind entails great difficulty when it comes time to explain how societies get from one steady state to another. Before the clear boundaries and organized violence of 1572 or 1793 were possible there must necessarily have occurred a period of flux. What did the first lonely converts to Calvinism in the 1530s think they were doing? Did they know they were starting a new church? What went through the minds of the delegates to the Estates General of 1789 on the first day of their meetings? No interpretation of the spectacle and pageantry of that session could answer this question.

And this is a critical weakness, because the problem of motives would never have arisen among social historians if the aim had not been to account for rapid social change. In periods of revolutionary upheaval the question of motives gains a particular urgency, for those directly involved as well as for historians. When rapid change occurs, the guiding hand of established practice fails to limit and structure the choices individuals may make and therefore the things they can reasonably want. The opportunities that a revolution opens up are unexpected and frightening; those who seize the occasion are bound to be strong-willed—whatever else they are—bound to have a depth of character that the old social routine would never have allowed them to reveal. Such were, for example, Robespierre, the obscure young lawyer from Arras, or Madame Jeanne Phlipon Roland *ci-devant* de la Platière, wife of an inspector of manufactures and moderately successful encyclopedist of Amiens, both of whom shone briefly and went to the guillotine. Before the crisis, like everyone else, they were preoccupied with careers that gave only a moderate scope to their talents and aspirations. This is an indispensable feature of any form of social stability. After the crisis, like everyone else, they found their motives subject to constant suspicion and were constantly uncertain of others, both in the Assembly hall and on the steps of the scaffold.

CRISES OF MEANING

Since the appearance of Davis's essay attempts have been made to compensate for this weakness of cultural interpretation by developing cultural theories that allow a place for a dynamic of change within them. A number of these have focused on the French Revolution, aiming to fill the explanatory vacuum created by the revisionists. In general they have taken the form of a "crisis-of-meaning" interpretation: The revolutionary crisis is reinterpreted as one involving not ancien-régime society itself so much as the social and political language of that society and the shifts, fault lines, and incongruities to be found in this language.

François Furet has developed a theory about the political function of discourse to explain the outbreak and gradual radicalization of the Revolution.[20] According to Furet, because the formation of public opinion was hindered and obscured by censorship and privilege before the Revolution, concepts such as the nation or the people had a vague and insubstantial quality to them that they retained through the 1790s. The blindness of the Montagnards and the violence of their rule were simply symp-

toms of a highly abstract political language born in the constrained atmosphere of absolutist repression. Through the structure of discourse, arbitrary rule bred arbitrary
rule. In the absence of any established consultative procedure, what was to prevent
the sans-culottes from assuming that they represented and spoke for the whole nation? But then, by the same token, what was to stop anyone from making such a
claim, including the Thermidorians and finally Napoleon himself? The bewildering
outbreak and course of the Revolution may, in other words, have social origins not in
the intentions, interests, or frustrations of any particular group but in the manner in
which language was used in the ancien régime to construct an idea of the social
whole.

Such an approach is actually compatible with the "stress-zones" idea, as well, because in both instances what is proposed is that problems occurred in the way symbols conferring power and self-esteem were distributed, so to speak, whether these
symbols were ennobling office or the idea of the nation. In 1789 France was in the
dangerous situation of having allowed public opinion to grow halfway to maturity in
the interstices of law and at the same time of having denied many people privileges,
offices, and exemptions commensurate with their wealth and education. It was possible for anyone to assert that he had the backing of that quasi-legal thing, public opinion, of the people, and that therefore he had a much more ennobling function to fulfill than any mere influence-monger at court. True freedom of speech, when it finally
came, could not eradicate the habits of decades of semilegal political talk; it was not
long before newly created authorities dispensed with free speech, all the better to assert their absolute claims to popular support.

Lynn Hunt has rightly criticized Furet's new interpretation of the French Revolution because, for all its powerful insights into the workings of revolutionary politics, it
leaves the social dimension almost entirely out of account.[21] According to Furet, "The
'people' was not a datum or a concept that reflected existing society."[22] This was because "a network of signs completely dominated political life."[23] As a result, "the Revolution replaced the conflict of interests for power with a competition of discourses for
the appropriation of legitimacy," and legitimacy was equivalent to "the people's
will."[24] The only respect in which the Revolution can have had a social origin is in the
forms of discourse to which ancien-régime society gave rise in preparing the way for the
Revolution's "network of signs." But in Furet's discussion these forms seem to arise entirely out of the interplay between Enlightenment political thought and royal absolutism. The question of social or economic change is passed over in silence.

Hunt has accepted the core of Furet's interpretation of revolutionary discourse in
her recent book, adding to it several penetrating observations.[25] She agrees that revolutionary discourse rejected the play of interests totally. And from this fact, she
shows how the discourse became necessarily radicalizing, giving everything in social
life a political significance: "In the face of ambivalence toward organized politics, especially in the form of parties or factions, new symbols and ceremonies became the
most acceptable medium for working out political attitudes."[26] Furthermore, fear of
conspiracy forced the revolutionaries to examine and reform every "nook and cranny"

of daily life and to elaborate revolutionary discourse into a complete, life-encompassing system.

Unlike Furet, however, Hunt goes on to look for a social origin of the "new political class" thrown up by the Revolution. She argues that the revolutionaries were recruited — increasingly as time went on — among the structurally marginal elements of ancien-régime society. Extensive research has allowed her to document this claim with numerous, vivid examples. Jacobin leaders came often from the ranks of the geographically mobile or uprooted, from people with Protestant or Jewish backgrounds, from those who had been ostracized from local society in times past for diverse offenses against propriety. The difficulty with this thesis arises not from the brilliant documentation Hunt provides but from the lack of an explanation of the occasion of Revolution. Such people would have been available for an adventure in political language building at any time in any society. Therefore, Hunt offers no counter to the unsatisfactory idea put forward by some revisionists that the Revolution was an accident, that it had no social origins, only social consequences.

Both Hunt and Furet offer an explanation for the extreme radicalization of the French Revolution that is disturbingly similar to explanations offered for the extreme moderation of German liberals in 1848. In both instances the revolutionary assemblies rejected factional politics outright in favor of a search for principled unanimity. The German liberals later denounced their own refusal to recognize the power of organized social interests. This, they later decided, is what defeated them. Yet a similar refusal, according to Furet and Hunt, is what forced the Jacobins forward into ever-more-radical experiments in pure democracy (saving the Revolution from "failure" along the way). The Jacobins no more than the German liberals were willing to admit the legitimacy of any interest other than the general one. Perhaps the difference lies in the Jacobins' ruthless pursuit of those they saw as enemies of the general interest, of the illusory "aristocratic plot."

In any case it seems impossible to accept Furet's claim that "the 'people' was not a datum or a concept that reflected existing society." The question is not whether but how it reflected existing society. It is not at present clear whether any vocabulary can merely reflect social relationships without at the same time shaping and influencing them, and being in turn shaped by them. What does Furet mean when he says that the Revolution "replaced the conflict of interests for power with a competition of discourses for the appropriation of legitimacy"? Does this statement imply that under normal circumstances the conflict of interests does not require a discourse of some kind or does not involve a contention over the legitimacy of different terms or forms of discourse? If so, it is surely wrong, and fails to distinguish revolutionary politics from normal politics.

Following Furet's interpretation of the French Revolution, it would be necessary to praise, rather than castigate, the German liberals of the 1860s who bowed before Bismarck's fait accompli.[27] They were in fact doing what they have been condemned (especially by themselves) for failing to do in 1848, that is, frankly recognizing the legitimacy of class interest and openly granting to the Prussian aristocracy a place in politics commensurate with its de facto power. They replaced the dangerous and anomalous "competition of discourses for the appropriation of legitimacy" with the normalizing "conflict of interests for power."

Lynn Hunt claims the opposite, that the Jacobin refusal of party politics paradoxically paved the way for the creation of a rich and lasting revolutionary tradition that eventually, after 1875, made possible a healthy and normal party politics in France. The German liberals' frank recognition of the interplay of interests, in the absence of an established republican tradition, she would presumably argue, permanently crippled parliamentary life in Germany. This is a more satisfactory view, but it is one that forces us to recognize a deep relationship between terror and the establishment of a stable parliamentary regime. In Germany, too, terror was used; only it fell out that it was wielded in the name not of liberalism but of an absolute monarchy that, through military victory, carried out many of liberalism's tasks. The failure of German liberals, then, was that they failed in 1848 to be illiberal in the application of their liberal principles, and in the 1860s they were again too liberal in the frank recognition of class interest. Liberalism is supposed to eschew terror and applaud the interplay of interests. This is precisely what German liberals did. [28]

These reflections lead back to a more fundamental question. Why was it impossible to establish liberalism in Europe by liberal means? For it succeeded only where it found fanatical violence to support it. Another way to put this question is: Why was the liberal political vocabulary (words like "nation," "people," "citizen," "class," "interest," "society," "contract," etc.) such a blunt tool for reshaping social life that it always caused extensive hemorrhaging on first application? This question, already raised in the most trenchant way by Ralf Dahrendorf, is difficult to answer because the liberal vocabulary is so far the only one ever consciously used as a political tool to reshape social life. [29] (The Marxist vocabulary is largely of liberal origin, after all.) It is difficult to answer because there is no other vocabulary ready to hand for talking about the social origins and social impact of the liberal vocabulary. Here is where all current efforts ought to be concentrated. But it is not clear at the moment how the method of cultural interpretation might be used to answer this question, since answering it would require one to have an idea of what society is. Mere interpretation of the meanings of texts, rituals, and practices can never reveal, on its own, why a particular set of texts, rituals, and practices (those of liberalism) could be instituted only through direct application of the state's most powerful instruments of civil coercion. It may be that cultural interpretation as a method has implications for what society is that would help to explain why this was so; but in that case, it would be necessary to spell out these implications, to build a theory of history on the basis of interpretive method. An attempt to do so will follow; but it would be worthwhile first to mention at least one other recent discussion of the French Revolution.

William Sewell's study, *Work and Revolution in France,* offers a third variant of the crisis-of-meaning approach to the French Revolution, one that has certain advantages over Furet's. [30] First, Sewell's inquiry is a search for the dynamics of change within social discourse based on the assumption that social discourse is both inevitable and powerful in any society. He is not required to claim that crisis may result from discourse's taking on an anomalous power; the power of social language is a constant for Sewell. Second, Sewell has criteria of his own for determining what aspect of discourse is worthy of study. He chooses to examine over time the changing discussion of that most concrete, most necessary, and most constant of social activities, labor. However drastic the alterations that a social order undergoes, some conception of human labor will reasonably have to hold a central place before, during, and after the crisis; and changes in that conception are likely to hold the key to larger shifts in general patterns of language and of practice. Sewell has been criticized for failing to integrate his account of changing language with actual changes occurring simultaneously in the practice of work. It is true that he does this only in a general, global way. Nonetheless, his decision to seek out the dynamic of change in social discourse by examining conceptions of work allows him to balance continuity and change in his account, so that the Revolution does not appear to be merely an accident and the later recurrences of revolution in nineteenth-century France do not appear to be mere repetitions.

By Sewell's account work turns out to have been for the Enlightenment that form of interaction with nature which was the origin of all true knowledge and order in society as well as the ultimate justification of the right of property. Nature was mechanical, labor the manipulation of the mechanism, property the right to labor's fruits. This was the critical wedge used by the revolutionaries to pry away all forms of property and privilege that had no possible origin in physical labor: feudal dues, venal office, guild restrictions, noble tax exemptions. But a competitive economic regime based on private property, Sewell argues, was bound to cause a growing tension between the implicit nobility of labor – as the paradigm of human action and the origin of all property – and labor's all-too-evident degradation under the free play of market forces. It was this "dialectic" that gave rise to artisanal socialism under the July Monarchy. Potential contradictions in subordinate ideologies, in Sewell's view, may lie dormant until that ideology becomes dominant in society. Then the contradictions become evident in practice and serve to stimulate the further elaboration of new ideological configurations.

Although the bulk of Sewell's effort is devoted to the interpretation of abstract political language, from Enlightenment texts, from the Revolution, and from nineteenth-century artisan movements, nonetheless his "dialectic" pivots on a concrete shift in the established practices of the workplace consequent on the enactment of laissez-faire policy. This is what split the masters, now competing property owners, from the journeymen and what gave to the latter a new understanding of the remembered solidarity of guild life. Of all the attempts at cultural interpretation of change so far made, with perhaps the exception of Raymond Williams's, Sewell's alone has maintained a vital role for the everyday order of work, survival, and authority.[31]

Yet Sewell no more than Natalie Davis makes allowance for the individual, particularly in the all-important account of the emergence of class consciousness between 1830 and 1848. Like Davis in "Rites of Violence," Sewell takes evidence at face value. He seeks to maximize the internal order he can find within that evidence

44

and, as a result, creates a picture of perfect unity, as if all artisans spontaneously agreed without much forethought on how they ought to act in the crisis moments. The evidence is treated as emanating from a single, fixed source, an artisan community, which in reality must have been less sure of itself, less unanimous, less coordinated than it appears. In fact, Jacques Rancière's recent work has shown that much of Sewell's own evidence was taken from the outpourings of a literate stratum of artisans who were as disillusioned about the life of work at some moments as they were full of praise for the nobility of labor at others.[32] Had Sewell been able to take this diversity into account, he could have actually strengthened his own argument by pointing out that the "dialectic" he analyzed had, in some respects, an inherent force of its own. Whatever their personal experience, certain artisans had to struggle with the idea of the nobility of labor because it was implicit in the dominant social order in which they lived.

Declaring independence for the cultural realm against the supposed explanatory power of material interests was an important step for historians to make in the face of the evident success of revisionism.[33] Studying culture in its own right meant denying that every human being secretly wants only money and power; it meant taking evidence of social meaning at face value and searching for whatever order could be found within it. But now that this declaration of independence has been made it ought to be unmade. The point was never to claim that culture has no links with physical existence; it was only to claim that these links cannot be understood by positing a simple and universal underlying human motive. The aim was not to see the individual as merely a creation of culture, a unit or locus within which cultural meanings are realized. The aim was only to prevent the individual from being oversimplified as nothing more than the point where material "factors" and "forces" registered their impact.

Following the interpretive method unreflectively, however, runs the danger of merely substituting one spurious universal motive for another. Instead of treating money and power as the ultimate aim of human desire, cultural interpretation can end up positing coherence in its place. Any explanation of change based on the idea of a crisis of meaning or a dialectic of implicit contradiction ends up assuming that human beings fundamentally desire coherence and meaning and eschew contradiction and chaos. How else could radical and conscious change be explained, in purely cultural terms, except as the consequence of a breakdown of coherence and a desire to reestablish it? Such an account of change is therefore disturbingly self-serving; it is deductive, a canon rather than a discovery, an assumption about the underlying motive of human action that is really a metaphor.

However, it may be that one has no alternative but to choose some such metaphor according to one's taste, to deduce the ultimate motive of human action from it, and proceed to tell pleasing stories about the social present and the past. This appears to be what many of the great thinkers have done, after all, not to mention many very successful historians. And it is the clear implication of the work of such figures as Hayden White or Michel Foucault that in historical understanding, one's choice of topos is utterly arbitrary and determines everything that follows.[34] One may posit that everyone ultimately desires money and power, or sex, or death, or coherence, or closeness, or physical comfort, or moral rectitude. One may see the action as comedy or tragedy, conflict or negotiation, or groping for meaning. Application of any of these assumptions to the past will yield a consistent pattern as well as a satisfying program of research.

MESSAGES FROM THE UNKNOWN

But the dilemma just described can serve as the starting point of a theory of history, once it is seen as a difficulty that goes beyond the merely methodological sphere. That so many initial assumptions can lead to plausible and internally consistent results has been a problem within history, not just within historiography. Not that those who made history have been conscious of it; few have. Nonetheless, the babel of voices, of claims and counterclaims, of systems and creeds, that ascends upward from out of the European past – the revolutionary preachings of Augustine, Aquinas, Ockham, Luther, and Lenin; Calvin's certainties; Shakespeare's ruminations; Descartes's doubts; Kant's deliberation; Hegel's obscurity; the delightful heresies of Montaillou villagers and Tuscan millers – how could all of this powerful and diverse persuasion even have been conceived in the first place if there was not a blankness and uncertainty at the root of our souls so absolute and so silent that it bears almost any interpretation imaginable? Even those who insist on seeing all this as so much ideological mystification in the service of the ruling class must admit that mystification which is at once so diverse and so effective implies an awesome gullibility, a cognitive apparatus completely detached from its proper moorings in class interest, utterly malleable. Is this not, after all, the experiential counterpart to that "behavioral plasticity" that is the dominant trait of the human species? Direct vision of this glowing formlessness is denied to most people precisely because of the way established practice prescribes motives, structures choices, shapes long-term goals, gives form to failure and disenchantment. Here most people find a dependable refuge; their contact with uncertainty is reduced to brief intervals, to idle moments of reflection with little relevance to everyday life, or else it is transformed into a safely diffuse sense of alienation.

If these reflections are even partly correct, then there is nothing wrong with assuming that the maintenance or reestablishment of a minimum of coherence necessary to the carrying on of social life is usually high on the list of aims of a large number of social actors. The one great advantage of this assumption over other assumptions about basic human motives is that it takes into account the difficulty of interpreting motives, not just as a methodological problem but also as a social reality, as one of the driving forces behind historical events. Here the contribution of the crisis-of-meaning approach can be essential, so long as one holds in mind the idea that difficulties about meaning are not exceptional events, as Furet seems to assume, but a more or less endemic characteristic of human affairs, which worsen into crises under certain circumstances. Uncertainty is a constant, and it is constantly combated by certain social actors.

One must not, however, leap to the assumption that those actors most likely to promote coherence in social life are those who stand to gain most from its maintenance. Such an assumption would merely lead back to a slightly altered notion of class interest that would beg the question of motivation in just the way that past research has shown to be so fruitless. Worse, such an assumption would be so vague as to preserve the notion of interest against all possible attack from evidence. Those who worked to maintain coherence would always be identified as standing to gain from it – a process resulting in a *quod erat demonstrandum* of satisfying, if delusory, neatness.

It is nonetheless clear that there is a connection between the search for coherence and the use of violence. If there were any doubt that individuals usually fail to agree on the meaning of – and thus fail to assent to – the cultural and practical forms in which they live, one need only reflect on the pervasive recourse to coercion. Human communities everywhere fall back on force and the threat of force to keep individuals in line, as well as to chastise, defeat, transform, or at least hold at a distance other communities whose alien practices and creeds represent an implicit challenge to the universality and self-evidence of their own. Violence has many meanings; soldiers may think they are fighting off devils incarnate or ritually murdering gods rather than killing fellow human beings. But whatever world of meanings organized violence occurs within, it almost always appears as a kind of *ultima ratio* whose outcome ratifies the correctness of that world of meanings. Ultimately, this is because those who suffer violence are physically removed from the stage of history. The implications of such removal may be, of course, variously interpreted according to what one supposes the world to be. Coercion, the threat of impending violence, has as many meanings as there are societies within which it is practiced, but the family resemblances of these diverse meanings are unmistakable.

Few systems of practice have ever long subsisted without incorporating within them a police and a military function. It is not just the marginals or the foreigners who need the implied threat of violence to control their actions; all people share a shadowy awareness of how easily they could become foreigners to themselves if there were no ingrained disciplinary fear to set limits on their everyday imagination or if the form of coercion altered suddenly and radically. Skeptics are invited to examine the life histories of French émigré royalists who ended up working for Napoleon or czarist officers who served in the Red Army. It is not just that martyrs like Thomas More are rare but that even the Thomas Mores must face a crisis of identity when coercion is suddenly trained against them. This is not to say that people want to be disciplined, nor, conversely, that they want to break free. The point of this inquiry lies just in seeking a way out of the continual, unreflective, and tiresome attribution of standardized motives to large classes of individuals that is the most salient weakness of modern social thought. We do not all secretly enjoy punishment or secretly long to escape. Plastic as we are, unknown as we are to ourselves, given the diversity and unpredictability of the desires humans are likely to conceive (even those already fully absorbed in a stable culture), our systems of practice seldom survive in the absence of coercion.

It follows that some part of the established practices of a society (insofar as it has any) must impose on some of its members a desire to coerce others, to engage in controlled violence, just as commerce imposes a desire for profit. Those who participate in the practice of violence may be ambivalent. From the time of Homer to that of Stephen Crane, in fact, ambivalence has been one of the essential ingredients of heroism; neither Hector nor the hero of the *Red Badge of Courage* wanted to go into battle.[35] Likewise, the history of warfare is full of evidence that points to the necessity of totally limiting the individual combatant's options, as well as of building solidarity among combatants on the basis of their shared entrapment in the cul de sac of the battlefield.[36] How this is done—by what codes of honor, in the name of what ideals, and with the threat of what sanctions—is profoundly important to the structure of the remainder of established practices, those that are sustained and supported by the coercive ones. In a relatively stable and complex society the entrapment of some individuals into exercising violence spreads successfully to others a milder sense of having limited options. They renounce possibilities that would otherwise be very attractive; they learn the practices at hand very well; they become either content or else deviant in prescribed ways. But of course the sustained exercise of violence can always backfire; enemy armies may take over, or a society's own armed force may break apart into warring factions. Its codes and conventions may have held inconsistencies, or bred active frustrations, or inculcated deadly rivalries that have debilitated or destroyed it. The existing practices may make conflict endemic, for that matter, by prescribing dueling and factionalism as part of the code of the warrior. Whatever the exact circumstance, the rest of society cannot escape the consequences. Even Christian monks may end up making a virtue of necessity, like Saint Bernard in the twelfth century conferring sanctity on violence even though his most sacred texts preached explicitly and repeatedly against it.[37]

Coercion does not result so much in widespread hypocrisy as in a felt need to reconcile existing contradictions, to emphasize those aspects of one's own desires that can be made compatible with the influence of coercion at the expense of those that cannot. The kind of enforced coherence that emerges in consequence may be shallow, full of holes. To the extent that coercion plays a role in resolving difficulties of meaning and desire, social life is riddled with badly kept secrets and poorly concealed incongruities. People think less clearly; their ability to confront the problem of their own existence is lessened. The moment coercion fails, crises of meaning of various kinds are ready to break out. Or rather, such moments do not result from the failure of coercion, as an effect from a cause; they are the failure of coercion.

But of course meanings are not the only things that life consists of. No amount of hermeneutical contortion can erase this truth, and no theory of history can afford to ignore it. There is something else besides meaning. To name this other thing, to give it a meaning, always offers a hostage to those who would argue otherwise, even if the name one gives is as guarded and empty as *Ding an sich*. One ought not to name this other thing "nature"; that is too definite a concept and too closely tied to the outlook of a specific civilization in a specific period. Perhaps one can call it safely the "world," without going further into it. It is because meanings occur in the world that there is history. The superiority of Sewell's approach to the crisis-of-meaning form of historical explanation arises from the fact that he left a way for the world *tout court* to have influence on the world of meanings. First, by keeping his eye on labor Sewell implicitly recognized that people need more than just coherence; they also need subsistence goods; and the consequences of such needs for a society can be far-reaching indeed. Second, by discovering that the drive behind ideological development emerged from the unintended consequences of putting formerly oppositional ideologies into practice, Sewell implicitly recognized that human actions may (and usually do) have consequences that entirely escape the mental horizons of their authors.

Such consequences can never be captured by an interpretation of the meaning of actions for the actors involved. Roman peasants plowing and sowing their fields in a two-field rotation generation after generation did not intend to exhaust the soil. The inventor of gunpowder did not intend to make medieval chivalry obsolete. Columbus did not intend to find a new continent. A materialist viewpoint is not justified if it leads one to oversimplify the problem of motives of individual actors and collectivities, if it, in effect, assumes that all actors are themselves – in a different but related sense of the term – "materialists." But it is equally shortsighted to neglect the fact that whatever our diversity in other respects, we all live in a single world with a definite and in principle determinable structure, a world whose unnoticed features can unleash enormous crises in one social order or gradually undermine another, a world in which the technical breakthroughs pioneered in one society can suddenly thrust it into contact with hundreds of others whose existence was unknown to it a few years before. In such ways the world provides those seed crystals that give shape to our protean human character, and the outcome is history. Just as a society's established practices shelter human beings from full knowledge of uncertainty, so history constantly probes and challenges, mercilessly exposing unwarranted assumptions and dashing the finest hopes of warriors and peacemakers alike.

Among the tremendous wealth of examples known in history of this kind of unpredictable intrusion of the unknown into human affairs, the arrival of new gunpowder and sail technology in the Hawaiian Islands after 1780 is a particularly instructive case. The Europeans brought first and foremost new tools of coercion, which the Hawaiians immediately took to using on each other, with stunning consequences. When Cook first made contact in 1778, the major islands were dominated by numerous tiny princelings (*ke-alii*) frequently at odds with one another and constantly competing against their own lieutenants (the rest of the *alii* class) for ascendancy. War was highly admired; preparation for it absorbed the lives of *alii* males in peacetime. But metal was unknown. In traditional warfare:

Often the campaign opened in a leisurely manner, with sacrifices, prayers, exhortations by spear-flourishing orators, and individual combat between champions, before the agreed moment of general attack. In the early stages the chiefs, resplendent in feather cloaks and helmets, directed the battle under the protection of a phalanx of warriors carrying long spears, but once the fighting was fairly under way and javelins and sling stones began to break up the stylized formations, the *aliis* joined their near-naked subjects in sweaty, hard-breathing personal combat. At close quarters it was a war of daggers and clubs and even bare hands.[38]

But after 1785 the islands became a regular stop for English and American trading vessels on the Pacific crossing. The Hawaiians traded water and provisions for adzes, guns, and artillery; they captured ships, enticed artisans and gun crews into their service, and put the new weaponry to use in their own endemic conflicts. After two decades of intermittent warfare the islands were united for the first time under a single king, the chieftain whose use of the new weaponry was the most massive and most effective. He established an impressive governmental machinery, exacting direct tribute from his dominions in the form of a wide variety of crops and artifacts; he carefully preserved his royal monopoly of trade with foreign vessels – the key to his early technical superiority – and ruled over a growing community of whites who served him in various capacities, as carpenters, armorers, marksmen, and advisers.[39]

Weaponry did not in any sense "determine" this outcome. It was equally "determined" by the exact nature of the Hawaiian status quo ante, by the ethnic and linguistic unity of the islands, for example, and, as Marshall Sahlins has brilliantly argued, by the ready adaptability of native categories to the newcomers' arrival.[40] No such outcome is known for any of the other Pacific archipelagoes. No one can say what role the talents and personality of the victorious chieftain, Kamehameha, played in these events. What is clear is that the old warrior code, with its emphasis on ritualized hand-to-hand combat and continuous factionalism, could not survive the introduction of metal blades and gunpowder, nor could the social order it sustained. This highly competitive and fluid code was, at the same time, what gave metal and gunpowder their transforming significance, pushing the Hawaiians to acquire the new weaponry with rapidity and to improvise new tactical skills appropriate to it. The old code and the new techniques of violence were explosively unstable in combination.

It is not necessary to suppose that people inherently desire power to understand the course of these events. Many of the known facts of the Hawaiian case appear more compatible with the assumption that individuals in the absence of established practices do not know what they want.[41] The arrival of gunpowder in Hawaii was associated with unprecedented confusion at first. It was difficult enough establishing conventions for trading with the incoming vessels, whose captains and crew behaved in ways that defied Hawaiians' initial expectations. Many incidents of blood-chilling violence between ships' crews and flotillas of Hawaiian canoes resulted from simple miscues. Apart from this problem, battlefield practices and relations among the Hawaiian chieftains themselves were thrown into chaos. In all these domains treachery, sudden betrayals, ambushes, poisonings, and broken promises, not unknown before, spread like wildfire. It soon became apparent that following the old battlefield etiquette ensured certain defeat; but no one knew what to put in its place. *Aliis* even went calmly to their death, in some cases, apparently because they were not sure whether to accept their own misgivings, whether mistrust was really the appropriate response to a particular situation.[42]

Of course, the state of the sources on these events is such that no interpretation can be advanced with great certainty. Hawaiian oral traditions recorded by unsophisticated white settlers hardly qualify as solid evidence. But their confusing appearance before the critical eye in fact speaks in favor of an interpretation along the lines sketched out here. The gaps and inconsistencies, the frequently questionable attributions of motive, that appear throughout early European reports are a concrete trace of the real confusion that reigned in the islands in that period.

Violence has so far proved indispensable to stable social life. But as physical action violence is part of the world and has an existence of its own independent of the interpretations and intentions of human beings. The significance of this conclusion is nowhere more apparent than in cases where the physical properties of violence change rapidly, dissolving the dependable meanings, conventions, and codes that had built up around it, setting society adrift in a heavy sea of dangerous improvisation and mistrust. The Hawaiian case had a dramatic and relatively happy outcome, the unification of the islands under a single ruler whose state endured to the end of the nineteenth century. But the new equilibrium can often take on more somber forms.

The established practices by which any society shelters its members from the daunting vistas of potential human diversity represent fragile barks constantly exposed to stormy weather and uncharted currents. Almost any set of established practices that fulfill physical needs – however poorly, however unequally – can be explained and justified by means of an appropriately elaborated world view using appropriately chosen metaphors. But it is not common for such configurations of practices and world views to subsist unchanged for any amount of time. Challenges may as easily arise from unexpected prosperity as from exhaustion of natural resources, or the sudden onset of famine or epidemic. The balance may be tipped toward rapid change by the forging of new contacts with the outside world, by unexpected and unsought technical breakthroughs, or even, finally, by unexpected reformulations of existing teachings that cast old practices in a new and critical light. Naturally, in most cases of actual change, some or all of these dimensions are in play at once. Rapid change, change that disrupts not only the satisfaction of immediate needs but also the comprehensibility of the surrounding world, constantly threatens human beings and human societies from within and without. The interpretation of meanings of specific texts or acts cannot possibly by itself capture the full scope of the historical drama.

EXCHANGE AS SYSTEM

But critics of the method of cultural interpretation do not usually characterize its inadequacies in the way just described. Among social historians in particular there has been widespread apprehension that interpreting the meaning of established practices or studying crises of meaning entails a too-ready abandonment of the old themes of money and power. As Eugene D. Genovese and Elizabeth Fox-Genovese put it, methods borrowed from cultural anthropology lead "away from the political content of class relations" and result in an attempt "to put everything and anything ('race,' 'culture,' 'socialization,' and ultimately Rabelais's *ergo Gluck*) in place of class confrontation – in place of the fundamental problem of power and order – at the center of the historical process."[43] As has been seen, the turn to cultural interpretation was partly motivated by a profound uneasiness over the whole concept of class confrontation. But now, perhaps, it is possible to reformulate Genovese and Fox-Genovese's dissatisfaction in less troublesome language.

Social classes are widely seen, and not just by Marxists, as arising out of the roles individuals fill in production. A good deal of the revisionist argument about the French Revolution discussed in Chapter 1, for example, has been carried out by showing that individuals in the ancien régime did not fill the roles in production implied by the terms "feudal aristocracy" and "capitalist bourgeoisie." The importance of the evidence on this point is accepted by all parties to the debate, both Marxists and non-Marxists, because there is a general consensus that one potential criterion of social class is relation to the means of production. Where opinions currently diverge is over the question of what to do about the concept of social class, once relations to the means of production prove to be so complex and confusing in their details that neat class lines cannot be drawn. This is, in effect, the dilemma that has arisen in the study of the nineteenth-century working class, so many of whose strata were not filled by pure and simple wage laborers, or in consideration of the relationship between the German "bourgeoisie" and the Prussian "aristocracy" after 1871, both of which groups were obviously capitalists by that time if measured by their roles in production. These problems are compounded by the difficulties raised when the complexity of human motivation is taken into account. It is no longer possible to deduce interest from role in production and exchange, and to account for political conduct by citing underlying interest. Genovese and Fox-Genovese are fearful that amid this welter of difficulties, the fact of domination and oppression will be lost from view. And they suspect that this outcome may be the result of a hidden conservative political agenda among those carrying out the research. Without inquiring into this latter fear, it is certainly possible to recognize the validity of the former one. What provision can be made to take domination and oppression into account in a theory of history generated out of an interpretive method that gives full recognition to the difficulty of knowing human desires?

What has been said already goes part of the way to meeting the objection of Genovese and Fox-Genovese, first, by recognizing the role that coercion plays in disciplining and shaping human desire and second, by recognizing the role that the world plays in generating change out of the unintended consequences of action. But this alone is not enough. In the Marxist tradition, class relations are exchange relations. That exchange relations are important to social structure no one doubts. Interpretive method cannot avoid coming to terms with exchange in generating a theory of history. It will be argued here first that exchange can be, like coercion, a fruitful source of unintended consequences, and second that exchange relations can have a disciplinary effect very similar to that of coercion. A full exploration of these two points will make it possible to take the pervasive fact of domination into account and to reevaluate the thrust of historical change that has derived from exchange practices. Some may object that not exchange but production is the central issue needing attention. Those relations to the means of production that organize production, however, and determine its vector of development are always exchange relationships, whether what is exchanged is products or labor or knowledge or household chores, whether exchange is organized by gift, by barter, or by open-market prices. Thus an interpretation of exchange relationships that shows how they make domination possible will bring the full Marxist agenda, including labor and production – not just the old scenario of class conflict – into the scope of an interpretive theory of history. At the same time, it will be possible to elaborate a critique of the concept of class based not just on detailed empirical evidence but on a critique of the whole history of economic theory, Marx included. Class, it turns out, is a concept as likely to blind one to the precise means by which power has been exercised in modern European society as are any of the revisionist challenges to its validity that have so far been made. These matters can only be sketched out here, but it is hoped that the character of the argument will be made sufficiently clear nonetheless. Several case studies follow in later chapters in which the theory is applied in some detail.

The first step in the discussion of exchange, then, is to explore the special way exchange activities can result in unintended consequences. The differences from the impact of unintended consequences on the practice of violence, as just discussed in the Hawaiian case, are striking.

Exchange, like violence, is an essential human activity that often has physical properties that escape detection and subvert the intentions of those humans who engage in it. This is as true of commercial trade as it is of all those forms of barter and gift giving that have flourished wherever human society exists. Cultural theorists have often discussed practices such as potlatch, "total prestation," or the exchange of wives between hostile clans as evidence that the desire for gain as it is known in the West is not a universal human motive but a peculiar construct of our culture.[44] No example has been cited more frequently in such arguments that the famous kula ring of the Trobriand Islands, first studied by Bronislaw Malinowski.[45] This well-known case also provides convenient evidence on a further point that should never be lost from view. Exchange of whatever kind for whatever motives always has the potential of implicating physical systems, and physical systems have an order of their own. Wrong as Western assumptions about *homo economicus* may have been over the last two centuries, this fact has been a central and valid concern of economists from the very beginning.

Kula is a grand system of gift exchange that encompasses an enclosed ring of island groups east of Papua New Guinea. Clan chiefs and their retainers go regularly on expeditions to nearby islands to exchange gifts of red necklaces and white armbands. The two forms of gift are complementary. A partner who receives armbands gives necklaces in return. The gifts as a result circulate in opposite directions, gradually completing a full circle of the archipelago over a number of years. The whole aim of kula giving is to establish one's prestige by the extravagance of what one gives away. But since one must receive in order to give, much energy and concern are also concentrated on how to acquire the best pieces. One could actually argue over whether the motives of the participants are altruistic or self-interested. Open bargaining is, in any case, frowned upon. The structure of the practice imposes generosity as the prescribed motive; there is, of course, plenty of room for private avarice, which is even ritualized in various ways.[46] It is in fact the peculiar mix of these two pulls on the individual that gives the kula its unique experiential flavor.

The useful aspect of kula gift giving for present purposes is that it can help to clarify, like a thought experiment, the relation between motives and exchange systems. The motivational requirements of a kula ring may be specified fairly easily. If the inhabitants of a ring-shaped archipelago did engage in gift exchange out of a desire to prove their generosity and if they always returned armbands for necklaces – that is, if this synopsis of Malinowski's interpretation of Trobriand motives were a correct one for some island ring (an unknowable thing, in the last analysis) – then and only then would there be a ring-shaped physical system in which necklaces flowed clockwise and armbands counterclockwise (or vice versa). As this statement underscores, knowledge of the existence and character of an exchange system is inseparable from knowledge of the motives of the participants. At the same time, the systemic potential, so to speak – that is, the possibility of things' traveling in a circle – can be a source of bias, helping to push gift giving of a particular kind to the fore as an established practice, limiting the options of actors, and therefore simplifying their motivational responses. So it is likely in a certain respect that motive and systemic potential will come to some kind of accommodation with each other. But it is not necessary that they do so, and a breakdown is possible at every moment. Human desire is like the wind, not like gravity.

Nothing has been said so far, either, of the precise quantity of flow in this hypothetical gift circulation. Obviously the flow of armbands and necklaces would not be of equal mass, nor would the two necessarily flow at an equal or regular rate, because each gift would be evaluated differently according to the beauty and rarity of its appearance. A number of mediocre armbands might be matched by the return of one exquisite necklace. Rate of flow in each direction would be extremely variable over time and not tightly linked with rate of flow in the other direction. Nonetheless, a circle could exist, and its existence would warrant one's speaking of an exchange *system,* not merely a set of exchanges.

What would happen in the case of breakdown or change raises further interpretive difficulties. If Trobriand Islanders suddenly stopped receiving necklaces from their kula partners, would they continue to give armbands with triumphant alacrity, burying their partners under unreciprocated gifts (just as they were being buried)? Or would the whole system come to a stop? In the former case, one can imagine crisis scenarios like the following:

A kula ring exists with two production points for gifts, one for armbands, one for necklaces. (See Figure 1.) Production of new gifts is necessary to make up for wear, loss, and some leakage out of the system (gifts given to inland partners, for example). Suppose there is a break in the circuit between islands C and D. Armbands would accumulate on island C, necklaces on island D. On island A gifts of both kinds would continue to flow in both directions, because A lies between the production points; flow would reduce to the trickle of new production, unless production increased. Islanders at A might be the last to recognize the existence of a problem. On island B, the flow of armbands would dry up quickly; only necklaces would be exchanged. Islanders at B might suppose at first that the crisis involved a shortage of armbands, since that would be their initial experience. If the circumference of the circuit were twenty-five miles, word would doubtless spread very rapidly of the disturbance in the normal practice of gift giving; coordinated effort to fix or compensate for the disturbance could be easily organized – if the meaning of gift exchange called for such effort. This would obviously require a public, sanctioned interpretation of the significance of the disturbance, hammered out in meetings or perhaps issued by clan chiefs. There might be disagreement, confusion, panic. If gift giving were sufficiently central, one might get a crisis of meaning, a search for replacements, organization of new practices exploiting previously neglected motives. If the circumference were twenty-five thousand miles, however, island A might experience no change for many decades. Its people might never hear of what had happened, until one day, after a century or so, it might happen that someone began to redistribute some of the huge accumulations from islands C and D – to advance his own prestige on island A, perhaps. Or one could imagine other scenarios of this kind by which the material disequilibrium would finally give rise to social consequences. To know what would happen in any given crisis would require an exact knowledge of the motives of those involved, both prescribed motives and private motives. But even the actors involved would be hard put to predict their own responses to an unexpected breakdown. To reconstruct what has happened in a past crisis situation, less difficult, nonetheless requires an even more exact knowledge of motives than that which is required to be sure the exchange system really existed in the first place. For one must understand how people would react to the unexpected if prescribed motives stopped simplifying their lives one fine day.

Economists have begun to understand the intimate link between variable human motivation and the existence and trajectory of exchange systems. Lester Thurow, for example, has strongly criticized the economics profession for treating preferences as exogenous factors "fully developed and immutable," the most important being our old friend the desire for money and power, what economists call "comparative net advantage." "What we want and like," Thurow insists,

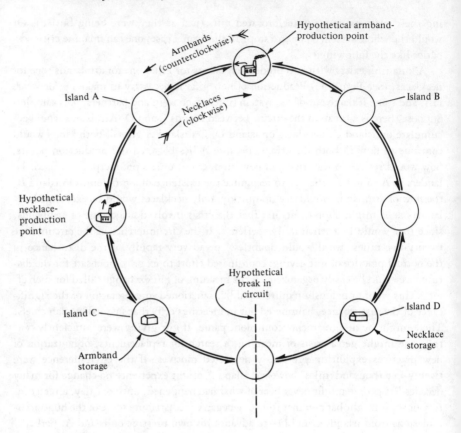

Figure 1. Diagram of a kula gift system

constantly evolves as we experience life. We will often do something deliberately, take a music appreciation course, for example, to explore or even alter our preferences. So some real theory of preference formation has to lie at the heart of the rebuilding effort in economics. No one knows where the reformulation of the behavioral assumptions of economics would lead, but it is clear that the current assumptions neither conform with what we know about human behavior nor produce models with much predictive power.[47]

Where such a reformulation may lead is to the conclusion that prediction is a will-o'-the-wisp. Where it must lead is toward the recognition of the intimate and fragile tie between system and motive and therefore the necessity of interpreting motives in all their complexity and variability before any even tentative knowledge of exchange systems is possible.

A special problem of exchange systems that makes them even more difficult to interpret, by comparison with techniques of violence, for example, is that they can easily transcend the local cultural horizons of participants in them. And unnoticed features of the system can have unexpected consequences. A system of exchange may be very different from what it is represented to be by local practices and meanings at some point within it. Recently gathered evidence shows, for example, that Malinowski passed on incomplete or erroneous reports about the production points of red necklaces.[48] This error had absolutely no bearing on his interpretation of the cultural significance of kula for the island of Kiriwina, where he worked, or other islands he visited. But if production were ever disrupted, such erroneous information could play a crucial role in the course of events. A matter of indifference to the ethnographer, such questions are often central to historical explanation.

Until recently, violence has been a more or less face-to-face matter; when it occurred those involved could see how it worked; alterations in the system were readily apparent even if not fully understood. Exchange, however, can easily create physical systems too large for any one person to observe their workings and often complex enough to defy model building. Erroneous notions extraordinarily fecund in their consequences are therefore comparatively common in the human understanding of exchange. This is especially the case in money-based exchange systems where credit and accounting make the total stock of money into a purely symbolic rather than a physical matter. Money is a counter; it is not symbolic in the normal sense – it does not signify in the way that phonemes, lexemes, or categories do – but it is not physical either. Even when precious metals remain the primary medium of exchange, misapprehensions can run rampant.

From at least the thirteenth century prices have played a role in European society too great to be ignored. And events very much like the hypothetical disruption of the kula ring just sketched have happened repeatedly. In the sixteenth century, for example, the Spanish imported large quantities of gold and silver from New World mines, triggering a severe inflation, the so-called price revolution that tripled prices between 1560 and 1640. It is certain in retrospect that inflation was an unavoidable outcome of Spanish spending; but this was not understood at the time. Price increases were often laid down to a general increase in greed. Historians first believed that this inflation might have hurt feudal lords and helped ambitious, middle-class merchants with good business sense. But this version of the social crisis brought on by inflation has been largely rejected. No such neat groups of sufferers and beneficiaries have been identified; yet it is still generally agreed that the inflation had powerful social consequences related to the Religious Wars in France, the Puritan rebellion in England, and the Thirty Years' War in Germany.[49]

A consensus has emerged among English historians that inflation helped in the breakup of the feudal retainer system.[50] Great lords, assiduously raising rents to keep up with prices, alienated their tenants, whose notion of price made no allowance for inflation. Formerly, these tenants had served as a ready reservoir of armed retainers, whose loyalty to local barons made possible the endemic civil strife of the fifteenth century. The exchange of loyalty and deference in return for protection, stable tenure, and a just — that is, unchanging — rent was broken down by the price rationality that inflation forced on the great. Research suggests that the great by and large remained great, but their greatness lost its military dimension. Centralized authority was bound to benefit (it was on the rise for other reasons anyway); and a struggle ensued over the nature of that authority, a struggle led (on both sides) by independent-minded, medium-sized property holders — the "gentry." This was, then, an extremely complex outcome to the mere increase in availability of specie, misunderstood as it was at the time. As with the arrival of gunpowder in Hawaii, it is impossible to attribute the whole crisis to the single "cause" of inflation, and it is unnecessary to suppose that the desire for money and power was the central human motive behind the struggle. Precisely what form power should take and what role money would play in the practice of violence were the issues raised by inflation. How practices prescribed motives necessarily changed, as practices changed. As a result, these events cannot be accounted for by assuming that what people really wanted was a constant. Power in 1480 was the number of retainers one could muster from one's rent-rolls; in 1640 it was the number of followers one could attract with a speech in Parliament, a pamphlet, or a sermon on the profligacy of the court. Perhaps this is to overstate the difference. But it appears certain, in any case, that inflation, poorly understood but universal in its effects, was one of the background conditions behind the emergence of a political public in the English state; and it is not necessary to see politics as the mere expression of class interests to follow the chain of circumstance and accommodation that leads to this outcome.

Another revealing example of error about exchange relationships is the case of Bengal spinners and handloom weavers in the early nineteenth century. Their trade at first benefited from closer commercial links with Europe in the late seventeenth and eighteenth centuries. But by 1800 Lancashire's machine-made cotton yarns and calico cloth began to supplant Bengal products in foreign markets. By 1815 Lancashire exports began to reverse the flow of goods, underselling Bengal products in their own domestic markets—aided, of course, by the growing British political hegemony in the subcontinent.[51] In this instance the novel link in the physical chain of social practices (the steam-powered spinning mill) was literally half the world away, unavailable to scrutiny, impossible to understand fully, but nonetheless decisive in its impact. The population of Dacca, a muslin production center dependent on export trade, fell from 150,000 to 30,000 within two decades after 1800.[52] Indian weavers soon found that they could keep a hold on the domestic market only by buying and using British machine-made yarn. It is estimated that over two-and-a-half million spinners were thus put out of work in Bengal alone between 1825 and 1830.[53] In 1828, one widowed spinner wrote that she had been reduced from relative prosperity to utter destitution by the influx of foreign yarn. "I had a pride," she said,

> that foreign thread would not equal mine in quality. But I saw afterwards it was better than mine, and I heard that it sold at three or four rupees a seer [less than half the earlier price]. If the foreign thread were sold at a good price it would do no harm. But instead it has ruined us. . . . So I beseech the spinners of the country sending this thread to consider my application, and see for themselves whether it is proper to send yarn to this country.[54]

Spinners in Europe who had undergone a similar experience at least knew what they were up against, those "jennies" (a shortening of "engines") or *mécaniques* (as they were called in Normandy) that they at first attacked but soon adopted for themselves.[55] The Bengal spinner knew of nothing but the disastrous price differential that hurt her pride and destroyed her living, and she naively appealed to the "spinners of the country sending this thread," whoever they were, to save her.

However fluid in practice, the Indian caste system, in addition, increased the difficulty of shifting to new occupations. There can be little doubt that England's lead position in the development of world trade had already made its effects felt on those English laborers who jumped into the handloom trade at its peak around 1780. This was not because they were maximizing mere monetary gain (as their subsequent refusal to leave the trade demonstrates) but because they were searching for an ideal of skill, independence, and self-respect already very much more flexible than what was available in Bengal.[56] The constant rate of change in commercial systems had already begun to have a sustained effect on English culture. In the meantime English wooden ships plied the waters between Liverpool and Calcutta in exactly the same way in 1780 as in 1810, carrying whatever would sell best. (Some may have continued on to Hawaii.) On the ships themselves, sails were unfurled in identical fashion; the authority of the captain may have altered slightly, but the lives and symbolic worlds of the sailors were little changed. Their practices were effectively identical, but their material significance and cultural impact were reversed because the system of exchange had changed around them. In 1780 their trade brought prosperity to Bengal; in 1810 it brought Lancashire yarn. Of course, within a few decades the steam engines that made the yarn in Lancashire would also eliminate the need for sail technology.

A SYNOPSIS

Although the theory of history being proposed here has not yet been completely laid out, enough has been said to warrant a pause for review. The remaining portions of the theory are better explored in the context of a brief discussion of the history of economic thought, which will be undertaken in the next chapter.

What has been said so far may be summarized as follows. The concepts of class and class interest are in crisis for two reasons: (1) because individuals' roles in production and exchange are seldom simple, so that their class identity is a difficult matter, and (2) because human motivation and perception are, in any case, too complex to ensure that class identity will offer any key to political behavior. The turn to interpretive methods of the last decade has been, in some measure at least, a reaction to the crisis of the class concept. But cultural interpretation as historians took it up proved a brittle tool for explaining change, and – even when crisis-of-meaning concepts are developed to cope with this problem – it remains an inadequate means of evaluating individual alienation in general and the necessity of terror in the founding of modern liberal social orders in particular. A way out of these problems is to elaborate a theory of history based on interpretive method. The starting point of this theory is that difficulties of meaning are endemic to societies, not exceptional. The near universal resort to coercion in human affairs is evidence of the inevitability of discord over the meaning of human social existence or the meaning of any publicly recognized set of principles for dealing with such existence. It must be said at once that coherence is not the only thing necessary for a minimum of stability in social life. Subsistence goods must be procured. In addition, the world has an independent existence. The actions and things that are the vehicles of meaning are also physical events and conditions that may have unintended consequences. Every set of social practices is therefore the expression of a three-sided struggle: the struggle for subsistence goods, the struggle to clarify cognition and to order desires, and the struggle to ward off, comprehend, cope with, the unintended consequences of this-worldly action. Individuals may not feel any of these imperatives at any given moment; they may play no part in individuals' actual motives; but if the sum total of people's coordinated actions does not achieve a minimum of efficacy on all three planes, crisis is in the offing.

Coercion and exchange are spheres of activity within which messages from the unknown frequently emerge. By comparison with the exercise of violence, at least up until World War I, exchange relations are an especially fruitful area for the generation of unintended consequences because these consequences so frequently occur at a distance from many who participate in creating them. (Modern mechanized warfare obviously presents similar problems for participants.) In addition, the understanding of the structure of exchange systems requires accurate knowledge of the motives of the participants, an extremely difficult thing to achieve.

What remains to be discussed is the way in which certain kinds of exchange relationships resemble coercion in that they create a potential for social discipline. The argument of the next chapter will be that within the language of classical political

economy this potential for discipline becomes invisible; it becomes in effect a consequence unintended by a theory of exchange systems that in other respects sufficiently
resembles practice to be plausible. Marx, or at least Marxism, did not adequately sur-
mount this drawback of the language of political economy, a fact that is evident in
the unavoidable simplifications of Marx's view of capitalism that result whenever
summary statements on class relations are created for popular consumption. Once
these matters have been spelled out, it will be time to see how the disciplinary potential of certain exchange relationships can help explain the French Revolution and
nineteenth-century social conflict. This will be the task of Chapters 4 and 5. The aim
is to produce a cultural interpretation of European history that puts power in its
proper place, that puts an end to the chase after neat but illusory social classes, and
that at least suggests some starting points for a redefinition of our inherited notions
of political liberty.

3 Growth of the liberal illusion

A SYSTEM OF EXCHANGE can easily have unintended consequences, consequences that can have a catastrophic effect on the fates of thousands of people while other parties to the system go on as before, blithely ignorant of the impact of their actions. Each participant sees only a tiny part of the whole. For the rest each must depend on hearsay. This was the dilemma that piqued European thinkers to reflect on trade with a new urgency in the seventeenth and eighteenth centuries. The vicissitudes of commerce increased with its volume; the reversals and uncertainties and bitter surprises to which it gave rise forced on consciousness a need to grasp the systemic underpinnings of trade's unintended consequences. Strangely, however, the eventual outcome of this reflection was a doctrine of indifference. The existence of system was perceived, but once perceived it was declared best left alone. The individual's ignorant carrying out of his business, indifferent to the larger consequences, was discovered to be beneficial to the whole. Western thinkers no sooner gained a new insight into the systemic nature of exchange relationships than they renounced all use of it. How did this come about?

THE DOCTRINE OF EQUAL EXCHANGE

The forms of exchange that a new group of economic theorizers wished to defend in seventeenth-century England were undoubtedly grounded in a desire for monetary profit. Speculation in grain, lending at interest, foreign currency transactions, and enclosures of common land were all highly structured established practices that involved individuals who had no desire to create broader, multivalent relationships with one another.[1] (Enclosing commons was in effect a renunciation of such relationships.) Furthermore, they were activities engaged in by persons already possessed of wealth above the common degree, activities made possible solely by the order and authority of the early modern state and the advancing technology of transport and communication. One could not engage in such practices without desiring to profit from them. The desire for profit was effectively imposed by their structure. But this was not true of most social practices at the time, whether or not they included monetary exchange as one of their elements.

62

From the beginning of modern economic thought, however, motives were assumed to operate with perfect uniformity within exchange systems. The recent works of Albert O. Hirschmann and Joyce Oldham Appleby have made this quite clear. "Is not gain the end of trade?" asked Edward Misselden in 1623 – for him a question that needed no reply.[2] Because all participants were assumed to want the same thing when they engaged in monetary transactions, the tendency was to see all such transactions as fundamentally similar both in their social causes and in their social effects. But this meant that the great diversity of motives for engaging in money exchange and the great diversity of effects of such exchange – some beneficial, some disastrous – were hidden from view. The common outcome of so much modern economic thought, the recommendation to leave trade alone, stemmed from an erroneous assumption about motives. This assumption first arose as a means of defending commerce against traditional Christian condemnation. Not just merchants, so went the argument, but all people sought their own gain. "Did not Moses in all his affliction with the children of God, aim at his own advantage?" asked Reverend Joseph Lee in 1656.[3] In doing so he helped plant the seeds that would later grow into the modern belief in the universal desirability of money and power.

In contrast to Lee, some early apologists of trade recognized the exceptional nature of the merchant's activities. Rather than insisting that gain was a motive shared by all, they praised the moderation and harmlessness of commerce by comparison with the depredations of warfare or the violence of religious fanaticism.[4] It was Voltaire who found a way of reconciling this second rhetorical strategy with the first. On the one hand, he praised the religious toleration of the commercial spirit. Commerce, like philosophy, moderated passions, disciplined desires; both were inimical to fanaticism and superstition. On the other hand, he argued that the real foundation of even the religious zealot's actions was self-interest. Voltaire gave this point a satirical bite in his definition of *amour-propre* in the *Dictionnaire philosophique*:

> A missionary traveling in India met a fakir loaded with chains, naked as a monkey, lying on his stomach, and having himself lashed for the sins of his compatriots, who gave him a few pennies. "What self-renunciation!" said one of the spectators. "Self-renunciation!" replied the fakir. "Let me inform you that I only have myself lashed in this world to pay you back in the next, when you will be the horse and I shall be the rider."[5]

In a flood of writings, Voltaire propagated the new truism: Everyone was really moved by self-interest. But commerce reduced and civilized the deleterious effects of this fact of the human condition, while religious orthodoxies all too evidently barbarized and exaggerated these effects.

Of course, at just this moment on the periphery of the expanding European commercial system, human beings were being reduced in Eastern Europe to bound serfs, and in West Africa to chattel slaves, dying in their thousands in the holds of "civilized" merchant vessels. Misery on a scale to match anything produced by the age of religious warfare – in the end on a far vaster scale, if one considers the whole long histories of Prussia or the American South that would follow – was being facilitated by commerce. In those distant places certain human beings sought, not monetary gain, but absolute overlordship, a desire imposed by the current practice of estate management and cash-crop cultivation. Commerce put the means into their hands and pointed the way. The Portuguese taught the Dutch how to manage slave plantations; the Dutch taught the English. Sugar prices and later cotton prices required slave labor; indentured servants were too hard to discipline and too scarce. Racial difference and African background were easily reinterpreted by English planters as making blacks suitable for slavery.[6] Even as it abetted massive terror, however, commerce also obscured the practice of terror from the view of traders and thinkers in London or Amsterdam. In these metropolises, slavery in the Caribbean and serfdom in Pomerania were as distant and invisible as was the mule jenny later to Bengal cotton spinners, or the production of kula gifts to Malinowski. In the comfort of a European salon, it was easy to evoke the image of two wealthy London merchants, one Puritan, the other Quaker, dickering over the price of their wares, and to treat this image as a paradigm of what commerce did to social relationships.[7]

ASYMMETRICAL EXCHANGE

In reality the social relationships surrounding the use of money and commodities in preindustrial Europe were far more varied, even if one excludes for a moment the extremes of the Atlantic slave trade and Eastern European serfdom. These variations, buried in the rural and neighborhood routines of life – easily overlooked by merchants' apologists – were nonetheless essential to the hierarchical arrangements of persons and the concentrations of authority that made society what it was. There were variations in the uses to which commodities were put and the effective experience of owning commodities. And there were consequent variations in the kinds of contact that existed between persons who engaged in exchange. These latter variations concerned what may be referred to as asymmetries in monetary exchange. By "asymmetries" is not meant here that the poor gave services or money to the rich of a higher value than what they received in return, though the word has sometimes been used in this sense. Here it is used to refer to something quite different, to the sheer difference in personal worth of the parties involved and the consequent divergence in their attitudes toward use values. Monetary exchange asymmetries have existed as long as money has been in use, and they survive relatively unchanged to the present day, despite the prodigious development of capitalism. Monetary exchange asymmetries, far more than slavery or serfdom, have influenced the distribution of social and political power over the last three centuries in Europe without ever being properly understood. Exchange asymmetries remain the principal means by which the use of money helps to create social structures. They therefore deserve detailed attention. They may be briefly described as they appeared on the eve of the eighteenth century as follows:

In preindustrial Europe a rich man could afford to buy clothes for hunting, clothes for dinner, clothes for town, clothes for home. He could have a chair for his desk and another in his parlor. He could have fifteen different dinner dishes served in as many days. He could pay a man to clothe him and another to bring his brandy. He could make land transactions twice a year, order major improvements to his house and park every decade. Each individual transaction played a very small part in his life.[8] A poor artisan, on the other hand, bought one shop and one set of tools at the beginning of life, one bed, one pot, one ladle, one apprentice. He slept in the same room as his family all year round. Each transaction bulked much larger in his life because the commodity involved was for him an essential and long-term feature of his life.[9] Over time he lost sight of the precise relation between price and good. His tools became worn, but those were his grooves and the rubbing of his hands that he saw on them. His linen became threadbare, but he knew exactly what the stains and tatters were from. In the seventeenth and eighteenth centuries, as now, most people got married once or at most twice (although then it was death rather than divorce that occasioned the repetitions). There may have been competition at the time of the courtship, but what did that mean fifteen years later? The same sort of disjuncture between purchase and use characterized the relation of the poor farmer to his plot of land, the poor weaver to his loom, the spinner to her wheel.

The poor had to live and work with what they bought while the rich soon sold it again or rented it out. A question to the rich of figures, balances, letters of credit, deeds, and bonds, property was for the poor a question of highly particular and peculiar utensils, four specific walls, one single piece of bottomland that had a tendency to flood in wet years, one address on a narrow street. By the eighteenth century, price could appear as a mere mathematical entity to one, a proper subject of scientific formulas and abstract theories; to the other it was a dangerous and unpredictable thing, a destroyer of lives and bringer of blessings, a capricious god, probably manipulated by unseen conspirators.[10]

In a sale of land between a rich and a poor man, their attitudes toward the land would be starkly different. The rich man might focus on the average annual yield of the acres in question; the poor man would wonder how easily the plow slipped through the clods of earth, how frequently stones were to be met with. Was there good drainage for a place to build his cottage? Who were the neighbors? It might be argued that a profit-maximizing rich man would also inquire into such things. But this misses the point. The poor man's interest was not in profit as such; it was in the pain he personally would feel when the blade of the plow struck a hidden boulder, the sleep he personally would lose when extra hoeing was necessary or when manure just spread was washed away by a sudden rain. The poor man's use of the commodity was immediate, life-encompassing, a question of smells and flavors, muscle aches and broken ankles; it would shape the character of his connection to wife and children.

It is exact for the eighteenth century to speak of men and not women in the exchanges discussed so far, but similar observations apply obviously to women. For the chambermaid in the rich man's house, it was a fateful day when she entered service and would be another when she left. Was the mistress of the house kind or domineering? Did the design on the silver make it easy to polish? Her annual wage built up very slowly into something that would buy her another fateful master, a husband. Two huge transactions, very small to a rich man, and her life course was settled. In addition, one very concrete way in which rich women resembled the poor was that they, too, were often insulated systematically from the kinds of transactions whose personal significance could be adequately expressed in a ledger.

From this stunning contrast in the personal use of commodities arose asymmetries in the personal relationships created by monetary exchange. It is important to remember that most monetary exchanges in rural areas and within the workshops of urban artisans gave rise to complex personal relationships, instead of simple, anonymous ones.[11]

In such transactions, the mere difference in the relative significance of a particular commodity to each party could give the rich a certain power over the poor very different in kind from the power created by coercion (although indirectly dependent on coercion). A landowner who leased out twenty farms could afford to make a few mistakes, to suffer a few setbacks, without feeling the pinch. Of eighteenth-century English landlords, for example, Mingay remarks that

> farms in hand meant trouble, expense, and possible loss, and at the least were highly inconvenient. Even the smaller landlords, who customarily engaged in farming, disliked having more land than they could properly manage. When the Purefoys had a farm fall into their hands [i.e., by losing or evicting a tenant] they found their comfortable days of leisure replaced by a "great hurry," and with the servants away looking after the farm, and the horses all "workt down," their normal life of entertaining and visiting was out of the question.[12]

But such inconvenience, which would have been much less to a large landlord, must be multiplied a hundredfold to appreciate the position of the landless farmer caught between leases. Such a person with a dependent family had a great deal at stake when seeking a lease. If he did not estimate the value of the land properly or did not convince the owner of his skill and energy, if he lost the farm or took it on at too high a rent, he was in serious trouble. But even if he was the perfect tenant, the landlord might refuse him for some extraneous reason without suffering much loss. This difference alone was often enough to elicit humility, deference, and obedience from the poor in their dealings with the rich.[13] However freely both parties entered into the transaction, the owner had only inconvenience at stake; the tenant feared destitution. The rich can afford to be capricious; the poor must therefore be careful.

This asymmetry in the stake each party had in given transactions, based as it was on a contrast in the use value of given commodities to each party, worked to give shape to a large proportion of European society by the early modern period. The poor's use of commodities was more varied and multidimensional than the rich's; it was comparatively difficult for the poor to reduce in any satisfying way this varied use to a single, quantitative monetary expression. Yet the poor's need, when dealing with the rich, to reduce all this varied usability of things to an accurate price value was great. They had to marshal all their shrewdness when facing a rich man. But theirs could never be the simple shrewdness of a profit-maximizing merchant.

A competitive environment raises no impediment to the impact of such asymmetries. If a prospective tenant is confronted with ten landlords or ten thousand, he still needs a farm desperately. His very survival and that of his family may depend on the kind of lease he can get. For the landlord, even a relatively small one who owns only three or four farms, the quality of any one lease agreement is never a life-or-death matter. This difference alone, no matter what the attending circumstances, will be sufficient to give the landlord a crushing advantage over his tenants if he chooses to use it. Few landlords will fail to do so; the structure of the situation prescribes a desire for submission and humility from tenants, whatever the landlord's private inclinations. Tenants more often than not will learn to offer these things as a matter of course.

Money is not an essential ingredient of exchange asymmetries. Asymmetrical exchange may be regarded as a large genus within which asymmetrical monetary exchange forms an important species. Marcel Mauss in his celebrated essay *The Gift* remarks that among the Kwakiutl,

> if a subject receives a blanket from his chief for a service rendered he will return two on the occasion of a marriage in the clan chief's family or on the initiation of the chief's son. But then the chief in his turn redistributes to him whatever he gets from the next potlatch at which rival clans repay the chief's generosity.
>
> The obligation of worthy return is imperative. Face is lost forever if it is not made or if equivalent value is not destroyed.[14]

In such a gift-giving relationship, it is not just the subject's need to return more than is received that holds him in thrall to his chief, but also the fact that the chief, with his ever-growing stock of valuable gifts, is never in danger of losing face before any one of his subjects. It is not the equality or lack of equality of what is exchanged that sets up the advantage of one party; it is the fact that what is exchanged is of only minor significance in one party's life and of major significance in the other party's. The whole of the two parties' social identities must be taken into account. This is why the word "unequal" fails to capture what is being described here; "asymmetrical" may be an awkward term, but it at least draws attention away from the thing exchanged, away from the reductionistic simplification of a quantity concept, and toward the whole imbalanced social configuration of the relationship. Being a geometrical metaphor, it invites the imagination to open up, where numerical metaphors encourage it to close down.

When money enters the relationship and when the thing exchanged for money is not ornamental or prestigious artifacts but either subsistence goods or else the means of making subsistence goods, the asymmetry takes on a very special shape. The peculiar shape of such a monetary relationship is so important that it warrants a step-by-step exposition.

First, the term "subsistence goods," as used here, means anything that satisfies needs which, in a particular case, are rated very high by the parties involved. People make hierarchies of needs for themselves; the survival requirements of the body and its nervous system must be creatively transformed by consciousness before they can become the object of action. Food, clothing, and shelter are often found high in the hierarchy of needs, but they are never alone there and will frequently be sacrificed for other goods in specific communities. Wine has been for long a subsistence good in many regions, just as in many others it has been regarded as an imported (and vicious) luxury. Special holiday dress on which great care is lavished is a subsistence good in most societies, however poor. Pilgrimages to religious shrines in times of sickness, the *Wanderjahr* of adolescent males, gloves, scarves, buckles, and pictures to hang on the wall all represent goods for which poor people have routinely sacrificed immense quantities of food, clothing, and shelter. It is misleading to leave them out when talking about subsistence or to suppose that the basic needs are merely biological or "material" in character. (More will be said about this in the first section of Chapter 4.) In asymmetrical exchanges of money for subsistence goods or for the means of making them, sanction for a failure to make "worthy return" is not (or not only) loss of face but directly and immediately loss of the ability to live and work.

Second, the unique characteristic of money is that it allows an extremely exact calculation of what constitutes "worthy return." Under the proper circumstances the rich may use monetary transactions to establish a highly flexible and detailed discipline over the poor tenants or laborers or outworkers they engage. Under the proper circumstances it is possible to exercise this discipline at a distance, from the library of a country house, the counting room of a warehouse, or an urban *hôtel particulier*. A field of force is set up in which one pole is represented by the account book of the wealthier party and the other is represented by the diverse bodily needs and familial obligations of his poor subordinate. A pen, by raising a rent figure at one pole, may cause physical pain in the stomachs and on the calloused hands at the other pole; or it may cause moral anguish when parents regard children in want.

One must know exactly what is exchanged to see how the disciplinary potential is set up. Sharecropping, for example, a very common form of relationship in rural Europe down through the nineteenth century, is like Kwakiutl blanket exchange in that it involves no money, but different in that it involves the exchange of a means of making subsistence goods (land) for a share of those subsistence goods. Use of farmland (and sometimes equipment) is exchanged for a fixed proportion of the yield. In such a relationship it may be necessary for the landowner to impose discipline through direct surveillance, the ultimate sanction being nonrenewal of the relationship.[15] Otherwise, the sharecropper may work only enough to ensure his own livelihood instead of maximizing yield, and the owner will then be left with a smaller harvest to split. If the sharecropper's right to renew is ever established, the owner's ability to discipline may become nil. In a farm lease involving money rent, discipline does not have to be exercised by direct surveillance; it becomes contingent on the landowner's ability to adjust the rent frequently. A nine-year lease in a period of rising crop prices will allow the tenant to retain all the benefit of the growing value of his harvests over the course of the lease. The tenant will have the option of translating this benefit into less-sustained effort or improved consumption or improved equipment or the purchase of additional land. Whatever the case, the field of force weakens. If crop prices fall over the term of the lease, the tenant may be driven to starvation or to abandoning the farm in despair. Discipline degenerates into destruction of the relationship.[16] In wage-labor and subcontracting relationships, still other factors determine the efficacy of potential discipline. (More will be said on this matter in Chapter 5.) In short, money in asymmetrical exchanges can be either a highly refined instrument of discipline or a very blunt one, depending on the circumstances.

Such exchanges establish only a potential for domination, for the exercise of discipline. The potential varies in form just as the exchange does. Whether or to what extent this potential is used by the wealthier party or responded to by the poorer one cannot be determined except by looking at specific cases. The potential's use may be blocked by other features of the situation; and it is always the case that idiosyncracies of the persons involved determine the exact nature of the relationship. Exchange asymmetries may be thought of as features of established practices to which individuals may or may not give assent and which are more or less difficult for individuals to ignore depending on the circumstances. The concept of asymmetry is not meant to straightjacket interpretation or to reduce complex relationships to a unidimensional flatness. It is a concept that interpretive method needs because it draws attention away from the mere meanings of the visible acts of social life and toward the disorderly, unrealized desires of actors. By looking at both the effects of coercion and the character of exchange asymmetries in a specific society one can develop one's own independent idea of what a society is and how its relationships are structured. One can then do more than merely interpret the ostensible meanings of texts, rituals, and practices; one can make a judgment about their effects on real relationships, that is, about their role in giving order to cognition and desire. By investigating the articulation of coercion and exchange with the ordering and fulfillment of desires and by identifying the unintended consequences of established practices (that is, those results of practices which their public meanings do not encompass), one puts oneself in a position to discern trajectories of change. Interpretive method is thus provided with a theory of history tailored to its needs, a theory that allows one to use interpretive method without losing sight of the role that our common this-worldly existence and our conflicting desires play in shaping human societies.

One important limitation of the concept of exchange asymmetry is that it refers exclusively to the structure of a dyadic relationship and says nothing about the larger social and political context within which that relationship takes shape. It is a microeconomic concept, so to speak, focusing on two isolated individuals. Asymmetrical exchanges cannot give structure to a society except insofar as some collective decision or the outcome of some collective conflict sets the terms within which these exchanges will occur. It would be misleading, therefore, to present a picture of the role such exchanges played in structuring European society about the year 1700 without saying something, however summary and inadequate, about how things got to be that way.

It is noteworthy that both G. E. M. de Ste. Croix and M. I. Finley (that is, a Marxist and a non-Marxist) identify the same distinctive feature as setting off Greek and all subsequent European civilizations from their Near Eastern precursors.[17] That feature was, in a word, money. From at least the seventh century B.C. exchange relationships involving money, property, and labor services constituted a new kind of social order on the northern coast of the Mediterranean Sea; and the state, as we now understand that term, grew up as a formalized arena within which conflict over such relationships could be contained and sufficient consensus created about the rules governing these relationships to avert constant civil war. The very idea that societies have states (or vice versa — that the two things are not in any case coterminous) arises from the fact that in Western societies law and custom create a private arena within which individuals come face to face with each other and strike vital bargains involving work, money, family, and the necessities of life. To separate state and society when speaking of the Kwakiutl — or of an early medieval manor, for that matter — is nonsense for the simple reason that neither Kawkiutl nor early medieval society was organized around two prevailing kinds of relationships: one kind ("social structure") involving asymmetrical monetary exchanges, the other ("politics") involving more-or-less-organized contention over the laws and customs that shape the first kind.

Three reasons may be cited to explain why the spread of asymmetrical monetary exchange was likely to transform social conflict. First, conflict resulted from the potential bluntness of money as a disciplinary tool. A bit of bad weather was sufficient in 600 B.C., just as it remains in 1986, to upset all calculations and to thrust thousands of farmers into crisis, putting them at the mercy of wealthy creditors or landlords. It was about 600 B.C. that Solon averted civil war in Athens and set that society on the road to democracy by decreeing that debts could no longer be secured against the persons of Athenian citizens. Defaulting debtors who had been sold into slavery were immediately freed; others liable to the same fate were declared free of their debts. From this reform arose that stark distinction between citizen and slave in Athens upon which civil equality and popular sovereignty were later built.[18]

Second, conflict in this new kind of Western social order tended to take the form of intervention by third parties in the common dyadic relationships that money creates. Politics and sometimes warfare have provided the sphere in which such third parties emerge — whether in the form of the state, of riotous crowds, or of invading armies. In Rome, for example, the failure of the Gracchi brothers to achieve legal reform in favor of the poor after 120 B.C. sealed the republic's fate. From that point on, the senate foreclosed any further use of state institutions to mediate between rich and poor. Within a few years Marius opened the road to autarky by taking landless citizens into his legions, paying them in cash for their services, and rewarding veterans with land. Loyal service to a victorious general became a form of protest against the senatorial aristocracy and simultaneously a route to independence from the enormous power of its private wealth. This particular form of protest was vitiated by its opportunism. Obviously the poor did not lament the passing of the republic and the creation of an unchecked monarchical state, but in the very long run they suffered a severe deterioration in their position under the empire, so severe that the distinction between citizen and slave again lost its meaning by about 400 A.D.[19] The precise structure of the state in Western societies is important first and foremost for the way it creates opportunities to regulate or modify the disciplinary potentials of monetary exchange. When discipline becomes too blunt, people caught on the painful end of dyadic exchanges will become available for political adventure. They will look for rallying cries, for allies, for certain forms of solidarity.

Why not call this "class conflict," as many historians do? The reason is that being subject to discipline through asymmetrical monetary exchange is not the same thing as having a specific relation to the means of production. (This point is discussed in greater detail in the final section of Chapter 5.) It would be easy, of course, to redefine the term "class" to apply to such disciplinary relationships, and many readers might be more comfortable with such a strategy. After all, everyone who uses the term "class" nowadays redefines it.[20] But that is also a good reason not to use it at all. A few moments after redefining it both writer and reader would be in danger of sliding back into the comfortable notion that it is natural or normal for a one-to-one mapping to exist between classes and political factions and that when this does not occur (which is virtually always) it is because of an intervening factor, a peculiarity, an oddity of ideological or economic circumstance that must be surmounted by the progress of history. This is just the opposite of what the historical record shows, which is that political movements draw on broad bands of support, coalesce around principles that transcend the concerns of specific positions in the social structure, and depend on the dedication of selfless innovators. All of the leaders and many of the supporters of the popular parties in ancient Athens or Rome were themselves aristocrats. As in the case of the French Revolution, fissures broke Athenian and Roman society apart along a jagged diagonal rather than a neat vertical or horizontal line. Solon, Pericles, the Gracchi, and Julius Caesar rallied broad coalitions behind them, coalitions that tended, more often than not, to recruit persons who suffered in a variety of ways from painful discipline exercised by wealthy exchange partners, or who feared they might suffer from it. The same could be said for any modern leader of a "working-class" movement, whether Feargus O'Connor or Lenin. Asymmetrical monetary exchange, when prevalent, creates predispositions, "raw material," if one likes, for political movements, but nothing so definite or deceptively clear as the term "class conflict" implies. The fact that the notion of exchange asymmetry refers only to a dyadic relationship and does not simultaneously refer to the collectivities whose conflicts and compromises create the social context around dyadic relationships gives it a flexibility that the concept of class almost unavoidably lacks.

Finally, conflict in Western-type social orders is shaped by the fact that money is confusing. It is perennially perplexing that apparently fair bargains struck between relatively (or legally) free individuals should result in one party's falling into the power of the other. On the one hand, is not the money proffered a just and reasonable measure for the service or good received? On the other hand, flattery and self-deception (themselves weapons of conflict) have assured as the centuries passed that the rich would feel justified in disposing of the fates of others. The poor were insignificant, lesser forms of being, polluted by their continual intercourse with the particular facts of their worn little cottage walls, degraded by long boring hours behind the plow. These two ideas – of the fairness of money and of the inherent superiority of the wealthy – remained in uneasy balance through all vicissitudes down to the modern era.

It was easy, as commerce and communication shriveled away at the end of the Roman Empire, to translate the disciplinary control of lease and sharecropping relationships into the juridical, military, and personal power of a lord over his serfs.[21] Across the subsequent millennium, relations surrounding the meeting of subsistence needs in European society shifted back and forth between the extremes of direct, coercive surveillance on the one hand and purely monetary discipline on the other. Monetization of labor dues combined with inflation hurt the lords of the thirteenth century. The Black Death was a further boon to the peasants that survived. But even in the darkest days of the century following the plague's outbreak there was never the slightest threat of social equality breaking out in landlord–tenant dealings. Some lords revived the legal strictures of serfdom to extract submission from the dwindling number of peasants. Others offered terms of tenure that were extremely favorable – payments low, security high – to attract new tenants to their abandoned farms. But tenants were never invited home to dinner. On the contrary, there was instead much discussion of the proper relation between villeins and lords, as the latter sought to coordinate the use of their lessened (but hardly threatened) asymmetrical advantages and coercive resources.[22]

With the return of demographic pressure in the fifteenth century, the balance tipped back even more firmly in the lords' favor. Commercial expansion and inflation from 1500 on, causes of the rebirth of serfdom in Eastern Europe, had more variegated results in Western and Southern Europe. The taste for money income among the rich led in some regions to enclosures (driving out villagers to create pasture land for sheep), in others to further translating of the vestiges of manorial rights into money payments, in still others to accumulation of land rented on short-term leases whose rents rose along with, and in the seventeenth century faster than, prices. There was no return to serfdom, however; those peasants who retained manorial land usually emerged with greater control of it and greater security of tenure by 1700.[23] But even when the extreme of this evolution had been reached in the eighteenth century, it remained perfectly possible for sheer differentials of wealth to confer personal power. Having comparatively less at stake in any transaction with the poor, the wealthy – whatever the origin of their wealth – were able to command fear and respect from the poor through their money alone if necessary, just as they had in Petronius's Rome or Alcibiades' Athens.

Growth of the liberal illusion

What gradually changed after 1650 or so, and eventually altered everything, was that social thought began to deemphasize the just preeminence and authority of the wealthy, which had been frankly acknowledged and celebrated in European culture for two thousand years. Instead, a new emphasis was placed on the fairness and precision of money as a medium of exchange between legal equals. It is not that people lost sight of the advantage of the wealthier party when they turned their minds to the matter. But it became increasingly difficult to give representation to this advantage within the new conceptions of the body politic that arose with the Enlightenment. The beginnings of this change in social thought have already been alluded to; it is now necessary to diagnose with greater care the weaknesses that resulted.

MONEY AS UNIVERSAL EQUIVALENT AND PRINCIPLE OF LIBERATION

As early as the 1640s in England, following the victory of the parliamentary army over the crown, one of the factions in the ensuing political struggle showed itself to be in the grip of strange assumptions about monetary exchange.

As C. B. Macpherson has shown, the Levellers in the famous Putney Debates did not demand universal manhood suffrage (as they are frequently supposed to have done).[24] Their disagreement with the Independents was over how much property was sufficient to ensure the political independence that was a prerequisite for the franchise. The Levellers wished to exclude from the franchise "apprentices, or servants, or those that take alms . . . because they depend upon the will of other men and should be afraid to displease (them)."[25] For precisely the same reason, the Independents' leading spokesmen, Cromwell and Ireton, wished to exclude a much greater number of persons: all tenants at will, copyholders at the will of the lord, and artisans and shopkeepers not members of trading corporations. Such persons were bound to be jealous of those who owned property; given the vote, they would use their new power to steal from the propertied or abolish property entirely. Artisans who were members of chartered guilds, by contrast, held a privilege that, like property, could be lawfully taken from them by no man. For the same reason, Cromwell was willing to admit to the franchise all tenants with copyhold by the custom of the manor (since the lord of the manor could not take their land away from them) and even leaseholders whose lease was measured in lives, a common practice that secured the tenant from eviction at the landlord's pleasure. In effect, the Independents felt that all other persons were "dependent on the will of other men" and would be either afraid to displease them or else anxious to rebel against them. The Levellers insisted, on the contrary, that unprivileged artisans, leaseholders at will, or copyholders at will were full "free-born Englishmen" who, unlike servants or apprentices, had alienated none of their birthright of liberty.

This debate would have been impossible had the feudal retainer system survived, since it was just the people the Levellers wished to enfranchise who had earlier pro-

73

vided the core of the great barons' private armies. Their dependence had earlier been self-evident. Now at this central moment in the genesis of modern theories of natural right, thanks to the elimination in England of direct nonmonetary services from leaseholder obligations, it was possible to demand that the "birth-right of all English men [to vote] be restored to all which are not, or shall not be legally disfranchised for some criminal cause, or are not under 21 years of age, or servants, or beggars."[26] The Levellers' claim that all such persons were sufficiently free to exercise the franchise implied that paying a money rent for land on a short-term lease did not deprive one of reason or make one envious of all property (as the Independents persistently charged). Money, by implication, played a liberating role; a servant or apprentice who lived under his master's roof owed obedience and subordination, but a leaseholder owed only rent. His birthright of liberty was intact. This general view of the role of money in society lies at the foundation of most modern democratic constitutions. It is fundamental to most versions of liberalism, whether democratic or otherwise. But it is a view that has been plagued with problems from the very beginning, since it assumes that the poorer party to a purely monetary transaction is as free as the richer.

The advantage that the Levellers sought by treating monetary relationships as politically neutral was obvious; by doing so, they eliminated the principal objection to the extension of the franchise and thus hoped to gain for leaseholders and unprivileged artisans that additional bit of control over their own lives, of liberty, which the right to vote conferred. But by the end of the seventeenth century, other thinkers recognized new uses for the Leveller argument. The idea that monetary exchange was a politically free form of relationship was found to dovetail nicely with the idea that gain was the operative motive in all exchanges. In both notions one particular kind of exchange came to serve as an implicit paradigm. In this exchange, money and tangible commodity are virtually the only things that pass between the two parties, who are indifferent to each other in every other respect and perfectly free of other entanglements with each other. In early modern society this kind of exchange was most commonly encountered only in exceptional circumstances: in long-distance trade between urban commercial centers, in banking and discount transactions, in certain land purchases, in the exchange of the petty commodities of daily consumption in cities. This most highly constructed, rarefied, and special form of exchange, albeit a rapidly proliferating form, was taken to reveal the salient characteristics of all forms of exchange.

The spreading confusion can be seen clearly in John Locke's *Second Treatise of Government,* where, as Macpherson has shown, he combines the arguments of the Levellers and the Independents into a single incongruous vision. For Locke inequalities of wealth had their origin in the state of nature. Of course, he forcefully asserts the general freedom and equality of all men in the state of nature, and justifies property on the basis of direct labor and use: No man may keep more than he works himself nor hoard goods that will spoil before he uses them. For these forthright views he is justly famous. Nonetheless, Locke goes on to remark that the introduction of money allows a person to hoard without spoilage. And money can be introduced in the state of nature "by a tacit and voluntary consent." "This partage of things, in an inequality of private possessions, men have made practicable *out of the bounds of society, and without compact,* only by putting a value on gold and silver and tacitly agreeing in the use of money."[27] Before civil society is founded, in other words, great inequalities already exist, but based on an underlying tacit consent of equals to use money. Elsewhere Locke readily admitted that those who ended up possessing nothing because of money and trade, living "from hand to mouth," were unable to "raise their thoughts above" to matters of state.[28] In practice, then, strict limitation of political participation was unavoidable, even under a government founded on recognition of the liberty and equality of all men. Wisely, Locke avoided saying exactly where he thought the line should be drawn between "active" and "passive" citizens, as the French later called them. He had everything to lose and nothing to gain from being specific.

Most of the great figures of the Enlightenment, knowingly or not, followed in Locke's footsteps on these matters. Montesquieu, despite his starkly different style of thinking, despite his flexibility and his omniverous empiricism, failed like Locke to see in the monetary power of the rich over the poor any threat to liberty. In his ideal constitution, everyone is allowed to vote for representatives except those "in such an estate of baseness that they are not considered properly to have any will of their own."[29] Like Locke, he did not specify whether Levellers or Independents had the better opinion on who was to be included in this group. In addition, those "distinguished by birth, by wealth, or by honor" must not be confounded among the rest of the people. "The common liberty will be their slavery, and they will have no interest in defending it, because the greater part of resolutions [voted by the people's representatives] will be against them."[30] Therefore they must form a separate hereditary corps with its own deliberative body having the power to veto tax measures – a House of Lords.

Of course liberty for Montesquieu did not require ideal conditions; true liberty eschewed extremes of any kind and flourished under government of whatever form so long as it was moderate. The early monarchies of Europe, for example, preserved the deliberative tradition of the Germanic tribes by establishing representative bodies (parliaments and estates) in the Middle Ages.

> Such was the origin of gothic government among us. . . . It had the disadvantage that the lower people [*le bas peuple*] were reduced to slavery [that is, serfdom]. This was a good government with the capacity to become better. The custom arose of granting letters of manumission [to serfs], and soon the civil liberty of the people, the prerogatives of the nobility and the clergy, the power of the kings were in such harmony that I do not think there could be found on earth a government so well tempered as was that of each part of Europe so long as it lasted.[31]

The preservation of property was as essential to government for Montesquieu as it was for Locke:

> The public good is always that each one conserve invariably the property which civil law gives to him.

> The constitution of Rome was founded on this principle, that only those would be soldiers who had sufficient property to answer to the republic for their conduct. . . . Marius took all sorts of people into the legions, and the republic was lost.

> The revenues of the state are a portion which each citizen gives of his property [*bien*] in order to secure the rest. . . . There is nothing which wisdom and prudence must more carefully determine than the portion that one takes and the portion that one leaves to the subjects.[32]

Without saying it in so many words, Montesquieu nonetheless made his views quite clear: Those without property are too jealous of the rich to be allowed full participation in government. Or else they have no will of their own and can contribute nothing to the wisdom of political deliberation. It is wrong for them to be held in bondage; debt bondage is particularly dangerous to a democracy; but serfdom is only a minor evil in a well-balanced constitution, an evil easily overcome. Freed serfs, possessed of their "civil liberty" but unable to participate in government (because incompetent) or allowed only a limited participation (because too prone to jealousy of the great), are therefore in the highest state of liberty that the *bas peuple* can hope to attain. Implicit in these views is a complete failure to think about the power that grows out of monetary exchange relations between the rich and the poor. Only if the poor are subjected to nonmonetary, juridical forms of direct or personal domination is there any disadvantage [*inconvénient*]. If, however, power over the poor arises solely out of the lesser stake that the rich have in any one transaction, it is liberty.

These views, or rather this way of talking about property – "views" is perhaps too strong a word – had a long and fruitful history. Few in the Enlightenment stood out against the combined authority of Locke and Montesquieu. The *Encyclopédie* merely passed on conventional wisdom when it declared civil society's origin to be the desire to protect property or defined natural liberty as the right to dispose of self and property in the state of nature, and civil liberty as the freedom from personal bondage.[33] The Declaration of Rights of Man and Citizen of 1789 likewise made property a right existing prior to government, which governments were created to protect.[34] The National Assembly abolished "privilege," that is, all property that did not take the form of direct disposal over natural objects, and it wrote a constitution with strict property qualifications for the franchise. In this way liberty and equality were supposedly achieved. Only Rousseau and a few other minor voices held out against the chorus of agreement, persistently denouncing the forms of dependence that grew out of active commerce and great concentrations of wealth. Even Rousseau felt forced to make a place for private property in his ideal state, yet it was a highly restricted one. Property was for him a limited right held by the individual directly from the state, which served the function of separating individuals from each other and subjecting them directly to the general will, so that they could not enter into debilitating dependencies among themselves. It is, in fact, one of the keys to Rousseau's originality, from the *First Discourse* to the *Social Contract,* that he mistrusted money.[35]

In the meantime the further development of economic thought continuously reconfirmed the prevalent equation of property with liberty by systematically obscuring from view the existence and impact of exchange asymmetries. The universality of the motive of gain was given ever-greater emphasis; money gradually came to be considered a universal equivalent, a medium that could express the significance of any feature of human experience. Eventually, this approach to money and motives virtually theorized exchange asymmetries – or any variability in motives for engaging in exchange – out of existence. One can trace this development from Montesquieu through Ferguson to Smith.

In *De l'esprit des lois,* Montesquieu treated calculation in money terms as an exceptional practice characteristic of the commercial spirit: "We see that in countries where people are taken up with the spirit of commerce, one trades in all human actions and all moral virtues: the smallest things, anything human beings demand, are made, or are given, for money."[36] Peoples without commerce, by contrast, engage in brigandage but also offer hospitality to travelers freely, without counting the cost. Commerce brings peace and civilization but also "a certain sentiment of exactitude [*de justice exacte*]."[37]

For Ferguson, as well, the motive of gain was a circumscribed characteristic, limited to those who engaged in certain occupations. A necessary division of occupations between those that were "liberal" and those that were "mechanic" was for him the underlying fact of social structure. A man in polished society seeks to "conceal his regard for what relates merely to the preservation of his livelihood." Such a man views the beggar, the laborer, and the mechanic as "degraded by the object they pursue and by the means they employ to attain it," whereas those whose skill creates objects of beauty are of a "superior class" because they earn "applause as well as profit." The highest station is reserved for those who do not act out of "the consideration of mere subsistence, and the regards of interest," that is, those with sufficient property to ignore these things.[38] The need to limit the political participation of the laboring poor arises directly from, among other things, their necessary concern for gain:

> Ignorance is the least of their failings. An admiration of wealth unpossessed, becoming a principle of envy, or of servility; a habit of acting perpetually with a view to profit, and under a sense of subjection; the crimes to which they are allured, in order to feed their debauch, or to gratify their avarice, are examples, not of ignorance, but of corruption and baseness.[39]

The weakness of Athenian democracy was that such persons were allowed to engage directly in political deliberations. Here the use of property to dominate the propertyless is passed over in silence. But the motive of gain is still seen as an odd, exceptional factor in social relations.

The change in tone from Ferguson's essay of 1767 to Adam Smith's *Wealth of Nations,* published nine years later, could not be more dramatic. For Smith, gain was not one of the degrading results of the division of labor but its original fountainhead. It was "a certain propensity in human nature" to "truck, barter, and exchange one thing for another" that first led to the creation of separate occupations and thereby to the gradual increase in the productive power of labor. The creation of the occupation of "philosophy or speculation" was as much a consequence of the pursuit of advantage as was that of making pins; and both inevitably became subdivided in their turn.[40] The pursuit of gain ensured the rational distribution of society's resources, because, as Smith put it,

> The whole of the advantages and disadvantages of the different employments of labour and stock must, in the same neighbourhood, be either perfectly equal or continually tending to equality. If, in the same neighbourhood, there was any employment evidently either more or less advantageous than the rest, so many people would crowd into it in the one case, and so many would desert it in the other, that its advantages would soon return to the level of the other employments. This at least would be the case in a society where things were left to follow their natural course, where there was perfect liberty, and where every man was perfectly free both to choose what occupation he thought proper, and to change it as often as he thought proper. Every man's interest would prompt him to seek the advantageous, and to shun the disadvantageous employment.[41]

"The whole of the advantages and disadvantages": By this phrase Smith meant to include money as one kind of advantage among others. A butcher, for example, whose job in Smith's view was highly unpleasant, received more money for his work than a tailor, because the extra money compensated for the unpleasantness of the work. Otherwise butchers would prefer to make garments. Money was not an odd or peculiar object of desire but the liquid medium that balanced and coordinated all desires. Following this line of reasoning, exchange asymmetries could be wished out of existence. Assuming that all enjoy "perfect liberty" in the disposal of self and property, lord and tenant or master and journeyman bargain with each other solely with an eye to their own advantage. The poor need not be ingratiating; the rich have nothing to gain from sychophancy. Each must simply convince the other that he offers advantageous terms, secure in the knowledge that the invisible hand of self-interest will move the other to strike a deal. The rich man's potential caprice, his comparative lack of stake in the outcome of what are for him minor transactions with a crowd of poor tenants or laborers or servants, is simply defined out of existence. Even if tenants are found to offer humility and obedience, or lords to demand them, then this may be said to be part of the price, one of the disadvantages weighed by the tenant against the advantage of access to land; obedience can be treated as merely one of the "rents" that the landlord finds it advantageous to receive. If one is robbed of political liberty and self-respect, it is merely a rent.

In France Quesnay and the Physiocrats, though less sophisticated than Smith, nonetheless perpetrated the same error. True, they held that the laborer was parasitical whenever he received more than a bare subsistence wage for his work – a view that seemed to ratify the laborers' lowly status. But in the contemplation of the abstract flow of wealth through the different organs of Quesnay's *Tableau économique*, one easily loses any sense that monetary exchange all by itself can create a vast variety of forms of submission and dependence.[42] One sees only a functional, and equal, mutual interdependence in which the great source of value is the fecundity of the earth, of landed property. As Smith's work became known, French economic thought was already treating money implicitly as a universal equivalent, and the French were prepared to recognize the superiority of Smith's thinking; by the end of the 1790s his doctrine had displaced Quesnay's as the new orthodoxy.

Pushing Smith's formula to its logical extreme makes it impossible to distinguish any exchange relationship from any other. The differences between the kula ring and the New York Stock Exchange, or between these and Prussian serfdom, are reduced to a matter of the particular mix of monetary versus nonmonetary advantages sought by each party. In the Stock Exchange, monetary advantage reigns supreme; in the Trobriand Islands kula givers prefer esteem to tangible wealth; Prussian serfs pay for their land with service, deference, and obedience instead of rent. Everyone is happy.

Pushing Smith's formula to its logical extreme is exactly what his disciples set out to do over the subsequent fifty years in England.

According to Nassau Senior, if a father did not minimize the expense of raising his child by apprenticing him out to "a farm yard or a cotton mill," if he engaged in the unprofitable "speculation" of giving him a more expensive education, it was because "with all men, except for a few outcasts, one of the greatest sources of immediate gratification" was to witness the daily improvement of his offspring. The apparent irrationality of the behavior involved a concealed trade-off of money for satisfaction.[43]

By contrast, a person who refused to enter into a demeaning relationship of dependency and deference could be said to be forgoing increased wages in return for "freedom of action," as J. S. Mill put it, quoting as follows from a commission of inquiry into the state of handloom weavers:

> He [the handloom weaver] can play or idle as feeling or inclination lead him; rise early or late, apply himself assiduously or carelessly, as he pleases, and work up at any time, by increased exertion, hours previously sacrificed to indulgence or recreation. There is scarcely another condition of any portion of our working population thus free from external control. The factory operative is not only mulcted of his wages for absence, but, if of frequent occurrence, discharged altogether from his employment. . . . The weaver will stand by his loom while it will enable him to exist, however miserably.[44]

Thus handloom weavers were merely exercising their "perfect liberty" as they starved on four shillings a week rather than enter a Manchester steam weaving shed, where they would have been forced to submit to the clock and the foreman's arbitrary discipline. By implication, factory workers sold obedience and time discipline for money. The same argument could be applied to any relationship of deference or obedience on one side and patriarchal authority on the other. Parent and child, master and journeyman, landlord and tenant—according to classical political economy, such relationships were actually between two equal parties freely exchanging money equivalents. Thus prostitutes sold their virtue, aristocrats their grain, miners their exposure to dirt and danger, it was said, at a price that exactly balanced their pains.

This is an interpretation that can fit any evidence, as it has been repeatedly remarked, because no one can say how much virtue or danger are worth to anyone else or whether they are even a question of money.[45] Any time a laborer's wage level is higher than expected, according to Nassau Senior, "we may infer, either that his employment is subject to some peculiar disadvantage, or that, in fact, rent or profit enter into his remuneration."[46] Such a procedure is immune from all possible disproof. For this reason, the notion of advantage that rests at the core of classical political economy can lay no more claim to validity (and no less) than Freud's notion of the oedipal stage or Luther's notion of the futility of works for achieving salvation. All are equally profound and instructive statements about the underlying nature of human motivation; all are equally metaphorical, nonscientific, essentially poetic. Money is numerical, however, whereas salvation or making love to one's father or mother are not. One can make calculations and projections with money. To do so looks like science, even though in reality the value of money is as variable and uncertain as the human soul.[47]

The idea that price created a mechanism that balanced the various advantages and disadvantages of particular uses of capital and labor, common on both sides of the Channel by 1780, was especially apt to appeal to the rich man's experience of life by the eighteenth century. The rich were constantly engaged in transactions large and small, able to gain a sense of the relative potential money value of otherwise quite disparate things. A rich man could appreciate that two new chairs for the library equaled the annual rent on a twenty-acre farm or that a stretch of parkland could be traded for the feudal right of *banalité* in a neighboring village. Within his day-to-day life money was something very close to a universal equivalent; it was not hard for him to feel the persuasive power of the ideas of Quesnay or of Adam Smith. Successful merchants, of course, were even more familiar with the game of monetary comparison. Only by soaring high above the fates of others could one view the ravages of eighteenth-century price swings for grain, land, or manufactured goods as a beneficial mechanism. But this is exactly how wealth already allowed some people to feel, that they rightly disposed of the fates of others. Smith and Quesnay told them, even better, that it was a public service for them to make shrewd deals, that trade at the "natural" price benefited rich and poor alike. Famine prices brought more land under the plow: a noble image to cover up the memory of mass beggary or of funerals for the dead children of the respectable poor.

The problem with any such approach to understanding exchange systems is that the very things human beings need most to understand about them, the unintended consequences of their operation, are explained away. The destruction of Bengal cotton spinners, the starvation of cottagers in times of high grain prices, the subjection and enslavement of persons whose labor is used to create commodities for international trade, the systematic curtailment of political liberty — all such things tend to be treated as merely functional elements of a beneficial equilibrating process. In reality, they are the very things one would most like to be able to anticipate and prevent by understanding the systemic functioning of monetary exchange.

It might be possible to calculate, for example, that an armed retainer in the fifteenth century provided on the average £10 6s. 2d. of military power per year. But it is important to recognize that if both parties to the deal opt for cash instead of service — a minor matter for the Smithean economist — the result can be a complete transformation of society, a new configuration of political institutions, the occasion for revolutions in mind and in the public forum. Matters vital to human liberty are at stake. It is obvious that if parents began apprenticing their children to the highest bidder, some significant social change would be afoot, and not a good one. But every shift in the monetary and nonmonetary mix of elements in any transaction, equally, has a direct social impact that no society concerned with freedom can afford to ignore.

It is therefore essential for a social historian looking at the age of laissez-faire to recognize that a pivotal confusion of the period lay exactly here: in the notion that unregulated monetary exchange was perfectly compatible with — indeed, was an essential precondition for — personal freedom. This is a most profoundly erroneous idea.

MONEY SUBSTITUTIONS AND DISCIPLINARY POTENTIALS IN THE PRUSSIAN REFORM

The folly of this new conception of liberty, linked to the idea of money as a universal equivalent, was nowhere more apparent at the dawn of the nineteenth century than in the terrible misfiring of the Prussian government's attempts to liberate the serfs after 1807. In Prussia all the misconceptions of Enlightenment economic thought bore fruit in practical miscalculations. It is an instructive case. Prussian reformers thought they were liberating serfs; in fact they were merely altering the disciplinary potentials within which serfs could be made to continue obeying their betters.

Important as the Prussian defeat of 1806 was in giving the government the resolve to carry this reform through, it was Adam Smith, not Napoleon, who provided an acceptable notion of liberation. Smith's thought had received an enthusiastic response within Germany, although virtually every German economic thinker qualified his acceptance of Smith with a certain number of reservations, as Marie Vopelius has shown.[48] With respect to the serf populations east of the Elbe River, most agreed that they were too backward, too uneducated, to maximize gain. To free them from their hereditary dependence without proper preparation would lead to disaster. Efforts to break them of their familiar work habits, to introduce them to new crop rotations and stock-breeding techniques, failed repeatedly, it was said, because they did not understand the first thing about their own interest. That Smith's theory did not apply to them, which was generally acknowledged, was also, by a peculiar slip, held to be the serfs' problem, not the theory's.[49] Smith's theory purports to be descriptive, but almost everywhere its influence led to a prescriptive outlook. The desirability of an eventual freeing of the serf class was disputed by none of Smith's German disciples, but few saw it as immediately advisable.

One exception, however, was Christian Jakob Kraus, whose position as professor at Königsberg alongside Kant gave him an inordinate influence over the future leaders of the Prussian bureaucracy. As early as 1791 he is reported to have spoken in favor of an immediate freeing of the serfs.[50] The only possible objection he could see was that the current value of estate land took into account the value of the labor dues that serfs owed the estate. It followed, by the Smithean law of universal money equivalence, that estate owners could have no possible grounds for objecting to the end of serfdom if they were given a money payment to compensate for the lost labor dues. This opinion, expressed privately and in his teaching, had altered by 1802, when he published a short treatise on the subject.[51] In this treatise he denied that estate owners had any right to compensation. The backwardness and low productivity of the serfs he attributed to the drawbacks of their condition. Rising grain prices discouraged those who had to buy a part of their provisions. The increasing frequency of estate sales and the extension of grain acreage on existing estates made wage labor a method of labor distribution that was preferable to, because more flexible than, the rigid counterproductive compulsion of service dues. Serfdom, in effect, interfered with the easy substitution of monetary and nonmonetary equivalents. Further, he insisted, it was a matter of simple justice "that the country people [*Landleute*] should be able to choose their overlords [*Herrschaften*], and likewise the overlords their people."[52] Without the freedom to change masters, the serf gained little from the host of laws designed for his protection. Kraus's was a vision of freedom highly restricted indeed; justice was established when the serf became free to change one overlord for another.[53] Self-betterment would result from the heightened insecurity of wage labor. Liberation of the serfs, in effect, involved no threat to the power of the estate owner, only a reformulation of the terms under which it was exercised.

Of the Oktoberedikt of 1807 that formally liberated the serfs in Prussia, Vopelius remarks that it was "thoroughly imbued with [Kraus's] spirit."[54] Koselleck notes that it was fundamentally conceived in terms of economic principles, quoting its own stated aim: "to eliminate all those things that have, up until now, hindered the individual from achieving that well-being which his own abilities make him capable of."[55] The edict established free land exchange, free choice of trade, and the abolition of hereditary serfdom. Noble estates (with their judicial and police powers still attached, but soon to be stripped of labor dues) would be open to anyone to purchase.

Guilds in the towns would lose their monopolies. At a stroke an unregulated economy of freely exchangeable properties and services would be created. But on the all-
important issues of compensation for discontinued labor dues, the edict was mute,
leaving the details for later clarification. Where Kraus's own opinion had varied,
there the reformers were internally split.[56]

Following Stein's departure in 1808, those in favor of compensation carried the day;
and Hardenberg's Regulierungsedikt of 1811 spelled out the terms on which compensations were to be made. Serfs who held their plots with nonheritable titles – these had
been the majority, however heritable their status as serf (*Erbuntertan*) – were allowed to
gain full property rights in their land, free of all labor dues, in return for a compensation to the overlord equivalent to from one-third to one-half the value of that land (or in
certain cases even more).[57] The compensation could be paid by direct alienation of land
to the estate owner, by a one-time capital payment, or by a rent payable in twenty-five
yearly installments.[58] Until such payments were arranged, although the serf was personally free, he continued to owe the same labor dues as before in return for his land.
(Serfs with heritable titles in their plots were not covered by the 1811 edict; compensation conditions were not laid down for them until 1821.)[59] These conditions were
much harder on the serfs than Stein had originally envisioned or Kraus had recommended in 1802, not only because of internal disagreements among reform bureaucrats but also because of stiff and rapidly expanding opposition from the provincial
nobility to the whole project of reform.[60] "The constitution of the [noble and common]
estates [*Stände*], founded on holy and long-standing agreements, was the most beauti-
ful bond between the landed nobility and the nation; it established their unshakable
mutual dependency, which in the past has held our state together through the most
dangerous crises," declared the deputies of the Kurmark nobility on the eve of
Hardenberg's 1811 Regulierungsedikt.[61] Hardenberg's circle hoped that the edict's
terms would soften this kind of opposition. In effect, the serfs were put in grave danger
of losing all rights in land – through indebtedness or because their reduced holdings
would no longer be viable – in order to win minimum compliance from their overlords.

Even this concession was not enough, however. Hardenberg originally envisioned
a three-year period for the establishment of compensation levels and the settlement of
modes of payment throughout Prussia, with the concurrence of local authorities. By
1815, he hoped, the serfs would be in possession of their land so that land taxes could
begin to be collected directly from them.[62] But the provincial nobles, thwarted in
their desire to undo the reform, resisted it by means of legal maneuver. The actual
nature of serf titles in many regions was extremely unclear, so that the possibility of
endless litigation remained open.[63] In the end the government had to set up special
provincial boards (the Generalkommissionen) with broad powers to rule on titles, re-
draw property lines, consolidate holdings, even move whole villages, in order to ensure that alienated land was equal in quality to that retained by the former serfs.[64]
These boards were open to influence, the experts on them often ignorant of law and
local unwritten custom. They faced many imponderables when attempting to determine the money value and legal status of all the diverse forms of labor services and

use rights. In general, their decisions were favorable to the nobility. They ruled, for example, that certain classes of titles to serf plots were too weak to justify the former serfs in retaining any land. Labor dues continued to be owed for plots held by these weak titles, but now as a rent rather than as the feudal obligation of an *Erbuntertan*. Thus, one group was removed entirely from the effects of the 1811 edict.[65]

What Kraus had imagined in 1791 to be an extremely simple matter of paying to estate owners an amount equivalent to the value of labor dues turned into a social and administrative nightmare. Most nobles were not at all content with a money equivalent; they wanted serfs. If they could not have serfs then the next best thing was to keep the land and reduce the peasants to a penniless proletariat, an outcome that German disciples of Smith before and after 1807 widely denounced as unfavorable to the nation.[66] But few of them asked why it was a goal so fiercely pursued by such a large proportion of the estate owners, noble and nonnoble alike. Were they merely maximizing gain? Or seeking to shore up a threatened sense of honor and authority that itself could have no money equivalent? The process of compensation dragged on through the 1820s and 1830s. As late as 1848, 16 percent of peasants had still not concluded agreements to buy out their labor dues, thirty-three years after Hardenberg's target date.[67] Many did lose their land, owing to the weakness of their titles (as adjudged by inscrutable boards of experts) or to their inability to make a go of it on reduced holdings. State credit was legally withheld from them, although readily available to estate owners. Peasants could pledge no more than 25 percent of their reduced holdings for private loans; modernizing investment was effectively denied them. Population growth swelled the ranks of the landless, whose condition by the hungry 1840s became piteous indeed, a kind of mass beggary.[68] Estate owners took to paying wages to their now free laborers by giving them small plots of land that they could farm in their free time. Such arrangements looked so much like a rebirth of serfdom that the government found it necessary to put a twelve-year legal limit on this kind of contract, forcing the poor laborer's status, by this access of insecurity, to remain juridically that of a "free" man.[69] This is how hereditary serfdom was turned into labor agreements between freely contracting parties in Prussia.

The outcome in Prussia was utterly different from what the reformers had envisioned. Hardenberg had promised in 1811 that "the state would thus acquire a new, estimable class of motivated property owners" and that "through the desire to enter this class, the cultivation of the soil would profit from more hands, and through their greater effort, because freely given, more work as well."[70] Up to 1848, in fact, roughly 350,000 peasants did gain ownership of some land in Prussia, although compensation payments and indebtedness made their position precarious and many now had to depend on wage labor to supplement the yield of their own meager acres. Even worse, the number of rural landless laborers in Prussia in the meantime tripled, reaching well over a million.[71] Hope of gaining access to land ownership was for this group nil; their insecurity was extreme in the best of times, their suffering during the potato blight and bad harvests of the mid-1840s second only to that of the Irish. The disappearance of armed retainers in England by the beginning of the seventeenth century – an earlier case of money being substituted for a service – helped pave the way for social revolution. The common conclusion of German historians is that the Prussian reform likewise was one of the preconditions of the very different social revolution that followed there in 1848. How simple it is to translate nonmonetary pains and preferences into money equivalents!

Certainly Kraus was right to imply that the abolition of serfdom constituted no threat to the domination (*Herrschaft*) of estate owners within Prussian society. Had it been otherwise, reform would have been judged politically unacceptable and Smithean economics would doubtless never have found a following in Prussia. That such a shift in disciplinary potentials could be called liberation, however, gave it considerable appeal in a revolutionary age. At the same time, those who opposed the reform were also right to insist on the fundamental nature of the change involved. Serfs exchanging labor services for land had always been profoundly disadvantaged by the asymmetrical character of their relationship to estate owners; historically this disadvantage had been enhanced by the juridical condition of hereditary bondage. In 1807 the bondage was dissolved; between 1811 and 1848 the exchange itself was gradually terminated and replaced largely by contractual exchanges of labor services for cash payments – wage labor.

The potential for discipline was not lessened in these new asymmetrical monetary exchanges so much as completely transformed. An old sanction was removed, the threat of punishment for flight. A new sanction was made available, the threat of joblessness. Lords lost the ability to say whom and when their serfs would marry; but population growth made joblessness more frightening.[72] An old, vague calculus of equivalents, involving plots of land (held by diverse, vague kinds of feudal title) in return for a certain number of days of service per year, inflexibly set by custom, was replaced in most cases by the highly flexible, highly precise calculus of money for work. The extremely intimate, diverse, and personal solutions that individuals in Prussian society, whether lords or serfs, had previously worked out to the problems of day-to-day survival within the existing array of disciplinary potentials had to be extensively rebuilt. Everyone's identity changed, and not in any simple way. The threat of joblessness, for example, was not likely to hold in place the people who had previously feared punishment for flight. New incentive pay schemes such as piece rates were not likely to stimulate the enthusiasm of those who had learned to be content with customary labor service measured without reference to output in days at the plow or days in the harvest. Others, who had chaffed under the old system, would feel relief at receiving ready cash payments measured by their effort. Those Junkers who had learned to be content with cracking the whip over their reluctant serfs' heads as they worked in the fields were not likely to feel immediately comfortable with the potential for control at a distance inherent in the precise calculation of wage levels. Yet other estate owners welcomed the change.

The problem that the Prussian reformers faced was that the new economic thinking encouraged them to treat the substitution of money equivalents for labor and land as a very simple thing, yet their own knowledge of Prussian conditions, as well as the protests their proposals aroused, told them that such substitutions were actually revolutionary in their consequences. The result was that their legislative proposals, imbued with the new economic thinking as they were, were at first extremely oversimplified. But even the later, more-detailed reform edicts failed to allow for the complexity and diversity of titles, land quality, use rights, and labor dues. Application of these measures was in consequence slow, complicated, and corrupt; the outcome capricious, but almost never in the serfs' favor.

The notion of exchange asymmetries allows one to see how the Prussian reform altered disciplinary potentials without in any way threatening their continued existence in some form or other within established practices. If one confined oneself to interpreting the texts of reform edicts and memoranda, one would never be able to see this, or to see what these texts had to do with the texts of Junker protests. Because the substitution of money for any element of an exchange relationship alters the disciplinary possibilites created by asymmetry, such substitution always constitutes social change. This has long been recognized partially and imperfectly. The German economist Georg Friedrich Christoph Sartorius, for example, remarked in 1806 that the choice of equivalents for labor dues and other use rights (*Nutzniessungen*) was not, as many imagined, an easy matter. If done improperly, the whole reform effort could go awry, he warned.[73] The irony is that the reform measures eventually enacted fit closely with Satorius's recommendations, but reform went awry anyway.

The very character of money is to be substitutable. Modern economic thought, from the seventeenth century on, has exploited this character of money in the building of theoretical constructs. Such essential ingredients of theory as the concepts of capital, value, price, income, wealth, yield or return, rent, revenue, and utility appear precise because they may be expressed in numerical terms in specific cases; but in fact each may refer either to money or to things, depending on the circumstances. Each such term therefore rests for its meaning on the ready substitutability of money for things. But in reality money substitution always involves a "cost," which cannot, in the nature of things, be quantified. Thousands of Prussian Junkers did not want their serfs' labor dues to be bought, no matter what the price. Nor is it possible to say, once those buy-outs began, what the "cost" was to the millions involved of the extensive changes in their routine, vital, day-to-day relationships, that is, in their very identities. Dependence on economic terms that obscure from view the fundamental difference between money and other things makes it extremely difficult to appreciate the full impact of introducing money equivalents into specific relationships. The very stuff of modern social history can be erased from the mind with this kind of language. Of course economic theory has often developed in the direction of taking into account distinctions between money and other things, as in the distinction between fixed and liquid capital, for example. (But note that other terms, such as "operating capital," remain inherently ambiguous.) The thrust of economic thought has always been, in any case, to get around such distinctions, to come to a numerical "bottom line" of, say, marginal unit cost or gross national product or standard of living – concepts that obliterate all those distinctions that might allow one to appreciate the indefinable "costs" of money substitution.

MARX'S VALUE

Begun as apologetics for merchant activities, the great project of economic theory failed from the beginning to appreciate the highly variable role of money in human relationships. Or rather economic thinkers struggled to deny the existence of such variability, at first in order to win social acceptance for commercial profit and interest on debt. The endeavor worked, largely because in the seventeenth century the complex and personal money exchanges of village and workshop were hard for theorists to see and the impact of commerce on New World slavery or Eastern European serfdom was obscured by distance. The idea of gain as a universal motive for trade fit nicely, as well, with the arguments of Levellers and later of a Whig apologist like Locke that monetary transactions were politically neutral and did not impinge on the political liberty of either party. By Adam Smith's era, it was possible to fuse a number of ingredients into a single, erroneous vision of economic practice. Smith's synthesis was the full-blown liberal illusion. Its ingredients were (1) the unlimited and easy substitutability of money for any other object of desire, and therefore (2) the universality of the underlying desire for "advantage" or gain; (3) the political neutrality of money exchanges, and therefore (4) the compatibility of free trade with personal liberty. Each of these ideas so neatly entailed the others, all so plausibly turned on the apparent truth of the first principle, that the theory seemed to sum up what the essence of money is, especially in the experience of well-to-do landlords and merchants who had little contact with either production or deprivation.

With Smith as their guide, economic theorists could now turn to the countryside, look directly at relations of sharecropping or serfdom, and see them purely as results of the search for advantage. Insofar as serf or lord might not be motivated by gain, this was actually a consequence, as German disciples of Smith agreed in a nearly unanimous chorus, of the backwardness and ignorance of the rural population. Astonishingly, not the theory but the people were deemed to be at fault. In Prussia reform introduced money and freely alienable property into lord—peasant relationships with the intention of liberating the underlying desire for gain that motivated everyone. If gain did not motivate everyone, then reform would make sure that people had no choice but to be motivated by it. Prussian reformers were victims by 1807 of a kind of doublethink that allowed them to carry out a program that went disastrously astray from the very first, without ever feeling the need to question the principles behind it. Sure of the superiority, liberty, and flexibility of money transactions as they were, they were unable to see resistance as anything but ignorance. No evidence whatsoever could overcome a conviction structured in this way.

Of course the liberal illusion, as it won disciples all across Europe, did not go unchallenged. In England and France, where free-trade reform measures began dislocating the lives of the laboring poor in dramatic ways between 1790 and 1815, limited freedom of speech and press, as well as spreading popular literacy, allowed plebeian theorists to mount a sustained attack on the idea that monetary exchange was politically neutral. But the challenge remained incomplete. Because this countertradition as it developed borrowed extensively from the vocabulary of its opponents, one or more of the elements of the liberal illusion entered persistently into the attackers' thought, depriving it of clarity, rendering it prone to misconception. This was true even of certain tendencies within Marx's thought. That this great champion of working-class revolution may have borrowed too extensively from the vocabulary of political economy is a claim that cannot be made without offering a minimum of explanation, however, especially in a period when his intellectual reputation is enjoying a vigorous renaissance. The discussion that follows in this section and the next attempts to spell this claim out as carefully, and as briefly, as possible.

The beginnings of the countertradition can be traced back to the last decade of the eighteenth century. Hébert, Babeuf, the *enragés,* and others in the streets of Paris during the Revolution sensed the threat of domination inherent in free monetary exchange between rich and poor, even so clearly as to point to the poor's more intimate contact with the day-to-day uses of things and with day-to-day deprivations as the starting point for disciplinary potentials. But these penetrating glimpses were never codified. More will be said of these sans-culotte beliefs and their limitations in the next chapter. In England Thomas Spence, Charles Hall, William Thompson, Thomas Hodgskin, Charles Bray, and others created a tradition of critique of political economy built on a labor theory of value derived from Smith and later, in part, at least, from Ricardo. There has been considerable controversy over the significance of these English plebeian theorists, as well as over the extent of Marx's debt to them. They have been called "proto-Marxists," "Ricardian socialists," and "arcadian socialists," each term emphasizing a different facet of their wide-ranging views.[74] Their starting point was the doctrine that those who labored were entitled to the whole product of their labor. In England, they argued, those who worked received back less value as income than they created by their effort. Hence the core problem was one of unequal exchange between the "industrious classes" (including self-employed artisans and yeomen) and the idle rich. But unequal exchange was not viewed as inherent in the exchange relationship itself so much as resulting from the corruption of parliamentary rule. Taxes voted by the rich members of Parliament to pay interest on state bonds held by the rich were one source of difficulty. Acts of enclosure and other laws that permitted the amassing of great landed estates were another. This English tradition of plebeian theory thus easily fed into the Chartist effort to wrest control of Parliament away from the privileged few.[75] Far from effectively challenging the central fallacies of Smithean theory, these early socialists sought to fight the theory on its own ground, armed with borrowed notions of production, capital, value, and competition. The role of money as a disciplinary tool within asymmetrical exchange could not be clearly delineated in this idiom. To use the concepts of classical political economy without falling victim to them required a mind of a very special order, something that did not appear until Marx came on the scene.

Some will object indeed that nothing has been said here so far that Marx did not anticipate. Marx's system began and ended with a radical critique of the basic concepts of political economy that was not so very different from the one being put forward here. Marx was, in one sense, perfectly aware of what are referred to here as exchange asymmetries. Nothing could have surprised him less, for example, than to discover that Prussian serfs, once freed, remained subject to the power of their former lords. He insisted repeatedly that bourgeois freedom meant "a degraded and almost servile condition of the mass of the people."[76] He recognized that this servile condition arose within the wage relationship itself and was not a result (as the earlier English tradition had claimed) of the manipulation by government of property law, central banking institutions, or public debt. The laborer was reduced to servility precisely because he was "the free proprietor of his own labor capacity" and because selling labor capacity was not the same thing as selling a cow or some surplus grain. To sell labor power is to hand oneself "over to the buyer for him to consume, for a definite period of time, temporarily." The laborer's freedom, in Marx's view, was an odd thing indeed. "The worker," Marx said, "must be free in the double sense that as a free individual he can dispose of his labor-power as his own commodity, and that, on the other hand, he has no other commodity for sale, i.e., he is rid of them, he is free of all the objects needed for the realization of his labor-power."[77] Such a state of "freedom" could result only from a prior historical process of radical predation, the so-called primitive accumulation, in which a great mass of people were stripped of productive resources.

But it is important to notice that the ironic play on the word "freedom" in this passage is characteristic of Marx's treatment of the language of liberalism and of political economy. His dialectical method made possible almost endlessly sustained ironies that gradually eroded his opponents' language from within by repeatedly pointing out the practical consequences of applying liberal economic categories to real societies in history. Marx played with political economy the way a cat plays with a mouse. Says David Harvey of reading Marx:

> To understand the concepts fully requires that we understand the inner logic of capitalism itself. Since we cannot possibly have that understanding at the outset, we are forced to use the concepts without knowing precisely what they mean. Furthermore, Marx's relational way of knowing means that he cannot treat any one concept as a fixed, known, or even knowable building block on the basis of which to interpret the rich complexity of capitalism. . . . Marx never treats any one concept in isolation as if it could be understood in itself.[78]

It is true, then, that the notion of monetary exchange asymmetries is fully anticipated in Marx; nothing has been added here that he has not already at least alluded to. In another sense, however, simply to use the term "exchange asymmetries" is to break with Marx, because it represents a terminological break with the basic categories of classical political economy (commodity, production, capital, etc.). Rather than following Marx's method of working to undermine economic categories from within, the notion of exchange asymmetry points to something that simply cannot be expressed using those categories.

The difference from Marx can be seen in his treatment of the concept of value. In classical political economy, value is an unproblematic notion and its relation to money is relatively simple. Commodities may not always trade at their exact value, but they always tend to do so, all things else being equal. Otherwise money could not have been so readily accepted as a universal equivalent. But Marx was painfully aware of the inadequacy of such a view of the relation between money and value. His critique of capitalism and of political economy as a theory of capitalism rests squarely on his conclusion that money in exchange transactions was bound to fail to represent value accurately. The simplest reason was that exchange value cannot be an accurate reflection of use value; that is, the myriad uses to which any commodity can be put are never successfully expressed by a single number. From this it followed that the use value of labor (a commodity) could not be expressed by the wage (determined by the cost of delivering labor power); that surplus value (the difference between the wage and the true value of labor's use) was not the same as profit (the difference between the wage and the exchange value of labor's products); and so on. By the time Marx finished following up all these consequences it appeared that money expressions, that is, all prices in capitalist economies, were no more than a vast and complex sham, a skein of appearances that fooled both capitalists and laborers alike. Further, money's failure to reflect value doomed capitalism to recurrent crises and eventual breakdown. The most conspicuous victim of this sham, the source of all value, the engine behind the curtain, was the laborer himself.[79]

Marx did not imagine that these wrongs could be righted merely by giving the laborer a truly just wage; to do so would be to put an end to surplus value, which was the underlying basis of profit, and therefore to capitalism and therefore to the wage relationship itself. Wage labor was inherently unjust, just as exchange value was inherently inadequate as an expression of use value. To quote David Harvey again, value in Marx is not "a fixed and immutable measuring rod tied to labor inputs." That is, it is not quantifiable in a mathematically consistent manner. Value is instead " 'a definite social mode of existence of human activity' achieved under capitalist relations of production. . . . The paradox to be understood is how the freedom and transitoriness of living labor as a process is *objectified* in a *fixity* of both things and exchange ratios between things."[80] By this point the classical political economists' simple term "value" is being made to carry such a heavy load of meanings that it may almost be heard to cry out under the strain. This is exactly what Marx intended.

Following Marx it is possible to speak of "free labor" without ever making the mistake of supposing that those who freely dispose of their labor are actually free. Simply by being forced to dispose of their labor in one way or another they are enslaved. Following Marx it is possible to speak of value as the most concrete sort of thing while remembering that its existence is contingent on the historical emergence of a particular form of social order. But it is also possible that constantly retaining in awareness all these qualifications and reservations about the terms one employs may eventually overtax the mind. The danger of inadvertently resting satisfied with an incomplete or reified usage of one or more key terms is great.

It is easy to forget that the imperative to accumulate, for example, which is the drive for profit that runs capitalism, results in the stockpiling of surplus value, which is a form of value; but value is "not a fixed and immutable measuring rod." As a result, neither the size nor the rate of accumulation can be measured in a "fixed and immutable" way; and it follows that capitalism's tendency to overaccumulation is not "fixed and immutable" either. The revolutionary crisis may never come, that is; or at least its arrival is not guaranteed by the process of accumulation alone. But was this Marx's view or not? Experts remain divided.[81] Presumably, every change in the social and political order results in a change in the constitution of value as well. "Accumulation," like "value," is one of those Marxian terms that, like the vocabulary of political economy, refer at once ambiguously to either monetary or nonmonetary elements of exchange relationships. What is accumulated is in the first instance cash, which is reinvested in stocks or bonds or in the direct purchase of further fixed capital. Various use values and exchange values are all juxtaposed to one another under this single umbrella term. This is just the point that Marx sought to draw out. But once he had made the necessary distinctions, he immediately collapsed them back into the technical terms that were at once the objects and the tools of his critique.

Here is another example of the dangers of Marx's approach. One imagines that one may confidently use the term "free labor," knowing that free labor is really enslaved and that the term "free" is borrowed from bourgeois political economy. "Free" then refers to the contractual freedom of a competitive market, not political freedom or freedom in any other sense. Familiar with dialectical reasoning, one knows that treating "freedom" as "enslavement" is not a problem. But a kind of dialectical complaisance may ensue in which one fails to ask whether the enslavement of free labor may not be inhibiting freedom of contract, inhibiting, that is, competition. If this were the case, then wages would be determined not by the cost of labor power but in some other way; the crucial relationship in the creation of value, the wage relationship, might not be constituted in the manner described in volume one of *Capital,* with cascading consequences for all the other key Marxian concepts.[82] This is just what will be argued here at the beginning of Chapter 5. But it might be worthwhile to anticipate at least a part of that argument now.

It is easy to show that "enslavement," that is, the monetary exchange asymmetries of wage-labor agreements, did inhibit competition, even in Marx's day, the heyday of unregulated trade. Even in industrial Lancashire, Marx and Engels's paradigm case of a competitive, capitalist social order, monetary exchange asymmetries – it can easily be shown – dampened the formation of a competitive labor market to a considerable extent.[83] One need only look back at the testimony of a certain Journeyman Cotton Spinner of Manchester, quoted by E. P. Thompson *in extenso* over twenty years ago. In 1818 — too early for the influence of Ricardian or other labor market theories to have clouded his vision — he described the situation in the cotton mills of Lancashire as follows:

> The master spinners are a class of men unlike all other master tradesmen in the kingdom. They are ignorant, proud, and tyrannical. What then must be the men or rather beings who are the instruments of such masters? Why, they have been for a series of years, with their wives and their families, patience itself — bondmen and bondwomen to their cruel taskmasters. It is in vain to insult our common understandings with the observation that such men are free, that the law protects the rich and poor alike, and that a spinner can leave his master if he does not like the wages. True; so he can: but where must he go? why to another, to be sure. Well: he goes; he is asked where did you work last: "did he discharge you?" No; we could not agree about wages. Well I shall not employ you nor anyone who leaves his master in that manner. Why is this? Because there is an abominable *combination existing amongst the masters*, first established at Stockport in 1802, and it has since become so general, as to embrace all the great masters for a circuit of many miles round Manchester, though not the little masters: they are excluded. They are the most obnoxious beings to the great ones that can be imagined. . . . When the combination first took place, one of their first articles was, that no master should take on a man until he had first ascertained whether his last master had discharged him. What then is the man to do? If he goes to the parish, that grave of all independence, he is there told — We shall not relieve you; if you dispute with your master, and don't support your family, we will send you to prison; so that the man is bound, by a combination of circumstances, to submit to his master.[84]

Things had been freer, he said before the introduction of the steam engine enlarged the size of individual plants. In the new steam-powered plants,

> various disputes then originated between the workmen and master as to the fineness of the work, the workmen being paid according to the number of hanks or yards of thread he produced from a given quantity of cotton, which was always to be proved by the overlooker, whose interest made it imperative on him to lean to his master, and call the material coarser than it was. If the workman would not submit *he must summon his employer before a magistrate;* the whole of the acting magistrates in that district, with the exception of two worthy clergymen, being gentlemen who have sprung from the *same* source with the master cotton spinners. The employer generally contented himself with sending his overlooker to answer any such summons, thinking it beneath him to meet his servant. The magistrate's decision was generally in favour of the master, though on the statement of the overlooker only. The workman dared not appeal to the sessions on account of the expense. . . .
>
> These evils to the men have arisen from that dreadful monopoly which exists in those districts where wealth and power are got into the hands of the few, who, in the pride of their hearts, think themselves the lords of the universe [emphasis in original].[85]

What this testimony shows, and it is in no way surprising or unusual, is that the mill owners frequently used monetary exchange asymmetries to thwart market forces. The reference to a combination among mill owners should not be given too much weight. H. I. Dutton and J. E. King have shown that formal organization among them was highly intermittent because informal consensus on hiring practices was easily achieved.[86] Not monopoly but sheer size differentials, "wealth and power got in the hands of a few," were the source of the owners' advantage. Backing them up was the active collaboration of parish officers and justices of the peace. All semblance of bargaining, of maximizing gain through bid and response, information flow, and the free choice of contractual partners, was denied to Manchester laborers. It was easy for mill owners to accomplish this denial because their stake in closing the most advantageous deal with any one laborer was tiny. They could forgo with perfect equanimity the benefit to be gained from successfully bargaining with one worker. They had much more to gain from repressing all bargaining opportunities for individual laborers; they could thereby dictate terms to all who worked for them. The Journeyman Cotton Spinner's firsthand testimony suggests that Lancashire mill owners well knew how to use the threat of joblessness as a disciplinary device. Doubtless by as early as 1818 threat of discharge was a response so widely resorted to as to represent an established practice that few mill owners would have dared dispense with; as such it had become a key feature of the social order. It must also be remembered that "unskilled" cotton spinners in Lancashire, although their earnings varied widely from person to person and from week to week, were nonetheless a relatively privileged group, earning considerably more than a subsistence wage by the standards of the time. Mill owners faced stiff competition in the world market for cotton yarns, but such competitive pressure did not translate into inexorable downward pressure on the wages they paid. By the same token, their employees' grievances focused not on the exact wage but on the disciplinary effect of the wage relationship.

This matter will receive more thorough discussion and documentation in Chapter 5. All that needs to be recognized here is that one cannot simply presume that market forces determined wage levels or that suffering in Manchester slums was a direct result of the impersonal law of supply and demand. Surplus value was therefore being extracted in this historic home of industrial capitalism by other than strictly capitalist methods, by methods that cannot be appreciated unless one has a language for describing them. David Harvey interprets the mature Marx as holding that both labor and capital "are forced *at certain moments* to take class action" that interferes with free competition in labor markets (emphasis added).[87] But what the Journeyman Cotton Spinner points to is a consistent, unremitting interference that makes the notion of free competition simply inapplicable. Yet competition in Marx's theory is the mechanism that assures the fundamental link between wage levels and the cost of producing labor power. The testimony of the Journeyman Cotton Spinner suggests that exactly what the laborer earns is, in any case, only an ancillary feature of an oppressive situation that cannot be thought of as an economic mechanism. Quite distinct from the question whether the wage received by the laborer adequately remunerated him for the value he created is the more comprehensive, less quantifiable question what kind of life he led, what kind of social relationships he had. The notion of monetary exchange asymmetry points to the imbalance of any relationship between large employer and penniless worker and to the disciplinary potential set up by formalizing such a relationship as a free contract to deliver labor for money. This imbalance arises out of the brute fact that equal amounts of money cannot possibly mean the same thing to different individuals. (Again, this matter will be more fully discussed in Chapter 5.) The whole problematic of value calculus, with all its metaphysical imponderables, simply misses the point. One does not have to calculate values very nicely to see who has the upper hand.

THE FETISHISM OF THE PROLETARIAT

With reference to the body of Marx's theory, the proposal being made here involves more a shift of vocabulary than an attempt to supersede, disprove, or undercut Marx. Marx was perfectly aware that what were use values to poor persons were often only exchange values to the wealthy. He was perfectly aware of the advantage any large property owner has in his dealings with propertyless persons. But by naming the combined effects of the contrast in use values and the advantage of size a "monetary exchange asymmetry," and by placing this concept at the center of attention (instead of treating it as a means to the end of appropriation or accumulation), one gains a whole new method for analyzing social relationships. Even more important, one becomes proof against certain dangers of oversimplification that arise with peculiar persistence in Marxist views of class formation.

Marx's mature views on the question of class were surely more complex than his early ones or those that Engels propounded in his first book. Marx even anticipated, as R. S. Neale has shown, some of the problems that historians have since encountered and that provided the subject of discussion in Chapter 1 here.[88] But there can be no doubt that Marx never renounced the underlying validity of the ideas expressed in the *Communist Manifesto* of 1848. In 1875, well after completing the first volume of *Capital,* he simply quoted directly from the *Manifesto* when trying to summarize his views on class:

> In the *Communist Manifesto* it is said [wrote Marx in 1875]: "Of all the classes that stand face to face with the bourgeoisie today, the proletariat is a *really revolutionary class*. The other classes decay and finally disappear in the face of Modern Industry; the proletariat is its special and essential product." . . .
>
> The proletariat is revolutionary relative to the bourgeoisie because, having itself grown up on the basis of large-scale industry, it strives to strip off from production the capitalist character that the bourgeoisie seeks to perpetuate. But the *Manifesto* adds that the "lower middle class" is becoming revolutionary "in view of [its] impending transfer into the proletariat."[89]

In the same document, Marx criticized the Gotha Program of the embryonic German Social Democratic Party for proclaiming socialism's aim to be "the abolition of the wage system together with the iron law of wages." "Quite apart from the false Lassallean formulation of the law [of wages]" that appears in the Gotha Program, Marx found that

> the truly outrageous retrogression consists in the following:
>
> Since Lassalle's death there has asserted itself in *our* Party the scientific understanding that wages are not what they *appear* to be, namely, the *value,* or *price of labor,* but only a masked form for the *value,* or *price, of labor power.* Thereby the whole bourgeois conception of wages hitherto, as well as all the criticism hitherto directed against this conception, was thrown overboard once for all and it was made clear that the wage-worker has permission to work for his own subsistence, that is, *to live,* only in so far as he works for a certain time gratis for the capitalist (and hence also for the latter's co-consumers of surplus value); that the whole capitalist system of production turns on the increase of this gratis labor by extending the working day or by developing the productivity, that is, increasing the intensity of labor power, etc.; that, consequently, the system of wage labor is a system of slavery, and indeed of a slavery which becomes more severe in proportion as the social productive forces of labor develop, whether the worker receives better or worse payment. And after this understanding has gained more and more ground in our Party, one returns to Lassalle's dogmas although one must have known that Lassalle *did not know* what wages were, but following in the wake of the bourgeois economists took the appearance for the essence of the matter.
>
> It is as if, among slaves who have at last got behind the secret of slavery and broken out in rebellion, a slave still in thrall to obsolete notions were to inscribe on the program of the rebellion: Slavery must be abolished because the feeding of slaves in the system of slavery cannot exceed a certain low maximum.[90]

Here Marx attempted to summarize the analysis of *Capital,* showing how far both he and Engels had traveled since the 1840s, when their views were much closer to those of Ricardo and Lassalle. But one could also say that Marx in this passage had still not come quite far enough. Was he not, after all, inscribing on the program of the rebellion: "Slavery must be abolished because, however well the slaves are fed, they are made to work too hard and an ever-growing proportion of this work is done gratis"? This is, of course, virtually a parody of the profound critique of political economy found in *Capital,* but it is one that Marx himself wrote, and he wrote it, moreover, when giving his fellow socialists advice about the very practical matter of formulating a party program. The "enslavement" of wage labor arises from the disciplinary potential inherent in a supposedly free contract between persons whose stake in the relationship is entirely different, or asymmetrical. It does not arise from unequal exchange, as Marx implied in this passage, whatever he may have said elsewhere. Unequal exchange, assuming that it can be accurately measured, is a result, not a cause, of enslavement. Whenever one seeks to summarize Marx's critique, even when Marx himself did it, the vocabulary of quantified values threatens to take over in this way.

Engels in his famous pamphlet *Socialism: Utopian and Scientific,* to cite another noteworthy example, simplified the analysis of *Capital* just as Marx did in his *Critique of the Gotha Program.* Gareth Stedman Jones has remarked that this pamphlet, first published by Engels in 1880, "became the most popular introduction to Marxism apart from the *Manifesto.*"[91] In the pamphlet Engels identified the distinctive feature of the capitalist mode of production as the development of a planned, coordinated division of labor within single large enterprises. Production is "socialized" in the sense that it is no longer left to individual producers to organize it however they like. No one can say of any end product, "I made this." Yet this socialized productive power continues to be owned by individuals, and its fruits are still appropriated exclusively by the owners. "The [capitalist] mode of production is subjected to this [private] form of appropriation, although it abolishes the conditions upon which the latter rests." And further on Engels concluded, *"The contradiction between socialized production and capitalist appropriation manifested itself as the antagonism of proletariat and bourgeoisie"* (emphasis in original).[92] This is the view of the underlying cause of class conflict to which Marx gave voice in the *Critique of the Gotha Program.* The focus is on the robbing of the proletariat by private appropriation (that is, on unequal exchange), which is justified by an increasingly outmoded right of property. Conflict begins over amounts exchanged, and the proletariat's special role in abolishing capitalism arises from the fact that a wage, however high it is, is always lower than it should be.

Of course, a socialist state would also appropriate surplus value in order to achieve all kinds of collective goods, from schooling and medical care to capital investment. This is a point that Marx emphasized in the *Critique of the Gotha Program.*[93] But socialist appropriation would be public, rather than private, regulated by and for the citizenry as a whole. It was not necessarily the amount of surplus value appropriated but the private character of the appropriation that was unjust, although private appropriation could and usually did become too large. The evil of private appropriation, even when not too large, was that it was inevitably plowed back into capitalist enterprises in order to ensure opportunities for continued or increased appropriation in the future. This was wasteful and irrational. To receive a wage was therefore to be victimized by a wasteful and irrational system in which owners of capital used the fruits of labor to increase and perpetuate their access to the fruits of labor.

Stated in this schematic way for purposes of popularization, however, Marxist doctrine can easily give rise to a kind of fetishism of wages. It may be a penetrating critique of the capitalist drive for profit, but it still fails to deal with the grievance of the Journeyman Cotton Spinner of Manchester. His sense of injustice arose from the discipline that the factory owners were able to exercise over a population of submissive, docile laborers who could not take the risk of bargaining or resisting under most circumstances because they had so much more at stake in their jobs than the owners had in keeping them on. This is a kind of discipline that a socialist state could impose with even greater ease than private employers, unless there were very rigorous and very extensive safeguards created expressly to prevent such discipline. On the shape of such future safeguards Marx and Engels had virtually nothing to say. What the Journeyman Cotton Spinner was suffering under was not the exclusive fate of proletarians strictly defined. Disciplinary potentials arise in many exchange relationships; their forms are as varied as the relationships themselves. They are as easily established under "feudal" as under "socialist" production. Hierarchy and control in a given social order are a function of the whole array of such disciplinary potentials and the uses made of them.

Failure to deal fully with the disciplinary potentials of wage and other exchange relationships has handicapped the Marxist tradition's treatment of class formation. The fetishism of wages has given rise to a fetishism of the proletariat. Almost inevitably wage laborers are believed to hold a privileged position in the hierarchy of suffering and to have a special propensity to rebel because of low wage levels and because the surplus value they create becomes someone else's private property. In reality quite the reverse is true. That is, earning levels are, if anything, symptoms, not causes, of oppression. They will be lower where disciplinary control is more fully established. But even this statement oversimplifies. The near-universal pooling of wages among members of laboring households has ensured historically that wage levels of individual workers have had only the remotest relationship to the "cost of producing labor power." Wage levels alone tell very little about the social situation of individual laborers. The extraordinary hardships suffered by female heads of households – in the nineteenth century, as now, forced to live on wages meant to serve only as a supplement to male earnings – testify to this fact.[94] The relation of any individual laborer's wage level to his needs and desires is complex in the extreme. The real key to comprehending the character of his social position lies elsewhere.

The fetishism of the proletariat has given rise in recent historical research to the problem of the artisan, referred to in Chapter 1 with reference to E. P. Thompson's work, a problem that is no nearer solution now than it was in 1963.

Indeed, one of the great puzzles of the last century and a half of European history is the now well-known fact that proletarians, strictly defined, took a back seat to skilled artisans in all revolutionary and trade-union movements down to and including the Russian Revolution. Some of the largest urban trades of the nineteenth century – carpentry or masonry, silk weaving on jacquard looms, bespoke tailoring, shoemaking, furniture making – involved small-scale artisanal ownership of capital and employment of labor. Yet the members of just these trades provided the shock troops of urban revolt and the principal popular support for socialist doctrine at least down to the 1920s.[95] Were they members of the working class? Answering either yes or no to this question is unsatisfactory, as is the common impulse to treat them as bearers of a backward-looking or transitional consciousness that was doomed to disappear with the rise of a true proletariat. To see them as caught up in the "process of proletarianization" echoes Marx's view of them, stated in the *Manifesto,* as a lower middle class or petty bourgeois class facing "impending transfer to the proletariat."

But this face-saving expedient arbitrarily identifies one form of relationship, proletarian wage labor, as the only true revolutionary form of oppression and then accounts for all political movements arising out of other relationships by a kind of teleological analogy to the proletarian position.[96]

Examining the monetary exchange asymmetries in which nineteenth-century artisan groups were caught up, however, reveals disciplinary potentials that both explain artisan desires for liberation and account for artisans' greater ability, by comparison to, say, mill operatives or unskilled outworkers, to express such desires. None of this analysis requires that one decide on their class identity.

It would be worthwhile to examine a concrete example. The memoirs of the Paris mason Martin Nadaud give a vivid account of his brief experience as a subcontractor in 1841–42 that allows one to gauge the impact of monetary exchange asymmetries on his political activism. Stripped of guild regulation, construction in the nineteenth century gave rise to an unusually rich variety of forms of enterprise. There was wide scope for small-scale, speculative subcontracting, and doubtless most skilled artisans dabbled in it from time to time.[97] Nadaud in 1841 was faced with an urgent need for money.[98] The family farm in the Creuse department was burdened with a heavy mortgage; his father, becoming too old to work on the scaffolding, had just retired permanently to the farm and could not hope to pay off the mortgage without his son's help. Nadaud and an old working companion concluded a favorable deal to do the masonry on two buildings for an architect named Totain and his general contractor, Giraud. The price set was good, but there were rumors that Totain and Giraud were *mauvais payeurs*, bad payers – that is, that cash, when due, would be short, late, or nonexistent. Real payments would require renegotiating the promised price downward. It was late in the season; rain and sleet slowed up the work. Nadaud and his partner worked on the walls alongside the journeymen masons they were paying (on a piece rate) to help them. A competition developed to see who could lay the most stone despite the cold drizzle and the icing up of the scaffolding. Teams were formed according to the various native villages in the Creuse from which the masons came. "The *enfants de Beaumont* never shirk on the job!" one mason shouted. "Nor do those of Perseix!" called another.[99] With village honor at stake, they set to work and finished a story before dark set in. Content with the progress, Nadaud and his partner bought their employees dinner. At 2:00 a.m., arm in arm, they and their fellow masons marched home from a suburban café singing "like men thrilled with themselves and with their noble feat [*comme des gens ravis d'eux-même et de leur belle action*]."[100] The next day all were on the site at 7:00 a.m. as usual. The masonry work was complete within six weeks, and payment was received as agreed. After paying off their masons and counting out daily salaries for each other, Nadaud and his partner had over two thousand francs of pure profit to divide between them.

Nadaud continued subcontracting into the following year, but never with as good results. He found contractors to be an untrustworthy lot, tricky, always big on promises and short on cash. Supply of materials was a difficult problem, as was keeping up the spirits of his masons and their apprentices. As he took on bigger jobs, he always had to commit his accumulated cash reserve to paying wages to his employees and could only hope that his contractors would honor at least a part of their obligations to him. One missed payment by a contractor would put him out of business. Despite the heady profits, Nadaud quit within a year and went back to working for others.

Nadaud's skills and his very modest capital gave him great freedom about how to lead his life, at least by comparison with the Journeyman Cotton Spinner of Manchester quoted earlier. He could work for a wage or employ others as an independent operator; he could pick and choose among the various contractors according to their trustworthiness and to the prices they offered. (Unfortunately, these two often varied inversely with each other.) Once engaged on projects, however, Nadaud became very vulnerable before the much larger operators he was working for, who might or might not pay him what was promised. Usually, it appeared, they did not. Once the work was under way, they used the asymmetry of the exchange relationship to gain leverage. Having committed his capital and his effort to a building, Nadaud was over a barrel; he was always willing, in the event, to take less than he was promised so long as he got something. General contractors all knew this. Eventually Nadaud learned to inflate his initial cost estimates in anticipation of the contractors' underhanded proclivity to renegotiate. But by this time he was growing so disgusted with the work that he quit soon after.[101]

Subcontracting also compromised Nadaud's relationship with his fellow masons. Rather than drive them on, he chose to invoke their sense of honor and their pride in their skills to ensure that they worked hard for him. But to him this was itself hardly an honorable way to make profits over the long run.

The milder disciplinary potential of asymmetries of the construction trade (by comparison with outwork or factory wage labor) involved masons in intermittent but painful moments of vulnerability. Most of the time they were free of direct supervision. Nadaud, an ardent republican, often wore his red Phrygian cap (symbol of the sans-culottes) on construction sites. No one objected. He and his colleagues talked openly of revolution and of the glorious 1790s in their bars after work. They were free to formulate political views of any kind, press laws notwithstanding. And they had just enough experience of the domination of large-scale capitalist operators to develop a lively distaste for the competitive regime. The reign of laissez-faire, as they saw it, had turned once-honorable work into a sordid kind of gambling for high stakes. Textile operatives in the same period, far more completely dominated by the authority and surveillance of their employers, had more to complain of but less opportunity to discuss their grievances openly. As a subcontractor, Nadaud feared destitution only once every few weeks. The Journeyman Cotton Spinner had to fear it every day; he dared speak only anonymously and in secret. Nadaud wore his *bonnet rouge* to work.

To say that "proletarianization" is what radicalized Nadaud is imprecise in the extreme and fails in particular to allow for a precise estimation of the disciplinary pressures that both spurred him and permitted him to express his political opinions. As the label of a tendency or direction in capitalist development, "proletarianization" is even less adequate. A century and a half after Nadaud, construction workers still alternate between subcontracting and wage labor; the world system shows no impatience with immense diversity in workers' fates, such as between, for example, Detroit assembly line workers and independent Guatemalan weavers.[102] What unites these people is not levels of remuneration but forms of discipline, forms that they share with many who are not manual laborers.

PRICES AND CLASSES

Since Marx's time, economic theorists have not even tried to defend classical political economy against Marx's onslaught. They have abandoned not only Ricardo's labor theory of value but the very notion of value itself as a false and misleading construct.[103] People do not exchange things because things have equal value, twentieth-century economists insist. Exchanges occur because people want what they are getting more than they want what they are giving up. Any one person's desire for a thing (that person's "preference") will depend on various factors, but especially on how many the person already has of those things that he or she is trading for. Each additional thing has what is called a "marginal utility," which usually drops as the quantity already possessed increases.[104] (This concept will be referred to again at the beginning of the next chapter.) The route that theory has taken since Marx has forced economists to give up on the idea that there can be any common, public measure of goods, of utility. Prices measure only the current, fleeting balance points between conflicting subjective preferences.

The most serious difficulty of this brilliant salvage job, which has rescued so much of the edifice of classical political economy from Marx's clutches, is that it cannot be disproved. It has no empirical content. Preferences are not measurable or observable, and therefore they can always be claimed to be adequately balanced by prices. The procedure is as arbitrary as was Adam Smith's original idea of advantage; it allows economists to continue to treat money as a universal equivalent whose substitution in exchange relationships offers no difficulties. It allows them to continue to believe if not in the universality of the motive of gain then in an underlying "maximizing" process behind the formulation of desire, to believe in the essential equality of all trading partners and therefore in the political neutrality of monetary exchanges.

Obviously, few economists today believe that everything has a price tag; two centuries after Adam Smith our culture is full of the wisdom disseminated by classic spoofs of economic theory like Dickens's *A Christmas Carol* or George S. Kaufman and Moss Hart's play *You Can't Take It with You*. All are obliged to admit that there are limits to money's usefulness, on pain of being visited by the Ghost of Christmas Past. But it is also easy to avoid specifying the exact limits to money's substitutability for other objects of desire by adroitly appealing to new theoretical refinements, most notably in recent decades to the notion of "market imperfections." A market imperfection is anything that prevents prices from accurately reflecting the balance point between supply and demand. Market imperfections are viewed as a pervasive characteristic of the real world; perfect markets are never encountered outside the theoretical constructs, or models, economists use to approximate that world. For example, the impediments to free bargaining that the Journeyman Cotton Spinner of Manchester complained of in 1818, discussed earlier, in the section called "Marx's value," can be dismissed as a market imperfection that slows, without preventing, the emergence of an accurate market price for labor. The widespread and diverse disciplining effects of exchange asymmetries and the various roles that the instrument of money plays in them can thus remain as invisible to the modern economist as they were to Locke or Ricardo. Some very recent theorists have arisen to challenge this collective blindness, but so far with only minor effects.[105] The four interlocking principles of the liberal illusion, which formed the persuasive core of the Smithean synthesis and became the creed of laissez-faire reformers from Potsdam to Westminster in the early nineteenth century, continue to be actively proselytized and to win adherents today.[106]

But this is not all. Beyond the precincts of professional economics people continue to use unreflectively terms like "capital," "income," "standard of living," and "value," which refer indifferently to money instruments, real use values, or combinations of the two. They continue to use words like "price," "interest," "cost," or "profit" in ways that imply acceptance of money as a valid instrument of numerical measurement. By such means the implications of the liberal illusion insinuate themselves into the thinking of persons who would not, on reflection, subscribe to the whole doctrine in its explicit form. Into this latter group fall many if not most practicing historians at one stage or another of their work.

The concept of price, for example, is full of paradoxes. Every time an advertiser announces that he has products of exceptional value, he implies that the price demanded is not an adequate measure of the worth of his wares. Yet we all accept without question that statisticians use such price figures to measure gross national product, rates of inflation, or productivity. A price is a number; therefore it must measure something, we suppose. But this is not so. The liberal illusion is merely an elaborate social vision built upon a much older and more widespread presupposition, one that is inherent in the use of money. This presupposition is that numerical measurement of what is exchanged between persons creates a valid, interpersonal standard that is at least potentially accurate and fair. This notion is as widespread and as old as its opposite, which always lurks nearby, that the use of money is inherently unjust and unfair. In the thirteenth century St. Francis of Assisi forbade his followers to touch money; even when they found coins lying in the dirt and picked them up and gave them to the poor, they risked moral contamination, he said. Two generations later the Scholastic philosophers were justifying commercial gain as the fair retribution for services rendered. Social thought in Europe ever since has oscillated between these two poles. But the whole question whether specific prices are fair or not can draw attention away from the undeniable fact that money serves as an instrument of discipline in many relationships. It becomes an instrument of discipline just insofar as the money involved has a different significance to each party, essential to survival for one, a matter of indifference for the other. This difference in significance cannot be expressed numerically. It makes the whole notion of a fair or accurate price irrelevant. If it were measured and adjusted for by some overarching bureaucratic authority, then everyone would be guaranteed the same income, and the use of money, although now certainly fair and just, would immediately lose all purpose since there would be no incentive to accumulate it.

It is easy to see that if the price of all foods were to double tomorrow, the impact on individual habits of consumption would vary widely, correlating in part with levels of wealth. Some poorer persons would not change their food consumption but would lower other expenditures to compensate. Others would consume far less food, some because they had no choice. Many wealthier persons would not consciously be aware of any alteration in their habits. Most persons would be affected in a marked way. Gradually the demand (and all prices) for other essentials (clothing, shelter) would alter significantly. There would be political consequences – strikes, election campaigns – whose character would be difficult to predict. Nothing could be simpler than to say what the new price of any food item would be: the old price times two. Nothing would be more difficult than to say what this change would mean to any individual or to the society as a whole. (Ironically, it is socialist Poland that has come closest to carrying out such an experiment, with the dramatic consequences witnessed in recent years.) A price is a balance point not between contending freely chosen preferences of detached individuals but between diverse disciplinary pressures and resistances to them; a price gains its significance within the context not only of all other prevailing prices at a particular moment but also of the whole array of functioning disciplinary practices that give societies their structure. A price measures nothing, because it represents something different to every person. Were this otherwise, the use of money would become immediately pointless.

One can see how acceptance of the potential validity of prices as measures spreads confusion to other concepts by reflecting for a moment on the common linkage of class with the notion of exploitation. Class relationships are widely seen as exploitative in character, with exploitation defined as the self-perpetuating extraction of surplus labor. The extraction is self-perpetuating when the ruling class uses the surplus to reproduce "the conditions of a new extortion of surplus labor from the producers."[107] But such a definition becomes troublesome the moment one begins to try to measure how much surplus is being extracted and by whom. This can be illustrated with a thought experiment about the current state of world trade.

A landless agricultural laborer in Costa Rica or the Philippines today may expect to earn roughly $2 a day working on a banana or sugar plantation. An assembly line worker in Detroit can expect to make close to $20 an hour in total compensation for making automobiles. Yet their labor is very similar, similar enough to be viewed as of equal intrinsic value. If the Detroit worker is exploited at all, then the Philippine worker is extremely exploited. One may in fact see the Philippine worker as exploited not by his employer alone but also, even principally, by other countries. Sugar is very cheap on the world market; if the Philippine worker's wages went up, it would price Philippine sugar out of the market. His wages must remain very low because analogous workers' wages in other tropical countries are very low. Competitive international trade is pumping somewhere between $150 and $200 per day out of this worker, assuming his labor is as valuable as the Detroit worker's is. Some of this surplus benefits growers and distributors. But most of it is being passed on in the form of low retail prices for sugar to consumers in industrialized countries. The Detroit worker who eats doughnuts and chocolate, drinks coffee or tea, eats bananas, or munches crackers cooked with palm oil is directly consuming the surplus of his fellow worker in the tropics. How can he then be considered a victim of exploitation himself?

One may object that the Detroit worker's labor is intrinsically more productive owing to the fixed capital base and advanced technology he works with. The $20 an hour he earns is only a small fraction of the value he produces using these highly productive tools. His higher standard of living is in part a result of the higher level of accumulated capital in his country. He is capable of producing five Cadillacs a year but is allowed to keep only two. Hence he really is exploited by the definition just presented. The Philippine worker's labor is not so productive. He is capable of producing five thousand pounds of sugar per year but is allowed to keep only one thousand. But this distinction offers no real justification for paying him less than the worker in Detroit: Both engage in drudgery; if anything the Filipino's work is far less pleasant. Why should he receive less in pay? Were he earning as much and being exploited at the same rate as the Detroit worker, sugar would cost $50 per pound. Chocolate, bananas, coffee, shirts sewn in Taiwan, and watches assembled in Hong Kong would see their prices increase by similar orders of magnitude. This means that the Detroit worker is receiving a hidden income of perhaps quadruple his nominal earnings, even if he spends only 10 percent of his wages on tropical and Asian imports. However one reckons it, the Detroit worker comes out as a member of the ruling class. Even those earning a minimum wage as street sweepers in Paris are raking surplus out of the Third World, by these figures; even they are making on the order of ten times as much as the Philippine worker by benefiting from the flow of low-wage imports. The whole population of the Western world, Japan, and several Arab countries must be considered members of the exploiting class. There are no class boundaries within these countries if exploitation is to be taken as a defining feature of social class.

Only by focusing on the disciplinary character of wage and other monetary relationships in these countries is it possible to reestablish a coherent approach to what is occurring within them. After all, these societies would not necessarily change so very much if prices of tropical imports were raised to their "proper" level tomorrow. Bananas, coffee, chocolate, cheap radios, stuffed animals, and fried snack foods could all be dropped from consumers' budgets without severe threat to the social orders of industrialized countries. The cost of clothing could double or triple without shaking them to the core. There would be turmoil, probably healthy turmoil. However, the real determinants of oppression do not lie in exactly how much intrinsic value is being pumped about the world with improper prices on it. They lie in the way relationships are organized. Only by looking at their disciplinary character can the relationships of Detroit and Philippine workers be seen for what they are, still dramatically different but fundamentally variations on a single theme of asymmetrical monetary exchange. This is not to downplay the fact that in the tropics direct threat of starvation keeps workers humble on the job, whereas in the United States it is fear of losing access to stimulants and to high-status consumer durables, or fear of exhausting unemployment benefits or defaulting on a mortgage. Who would not prefer the latter fate over the former? Still, the industrialized countries today present stunning object lessons in how easily needs can be made to keep pace with endless advances in productivity, so long as the fundamental structure of relationships remains unchanged. They show how wealthy people can become while continuing to feel that the wolf is at the door. People cannot be liberated merely by increases in their incomes. The low prices of tropical imports are criminal. But there is no fair way to use money.

Marx's dialectical treatment of the concept of value, however obsolete in the view of certain economists, is a good method for uncovering and tracing through the nonquantitative character of money-mediated relationships. But it has many pitfalls. If one supposes that the essential characteristic of the wage-labor relationship is the "extraction of surplus value," for example, it is a simple matter to forget that surplus value cannot be measured by money units any more than value can in any of its other manifestations. The value of labor is not expressed by the value of wages, or by that of wages plus profits, or by that of wages plus profits plus some extra amount of value passed through to purchasers by competitive pressures – or by any other figure that could be derived by manipulating money units. The very idea that the value of labor can be measured in numbers on a single scale is a mystification.

Doubtless, if Marx had ever given his ideas on class a full theoretical development he would have subjected this liberal concept to a dialectical treatment similar to the one that he applied to the liberal concept of value. Arguably, this is what E. P. Thompson and his followers have tried to do in the last twenty years.[108] If one defines capitalist class relationships as the extraction of surplus value, then there have been all along in capitalist societies many independent producers who, because surplus value is extracted from them, are among the exploited – wage laborers in reality if not in the conventional sense of the term, just as there have been wage laborers like the Detroit assembly line worker who apparently benefit from the extraction of surplus value. If one recognizes that surplus value cannot be precisely measured, then who is in or who is out of the category of the exploited working class is never easy to determine. It is likely in any industrial society, no matter how mature, that this class will include thousands of independent petty producers, like the mason Nadaud, like cottage weavers in nineteenth-century Yorkshire or twentieth-century Guatemala, like small farmers in North Dakota or Provence. All these groups have faced market conditions that forced them to labor endlessly for the smallest return. Not employers, but bankers, contractors, and grain and textile merchants, discipline such people through contractual relationships involving credit, or purchase and sale of produce. Large corporations will employ armies of relatively privileged white-collar workers – clerks, supervisors, technicians – whose subjection to discipline is, if anything, more complete than that of manual laborers, and whose wages shade upward to a level where they become in Marxist terms recipients of surplus value, a level that can never be precisely identified. It is impossible to shut these people out of the working class, even though some of them are its immediate oppressors. The working class must be left to identify itself by a coming to consciousness. This was Thompson's starting point.

It is just this range of difficulties in defining the working class that has pushed not only social historians but also recent Marxist theorists like Poulantzas, Wright, John Roemer, or Burawoy toward bold reformulations of the concept of class.[109] There can be little doubt that Marx himself would have eventually been forced by the rigor of his own theory to take the same path. Thus, in the present, the concept of class may be said to be undergoing active evolution toward a status that would be in every respect suitable for expressing the central argument of this essay, that money is primarily an instrument of discipline, not of measurement. However, as with terms like "value" or "capital" or "accumulation" in Marx, so with the new concept of class: Its resemblance to the old commonsense original is so faint that one can legitimately object to retaining the old word. The potential is great for confusion, for retrogression, for subtleties slipping from the mind when one turns to application of the concept to practical problems. It can hardly be objected if one sets it aside. The virtue of a concept like monetary exchange asymmetry is that it can replace both value and class in their dialectical guise with a new, open, unsubtle, nonquantitative expression. The weaknesses of the new concept can only be identified in use. As will be seen, these weaknesses do exist, but on balance they are easily outweighed by its strengths.

Historians have now reached a point where, to use the concept of class coherently, each practitioner must, and most do, redefine it anew.[110] Those who reject it out of hand are as few in number as those who use it unthinkingly in the old way. Most insist that it must be defined in a manner that allows it to refer complexly to any number of differences of wealth, status, power, or honor in society, differences that serve in diverse circumstances as rallying points for factional conflict or insurrection. Arno Mayer, Patrice Higonnet, Sean Wilentz, William Doyle, R. S. Neale, and Charles Maier – to name but a few examples – all take pains in the course of recent studies to use "class" or related terms like "bourgeoisie" or "working class" in carefully circumscribed ways, peculiarly appropriate to the immediate evidence they are dealing with.[111] But even if everyone carefully redefines such terms when working with his or her own evidence, is there not a danger that retention of the terms themselves will obscure from view the immense difficulties that now surround the use of these terms in all contexts?

Within any sphere that is foregrounded in a historical account, money substitutions always seem important, as when peasants with common rights are bought out, or seigneurial dues become freely alienable, or journeymen cease to take part of their wages as room and board, or government bureaucrats begin to receive salaries for their work. But in the background the great abstractions that provide the general frame of reference often remain ambiguous regarding the changing role of money in social relationships. Prussian Junkers remain "aristocrats" before and after 1807; tenants, sharecroppers, and smallholders are "peasants"; wage laborers whether paid by the piece or by the hour are "proletarians." It is not that there are too many details to take into account; it is that the whole prevailing mode of social thought generalizes with a vocabulary either borrowed directly from liberal theory or else infected by its assumptions about money's function as a universal equivalent.

The concept of monetary exchange asymmetries is being proposed here as a means of making a break once and for all with the liberal illusion, with all of its intricate consequences. Exchange asymmetries, in general, create disciplinary potentials within established practices; such disciplinary potentials structure the life choices of serfs and lords, mill operatives and mill owners, general contractors and masons or plumbers, in a great variety of ways. They do so by limiting options, not by determining the actual choices individuals make. They operate throughout societies, not simply at the fault lines between supposedly distinct and uniform classes. They set up, to borrow a metaphor from E. P. Thompson, a "field of force" within which individuals must respond, with either compliance or resistance, to disciplinary pressures brought to bear on them from above.[112] Asymmetries do not eliminate the mystery of human desire, but they provide a grid of stark alternatives that conceal and domesticate that mystery.

What remains to be seen is how this approach works in practice and what new view of the great modern transformation of European society it makes possible. The aim is not to wash out the sea change of liberal revolution, to dissolve all development within the uniformity of asymmetrical discipline. The aim is to characterize the change more precisely. This approach cannot work without being applied to specific cases; it merely offers a way of uncovering the character of social discipline in any specific community. Only after a number of such cases have been examined in detail will it be possible to begin again to build up a picture of the whole course of modern historical development. The remainder of this essay is therefore devoted to the exploration of two classic problems, the origins of the French Revolution (discussed in Chapter 4) and the new protest movements of the laboring poor in the nineteenth century (discussed through two case studies in Chapter 5). The Conclusion will then offer some fragments of a revised view of European social history in the industrial era.

4 Money and the rights of man in 1789

THE NOTION OF MONETARY EXCHANGE ASYMMETRY being put forward here is merely a novel combination of some old and common economic ideas. One is the notion of marginal utility, a theoretical breakthrough of the late nineteenth century. The other is even older, from the fable of Midas, the idea, namely, that if everything one touches turns to gold, one is in big trouble. These two ideas are actually closely related. The notion of marginal utility in its simplest form is a microeconomic theory to explain how individual actors respond to prices. How many units should an auto manufacturer produce? The first unit is very expensive, if it is the only one. All the fixed costs of plant, equipment, management, and labor recruitment must be borne by it. If one produces a thousand units, these costs may be spread over all of them; if a hundred thousand are made, costs may be spread even further. At any moment an auto manufacturer must make enough units so that when costs are spread over all units, costs fall below prevailing prices for autos in the open market. The cost of the last unit (the "marginal" unit) must be low enough to allow a satisfactory profit. The utility of the marginal unit (i.e., its utility in bringing in profits) is the determining factor in the firm's decision about output.

Marginal utility also deals with the responses of consumers to prices. The first car one buys is likely to be very useful, the second is likely to be slightly less useful. The tenth car one buys is likely to be almost useless, as a means of transportation at any rate (unless one has a very large family, in which case it is the tenth car each family member has that is next to useless). At a given price, therefore, one buys enough cars so that the utility of the last one bought (the "marginal" car) equals the price. If cars cost only $10 apiece, individuals are likely to buy many cars; the last one purchased need supply only $10 worth of utility. If they cost $10,000 apiece, most families will be able to get $10,000 worth of use out of one or at most two cars. Combining these two halves of the theory offers a complete theoretical account of how prices balance output with demand. Competing auto manufacturers must continue producing cars until the cost of the last one is as far below the prevailing market price as possible, so as to maximize their profits. But if as a result too many cars are produced to be useful to consumers at the prevailing price, manufacturers then lower the price as far as they can without endangering their profits, and the extra cars are bought up; or else they reduce production until demand comes back into line with a profitable price.

These are the bare bones of the theory of marginal utility. It has been viewed by many economists as a replacement for the labor theory of value of Ricardo and Marx. The amount of labor used does not determine value and therefore price, so the argument goes; instead, prices balance the utility of the marginal unit to exchange partners. Marxists have in turn criticized the theory as being only a partial and localized explanation of price formation. It is generally agreed, in any case, that in macroeconomics things get a good deal more murky all around. If many manufacturers cut costs by lowering wages or laying off laborers, for example, consumers may no longer buy enough to keep prevailing prices at current levels. An unstable downward spiral can result. Where competition is muted by bigness, manufacturers facing a slump during which demand sags may find it easier to raise prices to cover the higher cost of the marginal unit than to fight costs within the plant. If the higher price blocks sale of even a reduced number of units, manufacturers may raise prices further. Again, disequilibrium may result. This is notably what U.S. automakers did in the 1970s following the oil price shocks and the resultant sagging demand for big cars. Cars got more expensive, not less.[1]

Marginal utility is a good enough idea, however, to allow one to notice something profoundly important about money. Money – that is, any medium of exchange in a society where use of such a medium is necessary for access to basic goods – has a negative marginal utility. The first amounts of money individuals gain access to they must get rid of quickly. Only when they have a sufficiently large amount of money can they keep some of it. An impoverished day laborer comes into a sudden inheritance of millions. His very first step will be, not to reinvest it or even to count it precisely, but to spend a certain minimum providing for diverse needs he has been neglecting. He will buy simple things first: a big meal, new clothes, drink, a new car. His own previous earnings were so low that he always spent all of his money. The utility of a small enough amount of money, as money, is next to nil. The first carrot, the first loaf of bread, and the first shirt one gets are precious. The first ten dollar bill is got rid of immediately. Human needs at their simplest level are too diverse to be satisfied by any one thing. This was Midas's error and his doom. He could not wear gold, he could not hug it, he could not eat it. But this is true not only of gold. If one has nothing but ten loaves of bread, one will seek to turn some of the loaves into a medium of exchange, probably to buy some clothes first and then maybe a bit of cheese. On this level, the idea that gain is what people want breaks down entirely. What people want is a host of diverse things: music, roofs over their heads, conversation, meals, showers, newspapers. Until this diversity of immediate needs is gratified, one can want little else systematically.

WEALTH AS A POLITICAL PHENOMENON

The analysis just presented explains why the calculus of money equivalents is so untrue to the position of poor people. Of course, generalizations about the motives of poor people, like all generalizations about motives, are hazardous ventures. Different people will make widely differing decisions about their immediate needs. A miner may not care about coal dust and darkness as much as a bank clerk would. Some women may enjoy selling sex at a certain price because their personalities and their outlooks incline them to it; others may do it out of desperation, fearing starvation. Still others starve rather than do it. All people retain a measure of freedom to choose which deprivations and which sufferings they will undergo and which needs they will seek to satisfy first. Everyone may exercise this freedom to achieve high moral ends as easily as to fulfill mundane sensual inclinations. To feed my child I would at least try to work in a mine if that were my only immediate choice; childless, I might balk at the idea. Classical and neoclassical economists are right to insist that in such matters as choice of profession individuals can and often do attach a price to the various moral and physical features of the work. For each person there are a range of such features that can have a money equivalent, although both the range and the prices would be highly idiosyncratic. Such matters are not completely irrelevant to the explanation of wage levels.[2] But everyone has limits to the range of things that can be given a price tag in this way, limits that the poor are more likely to be confronted with than the rich.

These limits arise first of all from the structure of the human body. Its survival and health and the sensitivity of its nervous system are indeed matters an individual can choose to ignore, if that individual is prepared to do the work necessary to achieving such indifference. Even then, however, the possibility of death or disability cannot be willed away. No one can choose, for example, to do without food for a year in order to buy a new car. But far short of death or ill health the body is already exerting strong pressure against making certain kinds of choices. Some miners may grow to positively enjoy their work, but one seldom sees a tourist spa being set up at a pit head.

Besides the bodily limits there are also historical and social ones. Historically, human communities entered the world of money equivalents with a definite past in a world of household-based subsistence labor. Socially, people still enter this world today from a background of household relations of sharing, duty, and reciprocity in which money exchange plays no role or at most a didactic role (as when a parent solemnly pays a child for a household chore). Of course, some parents may charge working adolescents for room and board; others may put five-year-olds to work at productive tasks. But no one pays wages directly to five-year-olds or charges them rent. "Historically and socially speaking" – the terms become almost comical at a certain point – if children are not nurtured, not given gifts of unstinting concern and attentiveness at least for a limited time, then one does not have survivable human communities. French cities in the eighteenth century were not survivable in just this sense; so many infants were put out to rural wet nurses and so few of them survived to return that apart from the other causes of demographic decline, these cities would have quickly disappeared from the face of the earth had it not been for the continual inflow of peasant migrants.[3] Somewhere in French society children were receiving the minimum of care – otherwise "France" would have ceased to exist – but by and large it was not among the working populations of the cities. The limits imposed by the body cannot be strictly separated from those imposed by the expectations and the sense of duty historically given to individuals by the viable human communities that create them. It is from within these expectations and duties that the body's limits are interpreted and assented to. People frequently prefer their own pain to someone else's. Miners beg their children to try another line of work. Mothers go hungry before allowing their families to be short of food at mealtime. These are not just poetic images but real tendencies that social historians have come across in their researches.[4]

Such choices ought not be compared to the decision of an investor to add railroad stocks to his portfolio and drop computer stocks. The investor still goes home that night to the same bed and the same spouse as he had the night before. He does not have to trade off blackened and broken fingernails for a glass of beer as the miner does. To lump all such choices into the single bag of "preferences," as economists are in the habit of doing, is to confuse apples with oranges. In Chapter 3 the historical origins of such mistaken thinking were shown to coincide with the formulation of the modern liberal notions of personal and political freedom. The economic idea of preferences and the liberal idea of freedom share the drawback of treating two actors as equally free of constraint when one is deciding what pattern his china will have and the other is deciding if the surliness of his foreman is unbearable or if it must be humbly swallowed for the sake of his children. One of these persons is free; one is not. A wage-labor agreement might be adjudged an exchange of equal values – or even unequal ones in favor of the laborer – by someone applying any number of methods for calculating amounts of abstract "value" or "utility." What the notion of asymmetry points to is the completely different role that the exchange plays in the lives of the two parties. The laborer seeks first of all to satisfy his own diverse bodily needs and those of the people most closely connected with him who share in the household wage pool. Any surplus then may be used for entertainment, education, adornment. Often certain less strictly "bodily" needs will in fact be set before the provision of food, clothing, and shelter. Painful bodily deprivation will buy a newspaper or a costume for carnival. The employer, by contrast, wishes only to have a part of his relatively immense surplus of goods manipulated in order to facilitate further monetary exchanges. John Locke, Adam Smith, John Stuart Mill, and Milton Friedman have seen no essential differences between the two situations. Marx and Engels's gaze, firmly fixed on this contrast at certain moments, was turned aside by their desire to destroy political economy using as their weapons only its own misleading categories.[5]

Negative marginal utility is a widely prevailing character of money, one that is more or less coterminous with money's use as a sole or principal means of access to subsistence goods. This is a generalization about human motives that seems like a safe starting point for two reasons: (1) Rather than being a claim about what all human beings want, it is merely a rule for recognizing a pattern in the diverse desires that human beings evidently feel; (2) this pattern is anchored in the needs of the body and the needs of minimum social connectedness that are everywhere essential to human survival. It is not necessary to come up with some universally valid minimum list of these physical and social needs. There is no such list. One must merely recognize that when people turn to the use of money, they already have such needs, more or less flexible, more or less specific (and of course capable of being shaped by the experience of using money to satisfy them). The poor person who requires to get, and get rid of, money quickly in order to satisfy such needs is extremely vulnerable when he looks for money by dealing with anyone whose equivalent needs are already provided for. The contrast in their situations creates a disciplinary potential.

Of course, to say that the contrast in their situations "creates" a disciplinary potential is to speak in a highly abstract manner, for the sake of clarifying the meaning of a new vocabulary for talking about exchange relationships. The contrast does not antedate the potential, nor does one often find people consciously deciding to use the potential for discipline or, conversely, to bow to its use by another. One does not find societies deciding one fine day to begin using money and then discovering, to their surprise, that it creates unexpected vulnerabilities. Without being detoured into a long historical exploration of the origin of money, it is possible to say nonetheless that when one encounters money-based societies, one encounters certain kinds of disciplinary potentials in active use, exploited according to rules of established practice in a way that hardly allows individuals (rich or poor) much choice about how common forms of relationship will be conducted.[6]

One frequently finds that in established practice the disciplinary potentials of monetary exchange asymmetries are used to "create" – again, the unfortunate abstraction, but analyzing something that is alive requires artificial divisions and reunifications – to "create" personal authority. By authority is meant here the ability to command willing obedience, loyalty, allegiance. There will be people who will work hard to see things from their employer's or landlord's point of view rather than face the pain of pawning their shirts for bread. Others may quit rather than do this. Nor is it necessary that every underling a rich man depends on feel active loyalty toward him, but he can easily require that some of them do, especially those butlers, stewards, clerks, and foremen who attend on him personally or carry out sensitive orders. By established practice, more or less compulsory depending on the context, he usually does require it of them. From the rest of his underlings, warm allegiance may not be necessary; dissent or resentment may be tolerated to a degree. But it is rare indeed for a rich man not to exercise the option of dismissing anyone who is openly disloyal or disrespectful, however useful that person's service may be in other ways. Besides being personally unpleasant to its object, disrespect is usually a sign of deviance, a breach of convention that demands either considerable personal courage or personal derangement, but in any case marks one as unpredictable. Therefore even secretly sympathetic employers may well do the expected thing and discharge the offender. The cumulative effect of authority so maintained when it is spread throughout a society is to limit the possibility of political liberty severely, whatever form the constitution may take.

The ability to command the active allegiance of others is, after all, properly seen as a political phenomenon rather than an economic one, even if it appears within ostensibly economic institutions such as agricultural estates or factories. By established practice landlords or mill owners may use their personal authority, once consolidated, to improve their bargaining position even further in lease or wage agreements, and thus to increase their wealth. But this should not blind one to the inherently political nature of that authority. The mere possession of wealth is sufficient to ensure that a person can command active allegiance by picking and choosing his hirelings – capriciously, perhaps, insofar as immediate monetary advantage is concerned. Underlings as a result find it very much in their interest to think more about their masters' interest than their own. From this it follows that the mere possession of wealth confers political power. It is not necessary to put the wealth to use, through bribes, contributions, or other influence peddling, to get political power – although that is usually possible. Wealth is a form of political power already.

Some may object that the term "political" should be reserved for reference to the state, an institution that seeks to maintain a monopoly of violence. But wealth is always a creature of the state; property rights are nothing more than rules that allow differential access to state violence. Often such rights confer limited police powers directly on the owner of property as well. Coercion is an inherent feature of wealth, essential to any conception of wealth, including Locke's or Smith's conception of it as stored-up value resulting from labor. Besides, the state is as much a creature as it is the creator and regulator of monetary exchange. State institutions cannot become separate from social or economic ones without issuing a currency and establishing laws on property and exchange. States then become arenas for collective contention over the social discipline that monetary exchange makes possible. Or if they fail to serve as arenas of such contention, as when a monarch or an oligarchy fails to adjudicate successfully between contending claims, then control of state institutions may become the goal of collective civil violence. In either case, no such thing as merely "economic" wealth can exist, even where property is defined in such a way as to make it purely private, stripped of all feudal, police, or other public features. Exchange asymmetries can still confer on owners the ability to command, to coerce indirectly.

These observations shed a new light on the function of conspicuous consumption in money-based societies.[7] The wealthy, as their wealth increases, move into a sphere where money really is much like other things one can own, and additional amounts of it have decreasing marginal utility. The first million is extremely useful, the tenth million less so; the thirtieth million may be positively boring. Consumption patterns display the small marginal utility of the last million acquired. It may be squandered without disquiet. And squandering some in a highly visible manner announces how much one has left. Conspicuous consumption, by displaying wealth, issues a silent command to all who witness it to offer obeisance and to submit their wills to its possessor. The marquis's lace cuffs and powdered wig as he steps into his tobacconist's shop, the executive's leather attaché case and credit card as he orders a hotel room, announce to all: "You may need to please me. I, in any case, do not n- .d to please you."

By a kind of reverse association, as well, objects of consumption acquire an aura of political authority. The country house or chateau with its park, the gleaming carriage and four with coat of arms emblazoned on the door, the silk brocade jacket, the snuff box, the stockings free of street mud – these were eighteenth- and early nineteenth-century emblems of authority. The suburban home on an acre lot, the BMW and Mercedes-Benz in the drive, the tailor-made suit, the flight to London on a Concorde jetliner, and the Swiss-made watch are present-day equivalents.

As these lists of things suggest, some of the money whose marginal utility is next to nil to the owner will be lavished on personal needs of the kind that the poor are likely to feel most acutely. Provision of food, clothing, and shelter become sumptuously ritualized undertakings. Eating becomes high art. Clothes do not merely clothe; they caress, adorn, and reshape the body. Shelter is constructed to imitate the forms of ancient temples, feudal castles, or seats of government. This sort of consumption is conspicuous because it highlights the differences between wealthy persons and others, announces the freedom of the rich from urgent bodily and personal needs, and reminds others of the nature of the chains that bind them. Throughout any society in which the authority of wealth flourishes there may spread in consequence a hunger to achieve or at least partially to emulate the wealthy's standards of consumption, not because of any inherent utility possessed by luxurious and expensive objects, but because people crave to bask in the aura of authority and respect that surrounds such objects. Only by doing so can they feel that they are free from the discipline imposed by the need for money to satisfy their diverse personal needs. This is why it is misleading to try to trace the progress of society by putting a dollar value on the average standard of consumption achieved by the masses. The wealthy are always ahead, the things they use always different, commanding, calm, apparently conferring self-assurance on the possessor.

When the first ready-made wool suits came within the reach of a worker's purse in the early nineteenth century, the significance of wearing a suit changed; the mere fact of its being ready-made became the new mark of low status. Some time after nylon began to replace silk in blouses and stockings, smooth, shiny garments began to look cheap.[8] These facts are well known. Less widely recognized is that the treadmill of consumption is driven by the feelings of oppression that a life of obeisance to wealth incites and by a desire for that freedom of the will which, in money-based societies, comes only with wealth. Long after the ownership of suits had been democratized, aspiring socialists and union leaders continued to appear before their shirt-sleeved constituents in the most severely correct bourgeois dress. They sought to speak with authority. Nowadays almost any kind of garment is within the reach of a laborer's pocket, and the code is gradually being reversed. U.S. presidents appear in carefully chosen casual wear when returning from a holiday; job candidates wear suitcoat and tie as a sign of respect before interviewers decked out in Izod-Lacoste. The very rich can now dispense with their cravats without fear of losing authority. But business executives, bankers, and lawyers still follow the old ways; as hirelings they are in need of symbols of command. These observations are offered not as a full interpretation of the significance of consumption patterns but only to identify a tendency inherent in social life when the multidimensional social and bodily needs of individuals can only be satisfied through getting and spending unidimensional money.

R. H. Tawney, in an influential study that first appeared in 1926, *Religion and the Rise of Capitalism*, argued that a prerequisite for the creation of a capitalist social order was the gradual separation of religious, political, and economic activities and their isolation in distinct spheres of social life.[9] In feudal society political and economic functions had a religious dimension. Kings were anointed with oil as David was in the Bible. Knights and master craftsmen took religious vows like those of priests and bishops. Lending at interest was a sin. In feudal society a property was also a jurisdiction that conferred military, police, and judicial functions on its owner. Before capitalism could develop it was necessary for the state to recover these properly political functions for itself. It was necessary to simplify the right of property by stripping it of its extraeconomic elements, so that citizens might compete with one another on an equal footing over forms of wealth that were freely exchangeable and good for nothing other than private enjoyment or the generation of yet more wealth. It was necessary to establish that the lessons of the Sermon on the Mount should not apply either to statecraft or to trade. It was necessary for the state to redefine itself as a referee that interfered neither with the private religious beliefs nor with the private economic dealings of its citizens, merely seeing that certain general rules were obeyed. In viewing the cultural prehistory of capitalism as a gradual separation of political, economic, and religious spheres, each with its distinct functions and rules of conduct, Tawney was also enunciating a view of history that was already implicit in the writings of Locke on property and religious toleration.

And Tawney was only presenting a common presumption of historians when he identified the prime mover behind this gradual separation of spheres as the expansion of trade and the spreading use of money in daily life. Feudal lords wanted what money could buy and commuted the military and labor dues of vassal and serf to money payments. The success of merchants and bankers in increasing trade, revivifying town life, and satisfying the wants of others urged the wisdom of reconciling their acquisitive individualism with Christian charity. Money borrowed or stolen from these same merchants and bankers financed the efforts of central governments to dispense with the support of the feudal aristocracy and to undercut its authority. However much Tawney's views have been disputed in their specific application, no one has sought to challenge this general scenario, which is no less than an orthodoxy to which historians of all schools still subscribe as a prerequisite to arguing over underlying causes, long-term consequences, or fine-grain details.[10]

But the whole matter of the division of modern social life into separate spheres — political, social, economic, religious — is riddled with confusion and paradox. On the one hand the boundaries between these spheres when treated as areas of inquiry have never been clear in the least. Economists do not exclude religion from their sphere of attention; they treat it as a "service industry."[11] Students of social relationships can hardly exclude economic, political, or religious institutions from their investigations, and theologians are obliged to subject legislatures, enterprises, and families to judgment on the basis of their own religious and ethical beliefs. It has been evident for a long time to anyone who reflects on the matter that economic enterprises are focal points of political power and creatures of special political preconditions. They are therefore absolutely central to any study of polities. The subdivisions of disciplines in the social sciences and humanities that correspond to these various spheres are not inherent in the subject matter – that is, in the organic whole of human life – in any way. They appear more as mutual agreements among intellectuals to disagree about which abstract aspect or dimension of a lived reality – the social, political, religious, and so on (and one could add here esthetic, psychological, historical, or cultural) – is primary. Once the decision for one dimension is made it cannot be argued about because it imposes its own vocabulary, which reduces the other dimensions to the appearance of epiphenomenal functions or effects of the primary dimension: Thus Durkheim's doctrine that religion is merely a means of shaping social solidarities, or Freud's that political conflict is merely an outgrowth of infantile family jealousies, or Gary Becker's that marriage and divorce (eminently social and religious, not economic, practices) are influenced by a calculus of utility, or Robert William Fogel and Stanley L. Engerman's parallel analysis of slavery as an economically rational institution, or Charles E. Lindblom's insistence that great corporations actually fulfill public (and therefore political) functions.[12] The list of great modern thinkers the kernel of whose insight has been to treat one sphere as merely an aspect of another could be extended indefinitely. But in the end this shows only that the separate spheres are actually facets of a larger whole and the disciplines that serve them only separate viewpoints from which simplified projections of the totality of human practice can be made and subjected to convincing analysis.

But though it has been impossible to see any neat division between these spheres when treated as analytical tools, the division of our institutions into separate kinds, especially our political, economic, and religious institutions, and the rigid requirement that they not trespass on one another's territory are widely considered distinctive, advantageous characteristics of modern society. The separation of church and state means religious freedom. State-run enterprises are a threat to economic freedom. Industrial lobbyists in legislative cloakrooms threaten political freedom. Prayers in public schools threaten religious freedom. Institutional specialization is of the greatest importance to historians because it is seen as the triumphant outcome of a long evolution traceable as far back as the meeting of Emperor Henry IV and Pope Gregory VII at Canossa in 1077.[13] A decisive turning point in this evolution was in fact the century from 1750 to 1850, when alterations whose social origins are still much in dispute gave birth to liberal industrial society. Liberal society's essential conception of public virtue was simply to keep government out of business, business out of religion, religion out of government, and so on.

In practice, however, such separations are constantly threatened, just as in thought they constantly dissolve. And it is difficult to see how it could be otherwise. On the one hand there is "corruption," whether legal or illegal, in the form of money passing improperly from lobbyist to legislator, or mill owner to preacher, or defense contractor to procurement officer.[14] On the other hand there are the inevitable problems: It was Locke who insisted in his *Letter concerning Toleration* that religious belief was a matter of the "inward persuasion of the mind" and therefore not something that a magistrate could impose by force even if he wished to.[15] But was Locke unaware that such a view of religion is in fact a religious doctrine? Toleration is itself a kind of interference. Likewise, governments that follow even the most strictly laissez-faire economic policy thereby engage in what is inherently interventionist favoritism.[16] Enterprises, by making decisions about salaries, about employee discipline, and about what to produce, inevitably shape social structure and political conflict.

The hopeless idea that these institutions ever could function independently of one another depends at least in part on the belief in the political neutrality of money. In a proper liberal social order money is the one thing allowed to flow between and reunite these separate institutional spheres. Wages, taxes, charitable and political campaign contributions, consumer purchases, weld the social, economic, political, and religious spheres back into an interdependent whole. But this is unobjectionable only so long as one considers monetary transactions to be what the Levellers, Locke, and Smith insisted they were, exchanges that do not limit the freedom of either party. This is an untenable creed, and its correction implicates the whole structure of modern human existence as well as many of the diverse categories so far devised in the human sciences for analyzing it. This essay can pretend to do no more than modestly point out the need for reflection. The concept of exchange asymmetry is offered as an analytical starting point that is neither social, nor political, nor economic, but can be applied fruitfully to all human this-worldly interaction. A penniless Baptist preacher with a family looking for a congregation may find his freedom of conscience painfully constrained in a manner not totally dissimilar to that of a representative seeking re-election, a door-to-door encyclopedia salesperson, or a worker. In a cabinet meeting a minister of public works may be compelled to support a distasteful measure because of political favors the prime minister is capable of offering to him, just as a domestic servant holds his tongue when the master is angry. The concept can be applied to any relationship, serving only as a rule for searching out patterned complexities of motive.

But the specific character of *monetary* exchange asymmetries – and this point is central to the argument of this essay – is such that political and economic practices have never been properly separated out, and cannot be separated out. Political theorists and devisers of constitutions may ignore or define out of existence the palpable political power that attaches to property and wealth. Economists may cut it up and hide it in boxes marked "costs" (to those who bow to money's discipline) and "benefits" (to those who enjoy the personal authority of wealth). But it will not go away. The confusion has arisen partly because monetary exchange asymmetries "create" – or should one say "facilitate"? – a very local, very concentrated form of power that requires little more to shore it up than the poor's need to get money and to spend it quickly again.

It is, in this respect, very much like the power of early feudal lords, which required no apology or support other than a local need for military protection.

The difference between feudal relationships and monetary exchange asymmetries is that the former have as their background anarchy; the latter arise with the use of money and the relatively greater political order that the secure circulation of money entails. Feudal coercion is direct; a lord may whip his serf, a king may attack his disloyal vassal. An employer is allowed only to fire or adjust the wage of his employee. Control may be nonetheless quite effective in both cases. Nor is there any neat dividing line that allows one to say when feudal power is definitively gone and monetary exchange asymmetries become a principal support of local focuses of power. The long period from 1200 to 1800, in which money gradually came to mediate an ever-greater array of social relationships, with many setbacks and quirks, is full of evidence of the fluidity with which feudal and monetary forms of power can alternate or combine. This is especially true of those feudal institutions called manors (or *seigneuries* in French), whose adaptation to monetary relationships was so successful that they remained a pervasive influence in the eighteenth-century countryside. Fiefs, once the vital links between vassal and lord, had by contrast lost most of their significance long before 1700. Heriditable nobility, yet another feudal innovation, lived on, like manors, transmogrified but vitally important within an ever-more-completely monetized social order. This whole question of the peculiar symbioses that developed between feudal and monetary relationships stands at the heart of a problem that historians have been struggling over since the early nineteenth century: the social origins of the French Revolution.[17]

THE PERFECTLY SENSIBLE ANCIEN REGIME

Probably the best-known fact about eighteenth-century society is that commerce and manufactures were growing rapidly. It is not an easy matter, however, to come to an accurate appreciation of the full social impact of expanding commerce. Money can sometimes mediate relatively egalitarian interactions, and this has confused many observers. Merchants in the eighteenth century did not personally crack the whip over anyone's back. Both rich and poor participated in the expansion of commerce not only as asymmetrical partners in lease and wage agreements but also as buyers and sellers of tangible, transportable dry goods: cotton, grain, wool, flax, pottery, beds, cloth, looms, carts and carriages, pewter mugs, brass buckles and buttons, printed Bibles, novels, and broadsheets.[18] A rising tide of goods, of essentials as well as nonessentials for every purse, flowed across Europe in the good years between 1648 and 1760. The weather was favorable; grain, wine, beer, and fustian were plentiful; work was to be had, if not in agriculture then in cottage industry, making nails from wire or cheap cloth to be shipped to the colonies overseas. Back from the colonies came tea, coffee, tobacco, indigo, sugar, and rum to stimulate new tastes that quickly became habits. It took less money than ever before to have a share in some of the good things of life, and less still to scrape by. Swelling trade would have been impossible without the new strength of governments; on the Continent this strength was based on the growing bureaucracies that gave substance to monarchs' claims to absolute power. To ensure their loyalty and their competence, the new royal bureaucrats were hired without formal consideration of their personal wealth or social standing (although it was essential to have an education and the right contacts), and they were paid salaries from the royal treasury instead of collecting fees or emoluments directly from the subjects.

Obviously these developments had certain democratizing effects; but it is as important to notice their limits as it is to recognize their existence. The price of grain was the same no matter if it was produced on a large noble estate or on a modest leasehold; the greater the proportion of harvests that was marketed for cash, therefore, the greater the advantage to those who were assiduous and expert farmers, whatever the size of their holdings.[19] A similar form of social leveling occurred in the production of other commodities, especially textile goods. Several million rural cottagers across Europe turned to spinning and weaving at prices far below what urban masters were accustomed to charge. Life was better for these rustics than before; no longer obliged to wait to inherit the farm, they married younger and had large families.[20] (The children's labor power could be put to use almost at once in carding or spinning.) The impecunious younger sons of wealthy families likewise enjoyed a remarkable improvement in fortunes. By demonstrating a little intelligence and exploiting family contacts they could capture posts in the expanding government bureaucracies; a few years in the colonies with a very modest initial investment could net a comfortable nest egg. One hesitates to use the word "opportunity" with reference to activities like slave driving on a West Indies plantation, privateering on the high seas, pirating new editions of Rousseau and d'Holbach in Brussels, or lobbying for a job in Versailles. One hesitates to use the phrases "careers open to talent" with reference to the Prussian *Beamtenstand* or "the marketplace of ideas" with reference to the illegal book trade. Nonetheless, by comparison with what went before, eighteenth-century society was more open. It was possible for some people some of the time to get out from under the thumbs of fathers or landlords or to escape from the dead end of being well educated but penniless, well dressed but dowryless, in love but landless. The impact of such new openings was limited; doubtless the atmosphere of expectancy created by their existence was their most far-reaching effect.[21]

It is certain that the power of the wealthy was not threatened. Some few who were not rich were able to extract themselves from the immediate influence of this power and to become wealthy in their turn. Many achieved modest independence – although often it was by threatening the independence of others, as rural weavers and stockingers did to urban masters, or as bagmen did to rural weavers and stockingers, or as illegal peddlers did to guild-sanctioned shopkeepers and stall operators.[22] In other cases modest independence was the fruit of expert obeisance: of the hairdresser to his wealthy clients, of the bureaucrat to his superior, of the suitor to his beloved's parents, of the parson to the squire, of the writer to his publisher's views on intellectual fashion.

As in all previous centuries, the political power that attached to wealth was recognized by certain governmental practices. However, the precise shape of these practices was changing. As the power of central governments grew, they constantly evolved new compromises with the power of landed and commercial wealth.

The absolutist pretensions of the Prussian king, so efficiently and so rationally advanced in every other domain, came to an abrupt end at the edge of the Junker's estate. Within it, the owner retained extensive direct police powers and personally appointed the judge who ruled in all civil and many criminal cases. Those who lived on the estate needed its owner's permission to marry, to inherit, to travel, and to buy or sell property and owed work on the demesne in return for their own holdings. Here there was no question of authority being shored up only indirectly, by the threat of dismissal. Even the enlightened compilers of the Algemeine Landrecht of 1794 allowed Junkers the right to thrash their underlings personally, so long as it did no permanent damage to the underlings' health. The right of corporal punishment even survived the abolition of serfdom, when all the estate dwellers became personally free in 1807–11.[23] The issuance of the landmark edicts of those years at first caused little more than a ripple on the surface of the old order on most estates, a fact that underscores how easily contractual relations can be made to substitute for feudal bonds.

Further west in Europe the king's law had long since interposed itself between landlord and tenant, farmer and farmhand. But in England the king's law was no longer made by the king. There the relationship between landholding and parliamentary representation and the Whiggish proclivity to use every government function as a means to personal enrichment were little more than different means to achieving a reconciliation between wealth and the state similar to that arrived at in Prussia. Wealth was political power; the equation was as true in England as everywhere else. Few were the squires who could not depend on the constable and the justice of the peace to do their bidding most of the time, although perhaps without quite the alacrity that their equivalents in Prussia displayed. Few were the gentlemen farmers who could not depend on Parliament to fix up an act of enclosure for them, easing the local smallholders of their land and the landless of their commons.[24]

In France as in England, landlords no longer personally whipped those who worked their land. All that was left of serfdom in Louis XIV's realm was the so-called seigneurial system. This system was in fact a characteristic institution of the ancien régime; a discussion of its general features is therefore a good way to begin to appreciate the complex and ambiguous impact of expanding commerce on French society.

The *seigneurie,* or manor, despite wide variations from region to region, was generally a mere shadow of its former self.[25] Many of the lord's extensive powers over its inhabitants had been commuted to fixed money payments centuries before, and inflation had greatly reduced their value. This was generally true of the *cens,* a ground rent that had taken the place of labor dues on plots within the seigneurie. *Lods et ventes* and *saisine* (or *relief*) had held up better in value over the centuries. The former was a fee charged at every sale of a plot, the latter a fee payable on inheritance of a plot. Both represented the lord's one-time right to prevent such transfers. Either was likely to be the most onerous cash payment demanded from inhabitants of seigneuries. It is noteworthy that *lods et ventes* took the form of transaction costs, that is, of fees paid to allow money substitutions to occur. They could be high, over 10 percent of the land's sale price in some cases. Also of continuing value were *banalités* and seigneurial courts. The former were monopoly rights over the local use of flour mills, ovens for making bread, or wine presses and could be quite lucrative when leased to a local miller or baker. Seigneurial courts retained jurisdiction over civil disputes within the seigneurie and were principally useful in the enforcement of the other seigneurial prerogatives and dues.

By the eighteenth century money substitutions had all but extinguished the original character of the seigneurial system, as a result of which change persons who occupied plots of land within a seigneurie were almost equivalent to free property owners. Land within seigneuries changed hands freely and was as likely to be owned by a noble, a town dweller, or a monastery as by a peasant. Seigneuries themselves were open to purchase by nobles and commoners alike. Yet owning a seigneurie retained a cachet, a flavor of feudal status. There was a significant, but hardly complete, coincidence of seigneurial institutions with large landholdings. Big estates were likely to have seigneuries attached. Controlling the extensive farmland that usually went with a seigneurie gave one real power over the tenants and sharecroppers who worked it. The right to call oneself *seigneur* was a fitting ornament to this power. It was necessary to protect this power by careful management of the terms of leases and sharecropping contracts and careful control of sharecroppers' farming methods, as well as by occasionally taking a tenant to court or riding out local popular resistance to an eviction or a rent hike. These unpleasant tasks could, however, be handled by an agent who rented the whole package, estate and seigneurie, at a fixed rate.[26] An eighteenth-century seigneurie could thus be characterized as a bundle of rights to exact payments from certain property owners and mill operators, which was (almost) freely salable, which burdened the free salability of other properties, and which conferred very limited judicial powers and a faint aura of, if not nobility, then at least lordship. Almost everything about it could be easily represented in money terms, but there remained a nagging residue upon which no price could be placed. As for the proprietors whose lands fell within the seigneurie, it was legally impossible for them to unburden their properties from the seigneurial dues attached to them. No amount of money could perform this feat.

Leases and sharecropping agreements were quite varied in form, but in contrast to seigneuries there was practically nothing about them to impede the substitution of money for goods or services. Still, they retained many peculiarities which suggest that money transactions were not always the preferred mode of exchange in the countryside.[27] There were few leases (*baux,* or *fermages*) that did not demand some in-kind payments in addition to a money rent – at least a fowl or two, a cask of wine, or some work keeping up a road. Many leases specified that all or part of the rent was to be paid in kind, as a fixed amount of grain or other produce per year. Yet it is clear that this in-kind payment, when it actually fell due, was often commuted to money at the going price for the commodity in question.[28] These leases differed from share-cropping (referred to in some areas as *métayage*) because sharecroppers paid a set fraction of the yield, usually one-half, not a fixed amount.[29] Establishing a fixed amount of rent, whether of grain or money, insulated the landlord from both tenant incompetence and bad harvests; if rent was paid as a fixed amount of grain, then in years of poor harvests the landlord received a more valuable rent that he could sell at famine prices and the tenant had far less grain left than usual after paying his rent. In normal years the tenant had a strong incentive to achieve yields beyond a certain minimum, just as did tenants who owed money rents. In bad years he was more likely to be forced into debt or obliged to default on his rent, which put him at the landlord's mercy. In either kind of lease, with money or with in-kind rents, the lessee's own personal needs, not a threat of violence, were the immediate source of the discipline that kept him at work; he had certain fixed costs to defray before he could keep anything. Sharecroppers had to be watched more closely, as there was greater danger of their slacking off once a certain minimum yield was reached – enough for the family's needs after sharing out. Paul Bois quotes a revealing remark by an eighteenth-century mayor of Le Mans: "General usage [in this area] is to lease land at prices fixed in money with a few fixed payments in kind. In the neighborhoods of the towns, where surveillance is easier, there is also some sharecropping."[30]

For all these agreements renewal time, usually coming in one- to nine-year intervals, was a moment of high tension, especially during the years of rising grain prices after 1760. Peasants struggled to establish at least an informal right to renew and often remained in possession of a particular plot from one generation to another. Landowners struggled to raise rents in proportion to price increases for grain or to improved yields. Landowners often demanded more than timely payment of rent as well; they expected deference for themselves and their agents and in-kind payments of items for their own table that were more signs of respect than sources of income. The landowner liked to offer guests a bit of "his" wine or a dinner made from "his" fowl sent in fresh from the farm that morning.[31] Yet all these relations were contractual in character; and money, or goods valued in money and meant for sale, played a preponderant role in exchange relationships. Monetary exchange asymmetries were everywhere apparent in the countryside, offering crucial support to the concentration of authority at the top of the rural social order.

The legal constitution of French towns was corporate in nature; that is, guilds of master artisans, of lawyers, and of merchants jointly governed their towns under the tight control of the crown.[32] Such guilds erected strict controls over the way money was exchanged for goods or services within town walls, but they did not prevent money exchanges from predominating as the form of relationship that connected individual households and workshops. The relation between wealth and power was not ignored. Guilds, for example, strictly regulated the size of workshops specifically to prevent one or two masters from dominating local trade. And they sought to impose strict, explicit discipline on apprentices and journeymen.

Thus the significance of property in France by 1700 was largely a question of monetary transactions, and the bulk of the political significance of ownership was expressed through monetary exchange asymmetries, as shaped by corporate regulations, seigneurial monopolies and transaction fees, and the laws of lease, inheritance, and contract. Slightly different exchange asymmetries prevailed in sharecropping and in-kind rental agreements; but these remained contractual relationships with disciplinary potentials based on the diversity of the poor's personal needs, just as did money relationships. Direct coercion of productive labor was extremely rare and widely regarded as irksome and backward.[33]

Despite the widespread use of money this was hardly a capitalist social order, however, not only because of the guilds' resistance to free competition or great landlords' indifference to maximizing cash returns but also because of the special modus vivendi that the crown had achieved vis-à-vis the political power of wealth. This modus vivendi took the form of creating government functions, honorifics, and exemptions and selling them to the proper candidates. Almost anyone who achieved a certain level of wealth was expected to and did seek out appropriate government-distributed offices and symbols. Even M. de Voltaire received a title of nobility when the time came, as did the ruthless Lyon printer Duplain (so brilliantly described by Robert Darnton) after he had made a killing swindling his partners in the deal to publish a second edition of the *Encyclopédie*. Paul-François Depont of La Rochelle achieved *noblesse transmissible* twenty years after the death of his slave-trading father. (These things were done with a certain sense of pace and circumspection.)[34] The de facto political power of wealth was blessed by de jure functions and privileges. The upstart merchant who bought a seigneurie expected the peasants to call him *messire* and could make it rough on them in the seigneurial court if they refused.[35] Commissions in the army and offices in the royal courts and in municipal governments were the common adornments of the wealthy. Many of these positions, sold by the crown at stiff prices, conferred nobility on the holder. Even though noble status had been openly arrogated by landowners up to Louis XIV's time and constantly for sale ever since, nobility was still deemed to be hereditary by nature and therefore not something one ought to be able to buy. The fiction was maintained that those who received noble status from the king, although paying up front for it at ever-higher prices, did so because of some noteworthy service to the nation that proved their inherent nobility. This pretense was considered scandalous in many circles, especially among the old nobility (those whose families had arrogated the status at various times in the distant past).[36] But underlying all this trafficking in seigneurial dues and monopolies, in titles and offices and exemptions, was the bedrock of de facto political power that wealth conferred.

This is not to say that there was one single, clear dividing line beyond which certain wealthy people merely wielded power without feeling its pressure on themselves. In a society like that of eighteenth-century France, one could not afford to float adrift in the deluded belief that one's property and position were secure. The general struggle for advancement continued as it always had, and the rules of the game were constantly changing. In the age of Catherine de Medici, two centuries before, alliance with the great families of one's own region, and even participation in their private armies, had been essential to advancement of self and family.[37] By the time of Louis XIV, however, it was the king who had become the single great dispenser of pensions, land, and influence. A few hours at his side could yield stunning windfalls; contracts to collect his taxes or to supply his troops were avenues to immense accumulations of personal fortune.[38] At the same time, new taxes were constantly being proposed that could threaten the settled calculations of any landowner. After 1760 prices rose faster than rents; careful estate management took increasing time and effort. The need to find dowries for one's daughters; to buy offices or find benefices for one's sons; to maintain a town house in a provincial capital, an apartment in Paris, or (even more ruinous) a hotel room in Versailles; to keep self and family in clothes and furnishings appropriate to one's station, created constant worries that threatened the peace of mind of any wealthy man.[39] A generous inheritance could flow through one's fingers in a few short years unless one were careful. Those with more substantial holdings than oneself were always galling because their pretensions to superiority were so transparently based on the power of wealth alone. Those below, likewise, were obviously consumed with jealousy and unable to appreciate the evident meanness of their desires and their judgments. In this pitiless rat race, every advantage was a comfort: a finely turned piece of furniture, a family chateau in Anjou, the right to put the noble particle before one's name, exemption from the *taille* (the principal royal land tax)—these were the things that allowed one to sleep at night.

What more blatant demonstration could one hope for that the parallel between sovereignty and wealth was implicitly recognized and universally felt than the court ceremonial at Versailles? There the most ancient nobility vied for the honor to do for the king what they expected their hired lackeys to do for them: to help him out of his nightshirt in the morning, to bear witness to his glory by awaiting his pleasure all day. Some were not above the desire to get their wives into his bed at night. In both cases the prize was the same, control of the keys to the pantry.[40]

To understand ancien-régime society in France it is absolutely essential to rid oneself of the idea that separating religious, political, and economic institutions is an inherently rational or superior way of organizing social life. Applying this assumption to prerevolutionary France produces only consternation and befuddlement. On this score France looks like the land of Oz. Titles of nobility, judicial and fiscal offices, royal fiefs, seigneurial courts, local monopolies of trade, and the right to collect certain taxes were all bought and sold like so much beef on a butcher's scale. The king's most far-sighted bureaucratic servants thought they could promote prosperity by designating certain economic enterprises "royal manufactures" and by giving them fiscal privileges, contracts, and generous subsidies with no strings attached—hardly a procedure designed to produce lean, competitive operations.[41] Those seeking justice before a sovereign court in France found that a large proportion of the panel of judges had no legal training whatever. Sometimes a judge, barely out of his teens with a minimal education in an Oratorian college, sat because he had inherited the post as part of the family estate. Others equally unqualified bought their way onto the court after making marriage alliances with leading judicial families. To win a case before such a court required more than legal expertise; influence and favors were a normal part of judicial, as of most other, business.[42]

The church was organized in very much the same style as the judiciary or the guilds. Although the Catholic church owned outright roughly 10 percent of the surface of France, it nonetheless required aspirants to the priesthood to provide perpetual annuities for their own support before allowing their ordination. To become a priest one had to find a packet of up to three thousand livres, the equivalent of a comfortable annual income for a lesser member of the nobility. The right to collect the tithe was sold to big grain dealers, and the proceeds more often than not went to monastic houses or absentee clergy who did nothing for the local congregations. Bishoprics controlled vast fortunes; high noble families vied to place relatives in these powerful posts, which for centuries had been the king's to dispose of. The vows of monks and nuns to live according to the rules of their orders were recognized by the royal government as legally binding. Flight from monastery or convent made one liable to arrest and confinement by royal officials.[43]

None of these practices of church or government were either secret or illegal. At the same time it was fundamental to the outbreak of revolution in 1789 that many of them began to appear, to a significant number of people, to be abuses that cried out for reform. This perception seems so natural today that one has difficulty recognizing that it was entirely new, a product of eighteenth-century intellectual fashion. The idea of social reform caught monarch, church, guild, and judiciary unawares. When these – to us – bizarre practices were first elaborated it occurred to no one to see them as corrupt, except for a few sympathizers of the old nobility. If anything, in the context of the sixteenth and seventeenth centuries they were advances, because they were essential to the reconciliation of old nobility with new wealth and of the crown's growing pretensions with the political power of elite wealth in general. They were indispensable to the growth of the centralized state.

It is of the utmost importance to recognize that just these odd practices have made possible the revisionist onslaught on the old Marxist scenario of revolution discussed in Chapter 1. To buy a seigneurie that yielded at best a 3 percent annual return, to purchase a post on the Cour des Aides, to raise an annuity for the ordination of a son – these were "noncapitalist" forms of investment. The preoccupation of the whole elite, noble and nonnoble alike, with pursuit of such investment is what made it impossible to find a capitalist revolutionary bourgeoisie capable of playing the role Marxist historians have assigned to it. It has not been widely enough recognized, however, that Barrington Moore proposed an important line of counterattack to the revisionist approach almost before it got under way. In 1966 he characterized these very same odd practices as evidence of the penetration of "capitalist influences radiating out from the towns" into the countryside and into royal government.[44] The ready sale of government offices, commissions in the army, and seigneuries; the "business-like" management of the collection of seigneurial dues, tithes, and taxes by professional estate agents and tax farmers; the readiness of noble families to intermarry with wealthy commoners — all point to a frank recognition of the importance of money, that is, of cash, bonds, rents, and readily salable property. Perhaps it was the whole elite that was becoming bourgeois, or at least those most penetrated by "capitalist influences" on the eve of the Revolution.

It is not hard to find evidence that this is how contemporaries saw matters themselves. Robert Darnton has recently provided the striking case of an anonymous wealthy commoner of Montpellier, who said in 1768 that his was a city "where everyone is known solely by the extent of their fortune." "The distinction between noblemen and commoners [in Montpellier]," remarks Darnton, paraphrasing this observer's views, "could ultimately be reduced to a question of wealth, old-fashioned wealth that was calculated in dowries." Noble brides brought thirty to sixty thousand livres to their marriages; brides of wealthy nonnoble families brought ten to twenty thousand.[45] Moore's conclusions of 1966 remain quite persuasive today: "As it came to France, capitalism often wore a feudal mask"; "capitalist ways of thinking and acting were seeping through the pores of the old order"; the Revolution was a result of the peculiar "interpenetration of bureaucratic, feudal, and capitalist features characterizing French society in the late eighteenth century."[46]

George Taylor is of course correct to insist that land management, the exploitation of seigneurial dues, and the holding of venal office were noncapitalist.[47] None of these activities were judged desirable or undesirable purely according to the rate of return on investment they yielded. Good management of such properties consisted of minimizing costs and maximizing returns, it is true; and efforts in this direction were becoming more common in the eighteenth century. But even such rational management was noncapitalist in the sense that it had no effect on the techniques of producing commodities. Raising rents, reviving old seigneurial dues, or increasing the fees collectible through the functions of a venal office did not induce peasants or anyone else to improve the techniques of production.[48] These were not capitalist enterprises. Barrington Moore is content to use the term "capitalist" in a larger sense, however; for him what is significant about ancien-régime society is the trend toward treating money as a universal equivalent, as something that can accurately measure the worth of anything else, from a loaf of bread to the right to paint a coat of arms over one's door. Such a trend cannot help but lead toward capitalism in his view because a capitalist social order is one in which money's operation as a universal equivalent becomes the determining feature of all relationships. It does not matter whether a capitalist class is present in advance or not; the end point is still capitalism.[49] Both points of view seem thoroughly justified.

But then what kind of society was France before the Revolution? A feudo-bureaucrato-capitalist society? A feudal sponge saturated with liquid money? Something weird and transitional? There is no handy term in presently available social vocabulary to apply to this social order, as recent research has revealed it, because available vocabulary reflects an implicit assumption that feudalism and capitalism are opposites: the one, feudalism, confusing political and economic functions thoroughly; the other, capitalism, rigidly separating them out. But this becomes an untenable assumption as soon as one begins to treat wealth as inherently political in nature – that is, as soon as one rejects the whole idea that the political and economic spheres have ever been separated from each other or even visibly distinct as separate kinds of activity. Firmly rejecting this idea makes it possible to see eighteenth-century France as a perfectly sensible and coherent social order, one in which the political functions of wealth were openly recognized, adorned with public honor, and made to interpenetrate with proprietary forms of public office. Wealth bought offices; office was one kind of wealth.

A person with a fortune of 1 million livres in 1750, for example, almost inevitably exercised great personal authority over a host of lackeys, domestics, secretaries, tutors for his children, estate agents, tenant farmers and sharecroppers, farmers of his *banalités,* and suppliers of his food, clothing, and numerous shelters. The vestibules of these shelters would inevitably be filled with would-be protégés seeking favors, pensions, and free meals. By settling 150,000 livres on a daughter as a dowry and raising another 150,000 in cash, this person could undoubtedly find some sovereign court willing to confer ennobling office on him, or at least on a son if he himself had earned his fortune in trade. He or the son would then become one of perhaps sixty magistrates making up a royal *parlement,* sharing one-sixtieth part of the judicial power of this high court of appeal. What could be more sensible? The fact that he lacked legal training did not prevent him from ruling over the fates of the hundred or so peasant families who occupied his land, or over the impecunious writers and artists who hoped to decorate his salon. Why should it prevent his deciding other people's fates as well?

Few historians would disagree with Barrington Moore's view that the sale of offices began in France as "an indispensable device in creating the king's power and hence in pushing aside the older nobility and overcoming the barriers of feudalism to create the foundations of a modern state." Not only as a ready source of cash but also as a means to "rally the bourgeoisie," venal office, "the mana that never fails" was crucial to the creation of those social conditions on which royal absolutism depended.[50] But why should it be necessary to rally wealthy commoners unless wealth carries some political significance with it? No one would deny that it does, but rigorously carrying through the implications of this political significance for one's whole view of French, or European, social history is quite another matter. It is necessary to recognize that wealth's political significance arises in part because money cannot serve as a universal equivalent, that the spreading use of money substitutions constituted social change because it altered the disciplinary potentials of exchange asymmetries. Replacement by money of some other element in an exchange (say, labor or grain) is not a matter of social or political indifference.

From this conclusion it follows, by the way, that capitalist society as it exists in theory has never existed in fact, because its theory requires that money be politically neutral. After the Revolution in the nineteenth century the political significance of wealth was given full sway by the device of pretending that it had no political significance and that therefore those who possessed wealth could do whatever they wanted with it, engaging in supposedly free contracts with supposedly free poor persons whose lives in reality they dominated. This is the oddity; this is the difficult social order to account for. The power of freely exchangeable property flourished like little local weeds all over Europe in the nineteenth century, thanks to benign neglect (laissez-faire legislation) and to loud and repeated public pronouncements in favor of the liberal illusion that money was liberating. Strange society indeed!

THE ACCIDENT OF REVOLUTION

But then how did such a sensible social order as that of eighteenth-century France come to be dismantled in a great rush between 4 and 26 August 1789? What impulse was it that brought a duly constituted Estates General to hurl itself, and France along with it, into the utopian experiment of liberal society? What was the source of the appeal of the liberal illusion for people of the ancien régime?

The argument that the Revolution was merely an accident is always attractive. The year 1789 was an unusual one. The combination of demographic saturation in the countryside with an industrial slump, a fiscal crisis, and a severe harvest shortfall, under the reign of a weak and indecisive monarch, would spell trouble in any time and any place. It is plausible to argue, as Theda Skocpol has done, for example, that this was a governmental or institutional crisis, not a social crisis, whose effects were aggravated by land hunger and starvation in the countryside. But if one looks more closely at this list of unusual things that were happening in the fall of 1788 and the spring of 1789 it may be possible to see patterns that point back to new characteristics of eighteenth-century society and allow a coherent statement about the social origins of this grand crisis.

The first item on the list of supposedly unrelated factors, the demographic saturation of the countryside, was the result of the sustained good harvests of the mid-century decades; excess population was dealt with by subdivision of plots – that is, parcelization – in some regions and by protoindustrialization – that is, domestic manufacture in putting-out networks – in other regions. (The two strategies often combined, as in Normandy, Flanders, and elsewhere.) Whether protoindustrialization stimulated population growth is controversial, but it certainly encouraged cash-crop farming to feed the new cottage entrepreneurs, whose lives became dominated by day-to-day monetary exchanges.[51] Steadily smaller plots, the spread of domestic manufactures, increasing involvement with money – these are how French peasants coped. The contrast with Prussia in the same period is revealing. There Junkers determined the size of plots, not peasant indebtedness or peasant inheritance customs. Junkers decided when and whom serfs married, so that population growth had little effect on size of holdings.[52] Some sharecroppers in France may have been subject to similar direct control, but they were not a large enough factor to be characteristic of the rural population as a whole.[53] Very many sharecroppers, in any case, like most leaseholders, owned marginal plots of land outright on the side, sharecropping only an extra amount necessary to ensure survival. These were less easy for landlords to control. Leaseholders after 1730 benefited from rising grain prices during the run of the lease, but their greater number of surviving children, like those of owner-occupiers, had difficulty finding secure places in the rural order. Domestic manufacture – spinning and weaving for the most part – was a general resort of the landless and of those whose inherited plots were too small to cover taxes, rents, and subsistence needs. In land transactions, crop sales, and sale of home-manufactured goods, the flexibility and liquidity of money helped peasants cope with demographic pressure.

The second item on the list of contingent factors, the industrial slump, may have been generated internally. That is, it began before and was not caused by the free-trade treaty with England that went into effect in 1787. Cheap English manufactures flooding in after May 1787 did not help matters. But rising grain prices may have begun squeezing demand for manufactured goods in general by as early as 1784.[54] Domestic manufacture, on which several million rural inhabitants depended to one extent or another by the 1780s, became gradually less remunerative until the 1788 harvest failure dried up the demand for everything but grain in the starving countryside.

The third thing on the list, the harvest failure, was predictable. When it would occur was in doubt. But that a year of bad weather would sooner or later upset all the arrangements made to sustain the growing population was certain. This was a crisis of success; additional mouths to feed had survived out of childhood and found small niches in the social order because expanding commerce and the presence of freely salable and subdividable land made flexibility possible. Money substitutions and money calculations in a world increasingly dependent on money exchanges were an essential feature of the agrarian crisis of 1788–89.

The fourth item, the crown's fiscal crisis, was not an exogenous or purely "institutional" variable. The government became unable to raise further loans in the summer of 1788 not because its debt was too great to service but because lenders were now part of a politically conscious public – quite a new thing in history – and the disaffection of public opinion by that summer made lenders fear that the debt might be too great to service. The king's ministers did not proceed as though they were officials responsible to this public; they refused, in particular, to open the king's books to public scrutiny; they introduced major reforms and then as quickly withdrew the reforms, all without consultation. Tax reform was necessary; approval of new taxes was sought first from a government-picked Assembly of Notables in 1787, then from the royal parlements – strategies that ensured the crown's continued control both over financing and over information about that financing. The royal government would not admit that subjects had any intrinsic right to knowledge of the king's affairs. But both these efforts failed because notables and magistrates proved themselves sensitive to a perceived public desire for public consultation. Particularly remarkable was the ungovernability of the Assembly of Notables, a hand-picked group expected to look favorably on royal prerogatives; instead it insisted on open scrutiny of royal account books. Calling the Estates General in the summer of 1788 represented a royal capitulation to pressure from the entrenched elite who held offices and titles, pressure exerted in favor not only of the constituents of this group but also of a public opinion that they felt they had to mollify or whose champions they hoped to become. But even royal capitulation did not reassure those members of the public who provided the short-term loans called *anticipations* that were vital to government functioning on a day-to-day basis. In mid-August the Treasury ran out of money. Only the return to power as controller general of the noted Swiss banker Jacques Necker, on 25 August, brought a temporary end to this embarrassment. Necker's financial expertise, his liberal opinions, and his record of moderation in office was sufficient to restore lender confidence overnight.[55] Public opinion now turned to focus on the composition and voting procedures of the Estates General. Political discussion intensified amid a flood of pamphlets; numerous ambitious provincials began maneuvering to win election to this body. The government was able to limp forward on short-term credit.

A fifth factor, the weakness of Louis XVI, was at least in part, like the crisis in the countryside, a consequence of success. His great predecessor Louis XIV had built the prison house of glory at Versailles with full knowledge of what the world looked like outside. But Louis XIV's successors never knew anything but the elaborate, endless, and doubtless continually exhausting round of court ceremonial. Hundreds of deferential eyes were trained on poor Louis and Marie Antoinette every moment of their lives. How this was to prepare anyone to get a grip on public policy is unclear. Louis preferred hunting to matters of state with no apparent understanding of the folly such a preference implied. A figure like Marie Antoinette playing at being a peasant girl in a cottage was as much a product of the centralized peace and order Louis XIV had achieved as was the humble rural spinner she mimicked, making yarn from imported cotton and selling it to peddlers and carters from urban marketplaces.

Finally, the existence of public opinion was not an exogenous factor either and cannot be separated from the social order that produced both the world of the court and the world of the protoindustrialized, parcelized countryside. Public opinion was created by writers and journalists in search of the openings and protection necessary for successful careers. Furet is correct to emphasize the extent to which the optimistic assumptions and the vagueness implicit in concepts like "people" and "nation" were consequences of the faulty censorship of the absolute monarch.[56] But that is not all that went into the formation of public opinion in the 1780s. Thanks especially to the extensive researches of Robert Darnton, it is now possible to say much more than this about the social construction of public opinion in the eighteenth century.[57] It is here above all that the social necessity of a revolutionary crisis, and the reasons why it crystallized around the liberal illusion, become evident.

THE ZEAL OF THE LITERATE POOR

Darnton's efforts to build a systematic social picture of the "republic of letters" in the late eighteenth century allow one to see significant patterns in the biographies of well-known individuals. Jack Censer's recent work on journalists, it should be noted, complements Darnton's findings, as does Daniel Roche's examination of provincial academies.[58] The conclusions that emerge from such prosopographical exploration can be summed up as follows: (1) Adherence to principle became an important means of winning the attention of patrons within the world of literature, social and political thought, and journalism; (2) since adherence to principle ill assorted with flattery of one's patron, there was a malaise inherent in intellectual life that found expression in adherence to *liberal* principle and in a generalized attack on what came to be known as *privilege*.

The emerging pattern can already be discerned in the career of Voltaire. In his time, as later, writing was no way for an author to make money because publishers paid little or nothing for untried manuscripts. Writing therefore had to be aimed at making a reputation. Early on Voltaire learned to exploit the burgeoning book trade to win personal notoriety, not merely by writing beautifully but by launching scathing critiques of the existing order, published in defiance of censorship. His works are full of implicit mockery of censorship, in fact, because his critical remarks are almost always thinly veiled behind orthodox posturing, speaking by analogy, or implicit comparison. Even sleepy censors knew what he was up to; but commerce in books was too protean and too profitable and the activity of reading was too private, too easily concealed, to be controlled by the government.[59] In consequence the naughty Voltaire's *succès de scandale* brought him admirers, and with admirers patronage, and finally more than patronage, intimacy. Unfortunately, intimacy did not reduce his penchant for independence or his satyrical wit; between 1749 and 1753 he was forced to flee first Versailles and then Potsdam. But by this time his reputation allowed him to make extremely advantageous arrangements with publishers as well. He ended life as a wealthy *anobli* landowner. Astonishingly, this unknown skyrocketed to the social heights by denouncing society.

Darnton's recent survey of some three hundred writers at mid-century, coupled with Censer's survey of forty-two newspaper editors, shows how Voltaire's personal strategy for success had by 1750 hardened into a standard career pattern.[60] Darnton's survey was possible because of the existence of extensive police files on writers of all kinds; merely to write for publication was by mid-century considered a suspicious activity. Over 10 percent of those in the survey had in fact passed time in the Bastille or other state prisons for their activities, just as Voltaire had done twice early in his career. Many more were closely watched as particularly dangerous characters; others acted as spies by denouncing the seditious statements or writings of their fellows. Still extremely rare were those writers who lived directly on the proceeds of book sales. Many pursued literary or scholarly endeavors as an avocation, depending on their own offices, properties, or clerical income for their support. "Thirty-six percent of them," remarks Darnton, "worked as journalists, tutors, librarians, secretaries, and actors, or else relied on the income from a sinecure procured for them by a protector. This was the bread-and-butter element in the republic of letters; and, as it was dispensed by patronage, the writers knew which side their bread was buttered on." Likewise, twenty-nine of Censer's forty-two newspaper editors began their careers as more-or-less-successful men of letters and accepted newspaper jobs only out of financial necessity. In most cases, these jobs were procured for them by benevolent protectors.[61]

Darnton's and Censer's evidence also suggests that a great diversity of motives led patrons to offer protection to particular writers. A well-turned piece of light verse or a clever play performed by the Opéra comique was enough in some cases to win the writer financial security. Others had to write exactly what they were told, producing politically motivated pamphlets, most often denunciations of specific policies or persons carried out to serve the interests of a particular faction of court or a particular minister. Obviously, a great number of writers were content to see themselves as pens for hire and felt no particular compunction about insincerity. But the formation and dissemination of Enlightenment thought was dependent on the existence of independent voices, writers who were able to make their way without compromising their intellectual integrity beyond a certain minimum. Such persons attracted a special kind of patronage; their protectors sought to liberate them, to allow them within limits to say what they wished. Often, in fact, it was other well-placed writers and thinkers who protected the new voices.[62] Of course, once the availability of patronage for the new self-styled *philosophes* became evident, such patronage also attracted its quota of insincere and superficial practitioners. But *philosophe* pens for hire had at least to adopt the pose of independent commitment to principle.[63] In the careers of the great creative figures, d'Alembert, Diderot, Condorcet, or Rousseau, there can be no doubt that protection played a crucial role, but was never allowed to play an interfering role.[64] The ability to resist the pressures of protection in fact often took a degree of sangfroid and self-abnegation, of personal moral fiber, and of sheer luck that was rare in the extreme.

In Rousseau's work, finally, such resistance became a central theme of social and political commentary.[65] His reflections on the origins of inequality constituted a grand denunciation of any society in which some had to turn for protection to others. His *La nouvelle Héloïse* (1761) glorified the lives of three provincials of no importance, who would never have attracted the attention of the great: one a tutor who defied the master of the house by loving his pupil, one the pupil who returned that love, one the pupil's eventual husband, who accepted the situation with sincere goodwill. All conventions of society were defied without any sense of moral wrongdoing; quite the contrary, virtue could be recreated only by such defiance. Rousseau's *Confessions* (published in 1781) continued the same theme, not only because of his defiance of literary convention in admitting to dubious liaisons, acts of dishonesty, and failures of duty, but also because he narrated in great detail his stormy relations with all his patrons. All of them, despite their efforts to the contrary, ended up expecting things of him,

131

summoning him at inconvenient moments, pressuring him into closer relationships than he wished, or secretly plotting against him. He could not stomach such intimate and threatening constraint and spent the final years of his life, despite repeated offers of help from numerous quarters, in a state of gloriously independent penury.

As Darnton has remarked, the extraordinary popularity of Rousseau's novels and of his *Confessions* resulted from his attempt to make the printed word a more sincere, more emotionally full, and more intimate form of communication than face-to-face contact could ever be. This, too, implied a rejection of the day-to-day world of patronage, insincere deference, influence peddling, spying, and denunciation. To paraphrase Reinhart Koselleck's views, contact with the reading public through the medium of the book trade, with its growing Europe-wide network of publishers, distributors, and retailers, offered a new hope, under the circumstances, of speaking personal truth.[66] This was Rousseau's excuse for writing novels in the first place, since he considered fiction to be corrupting. The epistolary form of *La nouvelle Héloïse* mirrored this conviction; the novel consists of secret letters passed between persons who were in daily contact with each other but who dared not speak sincerely in the presence of third parties. Rousseau's emotional approach to the private, ungovernable act of reading struck a responsive chord that had lain unnoticed and unsounded before his novels began to appear in 1761. One can see the tensions inherent in the social structure of the life of letters in the very substance of Rousseau's thought, in the very special style of his expression. On the one hand, speaking directly to a reading public offered an experience of personal liberation not available anywhere else in society. The privacy of writing and reading and the social distance between reader and writer prevented personal entanglements that might disturb the motivational purity of the writer's vision and the reader's response. If one could gain some respect from a wide audience, therefore, one's own character and life were confirmed as worth while in a special way. On the other hand, such self-affirmation in no way freed one from the pressure of day-to-day personal needs, that is, not unless a certain kind of reader were willing and able to step forward and offer protection. Protection, however, plunged the writer into an odd sort of monetary exchange asymmetry in which he was very much subject to the whim of one other person. His ability to retain his commitment to the visions and principles that first motivated his successful writing might easily be threatened.

Of course the personal reactions of writers and patrons to this situation were quite diverse; it would hardly be appropriate to think of Rousseau's thin-skinned sensitivity as typical. But Rousseau does give one a sense of the contradictory pressures created by the intermeshing of the established practices of the book trade with the established practices of influence peddling and protection among the ruling elite. These conflicting pressures were necessarily confronted by all writers and are a special example of how expanding commerce in the eighteenth century was democratizing in an ambiguous way. Monetary exchanges freed rural populations from direct dependence on access to land and facilitated the subdivision of plots, but they also trapped the peasantry in the downward spiral of demographic saturation. Monetary exchanges allowed anyone with wealth to purchase titles, offices, and feudal prerogatives appropriate to his de facto personal authority, but they did not change the fact that such titles, offices, and prerogatives were normally seen as properly inherent in persons and families, not as marketable commodities. Parvenus were always made to feel like trespassers. Monetary exchanges of printed materials gave rise to a shadowy entity called public opinion without giving public opinion a formal means of self-expression or a formal role in political decision making. Monetary exchange asymmetries were ubiquitous components of social discipline; but expanding commerce allowed for the realization – or more often the partial and imperfect realization – of once unrealizable, even unthinkable, desires. Such desires included those of young peasants who wanted to marry without owning land as well as those of young penniless lackeys like Rousseau who desperately wanted emotional relationships untainted by the inevitable ulterior motives that went with the need for money. Some peasants found partial satisfaction in domestic manufacturing, some writers partial satisfaction in the insubstantial world of print. It was in such different and unexpected ways that expanding commerce shook the very roots of the social order, even though not a single leaf fell to the ground before 1789.

But why in this context did the core ideas of the liberal illusion so often provide the principles to which *philosophes* selflessly adhered? Part of the answer lies in what has already been said. That monetary exchanges could have democratizing effects was widely appreciated. Few ambitious writers who reflected on the matter failed to make the analogy between the need for freedom in the book trade and the need for freedom in other trades. The great emphasis placed in the *Encyclopédie* on public dissemination of detailed knowledge about all the *arts et métiers,* that is, all branches of manufacturing, which Diderot elevated to the dignity of sciences, is testimony to the importance of this parallel within the whole *philosophe* program.[67] The interests of the reader were like the interests of the consumer, those of the writer like those of the artisan. Both had to be liberated from the restraints of the great mechanism of royal regulation that presumed to enter into every detail of production of books, hats, shawls, fustian, buttons, *gâteaux,* and gazettes with equal heavy-handedness. Patrons' monopolies over sources of income looked very much like guilds' monopolies over the right to produce and sell specific products, or venal officeholders' monopoly over the administration of justice, or the church's monopoly over spiritual life. Naturally there were differences of opinion among Voltaire, Montesquieu, Diderot, Rousseau, Turgot, and others about whether parlements, guilds, the church, the nobility, or the monarch himself represented the greatest scandal. But, perhaps with the lone exception of Rousseau, no one ever turned a suspicious eye on monetary exchange as such. After all, monetary exchanges were among the most important sources of new possibilities within that society.

The prestige of England, especially in the first half of the century, is another factor that cannot be understated. English commerce, English naval power, English parliamentary government, English religious toleration, English science and learning, provided impressive evidence of an alternative form of society more prosperous, more open, comparatively free of pettifogging regulation and arrogant protectors. The combined authority of Locke and Newton was immense; the two seemed to provide a single coherent vision of the cosmos and of the human species' place within it. Even Rousseau, who attacked Locke at every possible juncture, left a place for a modicum of private property in his ideal social contract – just enough, held in trust from the sovereign, to ensure one's own independence.

By the time the Enlightenment had reached its maximum influence within France in the 1770s, it was possible to find numerous propertyless young thinkers pursuing their careers with a staunch, principled commitment to free trade and to the rights of private property. In the final decades of the ancien régime the game of patronage had begun to alter slightly because certain *philosophe* factions gained enough influence within the government to be able to hand out jobs to those who publicly supported their reform proposals. Madame de Pompadour in her apartments at Versailles was replaced by Trudaine and his son Trudaine de Montigny in the Bureau of Commerce and, more briefly, Turgot as important promoters of *philosophes'* access to government support.

The tireless and needy abbé Morellet, for example, was promised a post by Trudaine de Montigny in the Bureau of Commerce in 1769, but when his protector was unable to deliver on the promise, Morellet had to accept a pension from the bureau instead. As a result he was unable to do the necessary research for his ambitious new dictionary of commerce and spent the early 1770s writing vigorous polemics against Necker and in favor of Turgot's attempts to free the grain trade and to abolish guilds. Although perfectly sincere, these works, which took time away from Morellet's dictionary project, were produced at the request of Trudaine de Montigny and Turgot, persons who could at any moment terminate his government pension. Later on, connections in England brought him into contact with Lord Shelburne, whom he advised during the negotiation of the treaty that ended the American War of Independence. For these efforts he received a generous royal pension. With entry into the Académie française in 1784, Morellet was able thereafter to play an independent role.[68]

Occasionally one finds in the Bureau of Commerce's files traces of other aspiring writers hoping for government jobs who failed to make the grade. A certain Latopie, for example, submitted a long monograph on manufactures in 1773 in the hope of proving his suitability for a post of inspector of manufactures. Such a position would have put him in charge of enforcement of all government regulation of commerce and manufacture for a whole *généralité*. He hoped to impress Trudaine de Montigny precisely with his opposition to trade regulation, with his enthusiastic acceptance of the *Encyclopédie*'s belief in the dissemination of improved techniques of production, as well as with his observational skills. What remains in the file is one chapter torn from this long work, apparently of interest to someone in the bureau; the rest was discarded. A more suitable candidate for the post – or a better-connected one – was found among the bureau's own personnel.[69]

More successful than Latopie at this kind of self-advertisement was Roland de la Platière, who was to become minister of the interior during the ascendancy of the

Girondists in 1792 and who ended his life as a fugitive in 1793. He was the youngest of five sons of an old Lyons robe family that had fallen on hard times. Utterly without prospects, he tried to emigrate to the colonies in 1754 at the age of twenty, but he fell ill in Nantes before he could board the boat.[70] Shortly thereafter a cousin found him a post in Rouen as apprentice inspector of manufacturers, an entry-level position in the Bureau of Commerce's large civil service. He impressed his superiors by writing long, detailed tracts in the style of the *Encyclopédie* on production methods in weaving and dyeing. He proved to be an indefatigable investigator and technical writer at just the time when Trudaine and his circle were beginning to restaff the bureau with forward-looking free-trade advocates. At first he moved up quickly, but after he was made inspector of manufactures of Amiens in 1766 his career stagnated. By completely neglecting the regulation of trade within his territory and dedicating himself to furthering his own researches he did only what was expected of him. But his rigid adherence to doctrine, his imperious tone, his aloofness and independence — the very qualities that had ensured him early success — now began to work against him. His superiors resented his fractiousness; he was not a team player. But he was undeterred. He published a continuous stream of books on commerce and industry, all promoting freedom and technical progress; none sold well. His first sign of favor to his future bride, Marie-Jeanne Phlipon, penniless daughter of a Parisian engraver, was to leave a pile of his notes in her lap and ask her to put them in order. Later he sent more to her from Italy, where he was doing an investigative tour. Soon she was doing his proofreading, rewriting his prose to remove some of its cold, dogmatic qualities, negotiating with his publishers and his superiors in the bureau at Versailles. She was more politic than he but no less committed to principle. It is characteristic of the end of the ancien régime that a figure like Roland, rigidly committed to the Enlightenment doctrines of free trade and technical progress, should thereby win the protection of superiors so that he could systematically subvert regulations he was, in principle, paid to enforce.

Another future revolutionary, Jacques-Pierre Brissot de Warville, like Roland the youngest son of a large family who entered adulthood without any resources to fall back on, was less lucky in his search for protection. Like Roland, he wrote voluminously and was at least able to induce publishers to take his work, so that by the time the Revolution broke out he had published "thousands of pages on the appropriate subjects," as Darnton puts it, on "the fallacies of St. Paul, the absurdities of the French legal system, the glories and weaknesses of the British constitution," and also on the importance of private property. But all his efforts and his intellectual skills failed to produce a steady income. Darnton has examined the evidence that Brissot, in a moment of desperation while locked in the Bastille in 1784, agreed to become a police spy.[71]

Maximilien Robespierre, yet another selfless young adherent to principle, began life as an orphan and a scholarship student at the prestigious Louis-le-Grand school.[72] When he returned to his native Arras in 1781 at the age of twenty-three to join the bar, he too showed signs of a recalcitrant independence, an indomitable desire to champion causes by writing and publishing – even if he does not seem to have known what to believe in at first. He, however, never stooped to seeking protection. He took cases that offered him a chance to defend science and denounce privilege and obscurantism. He defended a man sued for putting a lightning rod on his house and another who had been accused of theft by a monk. (The monk had apparently made advances on that man's sister.) In the latter case he published his brief before the verdict, an unusual step apparently meant as an appeal to public opinion to bring its own judgment in the case. Like Roland, he too gave copies of his writings to women who attracted him. Before local judges he made a point of proving his independence with frequent denunciations of current law, of *lettres de cachet,* and of a criminal procedure that allowed the accused to be presumed guilty. His practice was never prosperous.

> One must be fair to everyone, even to Robespierre [said a hostile contemporary]; one must admit that he was never motivated by a love of money. On the contrary, he was quite exceptionally disinterested. He gave unpaid consultations for several years and disliked taking fees from his clients even when he had won their cases for them, even though he had no patrimony and was so hard up that he had to borrow clothes.[73]

It is not surprising that people like Roland, Roland's wife, and Robespierre came to consider Rousseau virtually a saint. Their admiration for him applied equally to his political tracts and to his sentimental novels and personal outpourings. In all these manifestations of his genius he was, above all, a figure who refused obeisance, however it was demanded. That they did not share Rousseau's distrust of money and did not place a high priority on restricting property rights is not surprising. These issues did not receive great theoretical elaboration in Rousseau's work; the main body of Enlightenment thought very strongly favored private property and free trade as characteristics of natural liberty. Rousseau's impact was much stronger in the sphere of personal comportment and self-consciousness than it was in the sphere of political theory. His emphasis on sincerity and virtue could easily be combined, at least for a time, with the attack on "privilege" – that is on the monarchy's whole complex, centuries-old modus vivendi with the political power of wealth.

MONEY AND LIBERTY ON THE NIGHT OF 4 AUGUST

The problem confronted by any social explanation of the French Revolution is that new social practices came out of the blue, apparently the product of sudden, spontaneous consensus among millions of persons who were acting outside known routine and who therefore may be reasonably supposed to have been acting as individuals for once, doing something they really wanted to do. The comforting feature of the notion of class, as well as of those substitutes for class proposed by revisionists, was that these notions pointed to underlying communities of interest hidden within society's structure which gave rise to the sudden coalescence of action that was such a stunning feature of 1789. What can possibly replace the explanatory strategy of class, however, once its tendency to oversimplify human motives is recognized?

Building on what has been said so far about ancien-régime society, the answer proposed here has two parts; the first part deals with the manner in which revolutionary practice was established, the second with the role of money substitutions in shaping new common perceptions in the midst of the revolutionary crisis.

The decisive steps in establishing revolutionary practice were taken by the government itself in the fall of 1788, when it decided to call the Estates General, and in January 1789, when it announced the procedure to be followed for elections to that body. The first step, as already mentioned, was a capitulation before the pressure of public opinion; the second ensured that election of delegates for the Third Estate would be carried out as a kind of formal consultation of public opinion. It has long been recognized that the royal capitulation created a power vacuum; but it did more than this: It also left a legacy of specific rules about how that vacuum should be filled. A very wide franchise was established; all males on tax roles over twenty-five years old were called upon to vote, and in rural districts the voting was in three stages, assemblies at each stage electing electors for the assembly at the next higher stage. Rustics were allowed to participate, but the three-stage process virtually ensured that only members of the educated elite would arrive in Versailles.

Many who had never written or spoken in public before began now to do so; but those who had habitually done so had great advantages. Thus a perfect arena was created for persons of roughly Robespierre's or Brissot's background to appeal for votes through pamphlets and speeches.[74] Many, like them, appealed for support precisely on the grounds that they had the principles and independence necessary to bring about a national renewal, that is, to ensure that public opinion's new formal role would become a lasting feature of government. One need not lose sight of the extreme oddity of Robespierre himself (or of any of the other future revolutionary leaders – Roland, Danton, Vergniaud, Marat, Hébert – a mixed bag indeed). One need not lose sight of the extreme diversity of their motives; one need not try to pigeonhole any of them as a representative of this or that class or substratum. But one does need to recognize that once the practices of consultation and of public electioneering were established by the crown, these new practices set limits on, as well as giving scope to, the kinds of things that individuals might do. Robespierre, Brissot, and the rest may have been well suited to the new situation, but they were not free to do anything they liked. Electioneering, like commerce, like the journeyman *tour*, dictated the kind of personal motives that could be expressed within it.

In 1789 these limits were quite different from their present form in twentieth-century democracies. There was no right or left, no party organizations; the Revolution had not yet given birth to the idea of a political spectrum. Few advocates of absolutism, for example, were motivated to campaign openly for election to the Third. Not till after the fall of Robespierre would electioneering begin to appear as a viable strategy to conservative political forces.[75] Electioneering and absolutism could not help but appear to be contradictory in 1789. An absolute monarch did not seek public advocates or public acceptance, he required only the submission of subjects. Of course there was uncertainty about what electioneering really did mean at first, but the established practices of the republic of letters, of journalism, and of hack pamphleteering could be readily adapted to the new electoral practices. As different as a Brissot and a Robespierre were, the electoral strategies and claims of each were superficially quite similar to those of the other and to their previous activities. The virtues of sincerity, devotion to the public good, and incorruptible independence were not invented in 1793; they were inherited from the ancien-régime game of selling books and seeking protection. And the frustrations once inspired by patrons could now be inspired by that greatest patron of all, the king. It is not surprising that delegates of the Third, especially those who were provincial lawyers, acted more radically at Versailles than did their social equivalents who stayed at home, as Berlanstein has found.[76] The mere fact of being elected to the Third, by winning three hard-fought elections in a row, significantly altered one's social identity, putting one on a stage where one had to play to public opinion, where one's success in doing so would be far more significant in shaping one's future than the mere fact of having been a lawyer or a merchant or a journalist previously.

That revolutionary practice, once established, not only survived but became the new means of exercising sovereignty was a consequence of the astonishing convergence of the summer of 1789 between the aspirations of the delegates of the Third to become a National Assembly, on the one hand, and the desperate struggles of the popular masses against hunger and fear, on the other. Was this merely fortuitous? The second part of this social explanation of the Revolution's outbreak seeks a common origin for both these phenomena in money's expanding role in society. Money substitutions and money exchanges had spread very far in this society, creating new freedoms and new strains, both of which can be symbolized at once by the cult of Rousseau and by demographic saturation.

In fact, these new freedoms and strains played a role in every one of the factors sometimes listed as having accidentally come together in 1789. Without the eighteenth-century expansion of commerce the king would have had no strong opponent in public opinion to reveal his indecision and uncertainty; there would have been no rural masses perched on the edge of starvation, no industry to decline, no government creditors nervously reading newspaper reports about the Assembly of Notables, and finally no figure like Necker whose popularity alone was sufficient to refloat government finances. In Necker, at last, France had a minister who viewed his mandate as coming from the public. Accordingly, he devised the broad electorate and the process of popular consultation that prepared the way for the meeting of the Estates General. This novel electoral procedure not only laid the groundwork for the development of revolutionary practice; it also raised new expectations in the countryside. The king, it appeared, wished to know of his people's sufferings and what could be done about them, just as the worst harvest failure in living memory upset all the carefully constructed strategies of rural survival.

By May, famine prices reigned in all the grain markets of the realm. Many owner-occupiers and tenant farmers who normally produced all their own food and sold a surplus would be looking to buy this summer, and brought none to market. Enraged bands of cottage weavers and spinners and landless laborers began marching out of empty marketplaces to seek out hidden grain stores in the barns of surrounding farmsteads.[77] Every band that passed exacted its tribute of grain or bread. Even substantial peasants saw that they would have a hard time getting through the three long summer months to harvest time. Somewhere, something would have to give. Village leaders across the country decided that organized resistance to taxes, tithes, and seigneurial dues was their best hope for riding out the storm. These were the exactions of the outsiders against which a village consensus of opposition was most likely to coalesce. In the electoral assemblies of the spring, the injustice of these burdens had been widely discussed. Once the village agreed to withhold all payments to outsiders, the smallholders, tenants, and substantial farmers could then unite to protect themselves from the marketplace crowds and the marauding bands of the landless. They could stand guard over the fields and ward off food rioters and tithe collectors alike. Some semblance of order could be maintained and property protected.

A great movement of revolt began spreading raggedly and confusedly across the country in June, gained momentum in July, and peaked in early August. For a few short weeks the veil was lifted, and the ironclad rigidity of certain centuries-old relations of exaction and discipline were revealed to be just as flexible as the united peasant community wished to make them.

As it turned out, attacks on property rights as such remained rare, as a massive assault on taxes, tithes, and seigneurial dues changed the social landscape of France. Theda Skocpol has argued that this was because a large proportion of the peasantry enjoyed the possession of at least a small plot and because leaders of the village assemblies who sparked the rebellions were often the more substantial peasant proprietors, who were usually both creditors and frequent employers of their fellow villagers.[78] Skocpol is certainly right thus to emphasize, as Lefebvre did in his researches on the peasant insurrection, that the existing array of established practices within village communities and the stark contrasts in wealth and influence of different members of the peasantry shaped and set limits on peasant collective action.[79] Spontaneous unity of purpose had a definite social background in the village just as it did among the delegates to the National Assembly.

But if property itself was immune to attack, why was there no general attack on leases? The majority of nonpeasant land, which constituted roughly 60 to 75 percent of all farmland, was exploited through leases – certainly north of the Loire at any rate. Most peasants leased some land; the more wealthy a peasant was, the more land he was likely to lease. Village leaders had as much to gain from attacking leasing practices as did the impoverished masses. The terms of leases, as already discussed, usually created a very crude form of discipline over the tenant. He had strong incentives to work hard; yet even competent, hardworking farmers could lose their leases and be forced into bankruptcy if a couple of unlucky years came too close together. The rewards and penalties were not very finely tuned; the injustices were often self-evident. There were protests against prevailing lease practices in at least some areas in the spring of 1789 as well as widespread, if scattered, refusals to pay rent. But leases did not rise to the surface as a great issue.[80]

The answer may lie in the flexibility of money. Leases were contractual monetary exchanges renegotiable at intervals, whereas taxes, tithes, and seigneurial dues were not. Leasing land was the most important recourse of the smallholder whose own plot was too small to support his family; leasing was therefore a crucial and relatively flexible survival strategy for the broad mass of marginal exploiters on their ever-smaller inherited parcels. Leaseholders were, however, responsible themselves for paying taxes, tithes, and dues on their leased land; these were additional payments in money and kind over and above rent, and they fell most heavily on the smaller peasant in bad years. It may be that rents on leases were regarded more favorably in this period of demographic saturation because they were, by comparison to other forms of exaction, chosen, personally agreed to, a means of access to needed resources. Tenants were hardly free vis-à-vis their landlords, but one certainly exercised a greater margin of control over one's fate within a lease agreement than one did when, for example, paying the heavy *saisine* fee required to inherit a tiny plot from one's own father or uncle. This hypothesis is identical with the conclusions of a host of observers, including figures as diverse in outlook as Tocqueville and Albert Soboul. Tocqueville, whom Soboul cited with approval on this point, explained peasant ire against seigneurial dues by emphasizing that they were "indissoluble and nonredeemable"; there was no way to shake them off the land to which they were attached.[81]

Seigneurial dues were the objects of widespread violent resistance in July and August 1789; chateaux were invaded to gain access to the seigneurial record books and deeds, to burn them. Seigneurs and their agents were mishandled, even murdered. (At least some of these agents were also locally prominent peasant proprietors and large tenant farmers who resisted the tide of village opinion.) The seigneuries' central farm buildings and chateaux were sometimes burned down. Seigneurial woods were invaded by armed bands of poachers.[82] Not only were seigneurial dues inflexible themselves, but their effect was to burden land transfers with heavy transaction costs, reducing the flexibility possible to peasant families that were already having difficulties finding means of survival for all their members. Attacks on seigneurial dues may therefore have been, just like popular price setting in local grain markets, a function of the spreading use of money-based transactions as a central feature of peasant survival strategies after 1760.

It has often been said that peasant attacks on the seigneurial system forced the hand of the new National Assembly, that the delegates voted to abolish the seigneurial system on the emotional night of 4 August 1789 only because they desperately wished to restore order in the countryside and to mollify the peasantry.[83] It was already becoming clear by the end of July that in the new constitutional order that the Assembly was to fashion, property would be a "sacred" right, existing above and beyond government, which it was government's essential duty to protect. This single principle could justify freedom of the book trade (and therefore of speech) and freedom of every other trade (and therefore abolition of the guilds), because all impediments on trade were government interference with the free disposal of property. This was hardly a surprising outcome given that an elected assembly was carrying out reforms under the scrutiny of, and in the name of, mobilized public opinion. The central problem the Assembly had to confront, however, in carrying out such a vast reform was that most impediments on trade in the ancien régime were themselves forms of property. Guild members paid thousands of livres for their masterships; book and newspaper publishers paid high fees for the exclusive rights to publish on certain subject matter. The ownership of judicial office, considered abusive because it removed government officials from accountability to citizen property owners, was also the object of very heavy private investment. The seigneuries were simply one more of these freely exchangeable forms of property that were nothing but impediments on other peoples' ability to enjoy and exchange their property freely.

In a previous era the introduction of money equivalents for judicial office, guild monopolies, and seigneuries had been a great if unintended step toward the general principle that money could serve as a universal equivalent. But to make the final step and implement this general principle, it was necessary to abolish all these peculiar properties because they prevented other properties from exchanging freely for money equivalents.[84] It is important to recognize that even the defenders of the seigneuries within the Assembly argued for their retention only on the grounds that they were freely exchangeable properties and therefore just as much deserving of protection as other forms of property.

In doing so, these delegates were putting themselves on weak ground. Yet the Assembly admitted that such an argument held a kernel of truth.[85] After all, thousands of nobles and commoners over the centuries had invested untold millions of livres buying seigneuries. Was the government now merely going to strip them of their valuable investments? The solution hit upon instead was to compensate them out of the pockets of those who would benefit from the disappearance of the seigneuries. Here one sees reasoning inspired by the liberal illusion at work, reasoning very similar to that which moved Prussian bureaucrats to end serfdom in 1807–11. Money is a universal equivalent; it follows that the value of seigneuries could be expressed in monetary terms. Money ought to be a universal equivalent; it follows that landowners should not have to pay a 10 percent fee to a third party every time they make a money transaction with their land, since this prevents the price from reflecting the land's real value. Money is a universal equivalent; it follows that the landowners who must pay the fee doubtless as a result paid less for the land when they first bought it. Money ought to be a universal equivalent; therefore landowners within seigneuries must be forced by the government to aid in abolishing seigneuries by buying out the seigneur. The Assembly here reformed property in a way that suggested that it needed no reform. Certain key facets of the seigneurial system were abolished without compensation, including the courts, the *banalités,* and the exclusive hunting rights over local forests. These were the features of seigneuries to which an aura of elevated personal status and authority most evidently clung. This special aura, perfectly compatible with the real authority that attached to most forms of property, had to be eliminated outright because property was now declared to be perfectly compatible with individual liberty and equality.

Did such a reform constitute social change? Cobban and certain other historians would say no. Barrington Moore and certain other historians would say yes.[86] One's answer depends on the extent to which one is taken in by the idea of money as a universal equivalent. The abolition of seigneurial property was either a simple matter or a complex one. But if it was a simple matter of money substitutions and nothing else, then why bother to do it? And if it was not, then was money really a universal equivalent? If money is a universal equivalent, then there is no need to make it into one; if it is not, then trying to treat it as one is bound to cause trouble.

The peasants, as it turned out, refused to pay the compensations mandated by the National Assembly, but that is quite a different matter. It is enough to have recognized that this reform followed the logic of the liberal illusion and became entangled in its peculiar contradictions. It is true that the peasants forced the Assembly's hand, but the peasants did not invent the odd principles that shaped and justified the Assembly's confused, compromise-ridden decision to, in its own words, "destroy the feudal regime *entirely*." It may well be, however – at least there are strong indications in the secondary literature that favor the idea – that peasantry and Assembly acted in rough accord at this moment because they were moved by convergent reflections on the social significance of contractual monetary exchanges. All saw them, by comparison to seigneurial exactions, at any rate, as allowing more scope to individual choice and more hope of satisfying diverse personal needs. Such views were not unwarranted under the circumstances. What was unwarranted was to see such a change as the realization of utopian hopes and as the full accomplishment of social justice in the countryside. A refinement of disciplinary potentials between owners and occupiers is not equivalent to justice. But the habit of principled, resolutely independent, abstract theorizing inherited by the Assembly from the men of letters who chafed under patronage in the ancien régime inclined many of the Assembly's members and of their constituents toward utopian illusions.

Strong confirmation that liberal principle played as great a role in the Assembly's reforms as pressure from the peasantry comes from a recent study by T. J. A. Le Goff and D. M. G. Sutherland. They have shown that the Assembly took no action to reform *domaine congéable* or *quevaise*, which were common in the west of France. Domaine congéable was a form of "divided ownership: the edifices (buildings, crops, and some trees) belonged to the tenant; the *fonds* (the bare soil plus the more considerable trees), belonged to a landlord, who leased them to the tenant or *domanier*." Quevaise "gave the peasant hereditary tenure of his holding in return for some rather heavy annual payments and corvées [labor dues]." These tenures were neither strictly feudal nor strictly contractual. In the case of the seigneurie it was easy to decide who was the real property owner and who was the benighted feudal oppressor. Hereditary leaseholds and divided ownership did not lend themselves to such facile liberal categorizing, however. Despite intense local protests against onerous rents and demands that terms of redemption be laid down in law for these mixed tenures, the Assembly took no action to reform them. Le Goff and Sutherland see this failure as the first in a series of Assembly missteps that turned the west toward counterrevolutionary uprisings.[87]

The Assembly nonetheless found many other forms of property that resembled seigneuries in being easy to condemn on liberal grounds. In reforming venal office, noble tax exemptions, and guild masterships the Assembly followed the lines laid down in its treatment of seigneuries: abolition with compensation for those facets that were productive of monetary income, abolition outright of those facets that seemed to confer an intangible aura of status or authority on the possessor.[88] Thus the real political power of wealth, embedded in the disciplinary potentials of monetary exchange asymmetries, instead of being adorned with public honors and functions was covered over and denied so that it became at once invisible and also the true foundation on which most political authority would rest in the new society. This happened because greater personal freedom had seemed for a long time to result from money transactions, and in fact had resulted from certain money transactions. But a greater margin of freedom for some is not the same thing as freedom itself. This was one source of frustration and confusion that afflicted defenders of the Revolution in subsequent years.

THE CONUNDRUM OF THE RELIGIOUS SPHERE

After the August reforms the government would henceforth do nothing with property except protect it; the buying and selling of government functions, of privileges and exemptions, was ended once and for all. By this means the political and economic spheres were forcibly (but not really) separated. Thousands of people chaffed at the disappearance of seigneuries, guilds, and property in office, feeling certain that money compensations were no substitution for what had been lost. But it is widely agreed that the great generator of open opposition to the Revolution was the reform of the church that the Assembly undertook.[89] It is also widely agreed among historians that the Assembly botched the job of church reform badly. But it is not always pointed out that it did so because it faced impossible choices and was not so much too radical as too conservative. How was the religious sphere to be dealt with? The church as it then existed was an integral part of the ancien régime, reflecting in every part of its structure that social order's peculiar—to us—but in fact quite sensible conflation of religious, political, and proprietary authority. Simply to cut the church loose from government unchanged, in secure possession of its vast properties and tithes and the power that went with them, would have been just as dangerous politically as it was for an elected assembly to meddle unforgivably, as it did, in the church's affairs.

Religious freedom was conceded after some hesitation, and granted in the Declaration of Rights. But the Assembly was nonetheless unable to see the church as anything other than a public institution, its personnel as other than public servants, its wealth as other than public property. They saw its internal organization riddled with the kinds of privileges and abuses that they were attempting to reform in society at large: the stranglehold of noble families on the episcopacy, the diversion of tithes and rents away from those clergy who actually served the people, the virtual sale of priesthoods, cures, abbeys, and bishoprics to well-placed candidates. This was just the sort of problem that plagued the judiciary, the publishing business, and commerce in general. The Assembly could not pass over it in silence.

At the same time the Assembly assumed that it inherited from the king all his traditional power over the church, just as it inherited the other elements of his sovereignty. Did not the Assembly itself include many duly elected representatives of the clergy? Instead of redefining sovereignty as having no jurisdiction in religious matters, it tried to remake the church in the image of a publicly responsible civil service. Acting in this manner made it possible for the Assembly to abolish the tithe without compensation (the public need not compensate itself) and to put its hands on the vast landed wealth of the church without the appearance of injustice. Peasant resistance to tithes and the government's urgent need for credit both forced the Assembly's hands in this area. But, again, these exigencies did not give rise by themselves to the odd mix of old and new ideas that shaped the Civil Constitution of the Clergy, as the reform package was eventually named. The fact that it required an oath of allegiance to its provisions from every member of the clergy is what sparked the most violent outrage. The king had always been a quasi-religious figure; his authority within the French church had been condoned by the pope for centuries. But could this quasi-religious role be transferred from a hereditary monarch to a constitution? That a priest should have to swear allegiance to a document drafted by elected members of the laity seemed to many to be incongruous in the extreme. And yet, apparently, so did the idea of a government existing without religious sanction of any kind. But, then, is this really surprising? Can a government be legitimate without being somehow connected with the sacred? This job was almost bound to be botched. But once it was, the escalating tensions that gradually led the Revolution toward its radical extremes were also unavoidable.

PROPERTY AND TERROR

As recent objections to the celebration of the bicentennial demonstrate, the Revolution still rouses strong emotions in France. What excites reaction now, however, is no longer the same thing as what stirred people then. Now the reforms of 1789 are considered obvious, necessary, an inevitable step in human progress, by virtually the whole political spectrum from Communists to Gaullists. It is what followed in 1792 through 1795 that sparks shame, consternation, and controversy. At the time, however, matters were quite the reverse. The reforms of 1789 sparked shame, consternation, and controversy; violence was necessary to undo them, or else to ensure their survival. That millions of French people were shocked and dismayed by the sudden dissolution of the old social order into the three quasi-detached, pseudo-independent realms of religion, government, and private property may seem more understandable now that the in many respects perfectly sensible character of that old order's arrangements has been underscored. That many supporters of the Revolution were bound to be disillusioned and perplexed by its failure to produce immediate and perfect human liberty is also understandable in view of the emotion-charged role of liberal principles in the lives of ancien-régime writers and journalists. The dismay of its opponents and the perplexity of its supporters pushed the Revolution toward Terror. But it is particularly the latter factor, perplexity, that must be understood if one wants to appreciate the special sense of desperation that harried the agents who instituted the Terror.

When the Revolution came, even as it defended and extended the right of property, it was unreservedly supported by many who expected it to put an end to the pervasive servility of social life that Rousseau had so deplored. As it became apparent that no such result was forthcoming, the fault was often laid at the door not of anything systematic about established practices but of individual character, of old habits that had to be overcome, or else of evil intentions that demanded punishment. Madame Roland wrote to Brissot from the family estate near Lyons on 1 September 1789:

> Our provinces resonate quite differently to the clamors of the aristocrats than does the capital. Not that there are more nobles, but the inequality of conditions is more marked, more keenly felt, more fanatically defended. . . . You see nothing but little financiers and little councillors wherever you look, sons of bakers and of barkeepers, who are furious today to be put on a plain with their parents. . . . Religion is lost! The state is dissolved! Anarchy has arrived! There is no more subordination! These are their favorite expressions. . . . The officers of a little *sénéchaussée,* the canons of a *collégiale*—unknown anywhere else but there where they exist—raise themselves up above other persons much higher than your councillors of the Paris Parlement or your big *abbés* do over a merchant of the rue Saint-Denis.[90]

The Revolution had "put all men on the same level," she said, and that is what these blamable individuals could not stand. But it had not, and that is why such concern for distinction and subordination lived on.

Robespierre made the same error as Madame Roland, as indeed almost all partisans of the Revolution did, opposing the ravages of the newly reformed property game but mistaking its effects as the consequences of individual character. Rather than recognizing that property was an institutionalized source of personal political power, Robespierre attacked the wealthy as lacking in virtue:

> It is the people who are good, patient, generous. . . . The people ask only for peace, justice, and the right to live. The rich and powerful thirst after honors, wealth, and sensual enjoyment. The interest and desire of the people is that of nature itself, of humanity; it is the general interest. The interest and desire of the rich and powerful is that of ambition, pride, greed, and the wildest fantasies of passions that are fatal to the happiness of society as a whole.[91]

During the Terror, the sans-culottes took this approach to its logical extreme, seeing the members of large subgroups of society as all individually guilty of treason and deserving of death. "The streets should be carpeted with the heads of merchants," cried a dyer of the Arsenal section in the Year 2. Albert Soboul has shown that the sans-culottes had no objection to property as such, only to large concentrations of it:

> Hence we have *Père Duchesne* [says Soboul], whose rage was inspired "by those big men who continue to swallow up the little men." After having declared, "Fatherland be damned! Merchants don't have one," Hébert swiftly explained: "Not that I should be looked upon as being against commerce. No one has a higher regard for the 'respectable man' who lives by his industry than I do." By this he presumably meant the independent artisan and shop owner, small production and small business. Hébert had no notion that the interests of the artisans might be opposed to those of the journeymen and workers.[92]

This last observation is true enough, but under the circumstances a minor point. What Hébert and other sans-culottes did see was the fundamental opposition between those for whom property was merely a question of dry calculations and advantageous deals and those for whom it represented a concrete, everyday means to a livelihood.

Another comment from the pages of *Père Duchesne* makes the point: "[The sans-culotte] knows how to work a field, how to forge, to saw, to file, to cover a roof, make shoes. . . . And since he works, you can be sure that he'll never be seen either in the Café de Chartres, or in pothouses where conspiracies are hatched and people gamble."[93] In this passage Hébert is on the verge of identifying the differences in use values at the core of monetary exchange asymmetries. What the sans-culotte movement proved unable to do was to theorize about this crucial perception. Its adherents lacked an appropriate vocabulary. Such things cannot be invented overnight. As a result, those who were too exalted to work with their property were lumped together as morally reprehensible: "Until the snobbish merchants, the aristocrats, the rich, etc., are guillotined or dispatched en masse, nothing will work out properly," declared a widow of the Indivisibilité section.[94] It was not just high grain prices that prompted this sort of denunciation. The texts Soboul cites show that speculation in basic foodstuffs was considered just one element in a general behavior pattern of the wealthy expressing arrogance toward their fellow citizens and a total disregard for the welfare of the nation. The sans-culottes were defending the property of the rich, declared Didot of the Réunion section, "and every day the rich aristocrat steals the property of the people: their rights, their subsistence, their liberty."[95] In this statement one finds just the sort of kernel of truth that is scattered throughout sans-culotte ideology. Liberty cannot survive in an environment of stark inequalities of wealth, in which the basic needs of some enslave them to others, in which the freedom to speculate is equated with the freedom to vote.

But this statement likewise contains just the sort of fallacies that clouded both sans-culotte and Jacobin social ideas during the turbulent months of 1793 and 1794. The conflation of the rich with aristocrats, the implicit confusion of large-scale merchant operations, with their rigid, well-defined rules and imposed motives, on the one hand, and consciously chosen political opposition to the Republic, on the other, shows a failure to reckon with the political implications of private property. Without some idea of how monetary exchange asymmetries systematically make disciplinary control possible, the revolutionaries were lost. It was impossible for them to appreciate that the very Revolution they were defending was not the establishment of liberty but the engine of a new, more subtle kind of political submission.

Once the sweeping reforms of 1789–91 had been carried out, the Revolution inevitably became a search by everyone involved to better his own position in the new, open political institutions and the newly simplified property game. Upward mobility and social subordination continued to generate anxieties and humiliations and to absorb the energies and calculations of all.

It was not just the unprincipled opportunists like those of the corrupt circle that formed around Danton who took advantage of the Revolution to enrich themselves. Even the austere, puritanical Rolands fell victim to the enticements of deference and the attractions of the trappings of power that Madame Roland had earlier denounced. On 23 March 1792, when Roland discovered that he was to be named minister of the interior, he and his wife spent a sleepless night in high excitement discussing whether he should accept the post. Thrilled by the honor, Madame Roland pushed her husband to accept; his objections were not hard to turn aside. The following morning a friend, Sophie Grandchamp, called and found them still in bed and exhausted from lack of sleep. Later, when she returned to their small rented apartment, she recounted,

> I thought I was dreaming when I entered the salon. My friend, who had seemed that morning on the point of death, had recovered her freshness and charm. She was surrounded by a number of people who were showering her with compliments. Roland took his share in these civilities and seemed quite satisfied. I threw myself into an armchair near the fireplace, and there observed the new personalities: the room was crowded with ministers, chiefs of state, and the principal deputies. Two lackeys, standing outside the door, opened one or two panels for the visitors, depending on their rank.[96]

Four days later they moved into the sumptuous official ministerial palace. How difficult it was for Madame Roland to recognize that her dedication to liberty was being not honored but violated by this "apotheosis of the devoted civil servant," as Gita May has called it, the fulfillment of a dream Madame Roland had long since forsworn.[97] The lackeys, the compliments, the influence, the elegant dwellings, the general servility of the old despotism, lived on to be enjoyed by the servants of the people, because the political power of property and money remained untouched.

This is why Robespierre could send Madame Roland, Brissot, Danton, Hébert, and all the others to the guillotine with the firm conviction that they were all opportunists and weaklings. This is why he shouted with rage at the Assembly the day before he himself was arrested in Thermidor of the Year 2, calling the delegates "scoundrels" and "oppressors of the people." He knew that something was dreadfully wrong, but he did not know what.

François Furet was certainly correct to argue that absolutism left a heavy imprint on the language of Revolution, visible in its abstractness and in the rigid manner of its application to specific cases.[98] But it is wrong to suppose that this is a sufficient explanation of the character of revolutionary political discourse. It is wrong to conclude that this discourse lacked any relevance whatsoever to the social reality of France, that "the people" or "the nation" were too abstract to refer to anything real. The problem was not that this discourse was out of touch with the social reality around it but that it was positively wrong about that reality. The revolutionaries believed that they had established in the name of the nation the political structure of liberty, that it only remained for individual citizens to live up to the institutions created for them – hence the extreme emphasis placed on civic virtue and civic duty, all the qualities associated with the word *civisme*. By autumn 1793 mere lack of *civisme* had become grounds for summary imprisonment and execution. But since private property remained a source of political power incommensurate with true freedom of thought and expression, it followed that the new political institutions failed to provide the social conditions required to create freedom. Not individuals as such, but society as a whole, continued caught up in the chase after that personal power and distinction which wealth provided (or else in the constant round of bowing and scraping that poverty imposed). The rules of the chase were altered considerably, but not fundamentally. A frenzy of suspicion and uncertainty resulted when no one acted free, even though all were deemed to have been given their freedom.[99]

The abstractness of the common terms of political discourse, likewise, resulted at least in part from the inability of specific individuals, on inspection, to live up to the noble visions inherent in a term like "people" or "citizen": What real human being under scrutiny would not be found wanting when viewed as a member of the sovereign and infallible people? Any person either would have too much money or else would be obeying, or fearful of, or courting favor from people with too much money. Of all those engaged in the pursuit of money – and who was not? – artisans who depended on a large clientele (but not those like wigmakers who depended on a rich clientele) came the closest to the abstract ideal of personal freedom. They were not subject to any one person's will, nor did they oppress more than one or two others. Their survival threatened by shortages, their freedom of expression relatively great, many of them became strong partisans of the Revolution. Apart from them, who but a few saints would either give away their money or else risk destitution by refusing to obey their superiors? The calls for civic virtue became extreme because the necessary social preconditions of liberty had not been established.

These observations gain strength from two recent studies of the sans-culotte movement under the Terror that have shed considerable new light on its social composition and its unique political idiom. Richard M. Andrews has shown that a good number of the most influential and most outspoken members of the movement can be considered "artisans" only by stretching the term to the breaking point.[100] Many persons listed as carpenters, joiners, masons, or furniture makers in official records of revolutionary committees and assemblies turn out on closer examination to have been substantial employers with as many as sixty journeymen at work in their shops. Besides speaking out in assemblies, these leaders used their own employees as nuclei for revolutionary gatherings in support of official demonstrations or insurrectionary actions. Still other sans-culotte spokesmen have been shown to be younger scions of old robe dynasties or of well-connected merchant families who cloaked their well-bred origins behind popular speech and dress. Andrews has attempted to assimilate his findings to the old class vocabulary, announcing the discovery that the sans-culotte movement was really led by bourgeois. But what he has actually shown, in effect, is that the reach of monetary exchange asymmetries extended into the very interstices of sans-culotte organization.

At the same time Michael Sonenscher has shown how strongly ancien-régime shop-floor language influenced the formation of popular political discourse in 1792–93.[101] Hébert's sans-culotte newspaper *Père Duchesne,* for example, spoke with the metaphors and in the name of the values not of former guild masters but of lowly, wage-earning journeymen. The combined effect of these two research projects is to create an image of the typical sans-culotte leader as a relatively well off employer, wealthy enough to stay in his bureau and leave manual labor to his journeyman, who dressed and spoke in a manner as close as possible to that of journeymen and artisans of little or no property and who used his own wealth to enhance his influence within the sans-culotte movement. The significance of small independent artisans in the popular movement as revealed by Andrews and Sonenscher is not that they were its principal source of support (although they remain an important ingredient) but rather that they were its principal source of inspiration.

The movement's own idealized self-image, to which everyone paid lip service, was that of the poor but independent workingman with no desire to dominate, or be dominated by, another. Such a person had indeed the kind of liberty that the Revolution was supposed to have granted to all, the liberty to speak his mind without fear and without unduly influencing anyone else. But even on the streets of Paris he was a relatively rare person. Almost everyone else, by the very nature of things, was likely to be either in a position of authority over others or subject to others' wills merely in consequence of the purely "economic" relationships he entered into. This was so obvious in one sense that anyone who desired political influence sought to look like a poor but independent journeyman or artisan, and so inescapable in another sense that many of those who sought to do so acted either to shore up the authority of their wealth or else in deference to such authority.

None of this should be construed as denying that the guillotine and the Revolutionary Tribunals imposed a very rigid and crude form of discipline of their own, based on the direct and massive use of state coercion. By its harshness and its haphazard application revolutionary justice was bound to force many into superficial compliance and routine hypocrisy, thereby increasing all the more the general atmosphere of mistrust.[102] Resort to such drastic measures was first made at a moment when Paris appeared certain to be encircled by enemy troops; the infamous September massacres of 1792 were an act of wartime, an attempt to prepare for an impending siege by eliminating probable traitors within. Revolutionary Tribunals were set up afterward more to contain the violence than to extend it. Terror in the first instance began as part of a civil war in which advocates of both sides were randomly intermixed and impossible to distinguish by appearance alone – an explosive situation. But it is certainly also true that the readiness to institutionalize terror owes a great deal to the impediments that monetary exchange asymmetries constantly raised against the realization of revolutionary hopes. The law of the Maximum, which set strict limits on prices for a wide array of subsistence goods in the fall of 1793, was backed up by the very guillotine that had first been used against nonjuring priests and counter-revolutionaries. The reasoning was simple: High prices threatened the poor of the towns, that is, the Republic's most ardent supporters, and undermined the stability of the assignat, the paper money that the government depended on to continue functioning. To charge whatever the market would bear could only be, under the circumstances, a blatant attempt to return to the ancien régime. The political significance of monetary exchanges was at this urgent juncture fully recognized and vigorously dealt with. Nonetheless, the Jacobin leaders viewed this interference with the right of property as only a temporary emergency measure. The Maximum, like so many other aspects of the Terror, resulted from a confused convergence of exchange issues with questions of allegiance and treachery. This convergence was an inevitable result of the Revolution's misguided attempt to create political freedom. Protecting unrestricted property rights, making them into the sacred starting point of law, was no way to inaugurate the reign of virtue. Patrice Higonnet in two recent works has brilliantly argued for a similar view. As he sees it, the Revolution fell afoul of the simple fact that private interest and public spirit must necessarily come into conflict with each other. To this it is necessary to add only that they must do so because private property is unavoidably a source of political authority, not because avarice conflicts with virtue in our souls.[103]

THE ILLUSION ENSHRINED

This argument has moved from a consideration of the social origins of the French Revolution to a critique of its aims. But it should not be surprising that a view of the Revolution's origins that seeks to dispense with the notion of class should lead on to a rejection of the idea that the Revolution's reforms were part of a necessary, obvious, and progressive transformation. It was mentioned in Chapter 1 – and François Furet has also carefully pointed out – that the old class categories of the Marxist scenario of revolution can be traced directly back to the makers of the French Revolution themselves.[104] It was the revolutionaries who first analyzed the Revolution as a class struggle (although they did not use that term) between the "aristocrats" and the "Third Estate" or the "Nation," terms that were easily equated later by Marx, as well as by historians like Lefebvre and Soboul, with the Marxist categories of "feudal aristocracy" and "revolutionary bourgeoisie." The reliance of the revolutionary reform program on the tenets of the liberal illusion has been sufficiently explored in this chapter to render it plausible that something like the notion of class interest (a uniform underlying desire for gain arising within different social roles) lay behind the revolutionaries' sweeping identifications of whole social categories with specific political factions. To condemn all merchants or all aristocrats was to see a connection between the interests of a specific social position and the outcome of a political struggle. The liberal illusion that informed the decrees of August 1789 has lurked behind class analyses of political conflict down to the present. To replace such class analyses with a different starting point necessarily involves a critical reevaluation of those reforms.

If one breaks with the idea that money can serve as a universal equivalent and if one attempts to carry through the consequences of this break to every corner of social thought, it is almost inevitable that one's estimation of ancien-régime society will rise appreciably. Money's negative marginal utility for the poor, arising out of the diversity and complexity of all human beings' physical and social needs, places in the hands of their wealthy exchange partners a powerful disciplinary potential whose precise shape varies with the exact nature of the exchange relationship. Wealth and personal authority are therefore likely to be coincident in any society that uses money as a medium for distributing capital goods and subsistence goods. The beauty of the arrangements that had grown up in France over several centuries for integrating such personal authority into the larger scheme of things lay in the frank and open recognition by crown, church, and aristocracy of the authority of wealth. It was also recognized that accumulations of wealth were often arbitrary, the outcome of luck or of an individual's special talent for adding figures in a ledger – things that did not at first seem apt preparation for the exercise of authority. This, too, was taken into account: The nouveaux riches were expected to transfer their wealth into appropriate forms of property, land and office, and to behave in seemly manner for one or two generations before being given full admission into the ruling elite. No sharp distinction was made among the authority of wealth, the authority of religion, and the authority of direct state coercion; all these different forms interpenetrated with one another, for a long time with no more than scattered cries of foul play.

The challenge to this social order arose not because a particular class or classes of persons within society found that their interests were being thwarted or bypassed.

The spreading use of money within rural communities and the knitting together of routine commercial links across great distances had variegated destabilizing effects. The rural poor in some regions were enabled to undersell urban guild masters in manufacturing, to eke out livings without access to land, to swell in numbers and make the provision of food to them through commercial channels more difficult. In other regions the disappearance of recurrent demographic crises led to parcelization of land and the increased dependence of peasants on part-time wage labor and on the leasing of tiny plots. Monetary exchange provided the flexibility needed for survival, altering the disciplinary potentials that held the peasants in thrall to their social betters. Dues, taxes, and tithes began to appear anomalous in this context. At the same time the swelling book trade provided a new outlet of self-expression to talented but poor writers who nonetheless had to depend on patronage for their income. The tension between the intimate freedom of the relation between writer and reader on the one hand and the intimate subjection of protégé to patron on the other created a climate in which zealous, principled opposition to the status quo flourished. The concept of money exchanges as an instrument of liberation had much to recommend it in this context in intellectual discussions of both the position of the ambitious writer or manufacturer and the plight of the rural cottager or farmer. Free trade and freedom itself were easily confused by those who suffered from the ancien régime's casual approach to the sale of offices, privileges, and monopolies. When the fiscal and agrarian crises of the 1780s both reached a head in the autumn of 1788, the stage was set for a sudden transformation.

Once the Revolution was under way, its progressive radicalization under the pressures of foreign war and domestic subversion was a highly likely outcome. The utopian project of the August reforms, which aimed at the accomplishment of a complete separation of religious, political, and economic spheres of activity within society, was totally at odds with the spirit of the ancien régime. Opposition from those who had taken no part in the heady victory of public opinion over the crown was bound to spread. Within the ranks of the Revolution's supporters, as well, perplexity about the source of their multifarious failures added to the atmosphere of mistrust and frustration that gave rise to the Terror. Having equated complete freedom in the disposal of property with a high ideal of political freedom, the revolutionaries sought to locate their difficulties paradoxically in the individual characters of large categories of persons. The rich, the merchant, the aristocrat, lacked virtue. Class interest, although the term itself was not used, paradoxically became the enemy of true freedom even as it was deemed in another sense to be an expression of freedom and one of the main beneficiaries of reform; after all, did not the Revolution have as one of its principal aims the freeing of merchants to speculate in grain?

France embraced money, gave it sovereign authority over all relationships outside of a few refuges – the family, the army, the prison – institutions, that is, whose functions could not be made to square with the liberal illusion even in the 1790s. (In the end, Napoleon made an arrangement with the church as well, which allowed the secular clergy and a few convent schools and missions to offer escape from the atomizing meritocracy he fashioned.) Apart from these rare fortresses of solidarity, the free play of money equivalents was given unbounded sway. The revolutionaries are to be forgiven if they did not understand why true liberty and civic virtue were slow to make their appearance afterward, just as the counterrevolutionaries can be pardoned for feeling that no amount of money compensation could make up for the loss of those beautifully sensible ancien-régime honorifics, privileges, and perquisites that had given life meaning for so many. Money is not an easy thing to think about. The fact that it seems so simple and straightforward is one of the main reasons why two and a half millennia have not sufficed for Europeans to come to a full understanding of it.

On the plane of European history the French Revolution appears as an event that enshrined the liberal illusion in fundamental law and confirmed its controlling position within political idiom. It is as if the very monetary exchanges that were occurring around people every day became as distant and unknown to them as colonial slave plantations or as the suffering of Bengal spinners. Paris at the height of the Terror, London at the passage of the Anti-Combination Acts of 1799 and 1800 or the repeal of the Statute of Artificers in 1814, Berlin at the time of the first reform edicts of 1807 – bastions of revolution or else of reaction within the new Europe – had this much in common: People never stopped seeing that journeymen feared and disliked their masters or that tenant farmers were humble and deferential to their landlords, nor did they ever stop understanding why heads turned when a wealthy merchant and his daughter entered a drawing room. But when they theorized about these matters they now tended to treat all such actions as outgrowths of a universal, underlying desire for gain.

5 Challenging one's master in the nineteenth century: from Silesia to Lancashire

THE POLITICAL MOBILIZATION OF THE POOR in the nineteenth and early twentieth centuries was one of the most significant developments in history, giving rise ultimately to both the welfare democracies and the socialist states that dominate the present world scene. But these great protest movements were not merely the birth pangs of industrial society, not merely reactions against the emergence of capitalism as normally conceived. This is because capitalism as normally conceived has never existed. The poor's social experience, out of which these protests arose, bore only a superficial resemblance to the experience that was deductively ascribed to them on the basis of the liberal illusion. As a result, their political reactions bore only a distant resemblance to the reactions that observers, whether liberal or socialist, expected them to have. As discussed in Chapters 1 and 3, a whole range of knotty problems of explanation has grown up out of attempts to account for the poor's repeated failures to live up to their supposed historic mission. But this mission was one they never espoused.

To say that capitalist society did not come into existence in the nineteenth century presents one immediately with a terminological difficulty. To call nineteenth-century society capitalist is a convention blessed by long usage and near-universal consensus; therefore the word "capitalism" could legitimately be said to mean social systems like that of the nineteenth century, whatever it was. The claim being made here might therefore be rephrased as follows: Nineteenth-century capitalist society in the historical sense of the term never became truly capitalist in the theoretical sense of the term because it never achieved a properly functioning market system. Such a system is a social impossibility.

This assertion follows in the first place directly from the critique of the liberal illusion presented in Chapter 3. It follows as well from the reformulation of the social origins of the French Revolution offered in Chapter 4. A market system requires for its existence the full and free convertibility of all objects of human desire into money equivalents and the full and free operation of a separate economic sphere of social life. It does no good to object that the market model has for long been supposed to be no more than an approximation of social reality; the weaknesses of this position were already discussed in Chapter 3 in the section entitled "Prices and classes." To insist that "real" markets only approximate the market model says nothing about what it is that keeps real markets from achieving a perfect fit, gives no indication of how bad the fit must be before application of the model is ruled out, and provides no way of deciding whether other models (such as the one being proposed here) are better or worse. It begs, that is, all the essential questions. To point out that the market system never emerged is therefore merely a plea that these essential questions finally be put on the agenda of debate. The aim of this chapter is only to begin the search for those rule-governed patterns that may lie hidden within the "imperfections" that the market model has never pretended to explain.

One aim of the previous chapter was to show that attention to such "imperfections" may help to explain why the reforms of 1789–91 inevitably led to the Terror of 1793. The French Revolution represented an abortive effort to realize an impossible social order. Had it been possible for money to function as a universal equivalent, had it been possible to give unlimited sway to property rights without threatening the political liberty of individuals, then capitalist enterprise of a theoretically pure sort would have become the sole means of organizing human activities. It is this fact that gives a limited sense to Barrington Moore's insistence that capitalism was "seeping through the pores" of the old order simply because money was so freely and widely used for gaining access to privileges, offices, and properties.[1]

Money can be introduced into many relationships without immediately limiting the personal liberty of those involved – as an equivalent of land, buildings, luxury items, books, or even of judicial office – so long as neither party to the exchange is in a situation where his money has a negative marginal utility. But in transactions between rich and poor, in which the poorer party needs to get and quickly spend money in order to survive and to ensure the survival of family or household, the richer party is thereby endowed with a power over the poorer. This power cannot itself be given a money equivalence. It is an "extraeconomic" element of political control that enters into the heart of most "economic" relationships, dashing once and for all any hope of establishing a purely economic sphere or a purely political sphere in social life, dashing at the same time any hope that the most important prices and wages in a society will ever be determined by market forces alone. It was this extraeconomic power that aroused the hostility of the sans-culottes against merchants and landowners and that found expression in their subtheoretical pronouncements against speculation in foodstuffs as the manifestation of counterrevolutionary commitment. This power helped counterrevolutionaries to rally support in the West and organize White Terror in the South. This power bound many poor sans-culottes to their rich employers within the core of the revolutionary movement itself. This power made hash of the dream of political liberty.

The assertion that capitalism in the theoretical sense is an impossible social order must also be supported by an analysis of "capitalist" enterprise as it actually emerged in the nineteenth century. In the two sections that follow, an analysis is presented that amounts to nothing more than a repetition of the indictment of the liberal illusion presented in Chapter 3. However, this analysis is formulated with the specific problem in mind of enterprises in a laissez-faire environment, with evidence and examples drawn from the nineteenth century. Once this analysis is complete it will be put to work to account for two episodes of labor conflict drawn from that same period, with the aim of showing that nineteenth-century protest movements failed to be revolts against capitalism for just the reasons that capitalism failed to appear when its cue was read out on the stage of history.

FAMILIES AND ENTERPRISES

Nineteenth-century enterprises failed to become fully capitalist, as any enterprise must fail to do, for four interlinked reasons: (1) Production and consumption cannot be distinguished; (2) households cannot be enterprises; (3) labor cannot be disposed of in a market; and (4) enterprises are political institutions. Each of these points must be dealt with in turn.

Production and consumption cannot be distinguished because what is product from the point of view of one exchange partner is an item of consumption from the point of view of another. Coal and iron ore are end products for mining concerns but raw materials to be consumed for steel plants. Steel is the end product of steel plants but a raw material to be consumed for machine builders. Every process of production consumes factors of production; even nonrenewable natural resources are consumed when they are wrested from the earth, in the sense that the limited stock of them is permanently depleted. Every act of consumption is a production process. Some analysts are in the habit of speaking of the "ultimate consumer," an economic actor who consumes without producing. Private individuals who buy for their personal consumption are by convention held not to be engaging in production. This is surely what Adam Smith had in mind when he asserted that "consumption is the sole end and purpose of all production"—a doctrine that argued against giving producers any protection from the freely expressed preferences of consumers.[2] Smith's doctrine makes no sense unless there are ultimate consumers; without them it is circular, and production has no purpose whatever except to feed further production.

Marx was among the first to make critical use of this difficulty. He recognized that the ultimate consumer, the private individual, under capitalism was engaged in a production process as well. He produced labor power for sale to enterprises engaged in production processes. Thus, in Marx's version, capitalism did become the endless, pointless, circular maximization of production. And the circle was doomed to break down because as the maximum labor output was demanded from producers of labor power for a minimum price, the private individual was continually in danger of being unable to buy and consume all of the prodigiously growing array of products fabricated for his sake alone by the very enterprises that exploited him.

Modern economists have sought to extricate themselves from this difficulty by distinguishing among three kinds of consumption by private individuals: (1) consumption to regenerate their labor power from week to week, (2) consumption to produce "human capital," that is, valuable skills and knowledge, and (3) consumption "for its own sake," as a freely chosen good.[3] Maximizing this third form of consumption then becomes the ultimate purpose of the economic system. These distinctions in theory cannot, however, be measured in practice. Lester Thurow has catalogued some of the difficulties:

> Much consumption is self-produced. The services provided by housewives are the most important, but all of our recreation, do-it-yourself, and personal-services activities require skills. A good deal of the family's standard of living is provided by the members of the family itself. The ability to self-produce goods and services constitutes an important current and future stream of benefits, and human-capital skills are necessary to produce these services. And though these benefits are never priced or sold in the market, they influence the human-capital-investment decisions that workers make. . . .

> Investments are often made for the express purpose of changing tastes and preferences. For example, prodigious amounts of money are spent on private investments in psychology and psychiatry to alter personal behavior. And as preferences change, the value of human-capital assets may also vary greatly. . . .

> With physical assets, maintenance costs and depreciation charges represent no special problems in making investment decisions. But with human beings, one is faced with the joint costs of production and consumption. Man must eat and sleep both to work and to consume. How are these costs to be allocated?

In addition, laborers clearly consume on the job – just as they produce at home – in the sense that they do what they like to do in the shop whenever possible and alter work processes to an unknown extent to fit personal inclinations. But neither on-the-job consumption of this kind nor on-the-job training (which creates most human capital) can be measured in money terms except by means of capriciously (often deductively) chosen values. A theory that distinguishes among human capital investment, consumption for maintenance, and consumption for its own sake thus "empties itself of all empirical content," in Thurow's words.[4]

It follows from these considerations that there is a range of social activities, loosely associated with what are called households or families, that constitute a vast noncapitalist sector of production within any capitalist system. This sector produces people and skills. The methods of production employed are not amenable to an economic analysis that depends on measuring with money units. In this respect the Marxist tradition, superior because of its long-standing recognition that private families are engaged in production, has nonetheless led some researchers down a blind alley. The idea that the family is a production process has been followed up by attempts to analyze households in terms of quantities of labor and of surplus product differentially appropriated by family members. Implicitly, families are analyzed as if they were enterprises. Among other things, the difficult question arises whether women must be considered a class, by analogy to the working class that animates all enterprise functions. Feminist historians over the last decade have struggled with but often rejected this idea, insisting instead on the need for a complete revision of the male-centered, money-oriented notion of exploitation implicit in the received concept of class. This is certainly the correct response, whether or not the concept of patriarchy, as some have argued, can adequately replace or supersede the concept of class struggle as the motor of history.[5]

Noncapitalist households in a capitalist society are subject to certain kinds of severe pressures, some of which can be measured in terms of take-home pay and living costs, others of which cannot, such as the steady impact on personality of rigid authoritarianism, insecurity, or tedium in the workplace, or the difficulty of deciding between paid and unpaid labor demands. (Women factory workers in the nineteenth century were regularly castigated by observers for failing to do housework, for example.)[6] The members of households must resist these pressures in order to sustain the ongoing, open-ended, unmeasured exchange relationships characteristic of households.

In Europe the great reforms of the revolutionary era made all men equal before the law but left women suffering in an inferior legal status in property and inheritance rights; rights to vote, assemble, and speak; and rights of the person (such as the right to be free of corporal punishment or the right to choose one's own residence).[7] The vast majority of households continued to be made up of partners with decidedly asymmetrical abilities to call on the coercive power of the state to settle disputes or dispose of property. Children, needless to say, had even fewer rights than women and less chance to exercise those they did have. These stark differences in legal status had nothing to do with the requirements of liberal doctrine in property, free competition, or the just reward of merit. In many respects, as Mary Wollstonecraft and others were quick to point out, law on women and families was in direct conflict with liberal doctrine strictly interpreted.[8] In effect, the reformers suffered from a massive blind spot, and their work from a massive lacuna. Families were somehow to be brought over wholesale and unchanged into the new competitive order without feeling its impact.

Law and custom made women victims of marked exchange asymmetries within marriage, but these were not monetary exchange asymmetries. The whole notion of a "family economy" can obscure the nature of the institution and of its problems. Husbands did not in any sense buy labor or products from wives, or vice versa. Doubtless there were instances of families in which practices actually resembled monetary exchanges, as when a husband left a fixed fraction of his pay with the wife each week or charged his adolescent daughter for room and board. In general, however, family relationships could hardly escape being either much more intimate and complex or else disastrously worse than buying groceries at a store or paying for a room with board above a neighborhood bar. If the daughter lost her job or became pregnant, the father who continued to charge room and board was making himself her enemy, not treating her with the impersonal civility of a landlord. If a wife broke her leg, the husband who advertised for a replacement was engaging in a ruthless attack on her. However impoverished working-class families became in the nineteenth century, however frequent the instances of domestic violence or family breakup became, these truths remained self-evident. Expectations attached to family relationships; relationships were measured against these expectations; and the tone of family life was set by them. These expectations excluded strict monetary accounting of give-and-take within the household except in those situations where it did not threaten the underlying presumption of family solidarity and where it promised to stretch wages further or to have a didactic value. These expectations, in tandem with the law, also reduced women to a subordinate status that even women activists questioned only infrequently.[9]

Households so structured were a bonanza for certain kinds of capitalist enterprises, and these enterprises quickly developed a parasitic relationship with working households. The capitalist sector did not operate on strictly capitalist lines because of the impact of the noncapitalist household sector on use of labor. In a large number of trades, especially primary textiles, knitting, and garment making, but not excluding mining, small metals, packaging, food, and retail, enterprises turned quickly to women and children for labor once restrictive regulations were repealed. Laissez-faire in the "economy" lead to the ravaging of "society," as it is sometimes put. This formulation of the female- and child-labor problem fails, however, to recognize that the family, that most important of all "social" institutions, cannot help but be an essential sector of the "economy" as well. Societies do not have economies; they simply are the same thing as economies viewed from different vantage points. This is a conclusion that the inability to distinguish between production and consumption makes irresistible.

Women and children brought with them into the workplace all of the ingrained presumptions of their own inferiority and subjection to authority that reigned in households. They calmly accepted wages one half those of adult males or less, wages well below subsistence needs, however calculated, because they were presumed to be only supplements pooled with adult male wages in the household. Resistance and aggressive bargaining by women and children were nonexistent or comparatively intermittent, and this situation caused a massive distortion of the pricing of labor – enough by itself to prevent free-floating prices from ever balancing properly the demand and supply of labor, that most important of all factors of production. (This is not to say, of course, that women played no role in protest movements.) Consumer markets were flooded with cheap, shoddy shoes, garments, stockings, artificial flowers, and other bric-a-brac that women and children could most easily be put to use at making. Low earning capacity in turn reinforced female dependence within the household, even as women and children were displacing adult males in the workshop, giving rise to a range of new tensions and hardships unknown to the peasant and rural outworker households of the eighteenth century.[10] It is not as if the family remained unchanged; it continued to operate by different rules from enterprise while it changed to fulfill an essential production function for enterprises. The result was a weird travesty of a market system that deeply shaped the operations both of households and of enterprises.

If the anomalous nature of households within a capitalist system did not dash all hope of creating a functioning labor market, then the impediments to free bargaining that adult males encountered were certainly enough to finish the job. These impediments were briefly discussed in Chapter 3 and will be dealt with again in the course of this chapter. They arose from the disciplinary potential of monetary exchange asymmetries between employer and employee. Here, as well, however, law and custom played a strong role in enforcing them. (Labor law reveals that liberal reformers had other blind spots besides those that made them unable to see women.)[11] Among entrepreneurs, especially in textiles and mining, it was a common practice both to hire by family and to pay wages to the adult males that were double what their wives and children received.[12] An employer who did this gained in authority – first, because he could, if he chose, fire not one but all of a household's wage earners, and second, because his wage levels supported customary expectations about the relative authority and worth of family members in relation to one another. He became both provider and moral protector for those households that depended on him for survival.

The net result of these distortions was to make enterprises into very peculiar intermediary institutions. They were neither entirely creatures of the market nor self-subsistent institutions of authority and control. The disciplinary potentials of monetary exchange asymmetries could be used instrumentally to ensure profitability or to make possible survival in a difficult boom-and-bust environment. Nonetheless, entrepreneurs appeared to seek maximum authority for its own sake, without reference to the ultimate use it might be put to, often at great cost in strictly monetary terms. Most enterprises in the growth sectors, whether mechanized or not, bought some of their factors of production in competitive markets and sold their output in competitive markets; they could not afford, as a result, to allow their methods of operation to fall behind the competitive standard.[13] At the same time competition for profit was hardly the only way in which enterprises influenced one another's practices. Enterprises were owned not by individuals so much as by families interlinked through marriages, partnerships, and long-standing trading ties. Competition might be muted by sentiments of solidarity; industrial families usually played prominent roles in local politics. There were any number of ways to coordinate action, and there were strong motives for doing so, especially where control of subordinate laboring populations was concerned or where reaction to a banking crisis, a slump, or a new machine (all equally viewed as potential disasters) was required.[14]

Enterprises were therefore hybrid institutions, little polities that survived by bringing products to market at competitive prices. A competitor's new machine could be countered temporarily with wage cuts, for example, if one had the necessary political authority over one's workers to convince them to go along peacefully. Power and profit were sought each for its own sake as well as for the sake of the other. The structure of existing institutions, as willed on Europe by the sculptors of the liberal revolution, imposed this symbiosis of power with profit on the established practices of enterprises. By ignoring the personal authority that wealth conferred, liberals created a situation in which the pursuit of personal authority within the enterprise became a competitively imposed necessity for all entrepreneurs.

DISCIPLINE AND HONOR IN THE WORKPLACE

In the context of a laissez-faire social order that innocently treated all monetary exchange as politically neutral, the disciplinary potential of the employer–employee relationship produced the most effective personal authority if employers followed what can best be called police strategies of control. Police strategies are essentially different from military strategies. Police operate on the assumption that they lack the resources to inflict violence on all those in their charge. If the population should ever act in unison against them, they are lost. Effective control arises from the judicious application of violence to selected individuals and from the vigorous pursuit of conspicuous opponents. If there are too many lawbreakers to pursue, then degrees of offense are distinguished (as, for example, between drug dealers and mere drug users), and the more egregious offenses are singled out for attention.

Monetary exchange asymmetries in nineteenth-century enterprises presented entrepreneurs with very similar possibilities and limits. Formally, employers, of course, had no police powers – and this was a marked contrast from the formal situation within guild workshops and rural seigneuries of previous centuries. However, employers' power to hire and discharge, to set wages, to assign tasks, to formulate work rules and fines, were almost unlimited because they arose from the now-unlimited right of property over plant and equipment. These disciplinary tools were like police violence in the sense that they were inadequate if the work force acted in unison. So long as there were conspicuous offenders of limited number, however, these tools could be used to great effect. Moreover, until the very last decades of the century, the state in England, France, and Germany emphatically reinforced entrepreneurs' disciplinary control by outlawing unitary action by laborers.[15] Such action was treated as breach of contract or as monopolistic restraint of trade; liberal principle was invoked to force the laborer to deal with his employer on an individual basis. Individual "freedom" was thus the best guarantee an entrepreneur could have that his limited disciplinary arsenal would suffice to ensure control. If and when he failed, the police were ready to intervene to protect the "freedom of work," as it was called in France. Police and entrepreneurs in close collaboration thus became, in effect, the jailers of hundreds of communities of working people, firm in their belief that they were defenders of liberty.

Under these circumstances notions of honor were likely to emerge as extremely important. Disciplinary measures were meant to shame as much as to inflict privation; summary dismissals or steep fines were, like everything else, imposed, not bargained over. Entrepreneurs justified their discipline by asserting that workers had failed in their duty or betrayed a trust. Those who suffered such shaming were likely to elaborate an alternative concept of honor in their own defense. The laborer on his side confronted a situation in which the weight of disciplinary measures fell most heavily on the first to resist. Those who acted alone were doomed to fail. Those who sought to organize collective action were certain to be punished if identified, if not at once then after the dispute was settled. One less risky method of resistance was sudden, spontaneous unanimity of action, unpremeditated insofar as this was possible. The best alternative was strictly secret organization. Playing upon the sense of honor of one's fellow workers was among the strongest available incitements to action or incentives for secrecy in the absence of institutional or organizational constraints. Honor brooks no compromise; it commands action at a level where other sanctions lose their effect. It was easy to see the whole range of day-to-day disciplinary practices of the employer as shaming and to accept the privations of a prolonged work stoppage or the risks of discharge as proof of one's courage in the face of danger.

Showing courage in the face of danger would, in any case, hardly be a novel activity for laborers accustomed to the nineteenth-century workplace. Hacking at veins of coal, manipulating molten metal, or tending lathes in workrooms packed with unprotected drive shafts and belts brought both men and women constantly into contact with physical danger. Almost everyone was touched sooner or later by fatal or disabling accident, to self, friend, or lover.[16] Layoffs during slumps threatened workers' health in other ways. Hard drinking – so often deplored by well-meaning observers of every political persuasion – was a small risk by comparison to the daily exposure of limbs and organs to mere work itself. That a certain unspoken sense of honor should grow out of this daily combat for survival was inevitable in view of the negligent designs of the employer's very machines, to say nothing of his disciplinary code.

Those laborers who were able to use the possession of skill as an instrument of resistance to the entrepreneur's disciplinary code were likely, as well, to see their hardwon skill and their countercode of honor as integral parts of a single way of life. From this point it was a very short step to begin praising the honor of manual labor in general, whether or not one particularly liked the work one was doing. Such praise could be easily linked to certain elements in the thought of Locke, Adam Smith, or the early utopians which suggested that labor was the source of all that was valuable in life. Here was the starting point for that whole flourishing ideology, the "socialism of skilled workers," which justified and promoted labor organization, which inspired the young Marx, and which dominated European labor movements down to 1890 or so, shaping the thought of Feargus O'Conner, Thomas Hodgskin, Louis Blanc, Pierre-Joseph Proudhon, and Ferdinand Lassalle. The whole gamut of mid-nineteenth-century socialist theorizers and ideologues took the defense of labor's honor as their first principle.[17]

Of course, laborers had brought well-developed notions of honor and work with them into the new workplaces of the nineteenth century. However moribund the guilds had become by 1800, guild traditions remained alive everywhere and set strict limits on the disciplinary innovations entrepreneurs could impose without inciting collective resistance. This was one reason why the decades from 1800 to 1850 were marked by nearly continuous turmoil. A number of episodes of open conflict coordinated on the national and international levels restructured the face of the whole European state system but in general failed to shake the reign of laissez-faire law and doctrine. By 1851, after the dust had settled, it was clear that the laboring poor had suffered a terrible defeat all across the Continent. The possibility seemed dead for the foreseeable future that third parties, in the form of the state or of large collectivities seeking to influence it, might be able to intervene in any significant way in the dyadic relationship between laborer and entrepreneur.

From the laborer's point of view, as the nineteenth century wore on, the workplace became replete with military significance, something like a prisoner-of-war camp in which two contending disciplinary orders confront each other, one formal and explicit, enforced by the employer and his prison guards, one informal and implicit, with no reward or punishment other than the honor or shame before one's fellows resulting from courage or cowardice in the performance of work or in conflicts with authority. Because discharge was the entrepreneur's ultimate tool, those laborers who were most committed to the honor of the struggle for collective goods were likely to spend most of their lives *hors de combat,* unemployed or as barkeepers or peddlers in working-class neighborhoods, where, as veterans of the struggle, they could win loyal clienteles.[18] This was a development unique to the nineteenth century; earlier such persons were forced to flee, forced into social banditry, or forced at least to hide their activities so completely that the eye of the historian misses them.

In keeping with their traditional place in households, women were seldom expected to submit to the danger of leadership roles in the workplace, although loyal support during an open conflict was obligatory, and routinely facing physical danger was demanded as much of women as of men. Women had honor, too, but it was traditionally of a different sort, consisting of fidelity and submission, not of endurance under personal attack. They brought a distinctly different set of expectations from their past into nineteenth-century wage labor and outwork. Their submission to workplace authority, despite some notable exceptions, was perhaps not as fraught with feelings of personal defeat. It is certain that women were less often able to achieve the collective agreement necessary for public expression of such feelings.[19] This is what made their labor so profitable in a laissez-faire context; they could be used in ways which were traditionally forbidden and for which they had no well-developed expectations.

But why did adult male laborers of the nineteenth century feel the need to resist workplace authority in the first place? What rendered it illegitimate in their eyes? Two answers may be cited. The prevailing ideology of freedom, which some laborers brought to the factory with them and which others gradually became aware of, was at many points incompatible with their daily experience, sufficiently incompatible to make possible a generalized sense of grievance. Neither freedom of speech nor freedom of contract was available to them in the workplace, for example. Whether or not they had heard of these new concepts, however, laborers were subject to instabilities unknown to their forebears. In the new laissez-faire environment, enterprises were compelled to join the lockstep forward march of technical innovation as well as to maintain control over laborers at least as good as that of their neighbors. Real competition in product markets would cut them down if they did not. Change was constantly necessary, disrupting each previously agreed-on modus vivendi. The wild swings of the business cycle up to 1851 made the atmosphere of uncertainty even more pronounced. Radical changes repeatedly instituted without advance notice or consultation, imposed with rigid discipline, affecting every aspect of work structure and wage measurement, were bound to spark discontent. When this discontent sought an outlet, it came up against the police-style disciplinary strategies of the entrepreneur, and the contest of honor was the outcome.

The whole history of the European left is saturated with a spirit of military-style honor, which has seldom if ever been subject to systematic reflection or investigation. The rhetoric of resistance is built around core notions of courage and cowardice that are not explicitly discussed. Heroism in the face of the joint power of the employer and the state is held to be the ultimate route to collective salvation. But this theme has remained unexplored in part because, by and large, the left has accepted that capitalism is what it claims to be, a functioning market system, its evil arising from the fact that money is a universal equivalent rather than from the fact that money cannot function as a universal equivalent. The discipline made possible by monetary exchange asymmetries has been visible to all, but utterly neglected in theory. Each laborer is seen as bound in honor, not to defend his or her honor as such, but to struggle for collective marketplace goods: for a better standard of living, for a better bargaining position, for shorter hours of work, for a greater share of surplus value—as if an extra shilling per week could serve as adequate incentive for heroic self-sacrifice. At sufficiently low earning levels, of course, a small increment of pay is a worthy goal of heroism because the bare minimum of personal needs is not being covered. But such wage levels have not prevailed in the industrial core since 1890 or so, at least not for adult males. And all along the more combative laborers have been those who were better paid. Even where low wages do prevail, however, defense of honor (not of interest) is necessary precisely because the negative marginal utility of money and the authority created by monetary exchange asymmetries render the language of "self-interest" and "preference" tendentiously imprecise. Honor remains at stake, as well, even when wages are high. One struggles, one does not merely bargain (even if negotiations play a role), to impose or to "win" through voluntary solidarity (not to "sell" the employer) a wage increase so that one's self-respect and one's survival can be jointly assured. Yet many on the left continue to think of these matters in terms of the market model, in terms of numerically measurable trade-offs, bids and counterbids; and the theme of honor that has cemented the working-class movement together from the beginning is passed over in silence. It is something too obvious to need discussion. It is passed on as a central ingredient in hundreds of strike and union organizing stories without ever being named.

More will be said of this tragic oversight in the Conclusion. What remains to be accomplished in this chapter is a careful exploration of two incidents of conflict that will give depth to the general claims that have so far been made. The incidents have been chosen specifically to show the roles that confrontation, spontaneity, heroism, and symbolic gesture played in nineteenth-century social protest, to show how these facets of protest were linked to the police-style discipline that was exercised through monetary exchange asymmetries, and to show how these terms of conflict were obscured as all parties gradually came under the sway of the liberal illusion. Comparing incidents from Silesia in 1844 and Lancashire in 1853–54 – the former a region where manorial institutions and protoindustrial production survived, the latter a center of the most advanced mechanized industry in Europe – allows one to see the underlying continuity of structures of discipline and codes of honor as "capitalism" emerged, as well as the role of liberal reform and liberal thought in obscuring the significance of discipline and honor in the new social order.

THE BEGINNING AND END POINTS OF MODERNIZATION

Silesia and Lancashire: Two regions of mid-nineteenth-century Europe could not have been more different, one completely rural, the other robustly urban; one only barely emerging from feudalism, the other harboring the most advanced form of industrial capitalism known to the world at that time; one ruled by the king of Prussia, an absolute monarch, unrepentantly clinging to his prerogatives, the other under a parliamentary regime with a wide suffrage; one governed by a centralized bureaucratic administration, the other allowing the most decentralized forms of local government to hold sway.

The two episodes of protest under examination were also starkly different in form. The Preston strike (object of a recent, intensive study by H. I. Dutton and J. E. King) was organized with the explicit, limited intention of winning a 10 percent wage increase; any suggestion of ulterior political aims was vigorously rejected by its leaders.[20] The laborers were calm throughout the course of the shutdown, which lasted seven months, from 15 October 1853 to 14 May 1854. At its height in early November the action involved forty-seven thousand operatives and 183 mills in five towns. The seventeen thousand strikers in Preston proper received roughly £105,000 in contributions to their strike fund, mostly from cotton-mill operatives in the rest of Lancashire; the strike committees distributed this money to the strikers in weekly relief payments of from four to seven shillings and even published their accounts at the end of each week.[21] Preston became the locus of conflict because, by common accord, Lancashire cotton workers recognized that Preston wages were low; if they were not soon equalized with prevailing wage levels in the rest of Lancashire, then mill owners in other towns would have good reason to revoke their own recent pay increases. This was the motive behind the generous contributions that flowed in from other towns. In other words, an explicit and widely accepted assumption that market

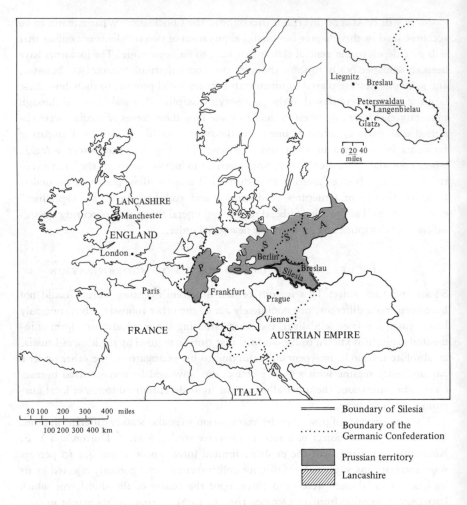

Figure 2. Europe in 1840, showing locations of Lancashire and Silesia. Inset shows villages of Peterswaldau and Langenbielau in relation to Breslau in central Silesia.

forces were in play lay behind the Preston action. Mill owners likewise justified their refusal of the wage demands by appealing to the threat of competition. They, along with most of the press and the home secretary, explained repeatedly to the strikers that neither owners nor laborers could affect the price of labor any more than they could control the direction of the wind.

During the course of the strike, as if in answer to this argument, efforts were made by strike leaders to move laborers out of Preston. Money was made available in the fall of 1853 to any family wishing to move to nearby Blackburn, where the mills were still working. By the spring, strike committees were offering to pay ship's passage for any family wishing to emigrate to America. Here was conscious manipulation of the labor market with a vengeance.

The strike ended soon after the outbreak of the Crimean War. Trade became unsettled; cotton sales had slumped over the winter anyway. Demand for labor was no longer deemed sufficiently high, so the strike was broken off. At first glance nothing could be more straightforward than the Preston strike: It was a market maneuver motivated by the enlightened self-interest of hundreds of thousands of Lancashire operatives who either participated or contributed money in the hope of increasing their earnings or at least keeping wages at current levels. The strike was a failure because the balance of supply and demand shifted against the strikers. Mill owners had begun bringing in strikebreakers in considerable number by March – all willing to work at current wages. And the declaration of war disrupted markets enough to convince the strikers that their cause was hopeless.

Like the verdicts of historians since that time, contemporary reaction in England to the Preston strike followed just this view of the matter. In fact, the political impact of the strike on the national scene, despite its long duration and the great numbers involved, was almost nil, and historians have shown very little interest in it since. But then, this is exactly what one would expect. In a modernized industrial society, purely economic dealings between private parties should not arouse public concern or require political intervention. The home secretary, Palmerston, pointedly took no action in the Preston affair. In the early weeks of the strike he received a petition from the weavers' strike committee asking him to mediate the conflict, but he failed to give an answer for over four weeks. His response when it finally came consisted of a highly condescending lecture on political economy coupled with a suggestion that the operatives give up their strike.[22] Dutton and King, in their extensive research of the Preston strike, found that almost no discussion of the event occurred in Parliament. It was covered regularly by the national press; the *Times* followed its unfolding, occasionally urging both masters and operatives to give up their obstinate behavior. Dickens published a firsthand report in *Household Words*. But soon after its end the strike was forgotten. The Webbs in their pathbreaking history of trade unionism said next to nothing about it; the 1850s, in their view, "are, for the historian of the general Trade Union Movement, almost a blank."[23] Until Dutton and King's recent study, upon which this discussion entirely rests, the Webbs' comment remained the common wisdom. English society was, in just these years, settling down from the stormy spring of early industrialization, of Luddism and Chartism, into the calm summer of a mid-Victorian consensus. The popular movement on the national level had suffered a final crippling defeat in 1848. Preston disturbed no one because it fit the pattern of a now unchallenged national consensus; all parties to the struggle accepted the basic tenets of political economy, differing only in their applications of its principles to the current state of trade.

The Silesian weaver uprising, by contrast, was a minor affair lasting only three days and involved at its greatest extent no more than six thousand persons. Four or five warehouses of merchant-manufacturers were pillaged, along with their adjoining dwellings.[24] The episode began with a parade of weavers marching before the warehouse of a merchant-manufacturer named Zwanziger in the village of Peterswaldau, singing an improvised song filled with derogatory remarks about Zwanziger and several of his colleagues. Zwanziger sent his servants out to catch one of the weavers; the servants took a young weaver inside and later turned him over to the police. The weavers came back the following day, 4 June 1844, bent on revenge; they attacked the building, did considerable damage, and then moved on to another merchant-manufacturer's warehouse late in the afternoon. The following day they attacked a third warehouse in neighboring Langenbielau, and during the course of this attack a small contingent of troops opened fire on the crowd, killing eleven and wounding at least twenty-four others seriously. By the evening of the fifth, both villages were occupied by Prussian troops. On the sixth there were a few more scattered incidents at outlying locations. About one hundred persons were arrested within a few days; eighty of them later received stiff prison sentences. The whole thing was over almost as soon as it began.

The Silesian weavers' action, despite its limited extent and short duration, caused an immediate sensation throughout Germany. This, too, was understandable. In a traditional society experiencing the first pangs of modernization, signs of the breakdown of old reciprocities and old deference and obedience should attract the greatest attention. Germany then stood before the great watershed of 1848; until the 1840s Germany had remained comparatively free of violent popular agitation. The *Kölnische Zeitung* of 23 June 1844 spoke for many when it ominously concluded, "This riot is a manifestation of the proletariat, which here repeats on a smaller scale scenes which we have long learned to expect from other countries."[25] Relief measures for the weavers were necessary, said the same paper in its 18 June issue; the government should not stand in the way of the "necessary struggle against the rising proletariat."[26] Werner Conze has called the Silesian uprising the highpoint of the spreading unrest of the 1840s that gave witness to contemporaries that Germany now suffered from the terrible English disease, "pauperism." What was to prevent the country from falling victim to the even worse French affliction, revolution? The new resonances added to the old term "proletariat" in these years summed up the anxieties of German public opinion.[27] Population growth was causing widespread unemployment; excess country youths were flooding the towns; early marriage, idleness, crime, and drink were everywhere. The old orderly society of estates was breaking down. But the Silesian incident was particularly frightening because it brought to public attention a large population of normally orderly, hardworking people who had stayed in the country working fourteen-hour days, managing their affairs with care, and who still fell into extreme poverty.[28]

Certain high government officials in Breslau tried to blame the troubles in Silesia on the press; its seems that several investigative pieces had appeared on the spreading misery in the weaving districts before the uprising occurred. But (again the *Kölnische Zeitung*) "hunger can neither be excited nor satisfied by mere words."[29] Wilhelm Wolff saw the same basic motive behind the disturbance. He noted that when weavers besieged the warehouse of F. W. Fellmann in Peterswaldau on the first day of trouble, Fellmann was able to save his property by offering the crowd money and bread and butter: "A piece of bread and a four-groschen coin were enough to hold at bay the rage of those driven forward by hunger and vengeance!"[30] However complex the nature of the problem or of its solution, the motive of the weavers was widely deemed to be painfully simple, their predicament woefully clear. A rootless wage-earning proletariat was in formation, and its wages were too low. Without higher earnings, many weavers could not be expected to survive. "In any civilized land in our part of the world, there is a certain minimum of needs for each human being," said Alexander Schneer, a Breslau official and author of the most important of these investigations, "and when these needs are not met, real destitution and misery are at hand."[31] Schneer associated this minimum with the standard of consumption of prisoners in Prussian houses of correction. "More than a small number of the inhabitants of the province that is called the pearl in the Prussian crown [Silesia] live materially far worse than those confined to our prisons."[32]

Schneer's concern with a precise definition of subsistence arose from his familiarity with the investigative literature on poverty coming out of England and France. He appears to have looked upon Louis Villermé's massive study of French textile workers as a kind of model, although he found no easy way to transfer Villermé's methods to Silesia.[33] Villermé had everywhere been concerned with average incomes and living standards.[34] In Silesia averages were meaningless because the complex surviving feudal regime conferred a very different meaning on a given wage level, depending on the exact number of feudal dues one owed. Schneer resorted to providing specific examples. He gave the exact names and addresses of some twenty families in several villages of the weaving district, providing a complete rundown of incomes, dues, taxes, and consumption standards for each one.[35] The level of misery was indeed impressive, although it appears that Schneer in his investigative travels had asked village officials to show him the poorest families. Averages aside, Schneer's evidence of widespread impoverishment despite hard, unremitting work at loom and reel was crushing, and the implications were frightening. The mismatch between merchants' profits and laborers' wages was, Schneer concluded, "the underlying ground of those woes from which our society suffers, the mischievous cancer from which it sickens; it is likewise the most threatening feature of our time."[36]

In Lancashire investigations of the proletariat were already an outmoded fashion by the time of the Preston strike in 1853–54. (Engel's famous *Condition of the Working Class in England in 1844,* written at the very time of the Silesian uprising, was partly modeled on an already well-established literature on Lancashire factory towns going back to the 1820s.)[37] The Preston strike inspired no one with a need to investigate further. In Silesia, however, Schneer's tour of inspection in the spring of 1844 was an unprecedented affair and may well have played a role, as his enemies intimated, in sparking a new self-consciousness among the weavers. Schneer visited over fifty villages during May and was in the area of Peterswaldau only eight days before the riots began, asking questions and visiting cottages.[38] His imitation of investigative methods pioneered further west led him to a parallel conclusion: Unregulated trade kept workers at the edge of subsistence.

Present-day historical evaluation of the Silesian uprising, although agreeing in part with this contemporary consensus, would nonetheless modify it in a number of important respects. The weavers' action was a manifestation not so much of the rising proletariat as of the contradictions involved in the peculiar "Prussian way" through the transition from feudalism to capitalism. Helmut Bleiber's study of Silesia in this period rightly emphasizes (and carefully documents) the uneven character of the relation between feudal (that is, manorial) and capitalist relations there.[39] According to his thesis, the particular contradiction in which the weavers were caught is that they were being treated both as serfs and as proletarians at the same time. This requires some explanation.

Like other Prussian serfs the rural inhabitants of Silesia had been made personally free in 1810, but their property holdings remained subject to most of the labor and money dues that had previously attached to their persons. The edicts designed to allow for dissolution of these feudal dues through money payments or the ceding of land to the lord had been much reduced in their application in Silesia. Feudal dues in Silesia had slightly different forms and often different names from those common in the other eastern provinces. Silesian Junkers argued successfully that the edicts did not apply to these special forms, since they were not mentioned in the texts of the new laws.[40] As in the rest of the east, there was little capital available to the peasants to help them buy their way out of feudal dues even where the law allowed it; the amounts of money or land to be paid by the peasants in such buy-outs were set in the first instance in local courts whose judges were picked by the local Junker. Appeals were handled by officials easily subject to Junker influence. In law, buy-outs were supposed to require ceding no more than half the land; but in practice, a piece of land in Silesia that had ben fully freed of feudal dues sold for as much as ten times the price it would have fetched before being freed.[41]

The inhabitants of Silesia in 1844 were in a social position in some respects comparable to that of French peasants on the eve of the Revolution. Personally free, they found their plots of land burdened with, in practice, unredeemable feudal dues payable in money, in kind, or in labor. In general these were much heavier than the French equivalents had been, however. Personal freedom since 1807 and the spread of protoindustrialization had encouraged early marriage, rapid population growth, and the subdivision of plots. Most of the weavers belonged to the rapidly growing feudal categories known as *Häusler* and *Einlieger*.[42] A *Häusler* "owned" a house and small garden (up to an acre, often much smaller) on which money and service dues were owed the lord. Einlieger "rented" their cottages but still owed certain feudal money dues and, like everyone else, paid stiff regressive state and local taxes. Feudal dues came in an extraordinary variety of forms, including the basic *Handdiensttage*, manual labor days; *Jagdgeld*, a money due to keep the lord from hunting on one's plot; *Spinngeld*, a money due for using a spinning wheel; *Weberzins*, a money due for using a loom; and *Schutzgeld*, a money due to compensate the lord for costs in case one were arrested and imprisoned at his expense. *Laudemium* (the equivalent of the French *lods et ventes*) was a 10 percent levy on any land transaction whether or not the land had been freed of other dues through a buy-out; *Grundzins* (the equivalent of the French *cens*) was a money due payable yearly on all land within the estate, owned or rented (again, whether or not it was free of other dues). These were the most common feudal dues, but there were many others. Bleiber provides colorful lists of such dues, most named for agricultural tasks once performed by serfs that had been commuted to money payments. (He also provides long lists of old use rights that were under attack, most important being the right to glean wood from the lord's forests in the winter.)[43] These dues all applied somewhere, some applied almost everywhere, none applied everywhere. Therefore, as already mentioned, it is impossible to make generalizations about average burdens; in any village amounts due would vary considerably from house to house.

Population growth in the weaving districts ensured that land for garden plots became increasingly rare; for many, feudal dues and all other expenses and needs had to be met out of income from weaving. When the linen industry hit hard times in the 1840s, therefore, and the potato crop began to suffer from a new blight, thousands of weavers – in an uneven and spotty manner – began to fall into the worst destitution. According to one estimate, current income for even the well-provided Häusler weaving family was only three times the sum required to meet feudal dues and taxes.[44] These obligations were fixed, moreover, so the slightest downward pressure on income was felt disproportionately in the funds available for subsistence. Obviously, by the summer of 1844 some weavers could no longer even meet their dues and taxes from current income, much less subsist – but how many were in this predicament is virtually impossible to know because of the patchwork character of the surviving manorial regime.

Therefore the Silesian weavers could not be considered a proletariat in the strict sense of an industrial wage-earning class reduced by job competition to a subsistence-level wage. In Silesia a subsistence-level wage would have been markedly different for each household. In addition, competition for jobs was muted by immobility. In law inhabitants had been free to move since the abolition of serfdom; in practice debts to shopkeepers, bakers, innkeepers, and merchant-manufacturers impeded movement. Those Häusler who still clung to half-acre gardens could not afford to leave. In addition, Junkers contrived to impede mobility by demanding certificates of morality from anyone who moved to a new estate. For a Junker to prevent someone from leaving his own estate, therefore, he had only to deny him such a certificate. Several observers remarked that Silesian weavers, in any case, seldom knew what was going on in the next valley, not to speak of employment opportunities in Breslau or Berlin.[45] There was no labor market in this still-feudal society and no price-clearing mechanism for setting wages. Many wages, as Schneer shows, were well below the level of subsistence (however defined) in the spring of 1844. Some weavers made use of their gardens, some turned to field work (those strong enough to do it), a few got help from the village relief fund, others starved.

Bleiber and other East German historians have rightly emphasized the special features of the Prussian transition from feudalism to capitalism.[46] Feudal, or manorial, dues continued to be payable throughout the eastern provinces even as the population shifted to industrial and wage labor for its principal source of income, and even as the Junkers turned to sophisticated new farming techniques to maximize yields on their demesnes. It is indeed odd when viewed from a Western European perspective that these specific feudal and capitalist social features should have coexisted side by side for fifty years into the nineteenth century. But there is nothing odd in general about the coexistence of "feudal" and "capitalist" elements; they could be found together in various mixes at various times and places throughout medieval and early modern Europe. Their peculiar coexistence in France is central to Barrington Moore's interpretation of the Revolution, for example. What was unusual about Prussia was the specific mix: The advance of capitalist rationality among Junker farmers and the spread of wage labor and domestic industry among the poor appear strange alongside the continuation of direct expropriation of both labor and money through manorial dues.

The weavers of the swollen manufacturing villages of Peterswaldau (with about six thousand inhabitants) and Langenbielau (with roughly twelve thousand) were caught between the scissors of a wage declining because of competition in international trade and fixed feudal dues still owing to their former overlords (in spite of their de jure personal freedom). They responded with an unpremeditated collective outburst.

No historian would argue today, as did the *Kölnische Zeitung* and Wilhelm Wolff, that the weavers were moved purely by hunger. Social history is beyond the point of seeing any collective action as blind or random.[47] The weavers methodically destroyed the wares, account books, and expensive furnishings of the *parvenu* merchant-manufacturers. They did not attack bread shops or do violence to persons; their interests were highly selective, their efforts well focused and coordinated. They were respectful, even submissive, to all officials who addressed them. At the same time, in order to get at the house of Dierig and Sons in Langenbielau and to wreak their notion of justice upon it, the weavers braved the fire of Prussian troops, suffering heavy casualties. They drove the armed soldiers off with stones. This was obviously a prepolitical movement; an almost biblical sense of justice spurred the crowds forward. Like the peasant uprisings of the sixteenth and seventeenth centuries, or the food riots of the eighteenth century, this weaver uprising had nothing in common with modern, politically conscious popular action of the kind so well represented by the Preston strike. It lay at the opposite pole from the rational, self-interested, deliberate withholding of labor engaged in by Preston mill operatives nine years later. Or so the standard wisdom on the history of popular political action would have it.[48]

Lancashire was in a modernized industrial society; the Preston strike reflected its individualistic, market-oriented structure. Silesia was in the first throes of a painful, hesitant transition from feudalism to modernity; the weavers' uprising broke out at the fault line where modern market pressures came into conflict with the old, feudal modes of exaction and standards of reciprocity. The merchant-manufacturers were doubtless attacked rather than the Junkers precisely because they readily lowered wages to starvation levels during a business downturn without the slightest paternalistic compunction, without any admixture of noble concern for the villeins' well-being. They symbolized modernity in a still-feudal social order. The strong reaction of public opinion to events in Silesia was therefore justified. These events were a sign of the times and an ominous precursor of the revolution that came four years later. Histories of Germany in this period almost inevitably mention Silesia in this context.[49]

Both the Preston strike and the Silesian riots served as the subject of well-known literary works. Preston provided the background for Dickens's *Hard Times,* Silesia the setting for Gerhart Hauptmann's *The Weavers.* Here as well the differences between the two events carry through. Dickens's broad and brilliant caricature of political economy and of the society that it spawned in the industrial North has only the loosest relationship with events in Preston. Few have ever felt the need to investigate the strike closely in order to come to a better understanding of the novel. Dickens's object was a whole social and political order; he spent barely forty-eight hours in Preston before writing it.[50] Hauptmann's 1893 play, however, aspires to be a genuine historical reconstruction. In recent years it has twice been republished along with extensive collections of original documents because study of the documents greatly enhances one's understanding of the multitude of facts and allusions that Hauptmann incorporated into the play.[51] Of course, he too aimed to indict a whole social order, that of his own Wilhelmine Germany; but since censorship continued there, Hauptmann hoped to evade it by sticking to the facts of a real historical incident whose implications no one could ignore.

As one contemporary review of Hauptmann's play remarked, "The author claims that his drama takes place in the 1840s in the location of the Eulengebirge. He is in error. It takes place – overlooking a few details – in the year 1890."[52] Hauptmann's depiction of the subjection of weavers to the power of the merchant-manufacturers had in fact too many obvious contemporary references to escape notice. Performance of the play was, after a celebrated court battle, outlawed. The different manners in which Dickens and Hauptmann went about using these two events reflect not only the impact of censorship, however. They reflect as well the very different places the two events held in the history of the respective countries. Preston's was a typical strike, part of a "blank" landscape, to which a novelist could turn – at random, as it were – for inspiration in creating his own characteristic portrait of a world. Silesia's was a signal event that could not be approached without the deepest respect for the documents; the slightest distortion would invite attack or incite misunderstanding. (It is a measure of Hauptmann's achievement that his play now virtually overshadows the event itself.)

On whatever level one looks – the material, the commercial, the social, the political, the cultural, or even the literary – the vivid contrasts between Peterswaldau and Preston stand out. Apart from their common dependence on international trade in textile goods (on which more will be said later), what do these two events have in common? Any conventional social historical account would put these two episodes of protest at opposite ends of the long and difficult road from premodern to fully modern social conflict. Silesia had barely begun the trek; Preston had finished it.

HONOR AND THE AVERAGE WAGE IN PRESTON

However, the facts may be construed in a different manner. Doing so makes it possible to tell a tale about the transition from premodern to industrial society quite different from the versions that are commonly told. By looking at the subtle interplay between coercion and exchange asymmetries, both monetary and nonmonetary, in these two regions it is possible to appreciate that the differences separating them were less marked than is normally imagined. For Preston, Dutton and King's superb narrative carefully brings out those elements of the struggle that bore little or no relationship to the expectations of political economy. Their constant attention to the political facets of the strike makes it a simple matter to reinterpret this event according to the argument of the present study.

Prevailing wages in Preston in 1853 were said to be low for Lancashire, 20 percent below the benchmark Oldham wage level.[53] This differential was of long standing. Dutton and King came across several explanations for it in the records. Preston's location was one: "Situated on the edge of the Fylde, Lancashire's main agricultural district, local manufacturers were provided with an abundant supply of cheap labor which kept wages down."[54] Elsewhere low wages were blamed on the character of the mill owners: " 'The cotton lords of Preston,' said Ashton Chartist Alexander Challenger in 1842, 'are the greatest tyrants in the country. It is well known that they grind their workmen down more than any other persons, getting their work done cheaper.' " Others blamed the "docility and willingness to tolerate low pay" of the operatives; indeed, Dutton and King conclude that the Preston operatives' "shameful reputation" for accepting low pay "exerted a significant influence" on their decision to strike in 1853.[55]

Stockport, another Lancashire mill town with a reputation for low wages, had struck successfully for a 10 percent increase in the summer of 1853. This was the immediate spur to Preston. At Stockport, too, shame was a central theme at the meeting where the decision to strike was made. Trade was flourishing, it was said;

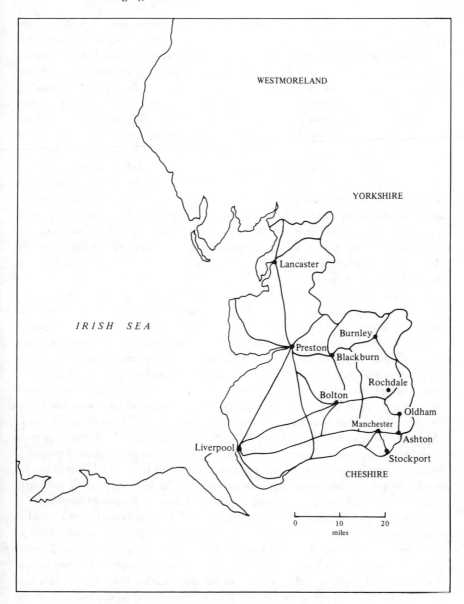

Figure 3. Lancashire, showing principal rail lines established by 1860

Stockport wages were 10 to 15 percent behind those of other towns. "At present the position of Stockport has retarded the advance of other towns," said one speaker. Another went further; Stockport had "stained itself among the list of manufacturing towns because it was paying the lowest rate of wages." At the meeting Stockport weavers agreed to "throw off the stain of reproach" by pushing for wage increases.[56] Within a few weeks they had won their demands. Preston operatives similarly, when they went on strike, adopted a slogan redolent with notions of honor and of valiant combat: "Ten Percent and No Surrender!" was their battle cry. Faced with the threat of a general lockout, the weavers heard their principal leader, George Cowell, tell them on 22 September that they would fight despite reports that "the workpeople of Preston are more chicken-hearted, more humble and docile, more flexible to the wishes of their masters than the workpeople of any other district." No longer would anyone be able to say that they were "the most rotten portion of the operative community."[57] It appears that some notion of collective honor was at work in Lancashire towns and that this notion was firmly attached to the idea of not letting oneself be cheated in the marketplace. Lancashire operatives felt a duty to their fellows to get all they could for themselves.

That town honor was an important issue suggests as well that labor may have been less than perfectly mobile in the Lancashire market. Preston's wages could not have been significantly lower than other towns' for a long period unless many people tended to stay in a particular town for life. How else could Preston's position near a farming region have been an advantage? Lancashire is not large; from Blackpool in the north to Manchester in the south is no more than thirty miles, a two-day walk on foot. Michael Anderson reports that most migration in Lancashire in that period "was of short distance only," even though twenty-mile walks in a day were readily undertaken for purposes of visiting. He found that 69 percent of Preston inhabitants in 1851 were born within ten miles of Preston. Only 12 percent were migrants from other Lancashire towns, a figure that Anderson interprets as resulting from extremely painful moves in search of work during depressions in the cotton trade. In other words, people did not move from town to town in good times looking for better wages because local kin and friendship networks were too important to survival.[58] Laborers moved so infrequently that 20 percent wage differentials could be sustained between communities no more than an hour or two from each other by train. Even in 1853 Preston operatives did not demand Oldham rates, only a 10 percent increase over their own rates, up to a level still below those of many much-closer towns, among them Blackburn, only six miles to the east. Rather than moving to a new town (moving the supply to the demand), they were willing to stay out of work for seven months, living on meager strike benefits, to win an increase that the next shift in the winds of trade might take back. (In effect, the next shift occurred before the strike was over.)

Perhaps these interurban wage differences could be accounted for by cost-of-living differences? If so, the operatives, their leaders, the mill owners, and the press were all completely blinded by money wages; even the strike's most determined opponents, whose learned arguments based on political economy appeared daily in the newspapers, failed to mention cost-of-living differences as a cause of wage differences. Preston mill owners explained the wage differences by citing the variety of machinery and production methods used in the industry – without explaining what relevance these things should have to the price of labor.[59] It is easy to guess why the owners were sidetracked into discussing equipment when trying to account for wage differentials. All adult male wages in Lancashire were paid on a piece-rate basis; the exact nature of the machinery therefore had a direct effect on the operatives' ability to earn money, as did anything that influenced their day-to-day performance. Recent investigations of these factors show that output was anything but predictable; earnings probably varied widely – 30 percent or more – from one operative to the next and from one week to the next.[60] The whole discussion of townwide averages was highly abstract for the individual operative. His situation may not have been so very different in this respect from that of the Silesian weaver subject to feudal dues. The importance of averages in Lancashire was that they made it possible to construct an estimate of the market price of labor – an item deemed to be of the highest significance by all, because theory said it was. The idea of the average wage was well suited to serve as a barometer of collective honor and shame in a society that granted such high prestige to the concept of the free market. Lancashire activists were well aware, in the aftermath of the defeat of Chartism, that the appeal of an issue like average wage level arose in no small degree from its apparently concrete, here-and-now character in contrast to the vast and vague hopes that had been attached to the People's Charter in the 1830s and 1840s. The strategy of making the town average wage into a point of honor proved capable of bridging the gap between the lived experience of workplace discipline and the prevailing doctrines of the liberal illusion. Fighting over wages could not be construed as a threat to the established order, yet it allowed a response to that sense of submission and shame which factory life generated. A space was discovered within which struggle was possible for concrete realizable goals that did not immediately provoke coercive state intervention.

The wage demand was nothing more than a shrewdly chosen pretext for fighting over deeper issues. Ostentatious market maneuvers made during the strike were likewise little more than elaborate bluffs. Although the strike committees offered to pay transportation for anyone leaving town during the strike, there were apparently too few takers to have any effect on the situation.[61] Dutton and King remain uncertain about the real purpose of the emigration offer: "Was it simply a tactical ploy designed to frighten the masters (in which it evidently succeeded)? . . . Or did it imply an unspoken belief that wages were after all dependent on supply and demand . . . ? . . . Perhaps [the weavers' delegates] themselves did not know."[62] The mill owners' efforts to bring in new laborers from outside the town were also rather unsuccessful – unless of course they, too, were only trying to frighten their striking employees. When the lockout was lifted in early February, almost no one returned to work; it was at that point that some firms began recruiting outside Preston, first in Manchester, then in Belfast, where 141 were hired out of the workhouse about the first of March. Workhouses in Yorkshire and Bradford were soon being scoured for candidates. The *Preston Guardian* predicted that "such unfortunates" would not be much good to their new masters.[63] The prediction was an accurate one:

> Birly Brothers sent a batch of hands back to Hull because they were (presumably by accident) damaging the machinery. There were reports of a strike at Horrockses of Irish knobsticks [strikebreakers] dissatisfied with the food provided for them. Richard Eccles had to dismiss two girls, said to be "abandoned characters" from Wapping, for their "wanton conduct in the mill," while wretched Richard Threlfall was forced by the magistrates to repatriate an Irish woman sacked when the remainder of his hands refused to work with her.

By the middle of March most of the mills remained closed.[64] The masters did not succeed in breaking the strike until local laborers began coming back to the mills.

There is considerable evidence, in other words, that market maneuvers in Preston were taken not for their own sake but only as gestures that were part of a larger code of combat. Demanding a wage increase was a point of honor, financing emigration a ploy, bringing strikebreakers from out of town a counterploy. Dutton and King do not believe that the strike was actually about wages at all; and they have an abundance of explicit statements to back this view from central actors on both sides of the conflict. Thirty-five firms signed a manifesto on 15 September announcing their intention to lock out the operatives one month hence if they did not give up their wage demands. The reason cited was the "spirit of tyranny and dictation" that inspired the operatives' leaders, who were "a designing and irresponsible body" of outsiders determined to foster "a feeling of dissatisfaction and estrangement" among the operatives. These outsiders, "having no connection with this town, nor settled position anywhere," wished to "arrogate to themselves the right to determine, and dictate to the operatives the means of enforcing conditions under which they shall be PERMITTED to labor."[65] To these charges George Cowell, principal leader of the weavers' committee (and a native of Preston), replied that trade was prosperous and that therefore "the masters have no excuse for resisting, save that they are not going to be beaten by the weavers. This is the whole of their argument, and it is now a struggle between Capital and Labor."[66] Mortimer Grimshaw, the only prominent out-of-towner on the operatives' side, a former weaver (whom no one would now hire) and well-known Lancashire orator, riposted in March in a speech to several thousand strikers:

> We have no desire whatever to manage or control the affairs of the employers. All we want is the right to live by our labor, to be paid that which is our due, to enter the mills free men and women, so long as we are prepared to do our duty as work people. What we claim is the right to be masters of ourselves, to resist all petty tyranny and oppression, to hold the right of private judgment, and to speak the free sentiment of our minds. And so far we intend to be masters.[67]

Cheering interrupted Grimshaw at this point.

Throughout the strike both sides insisted that they were resisting tyranny. The workers, their leaders repeatedly told them, were "factory slaves" in a state of "Egyptian bondage."[68] The masters regretted most of all the "alienation of . . . kindly sentiments of mutual regard" caused by "the tyranny and machinery of secret combination" of the operatives' leaders.[69] Was all this merely the rhetorical bluster of a period of crisis, from people whose eyes were really fixed on their pocketbooks? The question of "mastership," as Cowell called it, cannot be so easily dismissed.

Most of the forty-odd mill owners and their families lived within a few meters of fashionable Winkley Square in the center of town; they met regularly at the Literary and Philosophical Institution, the Winkley Club House, the Gentlemen's News Room, and the Theatre. In 1853 eighteen out of thirty-six town councillors were mill owners, as were five of twelve aldermen, eleven of nineteen magistrates, and four justices of the peace; so too were twelve of the eighteen mayors who served between 1836 and 1853.[70] In Silesia Junkers were given control of the police and local courts by law; in Preston the same effect was achieved informally by common accord without the intervention of central government. Mill ownership all by itself conferred sufficient political power to ensure a near monopoly of important offices. After all, other enfranchised property owners depended on the goodwill of mill owners for their own hopes of business success and admired them as examples of what success looked like. A rough ranking of persons in prestige and honor closely matched the ranking of firms by size. It was considered odd, for example, that the greatest mill owner of all, Thomas Miller, had never served as mayor. He was offered the post in 1845 but declined it. The following year he indicated a willingness to accept but was passed over for someone else; deeply offended, he swore never to take the job and stuck to his word, refusing a number of subsequent offers.[71] Miller was evidently used to getting his way. Even without office, he had great influence. After the strike certain strike leaders under indictments of conspiracy turned to him (not to the magistrates or the mayor) to have the charges dropped. And he arranged it within a few hours.[72] What Prussian Junker could have asked for more? Or what French seigneur of the ancien régime, for that matter?

Inside the mills the owners' power was both palpable and direct. When Grimshaw said that operatives wished to "hold the right of private judgment and to speak the free sentiments of our own minds," he was not inventing false issues. From the very first moment that a strike proposal was broached in the town, plans were also made to provide for those who would certainly be blacklisted during the conflict. Leaders were to be chosen, as much as possible, among persons not currently employed (hence the owners' charge that they were outsiders). A project was also launched to find money for a cooperative mill; one or two other such cooperatives full of blacklisted workers existed, but in the end sufficient sources of capital were not found in Preston.[73] Dutton and King speculate that the emigration fund was partially intended to make up for the failure of the cooperative project. They have, in addition, been able to confirm that Preston mill owners secretly established a blacklisting procedure in the summer of 1853, when the first signs of trouble appeared. This was common Lancashire practice. Before the lockout began at least three delegates were dismissed and two operatives collecting money for the strike fund were arrested for "begging" at Horrockses and Miller (the largest Preston mill, wholly owned by Thomas Miller). After the strike at least five hundred operatives were not rehired, doubtless not simply for want of "demand."[74] No relief fund was available then to help them. By June, however, once the operatives had been thoroughly overpowered, the owners eased their stance. It was then that Miller agreed to have conspiracy charges against the strike leaders dropped; he also announced a 5 percent wage increase — as if to demonstrate to his workers that sheepishness would go further with him than independence and to prove simultaneously that the price of labor was subject to the unpredictable fluctuation of supply and demand. When Miller informed the former leaders of his employees that conspiracy charges had indeed been dropped, he "complimented them on the good feeling which now prevailed between masters and men."[75] Doubtless no one in Preston dared at that point to "speak the free sentiments of our minds" in response to such a view; but there can be little doubt that many minds hid sentiments that could not be described as "good feeling."

Dutton and King have presented abundant evidence that the strike was a struggle for honor and independence against a powerful and overbearing set of mill owners. What they say of the peculiar position of women within this conflict confirms, as well, that workplace honor was a masculine issue, one in which women were expected to feel a vicarious involvement only. Although women represented a strong majority of those on strike, over two-thirds, there were no women in leadership roles, and women rarely spoke up at meetings or worked to collect money. One exception was Margaret Fletcher, who told the strikers in November 1853 that "it is a disgrace to an Englishman to allow his wife to go out to work." That women worked at all was made into an issue of male honor. Women struck, according to Mrs. Fletcher, to raise their husbands' wages.[76]

Those already familiar with large strikes of the nineteenth century may not find any of these details particularly surprising. But this in itself is extremely significant. It is instructive to compare the Preston strike to a free bargain as it is struck in an open market with full information. Traders on the floor of a commodity exchange, for example, do not waste time making speeches to each other about honor, tyranny, personal freedom, or "kindly sentiments of mutual regard." Deals are closed or refused on the basis of the exchange of a few proposed numbers, an operation that can be accomplished in seconds in a noisy hall with no more than a few simple hand gestures. Obviously this is not how labor services were traded in Lancashire, however "modernized" it may have been by 1853. Instead, mill owners, because of their ownership of extensive capital, were able to look with indifference on the outcome of any particular deal struck with a propertyless laborer. However good the laborer was with a power loom or a mule jenny, he could be fired forthwith if he breathed a word against his "master" or in favor of a strike. If he chose to refuse a wage offered him, however reasonable his counteroffer, he could be dispensed with easily and painlessly. The laborer might endure hardship as a result, but the mill owner's comfortable home in Winkley Square would not disappear. The laborer, with his pressing need to get and quickly spend money, was constrained to trade off not just labor but personal autonomy.

In the prevailing ideology of nineteenth-century England, owners and laborers alike were supposedly free individuals who had many of the same freedoms and rights: freedom of speech and of religion, freedom from arbitrary arrest, the right to trial by a jury of one's peers, the right to dispose of self and property without limit. But this list of rights did not generate an internally consistent social order; and conflict was bound to break out at the points of contradiction. Laborers were bound to see the owners as infringing on their rights and vice versa. Moreover, the laborers were correct; the property rights of the owners did in fact give them the opportunity to achieve, by the judicious use of police-style disciplinary strategies, the subjugation of a whole working community to their will; to exact the expression of "good feeling" from persons whose genuine sentiments were quite different; to prevent or inhibit untrammeled reflection (for it is very difficult to act one way and to feel another forever). Because common laborers were aware that they enjoyed extensive paper freedoms and because police-style use of the power to fine or dismiss was somewhat less daunting than direct police violence, it was highly likely that the mill owner's hegemony would meet with serious challenges from time to time. But it was also highly unlikely that purely local challenges would achieve any measure of success apart from memorializing the laborers' plight. "Tyranny" is as good a word as any for this state of affairs, so long as one recognizes that mill owners were themselves hardly free of constraint. The established practices that developed at the interface between international markets and local working populations during the industrial revolution in Lancashire imposed a desire for personal authority on mill owners. They had to pursue it with the zeal, and often, as in 1853–54, at the heavy cost, that accompanied their pursuit of technical proficiency in production.

LAWLESSNESS AND ASYMMETRY IN SILESIA

In Lancashire monetary exchange asymmetries prevailed in the mills, creating the conditions necessary for a police-style discipline that compelled large groups of laborer households to offer deference and obedience to the mill owners. Under the yoke of this discipline certain adult males became fractious at times; even in submission many felt the pain of unforgivable slights from day to day and unforgettable past defeats. Laborers found particularly injurious the de facto absence of freedom of speech at the workplace, a freedom that they learned to prize as distinctively English from a hundred sources, a freedom that the state guaranteed in theory. State coercion, however, had only to preserve property rights and to punish breach of contract to ensure that, a few episodes of trouble aside, calm submission to this lack of freedom persisted.

In Silesia monetary exchange asymmetries played a much less prominent role in determining the fates of those who worked for others. They operated in tandem with other forms of asymmetrical relationship, and with far more pervasive recourse to violence, to ensure submission from the vast majority. Junkers, besides collecting numerous money and service dues, had direct police powers over their estates' inhabitants and large control of the courts of the first instance as well. Displeasing the master meant not mere dismissal (as in Preston) but unfavorable court rulings on property matters, systematic harassment, even a public whipping or imprisonment. After 1807 Junkers also managed their demesnes increasingly along capitalist lines, seeking maximum return on cash-crop farming through technical experimentation and flexibility in response to shifts in demand. Some movement toward the abolition of labor dues and increased dependence on hired hands came as a result of Junker preference for the greater flexibility of wage labor, a preference that resulted from their keen pursuit of marketplace success.[77] To a certain number of inhabitants of his estate, therefore, the Junker stood in the relationship of employer; these included not just farmhands (permanent or seasonal) but also estate agents, stewards, and police officers, as well as the judge of the manorial court. To others he stood in the relationship of landlord; these included the Einlieger already mentioned, who rented household and garden. To both Einlieger and all the rest of the inhabitants he stood in the relation of manorial lord with the right to collect diverse manorial or feudal dues. To all inhabitants without distinction he stood in the relation of controller of police power without appeal and – because he chose and paid the manorial court judge – in the relationship of de facto judge and jury in all civil and many criminal cases. The Junker role was, finally, available to anyone, noble or nouveau riche, who could collect the money or credit necessary to buy a Junker estate at current prices.[78]

The Silesian estate in the 1840s was therefore very much a hybrid institution, part feudal, part capitalist, as has often been said. But this judgment is admissible only so long as one holds in mind that Lancashire spinning mills were also hybrid institutions in their own way, not entirely creatures of the market, little focuses of intensely exercised political control that survived by selling goods at competitive prices. A "capitalist" mill of Lancashire might be compared to a football game in which the two teams, laborers and employers, fought it out on their own, with the agents of the state looking on from the sidelines. If the ball came too close to the employer's goal, however, the state stood ready to intervene and make sure the right side won. In Silesia the state's agents were already on the field from the beginning of the game; they were identical with the employer's team. These special rules made for a game with a very different flavor, albeit one in which the ultimate outcome was no less assured from the beginning.

Nor did the Junker estate of Silesia (or anywhere else in the Prussian east) suffer from any undue instability as a result of its hybrid character. It was changing, and doing so in response to both internal and external pressures. But whether it was going through a fundamental transformation or merely adapting successfully to circumstance is a question not easy to resolve. Hans Rosenberg's seminal essay on east Prussian estates showed how they preserved elements of their hybrid character right down to the 1920s.[79] This hybrid character had been evident at least since the 1760s, when the grain and land markets began their long boom; or, if one follows Hanna Schissler or Peter Kriedte, it had been evident since at least the sixteenth century, because it was the international grain trade through the entrepôt of Amsterdam that made possible the recrudescence of Prussian serfdom in the first place.[80]

A fundamental "transition" that lasts two to four centuries and that is already in operation from the moment the status quo ante is first established can legitimately be mistaken for remarkable stability and vigor. The Silesian estate of the 1840s was, it appears, one of those perfectly sensible institutions of the kind that had flourished for equally long centuries in the French ancien régime. The ingredients were there in different proportions, but the characteristic — to us, incongruous — mix of political, juridical, and contractual forms was the same. It was perfectly sensible, for example, for the Junker to have great influence over the manorial judge through a peculiar kind of monetary exchange asymmetry and then, through the judge, to exercise considerable control over all judicial matters. By law the estate-court judge had to be a trained jurist; once chosen, he had life tenure; his salary, however, was paid personally by the Junker. These judgeships were usually given to *Justiziars* who lived in nearby towns and who held many such posts at once, so as to piece together a decent living out of the meager wages and fees. The judge was present on the estate only for court day, stayed as a guest in the home of the lord who hired him and who paid his wage, ate at the lord's table, and judged matters in which the lord was often one of the parties.[81] In this way the law provided a semblance of independence and expertise to judicial institutions while ensuring that they were really under the Junkers' control.

It was particularly sensible for the Junkers not to fear loss of personal authority as they shifted increasingly to dependence on wage labor, as opposed to feudal labor dues, in a period of demographic expansion and widespread underemployment. Bleiber quotes the following statement of one wage-earning farmhand from this period who chafed under the Junker's rigid discipline, a very rare bit of direct testimony: "Don't come here, we have enough people! What can a poor man do? Either he must make himself content with such treatment or, if he quits his job, he risks ending up lying in the road."[82] Fear of dismissal served just as effectively as fear of direct violence to ensure obedience.

It was equally sensible for the Junkers' various wage-earning servants to be often so zealous in their carrying out of his will that not even the faintest resemblance remained between their activities and the actual provisions of Prussian law. Many peasants were forced, for example, to continue seeking permission to marry and to continue paying the inheritance dues and other fees owed by hereditary serfs long after these had been abolished by reform legislation.[83] Max Ring, a doctor who practiced in Silesia before 1848, called the peasants "white slaves"; he told of incidents in which death had followed the infliction of corporal punishment on a villager without anyone raising a voice in protest. In the weaving village of Langenbielau, a Junker's policeman by the name of Meyer built a "whipping machine" that he prided himself on keeping going all day long. He repressed the begging that spread there during the hungry forties by having beggars whipped "half dead."[84] Eduard Pelz, the Breslau bookseller who bought a farm in Upper Silesia in the early 1840s, was astonished by the lawlessness he found in the countryside. In his writings he documented in detail how the Junkers' stewards and judges worked in tandem to dominate and systematically fleece villagers.[85]

That the Prussian estate never faced a decisive peasant rebellion of the kind that swept away the French seigneurie in 1789 is probably owing to its greater retention of instruments of direct control and of rights of direct expropriation in kind. Unlike the French seigneurial jurisdictions, Junker police and court powers went virtually unchallenged by the state; unlike most seigneurial dues, Prussian manorial dues were never fully commuted to money payments; most inhabitants continued to work regularly in the fields under the direct supervision of the Junker's agents or even of the Junker himself until such time as the dues were bought out. Nevertheless, the hungry 1840s in Silesia were difficult years for Junker authority, in some respects not unlike those of 1788–95 in France. This was especially true after the peasant uprising against labor dues in neighboring Galicia in 1846 gave Silesians an example to emulate. But the beginning of trouble antedated this incident by several years. Lawlessness was a coin with two sides. The policeman Meyer, for example, was murdered by an impoverished former Prussian officer whose children had been caught begging. There were numerous inexplicable fires of estate buildings and residences in the weaving district in 1844. On many estates in this same period dues and taxes were falling badly in arrears, not only because of sheer destitution. Poaching and pilferage, a way of life in normal times, reached unprecedented levels in the mid-1840s; forest guards reported that they were swamped by violators, most of whom were only exercising their former common rights to glean woods from the forests.[86] There is every indication that the social fabric was threatened in the mid-1840s by massive resistance, most of it local, informal, and uncoordinated. Junker discipline, whether exercised through monetary exchange asymmetries or through direct violence, had to be maintained through police-style strategies, just as did workplace discipline in Preston mills. There remained to the peasants, if they acted sporadically, spontaneously, and collectively, a significant margin in which to maneuver, however small by comparison with the situation of the Lancashire operatives.

One effect of Prussian legal reforms had been to make that margin slightly larger. Eduard Pelz, for example, instituted numerous lawsuits against local Junkers and their servants and began handing out free legal advice to peasants. Within months his fame spread by word of mouth; literally hundreds of peasants streamed to his door hoping to find out what the law really allowed or did not allow.[87] It was impossible for so much reform legislation to have been promulgated in Potsdam without some hint of it filtering through. In 1845, when the Silesian Landtag proposed a new law making possible buy-outs of certain peculiar Silesian feudal dues, the *Landtag* urged the king to act swiftly in the matter; the peasants would expect to hear word of the new law's promulgation soon. If they heard nothing, they would assume that the law was being concealed from them by their betters. When the king did not act, there were in fact troubles in Upper Silesia. From Kreis Beuthen, in early 1846, villages sent representatives to Berlin to find out what was happening; there were widespread threats to stop paying all feudal dues. The peasants believed, said one official, "that all those who can read conspire together with the lord and conceal from the peasants the truth about the law." That summer several villages in Kreis Waldenburg stopped delivering their dues. They claimed that the Oktoberedikt (of 1807) had abolished all dues, that this had been kept a secret from them for thirty-nine years, and that they therefore owed nothing. A certain tailor who was said to have been making speeches to them was arrested.[88]

A sign of the vigor of Silesian manorial institutions by comparison with French seigneuries in the eighteenth century is the fact that Junkers were at that time still able to invent and collect entirely new dues, whereas French seigneurial agents at best had only revived old ones. The spread of rural textile production, for example, gave rise to monetary fees paid by operators of spinning wheels and looms, the Spinngeld and Weberzinsen mentioned previously. Junkers thereby acquired a direct interest in the successful expansion of merchant-manufacturers' operations on their estates. It was perfectly sensible, therefore, for Junkers to tolerate merchant-manufacturers' efforts to use monetary exchange asymmetries as a means of disciplining spinners and weavers. The severity and arbitrariness of this new, independent form of discipline, however, finally sparked revolt in the weaving districts in 1844. But why were the main incidents of revolt aimed exclusively at merchant-manufacturers rather than at Junkers or their agents?

Exercising control over a putting-out operation presented special difficulties that were not encountered either on a Junker estate or in a Lancashire mill.[89] No direct supervision of the work was possible. The laborer had to be given full possession of the raw materials during the time he worked them up. To prevent him from absconding with them, Silesian merchant-manufacturers followed the common practice of extending materials on credit. In this way, even if the laborer sold the raw material while in possession of it, he had nonetheless acknowledged a legally binding debt to the person who originally supplied it to him. This gambit left the laborer legally free to sell his finished product to someone else, so long as he paid off his debt to the original supplier. The one drawback to this strategy of control was that merchant-manufacturers could easily find themselves in the painful position of having to compete against each other in buying back finished goods. Such competition might prevent them from paying prices to laborers that were low enough to ensure both hard work by the laborer (to ensure a living wage) and comfortable profit margins in the international market.

To obviate this danger Silesian merchant-manufacturers used several strategies.[90] First of all, a price agreed upon in advance was always subject to revision when the cloth was returned. A rigorous inspection could always reveal flaws and unevennesses that justified lowering the final payment. If the weaver objected, he was told that he could go elsewhere. To prevent him from actually trying to go elsewhere, some merchant-manufacturers would write the proposed price directly on the weft as it was given to the weaver. By common accord, other merchants would refuse to pay a higher price if the weaver offered his final cloth to them. He was forced to return it to the merchant who had given him the weft and to accept whatever that merchant offered. Some merchant-manufacturers would refuse to make offers on cloth until the end of the day, so that it was impossible to seek an alternative offer without losing part of the next day walking back to town. Finally, weavers were also offered advances on pay; once they were in debt they could be prevented from quitting or switching to another merchant-manufacturer by a demand that they pay off all their debts at once. In this way weavers were forced to accept whatever their merchants offered, in spite of the fact that weavers owned their own tools and had control over the raw material for significant stretches of time. All of these strategies turned on the monetary exchange asymmetry inherent in dealings between large-scale merchants and nearly propertyless weavers.

Whether Junkers admired the merchant-manufacturers' business methods is not known. It is certain, however, that the merchants admired the Junker way of life. The more successful ones bought land and built lavish living quarters adjoining their storerooms, making complexes very similar to the *Höfe* of Junker estates. The merchant-manufacturer Zwanziger of Peterswaldau, son of a weaver, was said to have amassed a fortune of 230,000 Taler in thirty years (60 Taler per year was considered a comfortable income for a family). He bought several estates in his own right and built a "palace," as the sources call it, in Peterswaldau, ostentatiously separate from his two warehouses. Relatively few merchant-manufacturers could equal his success, but those who approached his wealth spent it in the same way: on carriages, tutors and governesses, clothes, land, and houses. They kept to their place. They did not try actually to marry into the Junker caste, but they imitated it in detail. Dierig of Langenbielau married his daughter off with a hefty dowry to a local member of the clergy; modest steps up were acceptable when properly paid for.[91]

The sources make much of the fact that the weavers watched the merchant-manufacturers becoming ever richer and more pretentious as they themselves were generally impoverished. What they do not say is that this was a palpable political transformation as well as an economic one. As the weavers became ever more dependent on the large merchant-manufacturers, their new masters gradually took on the appearances of their old ones. The political implications of this change were not lost on the weavers themselves, as their actions in 1844 clearly show. Their minds not yet cluttered with the misleading abstractions of liberal thought, they had no difficulty understanding that they were engaged in a political dispute. Or rather, the problem of distinguishing among political, economic, and religious issues simply did not arise for them. This can be seen first of all in the song whose singing triggered the initial riot; it had been printed up on a broadsheet, and the printed version has survived.[92] It is entitled "Das Blutgericht" ("The Court of Blood"). In the first two stanzas the merchant-manufacturer's pay room is likened to a court and to a torture chamber. "The Zwanzigers are executioners, the Dierigs their deputies." They are all "Satan's brood, hellish demons, who eat the poor and all they have." Both religious and political imagery in the very first lines of the song make a clear statement about the character of the weavers' relations with the merchant-manufacturers. Then the song turns to the details of the pay procedure:

> Kommt nun ein armer Weber an,
> Die Arbeit wird besehen,
> Findt sich der kleinste Fehler dran,
> Wirds ihm gar schlecht ergehen.
>
> Erhält er dann den kargen Lohn,
> Wird ihm noch abgezogen,
> Zeigt ihm die Thür, und Spott und Hohn
> Kommt ihm noch nachgeflogen.
>
> Hier hilft kein Bitten und kein Flehn,
> Umsonst ist alles klagen.
> "Gefällts euch nicht, so könnt ihr gehn
> Am Hungertuche nagen."
>
> (Now comes a poor weaver
> To have his work inspected;
> If there is the slightest flaw in it,
> It's too bad for the weaver.
>
> When he receives his pitiful wage
> Still more is then deducted [as payment against his debt].
> He is shown to the door, and scorn and derision
> Follow him out.
>
> Entreaties, supplications are useless here;
> All complaint is vain.
> "If you don't like it, you can go,
> And gnaw on hungercloth.")

"Es kostet Blut" ("The cost is blood"), the song sums up; it concludes by denouncing the new liveried servants, the governesses, and the stately carriages of the merchant-manufacturers. The song is in correct German, and follows an *abab* rhyme scheme throughout, but it is often quite awkward in its attempt to stick to the proper form, and it has little of poetic grace to recommend it. Despite an intensive police investigation, the author was never identified. What it expresses is not just dissatisfaction over wages. The sense of grievance focuses on the moment of exchange, which is likened to a judicial procedure, to torture, to daemonic cannibalism. The weaver freely offers deference, pleading and beseeching for a wage that accords with his minimum needs. But humility counts for nothing with the merchant-manufacturer. There is at least a suggestion in the song that weavers had heard merchant-manufacturers appealing to their mutual independence as buyers and sellers in order to counter any suggestion that they owed the weavers some minimum remuneration. When challenged, the merchant-manufacturer depicts himself as merely passing through prevailing prices; the disastrous state of the international linen trade in 1844 is not his doing. If the weaver does not like the price offered for his cloth, let him take the cloth elsewhere and sell it. Let him take the cloth home and eat it for dinner. The line "Am Hungertuche nagen" makes reference to the weaver's special vulnerability to monetary exchange asymmetries. He has worked to make cloth but he cannot live on cloth; to satisfy his diverse personal needs he must get cash from the merchant-manufacturer and quickly spend the cash again. Otherwise he will die. For the poor, "The cost is blood." Merchant-manufacturers welcomed the power this situation gave them over weavers but accepted no responsibility along with that power. They accumulated the symbols of high position but none of the engagement of leadership. Not only was this a stark break with traditional expectation in Silesia, but it made of merchant-manufacturers the most conspicuous local target for resentment during the severe slump.

The Junkers in the weaving villages were comparatively distant figures who, rather than farming their own fields, rented cottages to weaving families and collected spin money and loom money through paid agents rather than exacting direct labor services. Thus a local Junker could pose as the upholder of the old rural order in the aftermath of the weavers' uprising, as a figure who understood mutual duty and who saw social life itself as an affair of honor. The following pronouncement, issued on the day after the outbreak of rioting, at least suggests how great a contrast existed between traditional Junker claims to authority and the upstart merchant-manufacturers' claims of mutual independence and lack of responsibility:

> I find Bielau on my arrival in a state I never feared to see it in. If there is still a spark of your old love and attachment for your feudal lord in your hearts, if any feeling for order and right still lives in you, I ask you, I adjure you, renounce all criminal undertakings and return to that state which it was for so long your fame to preserve. Do not believe that any interest other than your welfare and the good name of your community leads me to make this request. I cling to the conviction that, had some unhappy chance not taken me away from you these last few days, scenes which have—I must say it—shamed you perhaps would not have happened. Now having returned to you, I will try in your midst amicably to restore order, which in any case will be upheld without exception by force of arms. May God and your love support me therein. Count von Sandreczky-Sandraschütz.[93]

Here was a style of command to which the upstart merchant-manufacturers could not aspire. Their imitation of Junker consumption patterns only underscored in the weavers' eyes the sharp difference between the old code of military honor and the new one of counting-room trickery.

That both were forms of political domination it never occurred to the weavers to question. When the weavers attacked the merchant-manufacturers' buildings they destroyed everything with a remarkable thoroughness. Stocks of yarn and cloth, ledgers, and debt registers were the first targets; furniture, dishes, carpets, and drapery were next; finally the buildings' rich embellishments—plaster walls, ornate banisters, even roof tiles – all were hacked to bits with axes. No fires were set, no persons attacked (except while the troops were shooting). Crowds returned to Zwanziger's twice to continue the work of destruction long after the initial riot. Objects already broken were subjected to further, purely gratuitous blows. An eyewitness described the damage at H. H. Hilbert and Andretsky in Langenbielau as so extensive that furniture was barely recognizable from the little pieces that were left behind. The weavers took away from the merchant-manufacturers not just the instruments of commerce but also those things by which they had sought to enhance their stature in society, all the paraphernalia of substance and authority that, in the weavers' view, the merchants did not know how to use or have any right to.

Although the differences between the forms of action used at Preston and Peterswaldau are numerous and noteworthy, there is still one underlying similarity. In both cases collective action was organized to avoid giving the opponent conspicuous targets on which to train his disciplinary sights. In Preston this was done by choosing leaders among those already unemployed. In Peterswaldau it was accomplished by pure unpremeditated spontaneity. Until the moment Zwanziger's servants seized one weaver from the crowd outside his house, the action had not gone beyond the level of an ominous prank. For Zwanziger to capture one participant at random, however, was to throw down the gauntlet, to shift the terrain of confrontation from that of charivari to that of the battlefield, a terrain on which solidarity becomes a point of honor, on which the only safety for the individual lies in attaching his fate to the fate of the group as a whole. The systematic attacks of the following two days were organized in haste without much planning or forethought. All those involved were aware that reprisals would follow swiftly and that they had only a few hours within which to act. The shape of the action therefore had to be extremely easy to understand, as unambiguous and as suffused with meaning as possible. The attack on account books and on items of consumption, the blindly courageous unarmed resistance to Prussian troops, and the continued signs of deference to persons in authority appear to be indications that weavers did not wish to make difficulties, that they were only defending their honor, not shaming themselves. To risk death in such a cause is acceptable.

Such a spontaneous, unpremeditated defense of honor is indeed an old, even an archaic, form of social protest. It is not difficult to discover numerous parallels between the weavers' actions and the attacks of French peasants on chateaux in 1789, or the food riots that were so common a feature of eighteenth-century history, or peasant revolts against the royal fisc in the seventeenth century.[94] One crucial factor in the similarity of all these actions was that the populations involved were subject to police-style discipline. They confronted repressive forces capable of crushing individual resistance but insufficient to repress collective resistance. They confronted tax collectors, grain dealers, seigneurial agents, or merchant-manufacturers who were capable of exemplary harshness if allowed to deal with people one at a time or in small groups but who were unable to oppose a united community. They responded to situations in which such harsh discipline meted out on an individual basis had become not only unjust (injustice was routine) but degrading and shaming, because of prevailing prices or tax rates or population growth. Discipline broke down because pain meted out to the bodies of the poor no longer corresponded to obedience or deference but grew without limit.

"Primitive" rebellions, as they have been called, when viewed in this light, are not so different from the advanced, apparently rational and organized actions of industrial laborers like that in Preston in 1853–54. The greatest difference lies in the formal separation within a liberal polity of the discipline of monetary exchange asymmetries exercised by mill owners and the discipline of violence exercised by state officials. This formal separation, although it did not preclude close collaboration, at least opened up a space, a public sphere within which laborers could peaceably assemble, discuss plans, choose leaders (who were willing to be immediately fired from their jobs), collect money. But the underlying grievances were still translated into affairs of honor by the way in which police-style discipline was used and misused against the poor. And the ultimate coordination of state violence with monetary discipline in England as in Silesia left little doubt about the final outcome. (Even if Preston laborers had won their wage increase, for example, how could they have defended themselves against subsequent disciplinary campaigns to bring perceived strike leaders to their knees?) Viewed from one perspective the Preston strike really was something new in the history of social protest, an immense step forward; viewed from another, however, it was only a variation on a very old theme. Liberty for the individual remained a distant dream.

THE DRAMA OF EXCHANGE

What is remarkable about Hauptmann's play based on the weavers' uprising is that the issue of monetary exchange asymmetries stands at its center. This issue is the source both of the play's dramatic impact and of its universal appeal. The weakest feature of the play consists of those scenes that Hauptmann contrived to provide the audience with information on family budgets, living conditions, and consumption patterns. A recital of earnings and expenditures is inherently undramatic. Hauptmann showed considerable ingenuity in finding ways to interweave such information with the unfolding action of the play, but he could find no way to give it life.[95] The scene in the merchant-manufacturers' pay room, however, is alive with tension from beginning to end. Doubtless this is why Hauptmann chose to begin the play with it. To structure this scene Hauptmann took his cue from the weavers' song, "Das Blutgericht," and from certain discussions of the merchant-manufacturers' business methods in the sources. In his stage directions Hauptmann indicates:

> Most of the patient weavers [in the pay room] look like men standing before the bar of justice, where in painful tension they await a life-or-death decision. Or rather they all have a certain oppressed look, special to those used to receiving

alms, who have gone from disappointment to disappointment consciously attempting to be resigned and to make themselves as little as possible.[96]

Here Hauptmann reiterates the implications of the weavers' song: The poor in
dealing with the rich and the condemned in a court of law are caught up in political relationships.

The very first incident of the play involves a woman who, to get through the
week, is in desperate need of a few groschen more than her husband's cloth has
brought. The pay clerk says he is not authorized to make an advance. The woman
asks to see Herr Dreissiger (Hauptmann's name for Zwanzinger). The clerk snaps
back: "God knows Herr Dreissiger would have an awful lot to do if he took care of every little matter himself."[97] This is as much as to say, "Your life or death and that of
your family are nothing to him. A matter of a few groschen is of no significance to
him even if it could save your miserable life." Here in the very first lines of the play
the monetary exchange asymmetry between weaver and merchant-manufacturer is
perfectly and correctly depicted as the source of the latter's power. Moments later,
when the plucky weaver Bäcker, soon to be a leader of the revolt, receives his wage,
he refuses to accept the derisory sum offered. He protests loudly; Dreissiger is called
in. After an altercation Bäcker, now discharged from Dreissiger's employ, agrees to
leave but demands his money before departing. Dreissiger throws it on the floor.
Bäcker responds, "My wage belongs in my hand." Dreissiger orders a clerk to pick
the coins up, and Bäcker, taking them, leaves. The wage becomes a point of honor
in a political standoff. Deference is refused; from that moment the weaver's employment is at an end; but his defense of his honor soon inspires others. Later, when the
revolt breaks out, the crowd's methodical destruction of the merchant-manufacturer's pay room has been perfectly prepared for. Hauptmann is equally good dealing
with Herr Dreissiger's ostentatious dwelling; amid the chillingly luxurious furnishings, Dreissiger is basking in the homage offered by his clients – his children's tutor and the local clergyman – when the weavers march up singing "Das
Blutgericht" outside.

Dickens's novel *Hard Times,* by contrast, hardly deals with the relationship between mill owner and operative. The strike, rather than being at the center of the
plot, serves only as a backdrop to it. This is because Dickens was attempting to provide a critique of political economy as a social philosophy. In order to accomplish
this aim he invented Gradgrind, a schoolmaster dedicated to teaching political economy to his pupils, and with a sure instinct for one of the theory's great weak points,
he put Gradgrind's family at the center of the action. Had Dickens concentrated his
attention on the strike itself there would have been too little opportunity to parody
the dictates of the utilitarian creed. Doubtless Dickens thought that this was because
these dictates actually worked inside the factory. This is why the factory appeared so
flat and uninteresting to him. It was in the realm of the family that Dickens found
the ammunition for his blast. One cannot forget the image of Bitzer, who has suc-

ceeded in getting his mother admitted to the poorhouse and who now gives her half a pound of tea per year in spite of the fact that "all gifts have an inevitable tendency to pauperize the recipient." If Dickens had, like Hauptmann, attempted a careful reconstruction of the protest itself, he would have been forced to set political economy to one side. It was little more than a smokescreen used by both parties to confuse the enemy. Dutton and King's in-depth investigation led them directly to this conclusion.

CONFLICT WITHOUT CLASS

A number of important objections may legitimately be raised to the treatment of local conflicts proposed in this chapter. First, why should these two incidents not be treated as cases of class conflict? They seem at first glance to be quite straightforward instances of class conflict. Even if defined in a strict Marxist sense as referring to a shared relation to the means of production, the term "class" could be used with perfect consistency to refer to Preston mill owners and mill operatives as well as to Silesian Junkers, merchant-manufacturers, and weavers. That the Silesian weavers were not merely wage earners but stood in a special relation to Junkers who appropriated surplus through manorial dues poses no problem because they all shared this "transitional" position. One of the difficulties with the concept of class in recent historical research is that it can often be used in just such a consistent and satisfying manner in the context of intensive case studies. If one examines a town or region dominated by a particular industry, or even a limited mix of industries, social relations appear radically simplified. But one can pile a hundred such case studies on top of one another and they still do not add up to a consistent global analysis of class relations. It is when attempting to generalize across industries, trades, regions, and towns that one runs up against grave difficulties with the concept of class. Drawing neat class boundaries on a national level or deciding who is or is not a member of the working class in one of the great metropolises such as London, Paris, or Berlin is quite a different matter from identifying classes in a Lancashire mill town or a Silesian village.[98] As noted in earlier chapters, relations to the means of production turn out to be diverse and unstable and do not adequately parallel political comportment.

A matter as apparently simple as deciding who is or is not a wage laborer becomes fraught with paradox. Did Silesian weavers receive a wage, for example? Or were they owners of the means of production whose chances of profiting from such ownership were cut off by unfair trade practices? The issue can be ignored in a case study but not when one is trying to define the boundaries of a nationwide or continentwide class. Preston cotton spinners and power-loom weavers had a much higher standard of living than Silesian weavers, greater security of income, and greater or at least equal control of work rhythms even though they were apparently further down on the scale of "proletarianization." Compared to Martin Nadaud, the Parisian mason discussed near the end of Chapter 3, however, both weavers and mill operatives look underprivileged. Nadaud's family owned a farm, although it was mortgaged and apparently not self-supporting; he himself had the choice of being either a subcontracting entrepreneur or a very well paid wage earner. It is hard to see him as a member of the working class, if one takes the working class to mean propertyless wage laborers. And yet Nadaud is typical of the kind of worker who carried out the great protest actions that punctuated nineteenth-century French history. Or is he? Jacques Rancière has argued that masons and carpenters cannot be compared to tailors and shoemakers, the real shock troops of revolution, whose position was much worse because their skills were easily learned and provided no bargaining wedge and because women and children outworkers competed directly against them. Refinements and distinctions continue to be brought forward with no end in sight.[99]

There is no doubt that sophisticated concepts of class can be developed to deal with all of these difficulties – indeed, with any level of difficulty one might encounter in studying real societies. This is especially true if one is prepared to use notions of class that do not require one to place specific individuals like Nadaud or the weavers of Silesia either definitively in or definitively out of the working class. (Erik Wright's notion of "contradictory class location" is a good example of this kind of refinement.)[100] But taking this step, of course, means severing the word "class" completely from its etymological roots. The word was first borrowed from Latin to express the opposite idea about society, that people could be "classified" one way or another, that they belonged definitely on one side or another of various dividing lines drawn through society. At first these lines were not taken as having necessarily hierarchical implications. Class first came into use in its modern sense in the early nineteenth century to refer to the de facto groups that an atomized liberal social order threw up, after guilds, manors, and noble titles had been abolished.[101] Why retain the word, once one realizes that such classifying is inherently misleading, that individuals are too complex to be sorted meaningfully into discrete boxes?

A more telling objection to the approach exemplified by these two case studies might be that neither of them deals with national-level political movements. Class, whatever its weaknesses, has for long been the concept of choice for analyzing such movements; until one shows how the concept of monetary exchange asymmetries can improve our understanding of the national level it would be unwise to set class aside. All social vocabulary is approximate, after all; there is no reason to throw out a usable concept like class in favor of a new theoretical construct that will only prove to be equally approximate in due course. In response to this objection, several observations are in order. The principal limitation of the concept of exchange asymmetry – that it is a dyadic, microeconomic concept with no pretensions to explaining collective phenomena – is in fact an advantage in one respect. It does not prejudge what sorts of conflict are likely to occur on the level of the collectivity or the state. The two case studies presented in this chapter showed how particular forms of asymmetry biased local conflict in the nineteenth century toward collective defense of honor. To move from the local to the national level would require yet another kind of case study. An idea of what such a study would look like is suggested by the argument of Chapter 4, although this represents little more than a sketch, meant to be suggestive rather than definitive. Further, some work that nicely complements the analyses of local conflicts presented here has already been done on the national level for the nineteenth century.

Nothing would be easier, for example, than to combine the analysis of the Preston strike in terms of asymmetries as proposed in this study with the approach to national-level political movements elaborated by Gareth Stedman Jones in his seminal essay "Rethinking Chartism," as well as in other recent pieces.[102] In that study he challenged the well-established historiographical tradition that treats Chartism as the first working-class movement in English history. He pointed out that, whatever the makeup of its constituency, the Chartist movement was not working class in its political vocabulary, which it inherited from eighteenth-century radicalism. It was not working class in its diagnosis of the ills of capitalism, which focused on the point of exchange rather than the point of production, and on market conditions rather than employer–employee relationships. It was not working class in its ultimate goals, which, besides the franchise, included social reforms to protect independent producers that were reminiscent of the ideals of Thomas Paine or Thomas Jefferson. Stedman Jones argued that the rise and fall of Chartism must be explained primarily in terms of the state. It was the peculiar activism of the reformed Parliament after 1832, rather than the industrial revolution, that led the popular movement to focus on parliamentary power and franchise reform. Once this period of activism had passed, Chartism lost its attraction. With the full establishment of a liberal social order by 1850, the actions of the parliamentary elite receded from center stage, and the hope of using the state to alter the social order likewise turned to bitter disappointment.

It is easy to see the stamp of these national-level developments on the form of the Preston strike of 1853–54. The strikers' cautious refusal to look beyond the issue of pay and their insistence on justifying their action in terms of political economy show how completely the failure of Chartism had impressed itself on local calculations by this time. Of course, this strategy did not conceal from the strikers for a moment their primary concern with mastership and tyranny. Yet one can only conclude that the results were disastrous; neglect of the state was a mistake, pay raises can never of themselves ensure freedom from tyranny. The very economic sophistication of the strike was the workers' undoing. Better to be marching through the woods singing "Das Blutgericht." Elsewhere I have presented an argument about the French Second Empire that, like Stedman Jones's, treats national-level politics as a kind of drama that provides cues to actors at the local level about what kinds of claims are legitimate and how to struggle over them.[103] The important thing about such drama is not that classes line themselves up neatly behind one or another political faction but that actors in a diffuse way make their own strategies and hopes conform to the outcome of national conflicts.

It has long been recognized that one cannot call Chartism a working-class movement in the sense that its supporters were all proletarians strictly defined. That is, a very large percentage of Chartism's supporters were depressed outworkers; skilled millwrights and shipwrights who worked on a subcontracting basis; mule spinners paid by the pound who were employers in their own right of piecers and bobbin boys; and numerous small-scale shop operators, such as tailors and shoemakers, who dealt directly with the public. The journalists and barkeepers who came to lead the movement, in addition, found within the warm atmosphere of popular patronage welcome refuge from the chill winds on the laissez-faire tundra.[104] Monetary exchange asymmetries dominated the daily experiences of all these people, but in a variety of ways, just as those which plagued Silesian cottage weavers or masons like Nadaud varied widely. Chartism thus united people who were not a working class behind a program of radical reform not formulated to express working-class interests; their grievances concerned the programs of an activist state, and they correctly saw control of the state as a critical step toward reining in the unbounded pretensions of large property owners. Chartism was a movement of the "class" of the unjustly disciplined, of the unfree, both male and female; in this respect it remains a model worth emulating.

It is thus quite possible to account for the whole of English social history down through 1850 without evoking class interest to explain events either on the local or on the national level, and at the same time without for a moment losing sight of the fundamental justice of the popular movement's cause. It is not only possible to do so, it is necessary to do so, for the simple reason that the result is less approximate, less fuzzy, truer to the documents, than an approach that depends on the old scenario of class conflict.

One final objection to the case studies presented here might run as follows: They have merely sought to replace the concept of class interest with the concept of collective honor, a substitution that must be seen as a step backward rather than forward. Does it not amount to making a blanket claim about underlying human motives? Is not such a claim every bit as immune to disproof as the notion of class interest? On the contrary, the discipline that arises out of monetary relationships derives from the minimal survival needs of the human body and of human social connectedness. That there are such minimal needs requires no proof. Discipline is possible because only one party to an exchange has such needs at stake in its outcome. Discipline derives from an ordered diversity in the motives of those involved. If a worker could choose not to eat for a year in order to make his wage demand stick, then the employer would have no power over him whatsoever. The notion of interest fails to capture the stark difference between worker needs and employer preferences. In many capitalist enterprises of the nineteenth-century type, both centralized and decentralized, the resulting disciplinary potential could be realized only if the employer followed a police-style strategy of singling out conspicuous offenders for disciplinary action. This strategy had to be carried out within the limits of a nominally free contractual relationship most of the time; recourse to violence was possible only with outside help and only occasionally. Discipline used in such ways leaves open a window. A conception of collective honor can be an extremely effective means for mobilizing resistance in the face of such discipline.

No claim is being made that such notions of honor were universal or that they were even uniformly accepted by those who engaged in collective resistance under their aegis. The claim is that by analyzing the consequences that the irreducible needs of existence have for certain kinds of monetary relationships, one can discover a bias in favor of certain strategies for collective mobilization. There are all sorts of solidarity. The solidarity of the family is shored up by the profound emotional and physical pains often associated with its dissolution. The solidarity of nations in time of war is shored up by fear of quick justice for traitors and by fear of the sufferings of occupation in case of defeat. The solidarity of nineteenth-century workers' dropping tools in unison to protest an employer's discipline was fitfully and intermittently shored up with threats of violence from fellow workers but by and large had no other sanction than fear of obloquy. The term "honor" has been used here simply as a name for something that moves a person to act in the face of danger when equivalent danger does not result from inaction.

Although the two cases examined have both come from the realm of manufacturing, there is no need to limit the method of analysis to that realm. It could as easily be applied, as some of the discussion in Chapter 4 indicates, to peasants or intellectuals, notaries or bureaucrats, domestic servants or schoolteachers. With a sufficient number of case studies built up, nineteenth-century European society would begin to appear as a kind of field of force of authority in which everyone was caught up at his or her own particular position between the upper and lower poles. The advantage of the field-of-force figure is that it does not require one to draw horizontal lines representing class divisions at arbitrary points across the skein of social relationships.[105] A great deal of the authority in European society was by 1850 based on monetary exchange asymmetries, but by no means all of it, perhaps not even the greater part of it. Families represented a large preserve of (changing) authoritarian relationships that did not arise directly from monetary exchanges; so did armies and navies, schools and prisons, courts of law, and parliamentary factions. But the constant mobilization of the adult male laboring poor for conflict on the local level in the nineteenth century cannot be understood except by examining how monetary exchange asymmetries reshaped, and simultaneously did violence to, collective conceptions of male honor. Male honor came into play precisely because of the confused and inconsistent character of liberal reform, which brought competitive commerce into a new and painful relation with solidary working families. These conceptions of honor were only new variations on similar conceptions of honor that can be found mobilizing poor adult males in the earlier, precapitalist period. In this respect capitalist society represented not a radical break so much as a logical extension and refinement of forms of social control that had previously prevailed in Europe.

6 Conclusion: The poor and their partisans

By NOW A REVIEW of the key points that have been put forward in this essay and of their relationships to each other is long overdue. What follows is a skeletal outline, intended to recall and clarify for the reader the principal stages of the argument and to spell out their mutual connections.

THE ARGUMENT IN SUMMARY

The current crisis of the concept of class that was reviewed in Chapter 1 has arisen from the insurmountable weaknesses of that concept for use in the explanation of political mobilization and conflict. Research of the past twenty-five years has gradually undermined an older style of historical explanation pioneered by Marxists but widely used within the historical guild. This style was based on identifying political factions of the past with specific social classes. Study after study has revealed two problems with this style. First, neither leaders nor supporters of such factions were recruited exclusively or even predominantly from the classes whose interests these factions were said to represent. Second, in many cases the classes previously discussed as concrete entities, even as collective actors with a single consciousness and will, could not be identified on closer examination, or if their members could be located they proved not to have the characteristics requisite to qualify for membership in the class.

It was impossible, for example, to find a bourgeoisie in ancien-régime France with a way of life, sense of identity, or interests that distinguished it from the elite as a whole. In Prussia the Junker class was easily identifiable since its existence was based on legal title, but the behavior and interests of its members turned out to be sufficiently complex to prevent one from labeling them meaningfully either a bourgeoisie or a feudal aristocracy. In England it proved possible to identify a working class and a working-class movement during the industrial revolution only by throwing open the doors of class to "members unlimited" and redefining class in terms of consciousness rather than as a relation to the means of production. The supporters of liberalism in Germany in the pre-March era have been shown to be equally heterogeneous; no weak bourgeoisie but a motley collection of lawyers, professors, bureaucrats, shopkeepers, artisans, and journeymen dreamed of constitutional government, German unity, and the rule of that vague entity, the *Mittelstand.*

The list of recent discoveries like these could be extended at will, each one the fruit of important revisionist research programs in country after country. The progress of this revisionism has benefited as much from the work of historians calling themselves Marxists as from the work of others. Alfred Cobban in 1964 noted that the rich empirical research of Georges Lefebvre was itself the best source of evidence against Lefebvre's Marxist class analysis.[1] E. P. Thompson openly embraced the social heterogeneity that his evidence revealed among supporters of radical reform in England before 1830: One did not have to earn a wage to gain entry into his working class; one had only to recognize oneself as a victim of exploitation.[2] Many working within the Marxist tradition have hailed these developments as a welcome stimulus to deeper theorizing about the true nature of class in the capitalist era. But one must question where this deeper theorizing will lead. Will it not involve in the end recognition that Marxist theory (like economic thought in general) is fundamentally a set of more-or-less-revealing interlinked metaphors? If so, will not the new notions of class that are developed be so different from the old that retaining the term becomes more a matter of piety than of substance?

An important method to which historians have turned in the last fifteen years or so in the hope of rethinking (or else replacing) the concept of class has been the interpretation of discourse or of culture. But interpretive method, as discussed in Chapter 2, solves the problem of individual motivation in effect by ignoring it. The meaning of conventional actions, rituals, and practices is unlocked by interpretive effort and is then set at the center of the human drama, as the prime source of structure and order in society. This method has difficulty dealing with change for two reasons. First, it leaves out of account the impact of the unexpected or unintended; second, it fails to offer any explanation of how individuals respond either to rituals and conventions or to the unexpected. Rather than thinking in terms of monolithic cultures, therefore, it would be better to consider social life as ordered by established practices that are more or less rigid, more or less elaborate in their prescriptions depending on the case. (The examples of international trade, of a journeyman's *tour,* and of strategies of familial ascent were discussed in Chapter 2.) Established practices impose motives on participants, but they do not necessarily exhaust participants' abilities to desire, nor do they require unconditional allegiance of participants.[3] In Chapter 4 the eighteenth-century book trade was treated as an established practice that, in conjunction with the established practice of patronage, predictably gave rise to a sense of grievance among some writers. It was not necessary to assume that all writers felt the grievance or that those who did so responded in identical fashion (still less was it necessary to see writers as a social class), yet it was still easy enough to see how this conjunction of established practices helped provide one motivational source for *philosophe* skepticism and impatience with the existing order.

Conclusion

An ensemble of established practices, simply by being there, gives order to people's chaotic desires. One must either go along with established practice or rebel; rebellion may itself have established practices associated with it. Coercion maintains ensembles of established practices in the face of those diverse disorderly desires that, as part and parcel of the variability of perception and belief, are bound up in the human condition. Such ensembles usually have physical, systematic consequences. These ensembles are highly vulnerable as a result to two kinds of disruptive messages from the unknown, those that disturb the techniques of violence and those that disturb the physical systems that established practices give rise to.

Exchange is a particular kind of practice highly likely to have systemic features and highly fruitful in unintended consequences. The study of exchange therefore ought to be concentrated on searching out and measuring unintended consequences so that they can be anticipated and corrected for. Historically, however, economic thought in the West was built around a core presumption that exchange, especially monetary exchange, was always self-correcting and required only to be left alone to operate beneficially. This belief in the self-correcting nature of exchange was connected to a failure, in particular, to recognize the special difference between the desires that rich and poor usually bring to exchange relationships.

At this point, in Chapter 3, the argument of the book had come full circle. The notion of the universality of the desire for gain, originally identified as a weakness of the modern notion of class, was now discovered to have played a role in the erroneous development of economic thought and therefore in the events to be explained. As one of the four ingredients of the liberal illusion, fully elaborated by the time of Adam Smith, the notion of the universality of the desire for gain obscured from view specific, uniform, widespread differences between the motives that poor people brought to exchange and those that rich people brought to exchange. The poor were and are subject to diverse bodily and social needs of a pressing nature that can be satisfied only by immediately getting and spending money. The rich feel no such pressing needs. This difference can be called an asymmetry in exchange, the word "asymmetry" is used in preference to "inequality," since the latter term implies that this is merely a quantitative rather than a qualitative difference. There is a fundamental difference in the kinds of motives involved that no single umbrella term like "interest" can possibly convey. From monetary exchange asymmetry arises a disciplinary potential, a possibility of exercising direct power.

The notion of monetary exchange asymmetry therefore clarifies the relation between money and power, and does so precisely by noting the existence of an orderly diversity in the motives that people bring to exchange relationships. This diversity is rooted in the human body and in the minimal social needs of human existence. Money yields power to those who possess more than the margin at which it ceases to have a negative utility. Wealth allows the rich to discipline the poor through their bodies and through their sense of familial or other social duty. Everyone does not want money and power, but everyone does have a body susceptible to that discipline which follows in the wake of propertylessness in all money-based societies. There is a field of force that does reach out and pull our desires in specific directions; it reaches from the highest pole of power down and through to the lowliest redoubts of impotence.

Such power in the context of modern economic thought becomes a grand unintended consequence, an invisible consequence of commerce of the first order. Disciplinary potentials, even within the Marxist tradition, have a tendency to drop from view, even after their importance has been noted in passing, because economic concepts, founded on the validity of measuring with money units, implicitly refer back to a universal desire for (quantitative) gain that rich and poor are supposed to share as an underlying motive.

After all, if money is a valid public measure of anything, then it must be a measure of desire. In classical political economy as in Marx, money was held to measure (or to fail to measure) "value," something an equal amount of which would be equally desirable to all parties. Marginal utility theory made the advance of recognizing that prices might merely be compromise points at which the differing desires of exchange partners could meet. Each party's desire for a commodity varied according to that commodity's marginal utility, given the other objects already possessed by the party. But desire was still treated as being a uniform, politically neutral dimension of economic "preferences," things that, by definition, could be adequately expressed in numerical (and therefore monetary) form. The concept of monetary exchange asymmetry rests on the insistence that not all desires are alike, that reducing them to a single numerical dimension necessarily obscures differences of kind. This concept gives theoretical dignity to the common recognition that fear of starving is not the same sort of thing as preferring an 11 percent return to a 9 percent return on corporate bond holdings. This difference in kinds of desires is politically charged. Money exchange, by hiding this difference and its political implications from public view, by treating one person's first ten dollar bill as equivalent to another person's millionth ten dollar bill, at once creates and clouds over a kind of power that has been central to European society since well before the great liberating transformation of the end of the eighteenth century.

To mediate vital human relationships by using precise numerical units of account of whatever kind is to make society into a mammoth shell game, an endless Balzacian scramble. This has been frequently noticed before. But the concept of monetary exchange asymmetry points out that no solution can come from assuming that the shell game rests on an underlying uniformity of desire. The shell game is a painful and inefficient method of disciplining, trimming back, and cutting away at the underlying, exuberant diversity of desires – verging on the incoherent – which human beings regularly conceive of. An increase of liberty and a reduction of suffering can therefore come only from an orderly, but also radical, alteration of the disciplinary potentials of money exchange. It certainly cannot come from a mindless strengthening of the state, in which one mammoth asymmetry is allowed to swamp all the others.

Conclusion

Because the introduction of money exchange into manorial, judicial, agricultural, or other relationships always alters the disciplinary potential involved, money substitutions constitute social change. But such social change constantly threatens to become invisible to the extent that one accepts, or uses vocabulary that implies, the political neutrality of money or the universal validity of money as a substitute for anything else. This issue was explored through a brief discussion of the liberation of the serfs in Prussia after 1807. Monetary exchange asymmetries cannot be accommodated within the vocabulary of class, finally, because they create disciplinary potentials without regard to the exchange parties' precise relation to the means of production. The disciplinary potentials of asymmetrical relationships are themselves immensely diverse; even the subset involving monetary exchange covers a vast range. Tenant farmers, mason subcontractors, cottage weavers, writers, and mill operatives are among the kinds of persons subject to monetary exchange asymmetries who have been discussed in detail here. Marriage and sharecropping are two examples of asymmetry not involving money that have been briefly mentioned.

It might be objected that these examples vary precisely in accord with the variation in the modes of production that the relationships are embedded in. A mill operative in the nineteenth century was disciplined according to the requirements of a capitalist mode of production, involving the extraction of surplus value; a sharecropper of the sixteenth century according to those of the feudal mode, based on extraction of surplus product. But this objection is admissible only if one admits at the same time that writing books and giving birth to babies are processes of production. At this point "production" becomes indistinguishable from human action in general, and the word's status as a metaphor is revealed. It is interesting and important that Marx's underlying paradigm of human action was labor, rather than Hegel's concept of reason. But this substitution alone, together with the theory constructed on it, surely does not represent the final stage of human thought. It is admissible to explore for further revealing substitutions. If Marx's own thought began with such exploration, that is all the more reason to continue it today. The notion of production tends to imply that all products are of a kind, vessels of a certain quantity of labor, whereas it is the different ways in which these "products" articulate with the hierarchy of human needs that set up the possibility of discipline. What a relationship "produces," in any case, is the whole relationship itself, not the widgets or can openers that come out at one end of the factory.

With these considerations the presentation of a theoretical framework – aimed simultaneously at replacing the notions of class and class interest and at broadening interpretive method so that it could handle both change and political domination – came to an end. There followed two attempts to apply this theoretical framework, to see the kinds of historical explanation it gives rise to. First, the question of the origins of the French Revolution was reconsidered; second, two case studies of industrial conflict in the nineteenth century were presented. Central to the kinds of change under way in both instances was the gradual application to practice of the mistaken idea that human life is made up of separate spheres, especially the political, economic, social, and religious spheres, within which different and even contradictory rules of conduct apply. This idea arises naturally from the tenets of the liberal illusion because monetary exchange is held to be a politically neutral activity in which all parties freely seek their own monetary advantage. Economic and political behavior are therefore starkly different, or ought to be, for in politics people seek power rather than monetary advantage. (That money and power cannot be neatly separated in reality is widely viewed as an open secret, an ongoing scandal that must be accepted with Machiavellian resignation.) At the same time religious doctrine cannot apply in the economic sphere, especially Christian moral doctrine, because its altruistic (or alternatively intolerant) prescriptions threaten to disrupt the search for monetary advantage. Likewise, families must be protected from the corrosive effects of monetary exchange because they require a special form of solidarity to ensure the nurturance of new generations; they and other institutions must be confined to a social sphere. Those political institutions are best which confine themselves to the role of protecting the economic sphere from political, religious, or any other form of disruption, so that the self-equilibrating search for advantage can benefit all. And governments must also protect the social sphere from undue economic influence.

The need for a proper separation of spheres generated a program of reform in the period 1770–1820 that was carried furthest in France but that affected virtually every state in Europe to one degree or another. The whole history of realized social reforms in Western Europe since that time might be treated as an attempt to fine tune the relations among these spheres once they were separated. The modern welfare democracy may be seen as a social order in which income transfers, safety nets, child-labor and divorce-settlement laws, industrial development policies, and charitable and religious tax exemptions are manipulated with a view to allowing citizens once and for all to confront one another in a purified economic sphere as free, apolitical maximizers of advantage. But of course this whole effort is doomed because monetary exchange is inherently political in nature, just as family "reproduction" of persons and skills is inherently an economic function, just as the state's treatment of religion as a matter of individual choice is inherently a religious doctrine. The inherent and complete intersection of all such spheres throughout the whole of life as people actually live it requires not only that the true conditions of human freedom be entirely rethought but also that all the theoretical structures within the human sciences that have been built to account for the political dimension or the social dimension or the economic dimension of human existence be recognized as having unwarranted assumptions at their foundation.

A NOTE ON LANGUAGE

The term "monetary exchange asymmetry" is not a graceful one. But this ungainly expression was chosen for a purpose. Unlike terms such as "inequality" or "class" or "the economy," which are short, of long-standing usage, and therefore easily grasped by a large public, the phrase "monetary exchange asymmetry" draws the mind up short. If it is repeated more than three or four times, its meaning begins to fade. No one can plug it into a slogan; "Liberty, Fraternity, Symmetry" will never be any movement's battle cry. This is one of the concept's principal virtues. It seems stilted and abstract. As a result no one can use it without repeatedly rethinking what it refers to. The ever-present danger that social terms will be mistaken for social reality is at least reduced. At the same time, by firmly insisting that it replace a term so ubiquitous and indispensable as "class," I hope at least to open up some breathing space for fresh thought on the crucial importance of choice of words and of their theoretical context. Doing social history without being constantly aware of this problem is like navigating the seas without instruments: It is possible with great skill and with luck, but it is unnecessarily difficult and risky.

A further virtue of the term "monetary exchange asymmetry" is that it refers to a kind of relationship. It may be a drawback that this relationship is conceived of as dyadic and as existing in its own right without influence from context. This is the kind of drawback that any abstract social term necessarily brings along with it; warnings have been inserted in the text to alert the reader to this difficulty. Class terms, often said by their proponents to be about relationships, are all too frequently used in practice as if they refer to homogeneous aggregates of individuals who have no relations with one another or with anyone else except that of simply being in essence proletarian or bourgeois or aristocratic. This is a crippling drawback of the notion of class, one that makes jettisoning that notion once and for all strongly advisable. Human identity is simply not constructed this way. A class in the making is not a class; a class that is fully made, in this world of becoming, this vale of tears that is history, is dead.

FIN-DE-SIECLE CONFUSION AND THE NEW SOCIAL HISTORY

In this section and in the next an attempt will be made at least to sketch in an interpretation of the course of social history in the nineteenth century subsequent to the events discussed in Chapter 5. A full treatment of the German revolution of 1848, of the labor-aristocracy issue in Victorian England, and of the other historiographical issues discussed in Chapter 1 would doubtless take at least one extra volume. But some indication, however cursory, of how the notion of monetary exchange asymmetry might clarify, or at least shift the terms of, the ongoing debates is certainly required. At the end of Chapter 5, one is left with a rather grim picture of the possibilities and fortunes of popular protest. How does this square with the great victories of the European labor movements and socialist parties of the late nineteenth and twentieth centuries? Was not European society turned decisively away from laissez-faire orthodoxy toward a milder and more egalitarian welfare socialism? Does not this record of accomplishment, with the new conditions it has created, belie the assumption of inevitable subjection for the laboring poor implicit in the notion of monetary exchange asymmetry?

The aim here is not to deny the achievements of labor movements in Europe over the last century. It was the pressure exerted by these movements, in a context of advancing technical control over work processes and massive government stimulation, that created the high-wage economies we know today. Whatever the extent of their dependence on imports from a developing world where labor is still as cheap as air (which is of course a political fact as much as an economic one), it is still the case that these economies have created more comfort and security for the vast majority than was ever before imagined to be possible. This is an accomplishment not to be taken lightly.

But it is also a development that underscores the inadequacy of quantitative measures for diagnosing the malaise that afflicts capitalist societies. Why are there still so many poor people? In Western Europe today (and this observation would apply to the United States with particular poignancy as well) there are millions of people whose standard of living is by any objective measure higher than that of a large proportion of middle-class people of the nineteenth century and who are nonetheless by behavior and outlook poor. They appear to be low in self-esteem, indifferent to the liberating possibilities of literacy, lacking in hope for the future, politically passive. Not deprivation but domination is what lies behind such apparent self-surrender. One need only notice how the bureaucratic administration of transfer payments to the sick, the unemployed, or the disabled is designed to instill in them a feeling of being beholden, being inferior, being supplicants, unworthy by comparison with those who work and who willingly submit to a life of obedient drudgery. Physically safe from hunger and cold, welfare recipients are under constant emotional siege from the arid bureaucracies that hold them in thrall. The bureaucrats need absolutely nothing in return from the poor they serve, and they are therefore even more secure from challenge than employers. This is Nassau Senior's "lesser eligibility" in twentieth-century form, detached from exact quantities of money, realized in the asymmetrical structure of relationships. In the socialist states, of course, the assurance of personal security has been paid for at an even steeper price in personal subjection. But it remains true that the great achievements of the organized left in the democracies have been extremely ambiguous in their effects.

Looking forward from what has been said about Lancashire and Silesia in the mid-nineteenth century it is not difficult to see why this should be so. Down through at least 1920 labor strife in Europe continued to be dominated by the spontaneous defense of points of honor. Spontaneous defense continues to play a role today, in spite of the growth of union organization and mass political parties. The peculiarities of French labor law and union institutions have given this feature of labor conflict much greater prominence there than in Britain or Germany, but it is active in all three countries. The wide dissemination after 1880 of a simplified Marxism among socialist and union militants, however, helped to ensure that their view of labor's predicament remained cast in terms of the liberal illusion. This kind of Marxism imposed a sharp distinction between wage laborers (the exploited by definition) and all others which made it difficult to appreciate the plight or articulate the grievances of shop op-

erators, tenant farmers and owner-occupiers in the countryside, or outworkers, especially the millions of female outworkers whose home work provided a broadening
flood of cheap consumer goods. Small farmers were abandoned to the wiles of a new
conservative populism in Germany; in France socialists occasionally made gestures of
support toward them, but with little long-term success.[4] The sufferings of workers
were confidently attributed to the operation of a competitive labor market. It was
widely recognized that individual workers could not bargain on equal terms with employers, but rather than using this recognition as a starting point for a thoroughgoing critique of accepted economic concepts, militants and left intellectuals by common consent called loudly for government sanctioning of collective bargaining. The
problem was treated as a glitch in the system rather than a gaping hole in the theory.
Few believed that union recognition was the only remedy necessary; but even fewer
thought to question the idea that bargaining was an appropriate concept for thinking
about the ongoing war between employers using their police-style discipline strategies and laborers defending their prisoner-of-war notions of honor. The fundamental
problem of the laborer was seen as arising from free competition; wages always
tended toward bare subsistence, it was assumed, and hours at work toward the physical maximum. Employer discipline strategies, including the all-important question
of the form of the wage payment, were viewed as a secondary issue at best, not least
because they were difficult to generalize about, never having received general theoretical reflection. In short, instead of thinking about the diverse forms of exchange
relationships that gave rise to unjust disciplinary possibilities, militants quickly categorized people as in or out of the working class and treated all those inside it as experiencing a uniform fate.

From this starting point, activists of the time elaborated three distinct visions of
a future to work for, each one coupled with a distinct explanation for the dramatic
strikes that laborers repeatedly unleashed in the decades before World War I. The
first view, and probably the most common one in the two decades after the Paris
Commune—at least on the Continent—was that a revolution was necessary and that
conditions for its outbreak were ripening rapidly. Sudden, large-scale, spontaneous
strike efforts occurring here and there from month to month were seen as an indication that laborers from their own work experience were naturally led toward root-
and-branch opposition to the existing order. Beginning about 1890, however, the
need for a revolution came into question. Associated in Germany with the label "revisionists" and in France at first with the term "possibilists" and later with the
term "ministerials," a diverse group of socialist officeholders, union officials, and
intellectuals came to believe that fundamental change might be possible without
revolution.[5] Those who espoused this second vision pointed to their own success in
electoral politics and union organizing, as well as the gradual amelioration of the laborer's plight through legislation and collective bargaining. Spontaneous strikes
among laborers without union representation, which continued to be the predomi-
nant form of worker action, were seen by the revisionists as evidence of a need for
firm leadership. Laborers were right to seek to defend themselves against the rav-

ages of competition, but they could hope to do so effectively only if they organized, disciplined their impulses toward wasteful rebellion, elaborated specific negotiable demands, and presented the employers with a calm united front.

Naturally these views sparked controversy and forced the defenders of revolution to sharpen their analyses of state power and its relation to capitalism. Piecemeal victories, they insisted, would never add up to fundamental change. In the end the revolutionaries began to point to the very existence of revisionism as evidence of the need for revolution. This strategy gave rise to the third view, elaborated by Lenin in 1903, that working-class movements in the natural course of events would tend to become complacent and accommodative in outlook. Without help from an elite vanguard, the working class – whose true class interest lay in the realization of socialism – was capable only of achieving a "trade-union consciousness" far short of the revolutionary class consciousness it needed.

Of course, there were many variations on these three basic approaches. The Guesdists in France, for example, insisted publicly on the necessity of a party takeover of the state apparatus; they treated unions and strikes with indifference. Highly reminiscent of Lenin in these respects, they nonetheless acted after 1893 very much like revisionists whenever election time rolled around. Rosa Luxemburg and her followers in Germany resembled the anarcho-syndicalist Confédération générale du travail (CGT) in France in that both expected the revolution to occur through the spontaneous strike actions of the masses, although Luxemburg and the CGT differed markedly in their views of the role of the party and of the shape of postrevolutionary society. British trade unions came early under the influence of the Liberal Party and only gradually and hesitantly moved in the 1890s toward an endorsement of socialism, accepting the need for a separate labor party only in 1906. British radicals like Kier Hardy were extreme moderates by Continental standards.

But across all these quirks and national variations there was a strong undercurrent of consensus when it came to diagnosing working-class ills in quantitative ways. The industrial worker of the new age was overworked and underpaid. The CGT expected to rally the working class to a revolutionary general strike in 1906 by calling for the eight-hour day. When spontaneous strikes caught union officials by surprise – at Anzin in 1884, in the Ruhr valley in 1889 and again in 1905, on the London docks in 1889, in the Nord in 1890 and 1903, and on thousands of other occasions large and small – the militants' first impulse was to elaborate wage and hour demands in the workers' name.[6] In legislative assemblies socialist and labor delegates pushed for limitations on hours, minimum wage laws, and old-age pension plans. The central question of workplace discipline and control was seldom broached, and not only because this issue was viewed as too explosive. Despite general and oft-repeated denunciations of private property, no one ever couched his critique in terms of the political power that arose within the wage relationship, at least not on the level of theory.

The left's failure of vision can be seen in sharp relief by comparing a passage from Rosa Luxemburg's *The Mass Strike* of 1905 with one of the events she was referring to as it has been revealed to us by a number of recent studies. Laborers of the pre–World War I period are vastly better known to historians now than they were twenty or even ten years ago, thanks to a spate of recent monographs. Practitioners of the new social history have often themselves failed, however, to get beyond the terms of the old prewar debates and to appreciate the significance of their own findings. The well-known Ruhr mining strikes of 1889 and 1905 – two of the most important labor conflicts of the Wilhelmine period – offer a convenient opportunity to measure the distance between workplace realities and public assumptions that hampered Rosa Luxemburg and continues to plague historians today.

Luxemburg, no schematic Marxist herself, argued that revolution was both possible and necessary: necessary because trade unions could never secure the laborer against the depredations of capital, possible because (and here the stark contrast with Lenin) the extreme poverty of the working class pushed it toward revolutionary outbursts. Thus in 1905, in the aftermath of the second great Ruhr mining strike and in the midst of a revolutionary crisis in Russia, she argued that Germany was as prone to revolution as the Czarist regime:

> Let us consider *the poverty of the miners.* Already in the quiet working day, in the cold atmosphere of the parliamentary monotony of Germany – as also in other countries, and even in the El Dorado of trade unionism, Great Britain – the wage struggle of the mine workers hardly ever expresses itself in any other way than by violent eruptions from time to time in mass strikes of typical, elemental character. This only shows that the antagonism between labor and capital is too sharp and violent to allow of its crumbling away in the form of quiet systematic, partial trade union struggles. The misery of the miners, with its eruptive soil which even in "normal" times is a storm center of the greatest violence, must immediately explode in a violent economic socialist struggle, with every great political mass action of the working class, with every violent sudden jerk which disturbs the momentary equilibrium of everyday social life. Let us take further the case of the *poverty of the textile workers.* Here also the bitter, and for the most part fruitless, outbreaks of the wage struggle which rage through Vogtland every few years, give but a faint idea of the vehemence with which the great agglomerate mass of helots of trusted textile capital must explode during a political convulsion, during a powerful, daring mass action of the German proletariat. Again let us take the *poverty of the home workers, of the ready-made clothing workers, of the electricity workers,* veritable storm centers in which violent economic struggles will be the more certain to break out with every political atmospheric disturbance in Germany; the less frequently the proletariat take up the struggle in tranquil times, and the more unsuccessfully they fight at any time, the more brutally will capital compel them to return, gnashing their teeth to the yoke of slavery [emphasis in original].[7]

Luxemburg referred to the workers as helots and as slaves in this passage and alluded to the irrelevance from their point of view of representative institutions and parliamentary politics. Like so many others, she was perfectly aware herself of the political implications of wage-labor relationships. But what Luxemburg expected to be decisive for the workers' propensity to take action was not their political impotence but their extreme poverty. Or rather, she spoke of poverty as a political state, as if this were self-evident. But this recognition alone was not enough to turn aside the basic claim of the revisionists, that incremental improvements in wages and working conditions might accumulate into a complete political emancipation. Both she and her opponents lacked a vocabulary for analyzing the generation of discipline in monetary exchange.

In contrast to Luxemburg, reformists and trade-union officials in her own party advised their followers strongly against spontaneous strikes as a poor method of obtaining results. In doing so, they embraced even more fully than she the centrality of a quantitatively conceived material well-being in workers' lives. Ruhr miners were chided in 1905 by the SPD mouthpiece *Vorwärts,* for example, for their unplanned walkout.[8] They were compared unfavorably to British miners who had already long enjoyed what the Ruhr miners were hoping to obtain – compensation for time traveling to the mine face, the right to elect their own checkweighmen to keep track of output, payment for partially filled tubs, union recognition. In Britain, *Vorwärts* remarked, union negotiations preceded walkouts, and strikes were aimed at winning essential concessions, that is, increases in pay. The whole thrust of the piece was to suggest that Ruhr miners were lagging behind, were failing to understand their position in society. Not revolutionary élan but inadequate thought and preparation lay behind the spontaneous outburst of the strike.

Over the long term Luxemburg's views have fared much the worse in this debate. The practitioners of the new social history have come down solidly on the side of the reformists, at least in concurring that the European working class of the end of the century was immature and not at all ready for revolution. Activists, it has been shown, continued to come predominantly from the high-skill, high-pay end of the spectrum, and in particular from trades like construction and metalworking where apprenticeships still had meaning and traditions of organization and political action stretched back at least to the 1830s. Among such well-organized laborers moments of high militancy resulted not from misery but from technological challenges to the current organization of work. True proletarians were still in the minority within the working class and, even where numerous, often quiescent. Collective action when it occurred among them was highly ineffective and poorly focused.[9]

As it happens, two recent studies of the Ruhr miners mentioned by Luxemburg have quite independently come to conclusions that confirm this overall pattern. And the evidence in favor of their conclusions seems incontrovertible. What enabled the Ruhr miners to launch such dramatic, unplanned strike movements as those of 1889 or 1905, both Barrington Moore and Klaus Tenfelde argue, was the long-standing organization of work in small stable teams whose tasks remained untouched by mechanization, as well as the unbroken tradition of miner brotherhoods (*Knappschaften*) that went back to precapitalist days. These strikes were therefore not harbingers of a final mature confrontation with capitalism so much as initial responses to it. Tenfelde sees the 1889 episode as an important early step in the miners' gradual realization that what they needed was not a traditional brotherhood but a new kind of organization, a modern labor movement capable of "bringing into question the profit orientation and the omnipotence" of the owners of capital.[10] Their grievances were born of their still-recent "subjection to the lawfulness and dynamism of industrial markets,"[11] but their means of expressing these grievances were inappropriate because based on the old dependence on government oversight and guild corporatism. The most dramatic moment in the 1889 conflict came when the miners decided to send a deputation directly to the kaiser. This gesture proved to be a great public-opinion coup, bringing much favorable comment in newspapers and drawing rooms, but it did little to save their strike from failure. Whatever the kaiser may have said to the humble miners during their unprecedented audience with him on 14 May in Berlin, Tenfelde points out, the Prussian bureaucracy refused to interfere with the freedom of contract between mining employers and their workers. The mine owners' continued intransigence soon disheartened the miners; and most of the eighty thousand strikers were back at work within a few days of the imperial audience. Doubtless this dramatic failure was one of the things in the back of Hauptmann's mind as he wrote his famous play three years later.

The 1905 strike, according to Moore, was equally a transitional movement.[12] Unions resisted its outbreak, stepping in to lead only reluctantly after it was under way. Miners appealed again to government and public opinion for support rather than seeking hardheaded negotiations with mine owners. Again the strike ended in failure, this time when the Reichstag (not the kaiser) began making gestures toward intervention with proposed mining-law reforms. Granted that these reforms, when introduced the following year, went "a considerable distance" toward meeting the miners' principal demands, the episode as a whole still represented something quite different from Luxemburg's imaginings.[13] It was an action by essentially obedient workers, according to Moore, workers indifferent to political doctrines, seeking only a "little elbowroom" within the framework of the prevailing social order.[14] Moore fully agrees with Tenfelde that the miners' traditions of fraternal and loyal corporatism and of work-team solidarity "were both a handicap and an advantage in the miners' long efforts to discover and create effective forms of collective self-help, the strike and the unions."[15]

This ambivalent conclusion is not unlike observations one can find in a good number of recent works. Working-class activism in the prewar decades has been found to be not quite what it ought to have been. Unilinear notions of the gradual, untrammeled growth of a European labor movement have given way to more ambiguous evaluation. Strikes in these years were less rational but more expressive than those organized by well-oiled twentieth-century union federations. The last-ditch struggles against mechanization by declining artisans appear to historians as at once stirring and yet also poorly conceived. Even the successful establishment of working-class parties has been seen as part of a pattern of accommodation and growing cultural conservatism.[16] Both Moore and Tenfelde, for example – to return to the Ruhr for a moment—pause to remark upon the limited political successes that miners achieved in 1889 and in 1905 by turning their strikes into shows of loyalty. At the same time, these two observers remain impatient with such obviously immature gestures as sending a deputation to the kaiser or calling off a strike the moment the Reichstag shows signs of intervening. But if one reconceives the miners' position in terms of monetary exchange asymmetries and the struggle over honor, instead of thinking of miners as free purveyors of a labor service, the apparent immaturity of these gestures takes on a new color.

When the Prussian government abrogated its close control over mining operations in the Ruhr between 1851 and 1865, instituting a thoroughly laissez-faire regime, mine owners were quick to take advantage of their new freedoms, increasing the size of their operations and the depths of the shafts and reorganizing work discipline. But the miners experienced no new freedoms. They continued to negotiate separate bargains for the working of each seam as before; only now, without the protection of the state, the bargains could be broken or rewritten at will by mine management. They were therefore not bargains at all, but concessions from a position of overwhelming power. Miners had no choice but to accept what was meted out to them; owners had no one to oppose them.

In both 1889 and 1905 mine operators had refused to negotiate with striking miners or even to recognize the strike as a valid form of collective action by their employees. It was evident that police-style retaliations against anyone identified as a leader would immediately follow a return to work. The strikers were in effect being treated by the mining combines as disobedient individuals who had failed in their duty and were therefore liable to punishment. The liberal concept of free contract was invoked only insofar as it justified nonrecognition of collective appeals or proposals. The strikers were to be shamed like children. Caught in this position in both 1889 and 1905, they went over the heads of their employers, appealing directly to the government. And government recognition by kaiser or Reichstag was in itself an immense victory over the employers' refusal to see their action as anything but shameful disobedience. Once this point was won, returning peacefully to work represented an open display of loyalty, to the kaiser or Reichstag first and foremost and only secondarily to the employers. A display of loyalty can be a very powerful form of protest within the context of monetary exchange asymmetries. Loyalty demands, and what it demands is a kind of reciprocity that cannot be expressed in a ledger. A return of equal loyalty is the only possible fair response. But if employers were indeed ever to become loyal to their employees, then their properties would by this very step become useless to them; they would lose the freedom to maneuver—the key to domination—that such rights confer. Employee loyalty is thus a most desirable and also a most fearful thing to any employer; he is forced by the need to protect his property both to accept it and to hold himself prepared to betray it. The miners' gesture of 1889, the decision to send a delegation to the kaiser, struck directly at the heart of the asymmetrical discipline under which they lived out their lives. At the very moment this decision was taken, union militants in their own meetings, secure in their economic literacy, were busily formulating irrelevant wage demands.

Obeisance to the kaiser literally shamed the government into a significant shift in policy. As Klaus Saul points out, from 1889 on the clear trend of all mining legislation was toward the reimposition of government control. Within a few years government officials were given the power to intervene in employer–employee relations, and new occupational tribunals (*Gewerbegerichten*) were given authority to handle labor contract disputes. The Reichstag intervention following the 1905 strike amounted to a state-imposed settlement in favor of the miners.[17] But the effectiveness and appropriateness of the miners' actions ought not to be measured merely by their noteworthy political impact. The point is to see these collective movements as the acts of defiance they were and to recognize that defiance was better suited than bargaining to the direct political submission that was daily exacted from the miners by the huge mining combines.

It might be possible therefore to reformulate Moore's observation as follows: Strikes and unions were both a handicap and an advantage to miners, whose traditions of brotherhood and obedience gave them a surer insight into the problems of the capitalist era than anything the SPD had to offer. Or one might reformulate Luxemburg's view in this manner: Not their poverty but their subjection to police-style disciplinary strategies, which were aimed in particular at eliciting feelings of shame in the miners, led them toward occasional violent "eruptions" – the ever-present volcanic and meteorological metaphors are highly misleading – that is, toward safely spontaneous enactments of an alternative code of honor and shame. These enactments were revolutionary in a way that Luxemburg's economic notion of misery prevented her from seeing.

In fact, a third study of Ruhr miners appeared almost simultaneously with those of Tenfelde and Moore, David Crew's *Town in the Ruhr: A Social History of Bochum, 1860–1914,* which reaches conclusions very close to those being proposed here. In all substantive matters, Crew's extensive quantitative evidence of Bochum miners confirms the findings of Moore and Tenfelde on the importance of the miners' work teams and traditions, on the significance of work organization in miners' strike grievances, and on their failure to organize under the umbrella of either SPD or Catholic unions and party sections. But Crew finds this failure to organize to be attributable to the SPD and the Catholic Center Party and their unions rather than to the miners, given the stage of capitalist development Germany had then reached. "In that stage of large-scale, heavy-industry-based, 'organized' capitalism," he remarks, "the link between liberal ideology and social reality must have seemed far more tenuous, not only in Bochum, but in Germany as a whole, than perhaps it had during the early phases of the English Industrial Revolution."[18] In effect, Crew observes, unions and parties were unable to demonstrate any ability to defend miners against the great political weight of the mining concerns. Miners had no particular reason to believe that such classically liberal activities as joining associations, voting, and bargaining could do much to improve their position. "This may in turn suggest," concludes Crew, "that rather than continuing to 'ghettoize' recent German history as an exceptional case, more could be learned by attempting to situate the German experience within the framework of capitalist development in Europe and the world as a whole."[19] Just so. The only improvement needed to Crew's conclusion would be to add that at no phase of capitalist development or precapitalist development – not in Silesia, Lancashire, or the Ruhr – have liberal forms of political or economic activity, confined to their proper spheres as liberalism has defined them, offered a satisfactory means of expressing the grievances of propertyless persons.

Not just Ruhr miners but workers in many industries in all three countries under consideration engaged in movements of protest in the pre–World War I period that were revolutionary in a manner that both contemporaries and historians have failed to recognize. I have elsewhere analyzed a number of French textile strikes in detail, showing how they were for the workers complex gestures of *insoumission* aimed at the unchecked, overbearing power of mill owners over their local communities – gestures that could not be contained or directed into prescribed channels by harried and confused union militants.[20] Don Reid's recent work on the famous Decazeville metalworkers' strike of 1886 points to a similar interpretation. The large firm that dominated the small industrial town in southern France sought to extend the influence of exchange asymmetries beyond the workplace into the community. The firm recognized that small retail properties in the town were refuges of political independence, and it sought to destroy republican retailers and barkeepers by taking control of a consumers' cooperative and dictating that its employees had to spend their pay in this cooperative. It was such policies rather than work grievances that sparked the 1886 strike, according to Reid, and motivated the murder of the firm's director, Jules Watrin, an act that catapulted Decazeville into the national limelight. Journalists and political figures rushed from Paris in the aftermath of the incident, the former to document the violence of the workers' feelings, the latter to preach to them about the necessity of a disciplined movement. But it may be safely concluded that none of these visitors understood the true nature of Decazeville's grievance, the desire to breathe free air at least when not at work and to have the chance to be republican in what was after all in theory a republic.[21]

With the industrial revolution the power of monetary exchange asymmetries has become more difficult to exercise with perfect uniformity. The greater intensity of product competition and the resulting greater frequency of technical change force continual renegotiation of the terms of submission. The notion of contractual equality has justified a kind of domination at arm's length in which submission is demanded but nothing promised in return. But this notion is also a fragile fiction that workers have never fully accepted. Socialist and syndicalist thinkers wrongly attacked the contractual freedom of workers and employers as the root of all evil instead of seeing it as a sham based on a misapplied analogy with marketplace exchanges of tangible commodities. Their efforts to counteract with organization the effects of free competition met with only limited success. They would have failed completely without the occasional technological transformations that undermined obedience from below by robbing laborers of even their present slim security. These were what brought strikes and occasional bouts of unionization; these were what brought laborers to the ballot box with socialist lists in their hands. But none of this activity – none of the sword rattling of radical orators or the resolutions of union congresses or the growing parliamentary strength of the anticapitalist left – could have the desired effect as long as the position of the poor was so profoundly misconceived. A symptom of the depth of this misconception may be seen in the fact that all working-class movements, whatever their formal doctrine, were forced by circumstance to fight for a bare minimum of enforcement of civil and contractual liberties. Socialists in France and Germany no less than the Labour Party in England became willy-nilly champions of the right to strike and good-faith negotiations, of universal suffrage, and of parliamentary rule in their respective countries, because even where democracy existed on paper it remained so little respected in practice. The very liberties that the socialists in theory criticized as the engine of working-class enslavement they ended up defending in practice because they found them nowhere in society as it was.

The great labor movements of the end of the nineteenth century were odd amalgams of liberal influence and popular striving. Leaders like Rosa Luxemburg, Jules Guesde, and Jean Jaurès sought to characterize popular aspirations in terms borrowed from a tradition of economic theory that treated money as an adequate measure. Deprivation and overwork appeared central to them as a result; they understood laborers' powerlessness intuitively but had no words for distinguishing it from their mere lack of quantities of things. As a result, laborers continued their sporadic war against employer discipline without ever fully rallying to the formal organizations and explicit ideologies their leaders created. If the whole regime of quantitative thinking had been somehow overthrown, the supporters of this movement might have seen that, not more or less money, but money itself, was a source of tyranny. Only then could the formal and informal wings of the popular movement – the spontaneous and the organized – have built upon, instead of vitiating, each other's strengths.

THE NONEXISTENT NORM

Since about 1960 there has been a growing mood of confusion and doubt among historians over the inexplicable oddities of national histories. In 1978 E. P. Thompson reissued his "The Peculiarities of the English," and two years later Keith Nield published an article that reviewed the sparkling debate between Thompson and Perry Anderson that "Peculiarities" had touched off back in 1965.[22] The question at issue was why the English working class, which had been so resolute and politically active in its own defense before 1848, thereafter settled into a calm acceptance of the British status quo. This is an old problem that troubled Engels before his death and has as yet found no answer; if anything, the range of available explanations is getting wider, not narrower.

In 1980, the year Nield's article appeared, Geoff Eley and David Blackbourne published their *Mythen deutscher Geschichtsschreibung,* containing two essays that questioned the reigning explanations for the German catastrophe of the twentieth century.[23] In particular, Ely and Blackbourne trained a critical gaze on the idea that the German revolution of 1848 had been an unmitigated failure and that the German bourgeoisie had, as a result, never taken its proper leading position in a modernized polity. They questioned the idea that the bourgeoisie left the levers of power in the hands of obscurantist aristocrats, so that these levers were all the more easily seized later on by the Nazis. Eley and Blackbourn were not persuaded that German society failed to become bourgeois, or the German polity to become liberal. They questioned, in particular, the use of an idealized model of English history as a norm against which to measure German failure. In the expanded English version of their essays published in 1984 (which they significantly named *The Peculiarities of German History*), Eley and Blackbourn noted that the original German version "received lengthy reviews in the quality press and in the nonspecialist weeklies . . . was discussed in a radio broadcast, and its theme became the subject of panel discussions at a number of conferences."[24] As one of their critics remarked, if Eley and Blackbourn were right, "then where did Nazism come from?" This was the question that attracted so much public attention to the book in the Federal Republic.

Doubts among historians of France about the peculiarities of its recent history are of equally long standing and remain equally unresolved. Of special concern has been the cause for the disunity of the left. The French working class has been far more militant than those of England or Germany if one looks at willingness to engage in violent insurrections, unpremeditated general strikes, and small-scale, unplanned strikes and demonstrations. But the working-class movement has never been unified or well organized. Even after the creation of a single socialist party in 1905 (accomplished not without mental reservations all around), the bulk of the unions remained aloof from all party institutions down to the 1920s, by which time the socialists had split into bitterly opposed moderate and Communist wings. Worse still, union membership has remained unusually low, and working-class influence on legislation, with the exception of a few brief if important episodes, has failed to provide the powerful legal advantages enjoyed by German, British, or even U.S. labor unions. By comparison with the Germans' SPD, in particular, with its monolithic unity, its discipline, its clear chains of command, French labor has cut a poor figure indeed in the last century. Especially worrisome has been the long list of French politicians who began their careers as socialists and revolutionaries appealing to working-class constituencies and ended up as conservative centrists or even fascists. Among many others, Alexandre Millerand, Aristide Briand, Jacques Doriot, and worst of all Pierre Laval, the architect of Vichy, having acquired a following as socialists or anarchists, sailed resolutely to the right when the winds of opportunity shifted.[25]

Of course, from the vantage point of U.S. social historians all three of these countries have long been considered jointly to constitute a norm against which American "exceptionalism" can be measured. Although beyond the scope of this essay, it is worth noting in passing that Sean Wilentz's work has recently served as the focus of controversy over whether U.S. working-class consciousness and political traditions are to be adjudged sadly lacking or uniquely creative by comparison with Europe.[26]

These questionings and controversies have all been important, seminal, vital. But one truism must also, at least occasionally, be taken into account. It is impossible for there to be only exceptions. All too often when historians are characterizing the exceptional features of one nation's history they fail to examine the evidence that their implicit norm is also in its own way odd. If one compares the French or the British labor movement against the SPD of the pre–World War I era, it is easy to make the former two look weak and ineffectual. But one must not engage in such a comparison in a vacuum, as if the SPD grew up under normal circumstances. German historians have long remarked the impact of Bismarck's antisocialist laws and the relative impotence of the Reichstag in the German constitution as factors militating in favor of socialist unity and organizational centralism in the Wilhemine period. The laboring poor were ostracized by society, shunned by the state; in the SPD they created a special refuge. In addition, German historians have long noted the failure of SPD unions to achieve effective organization outside the skilled sectors or to prevent even their members from falling in with the jingoistic patriotism and militarism promoted by the empire and the ruling elite.[27] Such concerns reveal German workers as looking a lot more like British labor aristocrats than British historians usually realize and as enjoying less autonomy and self-consciousness than those mistrustful French individualists who seldom joined unions and disliked voting for anyone who wore a suit and tie.

When one considers recent intensive local studies like those of Crew and Tenfelde on the Ruhr or that of Mary Nolan on Dusseldorf side by side with similar studies from France or Britain, like those of Rolande Trempé, Joan Scott, Michael P. Hanagan, Robert Q. Gray, Geoffrey Crossick, or Patrick Joyce, one cannot help but feel that the national oddities so much in the limelight of late are rather superficial and that the deeper day-to-day social routines of industrial communities were relatively uniform across the whole of Western Europe.[28] Employer paternalism and struggles over workplace control have been objects of intensive research in the last few years, and here particularly the national differences seem utterly washed out by the similarities. Many unionized Lancashire factory workers, as Joyce has revealed them – voting for Tories, cheering the empire, and deferentially celebrating when the mill owner married or when his son came of age – are remarkably similar to the German workers of Chemnitz, an SPD stronghold discussed by Barrington Moore, who notes that they loved parades and uniforms and believed fervently in German national superiority.[29] Krupp's cradle-to-grave paternalism was certainly no more elaborate or effective than that practiced by the French firm Le Creusot.[30] The quick and near-unanimous rallying of workers to the national cause in 1914 in all three countries is becoming more understandable as specialized studies continue to probe the vigorous hold of employer authority and the unshaken prestige of the wealthy's consumption patterns in industrial communities in the late nineteenth century.[31]

At the same time, an entirely different kind of worker action is coming into focus. Petty resistance, one might call it; Lüdtke has adopted the German word *Eigensinn* ("willfulness" or "obstinacy") to describe the detailed and pervasive acts of disobedience, sluggishness, or obstruction that laborers engaged in on the shop floor in an attempt to protect themselves against employer discipline.[32] This is a form of opposition that lay at the roots of many unplanned strikes but that formal unions and parties were never able to draw on. European society by the eve of World War I was increasingly shaped by those peculiar forms of discipline and resistance that monetary exchange asymmetries in large enterprises gave rise to. In this respect, the direction of current research seems to be offering significant confirmation to the argument of this essay.

One cannot help but agree with Blackbourne and Eley that the German divergence from a Western model has been exaggerated and that a shared, even converging, evolution united French, British, and German societies as they entered the twentieth century. Whether one calls this a liberal or a bourgeois social order, however, depends very much on how one defines these words. European society was by then as liberal or as bourgeois as it would ever get, but this means that it was still a long way from resting on a capitalist economy as Ricardo, Marx, or even Milton Friedman would define capitalism, and still a long way from offering political liberty to the individual in the strict theoretical sense required by liberal intellectual tradition. The failure of a strictly liberal or strictly capitalist social order to emerge, the failure of reform efforts to separate the political, religious, economic, and social spheres from one another properly in any of these countries, is underscored by a comparison of the French Revolution as discussed in Chapter 4 with the road to unity that Germany traversed between 1848 and 1871. It should now be apparent why it was necessary, as mentioned in Chapter 2, to be illiberal in the imposition of liberal reforms on society, why these reforms tore asunder the social fabric in a way that could only seem nonsensical and unjust to many, and why, as a result, the French Revolution was in a deep sense as much a failure as were the efforts of the Frankfurt Parliament and of Bismarck to give Germany a lasting unity.

Extensive recourse to coercion was necessary to impose liberal social orders in Europe not just because old habits held the multitude in thrall, nor just because the machinations of benighted reactionaries threatened to undo the victories of virtue. Coercion was necessary because liberal reform did not produce dramatically new and free social relationships. Liberal reform did not liberate most people; it provided some with momentary windfalls (as in the abolition of the tithe or of seigneurial dues); it gave to all new opportunities to fight their way out of (and new chances to fall back into) the subjection of propertylessness. State coercion was formally separated from the disciplinary activities of property owners (but seldom remained so in practice). A narrow public sphere was opened up, allowing some freedom of speech and assembly in some times and places, creating opportunities for defensive action that it took much experience, and often luck as well, to use effectively. The disastrous mistakes repeatedly made in the popular movements of the first half of the nineteenth century provide abundant evidence of how difficult effective use of the new public sphere was. Either English or French experience can be cited here: Peterloo, Owenism, Chartism; the revolution of 1830, the Lyons uprisings of 1831 and 1834, the revolution of 1848 in Paris from February to the June days, the Commune of 1871 – these represent an awesome collection of miscues and misperceptions, paid for at a heavy price. Only after 1870 did popular movements begin to find forms of organization and defense that effectively took advantage of the limited kinds of public freedoms that liberalism promised. Even then it required constant vigilance to ensure that some of the promise was delivered on.

There was little reason for the common people or the educated poor or underprivileged professionals to exult in the accomplishment of a liberal revolution except insofar as they were swayed by the attractive wiles of the liberal illusion. Persuasive as this illusion was, it left many millions unconvinced. Still others remained caught up in disciplinary practices that prevented them from voicing support or even from reflecting sufficiently to make a decision. Coercion was required to bring the unconvinced and the coerced along, but those who accepted the liberal illusion were bound to fail to see precisely how or why so much coercion was necessary. They could not help but suppose that blindness and malice were the only things that could prevent people from devoting themselves to the cause of liberty. If liberal reformers turned to coercion, therefore, they usually overdid it. The Frankfurt Parliament of 1848 and the National Assembly of 1789 were in this respect identical. Both failed to appreciate the level of genuine popular opposition their glorious reforms were bound to stimulate as well as the potent means many private individuals had for stifling the political expressions of their subordinates. When opposition made itself felt, those who shrank from violence in both assemblies were eliminated.

In Paris a series of ever more violent rumps, determined to defend liberty, scattered indiscriminate death in all possible directions until even their popular supporters retreated in confusion from the political scene. In Frankfurt the Parliament itself was dissolved by a combination of crowd action and military intervention. In what sense was France lucky to have benefited from the ministrations of a Fouquier-Tinville while Germany was unlucky to have been served by selfless idealists like Robert Blum or stolid intellectuals like Friedrich Dahlmann? A.-Q. Fouquier-Tinville clung to his job as judge on the Revolutionary Tribunal, sending hundreds to quick execution, because he badly needed the salary to support his large family.[33] The Fouquier-Tinvilles are the problem of modern history, not its saviors; like the thousands of Germans who fearfully joined the Nazi Party in the months after Hitler's seizure of power, they are what needs most to be explained to a traumatized posterity.

After the failure of the Frankfurt Parliament there were many German liberals who quickly came to the same conclusion as their French predecessors. Organized violence was necessary, after all, to defend liberty. It is increasingly clear that Bismarck's program of the 1860s was almost entirely of liberal provenance, a fact that was obscured for a time beneath the abuse heaped on him by postwar liberal historians like A. J. P. Taylor.[34] The seizing of Schleswig-Holstein in 1864 had been originally demanded in the Paulskirche in 1848; the subsequent wars on particularism and particularism's greatest historical champion, France, and the constitution of the new Reich both realized old liberal dreams. Even the despicable and poorly motivated *Kulturkampf* against the power of the Catholic church within the largely Protestant Reich in the 1870s was approved by numerous liberals of anticlerical bent in the Reichstag. This latter campaign bears more than a superficial resemblance to the French Civil Constitution of the Clergy of 1791. Both attempted to make priests into civil servants and to control official church teaching; both resulted in the wholesale jailing of priests and bishops; both were followed by reconciliations that, by restoring to the church a reformed autonomy, transformed it into a grudging partner of the status quo.

Bismarck was no liberal, but he delighted in undercutting the liberals' support by doing what they wanted done with greater flair and resolution than they were able to show (not being at the head of an army and loyal bureaucracy). Because he carried out liberal programs in dictatorial fashion, Bismarck has been compared with justice to the Napoleons; but this comparison underscores the normality rather than the abnormality of German history.[35] Liberal France required two bouts of Napoleonic dictatorship, from 1799 to 1814 and from 1855 to 1870, to ensure the creation of a stable liberal order. Bismarck's period of ascendancy was only slightly shorter in total and ended only slightly later.

The argument is sometimes made that England provides the real model of a peaceful transition to liberal society, with its long enjoyment of governmental stability and gradual reform from 1689 to the present. Even the seventeenth-century upheavals there were mild by comparison to the French Revolution or the bitter conflicts of German revolution and unification. But Barrington Moore rightly argued some years ago that governmental stability is not the same thing as social peace and that the piecemeal use of coercion in England over the long run probably matched the more fitful interludes of violence experienced elsewhere.[36] One need only recall the slow destruction of the small-scale owner-occupiers in the countryside from the late seventeenth through the early nineteenth centuries, the frequent suspensions of civil liberties, the heavy-handed rebuffs delivered by Parliament to popular lobbying after 1792, and the selective repression of popular assemblies and the popular press between 1810 and 1848. This is not a particularly distinguished record even when judged by the modest standards of Whig liberty.

The German Empire that Bismarck fashioned stands out in that it was not a full-fledged parliamentary regime. But in some respects this made it more consistent with the forms of institutions found in other spheres of society. The Reichstag under Bismarck was rather like a union committee in an English, French, or German factory of the time, able to speak but unable to make its will felt, tolerated at sufferance, consulted only on the rare occasions when wages were to be lowered (that is, the budget increased), and bullied into submission by various expedients even then. Germany was in this respect a more coherent polity than either England or France.

In England and France, it is commonly supposed, in contrast to Germany, liberty and popular sovereignty were by the beginning of World War I the guiding principles of the state. No better demonstration of the folly of such a belief could be found than the First World War itself, with its millions dying under the incompetent leadership of generals whose power went unchecked by any reasonable process of review or consultation, with its thousands of "free" journalists willing to tell the endless lies about the front that prevented the public from putting an end to the long and indecisive horror. The war was a fitting conclusion to a century of tyranny in all "economic" and "social" institutions, justified by an appeal to a delusory notion of liberty in the "political" sphere. Habits of obedience hamstrung all efforts to understand the destructive military potential that the industrial revolution had created. This chilling norm had no exceptions.

HONOR VERSUS SYMMETRY

The struggle over honor continues unabated in millions of workplaces and offices today, at times muted, at times abetted by the plans and commands of national union bureaucracies. These latter institutions, the great unions and union federations, have their dark sides, as everyone knows. A local president of one of the large U.S. national unions was recently reported to have said to a meeting of disgruntled members, "Let me tell you, the dues of all the people in this room wouldn't pay for the hubcaps on my Cadillac."[37] This comment reveals a monetary exchange asymmetry of a particularly sinister, if prevalent, kind – sinister because it has grown up within an organization whose bigness was originally intended to counteract the asymmetrical power of the employer. Of course, such developments cannot be understood apart from the structure of labor law, which varies significantly from one country to another, so that union influence is quite difficult to generalize about but usually domesticated by state intervention. Still, it is no accident that unions are so widely suspected of serving an integrative function and so widely viewed as needing shake-ups from below. They can lose touch with membership for the very reason that employers can afford to ignore laborers' grievances, because they are big and the laborer is little. Union reform, like labor conflict, is therefore unreflectively discussed as yet another field of combat in which individual heroism is to be displayed and collective honor defended.

The whole question of the modern left's unreflective dependence on a combative code of honor is in desperate need of further study for two reasons. First of all, the union movement has grown up without ever finding a theoretical guide that could uncover the centrality of honor and shame within workplace relationships. Unions have constantly built upon a militancy whose real shape and origins have never been examined, and they have as a result predictably thrown their organizational weight against spontaneity, against the rapid response to insult, damping down the constant guerrilla warfare over discipline so essential to laborers' self-respect, with the result that laborers often feel doubly cowed, doubly oppressed, boxed in, betrayed by their own organizations. Their very victories lead them back to a new kind of powerlessness. The weakness of the French labor movement may in this context be counted as a real strength.

Secondly, however useful notions of heroism and honor may be in struggles against a pervasive police-style discipline, the question must be raised whether a movement that imposes a desire for honor on its supporters through the established practices it creates is appropriate for building a new society. That honor codes are appropriate for establishing counterhierarchies based on "combat records" and shared hardships, that they help make a new elite feel empowered to act autocratically for the good of all (why consult democratically with the cowardly multitude?), has been amply demonstrated by the disastrous histories of certain postrevolutionary societies in this century. Particularly unfortunate has been the way in which notions of class have been put to use as badges, of honor or alternatively of shame, with which to reward the loyal or punish the opposition. It is not surprising that this has been such a successful strategy for rallying support, since the notion of class was born in a period of great civil strife in Europe. However, it is at least necessary to examine whether the constant drawing of lines in the dust is the best way of establishing those decisive new practices that will lead society out of conflict and fear, away from the necessity for mutual robbery imposed by capitalist individualism.

These issues cannot be fully explored here. One thing is certain. Such issues can never receive the attention they deserve so long as those who challenge the status quo remain in the grip of an accountant mentality, formulating their aims with the help of consumer price indexes and cost-of-living allowances or charts showing the inevitable tendency of capitalism toward crisis. So long as it is accepted that the economic sphere is one in which numbers hold special sway and in which relationships do not have to be judged by the same standards as prevail in families or in democratic institutions – an idea as common in most socialist states as it is in liberal ones – just so long will the progressive forces in society drift ineffectually or else, if they chance to gain influence for a while, fail to change the imbalances of power that crush freedom on every side. The challenge that feminism has raised to the established left will also continue to go unanswered until a larger conception of freedom is developed that gets beyond paycheck fetishism, that can be used with equal sureness to identify the injustices of familial, workplace, party, and governmental relationships alike.

What would such a conception of freedom look like? This essay has been aimed at making at least a small contribution toward answering that question. If the notion of exchange asymmetry has been of any use in diagnosing the ills of capitalist society and the failures of liberal and Marxist language, it is only because it points by implication to a concept of personal freedom starkly different both from Lockean independence and from socialist material sufficiency. For Locke, property was the key to liberty because property insulated the individual from the need to depend on anyone else's will. But such independence is possible only for a minority and indeed arises from the inevitable dependence of the penniless on those who have property. Socialists have from the beginning objected that the masses must be rescued from want, for without material sufficiency there can be no personal liberty; but it has never been made clear how such a rescue effort could be accomplished without tyrannical centralization of control.

Humans are inevitably connected to and dependent on each other; Lockean independence is an impossibility. But it is one thing to be connected and mutually dependent and quite another to be oppressed. Without going into detail here, it is easy enough to imagine a symmetrical relationship, that is, one in which both parties exchange things that are essential in the same way to each party. In such a relationship neither party can afford to jeopardize the relationship more easily than the other. Of course, this image is entirely too abstract and would appear to fit relationships as diverse as petty commodity production and exchange, mutual assured destruction, or a love affair. But then, a model that can be applied in all spheres is just what is needed.

This is not the place to press on toward greater precision. Still, it is worth remarking in conclusion a certain resonance between this notion and the concern of theorists as divergent as John Rawls and Jürgen Habermas in recent years with constructing a model of the social conditions necessary for impartial deliberation. For Rawls, impartial deliberation is impossible to organize, but by theorizing about conditions necessary for its occurrence, one can arrive at a rough estimate of what would be decided about social justice in such deliberation. Rawls describes an "original position" in which persons are denied knowledge of their social identity, their wealth or poverty, their intelligence or dull-wittedness. If people in such a position were asked to decide upon the kind of society they wished to live in, Rawls argues, they would be risk-averse and would vote for the creation of that social order in which the least advantaged would be as well off as possible. This therefore is the most just social order.[38] Habermas, speaking from an entirely different tradition, attempts to analyze the origin and character of "the coordinating power of speech acts," that is, of their power to coordinate the actions of many individuals. This is a power that cannot be explained by reference to institutional contexts of control, command, negotiation, or compromise because it is necessarily prior to the organization of such contexts. It is this coordinating power, Habermas argues, that must serve as the object of a reintegrated human science that is at once sociology, philosophy, and linguistics. Likewise, it is through an appreciation of this power that a critique of modernity will become possible.[39]

What these theoretical efforts share with the notion, implicit by negation in the present essay, of a symmetrical relationship is a concern with uncovering the conditions in which human connectedness is itself liberating. The liberal tradition has from the beginning sought liberty through disconnection; and the opposing ideologies that have grown up around it have sought only to deny disconnection, to undo it, without sufficiently understanding what kind of connection ought to replace it. In the capitalist world great monolithic institutions such as state bureaucracies and enterprises are controlled autocratically from the top down, with utterly inadequate corrective constraints imposed fitfully from the outside through electoral or market choices. An ideal symmetrical relationship would be one that really is *self*-correcting. No one could be disciplined by another except insofar as mutually essential relationships began to go badly in consequence of an ill-considered choice or action. Dissatisfaction would be registered immediately and felt mutually. This kind of discipline would allow one to confront the difficult mysteries of one's own existence and desires, without the comforting interference of domination.

Short of achieving utopia, however, it is not difficult to think of some simple reforms to correct the more blatant evils of monetary exchange asymmetries, reforms that any society that values democracy should enact at once. The standard list of civil liberties enjoyed in most Western democracies – freedom of speech and religion, freedom of assembly, right of due process – is the product of a long historical evolution; these liberties were developed to protect citizens in their extremely asymmetrical relationships to the state. That they often do not work well is as widely recognized as is their immense value. All wage laborers should be given similar protections against dismissal or wage cuts. This reform might not be so difficult to accomplish as it at first seems. Employment at will as a legal concept has already been under fire for some time. Introducing the whole panoply of civil rights into the workplace would entail the application of established practices that are widely disseminated and extremely familiar. At the same time it would amount to a social revolution; without ending private property one could reduce its arbitrary power dramatically. It is only necessary to think what a difference such liberties in the workplace would make for journalists and editorialists, and therefore for the whole process by which public opinion is formed. Indeed, without such protections it is ridiculous to suppose that we enjoy real free speech in the public sphere, where self-expression is currently guaranteed only to those who can afford to "speak" loudly enough to be heard. Their voices are magnified by the talent they buy (that is, dominate).

And this is just a small fraction of the change that would result. In the short term it would also be necessary to do something about the family, that vast neglected sector of the "economy." Reforms which ensure that men do not have a lesser stake in the relationship than women do – the right to abortion, carefully constructed divorce and child-custody laws, the equal right of partners over all property and resources – have already been proposed or enacted in many places. Legal precedent is now available for treating the housekeeper and caregiver as making an "economic" contribution that can be measured in proportion to the earnings of the wage-working partner. But nonfamilial "economic" institutions are still in a position to demand so much work outside the home from members of households that they ensure that one partner must remain behind loaded down with unrewarded, unrecognized, and superhuman tasks to perform. What good are free speech and freedom of assembly to a housekeeper and caregiver if there are no child-care institutions, no help with the laundry or the floors, no means of constraining a wage-earning partner to contribute to upkeep in case of separation? Failures of reciprocity whether in the home or in the factory can easily foreclose the exercise of citizenship rights in the supposedly separate political sphere.

In the short run, put simply, there would be no harm in continuing the struggle to ensure that all become actually able to enjoy the liberties they supposedly already have. The effort would move society toward a practical search for those new notions of the individual and of human connectedness that are needed if the species is ever to escape from the current worldwide imperium of what M. I. Finley has aptly called "number fetishism."[40]

Notes

Preface

1. William Lloyd Warner, *Yankee City Series*, 5 vols. (New Haven, Conn., 1941–59).

1. The crisis of the class concept in historical research

1. See the introduction to Theda Skocpol, *States and Social Revolutions: A Comparative Analysis of France, Russia, and China* (Cambridge, 1979), 3–43.
2. Some noteworthy examples are François Furet, *Penser la Révolution française* (Paris, 1978), trans. Elborg Forster under the title *Interpreting the French Revolution* (Cambridge, 1981); Lynn Hunt, *Politics, Culture, and Class in the French Revolution* (Berkeley, Calif., 1984); Charles Tilly, "Did the Cake of Custom Break?" in John M. Merriman, ed., *Consciousness and Class Experience in Nineteenth-Century Europe* (New York, 1979), 17–44; Arno J. Mayer, *The Persistence of the Old Regime: Europe to the Great War* (New York, 1981); and David Blackbourn and Geoff Eley, *Mythen deutscher Geschichtsschreibung: Die gescheiterte bürgerliche Revolution von 1848* (Frankfurt, 1980). An enlarged English version of this last work has appeared under the title *The Peculiarities of German History: Bourgeois Society and Politics in Nineteenth-Century Germany* (Oxford, 1984).
3. This view of the Revolution was elevated to the status of an orthodoxy by the work of Georges Lefebvre, especially his *Quatre-vingt-neuf* (Paris, 1939), trans. R. R. Palmer under the title *The Coming of the French Revolution* (Princeton, N.J., 1947; New York, [1960]).
4. The term is George V. Taylor's; see his "Noncapitalist Wealth and the Origins of the French Revolution," *American Historical Review*, 72 (1967):469–96. It has been echoed by François Furet, who speaks of the "revenus fonciers" of the old-regime elite as neither capitalist nor feudal in form; see his "Le catéchisme révolutionnaire," *Annales: Économies, sociétés, civilisations* 26 (1971):255–89, quotation from 273 (this article has been translated as "The Revolutionary Catechism," in idem, *Interpreting the French Revolution*, 81–131). A thorough review of this debate has been provided by William Doyle, *Origins of the French Revolution* (Oxford, 1980), 7–40; his attempt to provide a defensible revision of the Cobban approach in the rest of this study is also highly provocative.
5. See Doyle, *Origins*, 24, 28; and Guy Chaussinand-Nogaret, *La noblesse au XVIIIe siècle: De la féodalité aux Lumières* (Paris, 1976), especially 39–64.
6. Alfred Cobban, *The Social Interpretation of the French Revolution* (Cambridge, 1964), 54–67; Denis Richet, "Autours des origines idéologique lointaines de la Révolution française: Elites et despotisme," *Annales: Économies, sociétés, civilisations* 24 (1969):1–23.
7. Jean Meyer, *La noblesse bretonne au XVIIIe siècle*, 2 vols. (Paris, 1966); Chaussinand-Nogaret, *La noblesse*, 65–117; Lenard R. Berlanstein, *The Barristers of Toulouse in the Eigh-*

teenth Century (1740–1793) (Baltimore, 1975), 153–54, 184–85; Robert Darnton, *The Literary Underground of the Old Regime* (Cambridge, Mass., 1982; this is a collection of Darnton's papers on impecunious writers in the prerevolutionary period); Colin Lucas, "Nobles, Bourgeois, and the Origins of the French Revolution," *Past and Present,* no. 60 (1973), 84–126. "In explaining the democratic assault on despotism and aristocracy," Taylor remarks, "it is unnecessary to conjure up a social struggle rooted in economic change" (Taylor, "Noncapitalist Wealth," 491). See also Doyle, *Origins,* 20.

8. Chaussinand-Nogaret, *La noblesse,* 123. (Translations from French and German sources are my own unless otherwise indicated.)

9. See Darnton's biographical sketch of Jacques-Pierre Brissot, for example: "A Spy in Grub Street," in Darnton, *Literary Underground,* 41–70.

10. Georges Lefebvre, *La Révolution française,* 2d ed. (Paris, 1957), quoted from the translation by Elizabeth Moss Evanson, *The French Revolution,* 2 vols. (New York, 1962), I, 102.

11. Ibid., 134.

12. Chaussinand-Nogaret, *La noblesse,* 228.

13. Michelle Vovelle, *La chute de la Monarchie, 1787–1792* (Paris, 1972), 24. Part of this same passage was cited, in a different context, by William Sewell in "Etat, Corps, and Ordre: Some Notes on the Social Vocabulary of the Old Regime," in Hans-Ulrich Wehler, ed., *Sozialgeschichte heute: Festschrift für Hans Rosenberg zum 70. Geburtstag* (Göttingen, 1974), 49–68, quotation from 65.

14. Vovelle, *La chute,* 62–73.

15. Taylor, "Noncapitalist Wealth," concludes that this was "an unplanned, unpremeditated revolution" (492). Doyle, *Origins,* repeatedly stresses the role of chance and of the unexpected concatenation of simultaneous events.

16. David Landes, *The Unbound Prometheus: Technological Change and Industrial Development in Western Europe from 1750 to the Present* (Cambridge, 1969), 41–80, for example, emphasizes the distinctness of English society in the eighteenth century. Other characteristic statements of this view include T. S. Ashton, *The Industrial Revolution, 1760–1830* (Oxford, 1948); and Phyllis Deane, *The First Industrial Revolution,* 2d ed. (Cambridge, 1979).

17. The classic statement of Prussian distinctness is Hans Rosenberg, *Bureaucracy, Aristocracy, and Autocracy: The Prussian Experience, 1660–1815* (Cambridge, Mass., 1958); or see Otto Büsch, *Militärsystem und Sozialleben im alten Preussen, 1713–1807: Die Anfänge der sozialen Militarisierung der preussisch-deutschen Gesellschaft* (Frankfurt, 1981). Büsch states that the maintenance of the Prussian military system "required unconditionally the upholding of the society of estates [*standische Organisation der Gesellschaft*]" (167) and therefore resistance to the flow of social change. No problem of ambiguity about the status of estates in society, he implies, arose before the liberalization after defeat at Napoleon's hands in 1806.

18. Quotation is from G. E. Mingay, *English Landed Society in the Eighteenth Century* (London, 1963), 167. Dowries got out of hand, Mingay says, in the eighteenth century; only the increasing availability of mortgages and the unexpected tripling of land rents after 1760 saved the gentry from disaster: "These two factors made it possible for landowners to continue on their path of making increasingly generous family provision while raising their standards of consumption." Thus luck—in the form of an expanding economic environment—not peculiar management skill, ensured gentry prosperity (idem, *The Gentry: The Rise and Fall of a Ruling Class* [London, 1976], 113).

19. E. L. Jones, *Agriculture and the Industrial Revolution* (New York, 1974), 70, 72, and work cited there: M. A. Havinden, "Agricultural Progress in Open-Field Oxfordshire," *Agricultural History Review* 9 (1962):73–83.

20. P. K. O'Brien, "Agriculture and the Industrial Revolution," *Economic History Review*, 2d ser., 30 (1977), 166–81, especially 173, and works cited on 170. The main response of large landowners to rising prices was to increase the number of acres under the plow — hence the popularity of enclosures. But this was a rather passive, unimaginative reaction not to competition but to its absence. Prussian Junkers responded in identical fashion to the same stimulus. In both cases the result was lower yields per acre. See Mingay, *The Gentry*, 97; on Prussia, see Hanna Schissler, *Preussische Agrargesellschaft im Wandel: Wirschaftliche, gesellschaftliche, und politische Transformationsprozesse von 1763 bis 1847* (Göttingen, 1978), 59–61, 80.

21. Patrick Joyce traces family origins of the factory-owning groups of Lancashire back into the eighteenth century in *Work, Society, and Politics: The Culture of the Factory in Later Victorian England* (New Brunswick, N.J., 1980), 6–29. H. I. Dutton and J. E. King, in *"Ten Percent and No Surrender": The Preston Strike, 1853–1854* (Cambridge, 1981), 79, discuss gentry connections of Preston mill owners. Lawrence Stone and Jeanne Fautier Stone point out that industrialists' connections were more often with the lesser gentry than with the exclusive pinnacle; see *An Open Elite? England, 1540–1880* (Oxford, 1984), especially 193–239.

22. See John Seed, "Unitarianism, Political Economy, and the Antinomies of Liberal Culture in Manchester, 1830–50," *Social History* 7 (1982):1–25.

23. Commercial interests in Parliament often resisted Ricardian orthodoxy; see Barry Gordon, *Political Economy in Parliament, 1819–1823* (London, 1976), 16–33. Dutton and King, in *"Ten Percent,"* 79, report that many mill owners were avid Tories, and generally in that study they discuss the owners' flexible attitudes toward economic theory.

24. For a general introduction to this issue, see Peter Kriedte, *Spätfeudalismus und Handelskapital: Grundlinien der europäischen Wirtschaftsgeschichte vom 16. bis zum Ausgang des 18. Jahrhunderts* (Göttingen, 1980).

25. This parallel has been discussed by Elizabeth Fox-Genovese and Eugene D. Genovese, *Fruits of Merchant Capital: Slavery and Bourgeois Property in the Rise and Expansion of Capitalism* (Oxford, 1983), 394–96.

26. Schissler gives this date in *Preussische Agrargesellschaft*, 59.

27. Ibid., 66–69, 75.

28. Ibid., 70–71.

29. Ibid., 115.

30. Nichtweiss is quoted in ibid., 221; Schissler's own conclusion is on 103.

31. Robert Forster, *The Nobility of Toulouse in the Eighteenth Century: A Social and Economic Study* (Baltimore, 1960), concludes: "Shrewd and economical, this provincial nobility had long since abandoned the aristocratic tradition of *largesse*. As with other expenses, the burden of the family settlement was met in a businesslike manner" (151). See also François Bluche, *Les magistrats du Parlement de Paris au XVIIIᵉ siècle, 1715–1771* (Paris, 1960).

32. A convenient summary of the consequences of the Prussian agrarian reform is in Peter Brandt, Thomas Hofmann, and Reiner Zilkenat, *Preussen, zur Sozialgeschichte eines Staates: Eine Darstellung in Quellen* (Reinbek bei Hamburg, 1981), 99–115; see also Schissler, *Preussische Agrargesellschaft*, 106–15; and Reinhart Koselleck, *Preussen zwischen Reform und Revolution: Allgemeines Landrecht, Verwaltung, und soziale Bewegung von 1791 bis 1848*, 2d ed. (Stuttgart, 1975), 487–559.

33. Schissler, *Preussische Agrargesellschaft*, 156. See also Brandt, Hofmann, and Zilkenat, *Preussen*, 106; and Hans-Ulrich Wehler, *Das deutsche Kaiserreich, 1871–1918*, 4th ed. (Göttingen, 1980), 24–30.

34. See Koselleck, *Preussen zwischen Reform und Revolution*, 514–20; and Hans Rosenberg,

"Die Pseudodemokratisierung der Rittergutsbesitzerklasse," in Hans-Ulrich Wehler, ed., *Moderne deutsche Sozialgeschichte* (Cologne, 1966), 287–308.

35. See Darnton, *Literary Underground;* Jacques-Louis Ménétra, *Journal de ma vie: Compagnon vitrier au 18ᵉ siècle*, ed. with a commentary by Daniel Roche (Paris, 1982); and Chaussinand-Nogaret, *La noblesse*, 65–117. On the *basoche*, see Bailey Stone, *The Parliament of Paris, 1774–1789* (Chapel Hill, N.C., 1981), 176–77; and George Rudé, *The Crowd in the French Revolution* (Oxford, 1959), 29–33.

36. See Richard M. Andrews, "The Justices of the Peace of Revolutionary Paris, September 1792–November 1794 (Frimaire Year III)," *Past and Present*, no. 52 (1971), 56–105; and idem, "Social Structures and Political Elites in Revolutionary Paris, 1792–94: A Critical Appraisal of Soboul's *Sans-culottes parisiens*," in Fourteenth Consortium on Revolutionary Europe, *Proceedings*, ed. Harold T. Parker, Louise S. Parker, and William M. Reddy (Athens, Ga., 1986), 329–69; a version of this paper has also appeared under the same title, in the *Journal of Social History* 19 (1985):17–112.

37. Schissler's analysis is particularly informative on this point (*Preussische Agrargesellschaft*, 115–44).

38. William H. Sewell, *Work and Revolution in France: The Language of Labor from the Old Regime to 1848* (Cambridge, 1980), 78–83; François Furet, "The Revolutionary Catechism," in idem, *Interpreting the French Revolution*, 81–131.

39. See the review essay by Theodore S. Hamerow, "Guilt, Redemption, and Writing German History," *American Historical Review* 88 (1983):53–72; see also Blackbourn and Eley, *Mythen deutscher Geschichtsschreibung* or *Peculiarities of German History*. Current orthodoxy is represented in Wehler, *Das deutsche Kaiserreich;* or more recently in Michael Stürmer, *Das ruhelose Reich: Deutschland, 1866–1918* (Berlin, 1983).

40. See Geoff Eley, "Deutscher Sonderweg und englisches Vorbild," in Blackbourn and Eley, *Mythen deutscher Geschichtsschreibung*, 7–70. (The English version, "The British Model and the German Road," is on pp. 39–155 of Blackbourn and Eley, *Peculiarities of German History*.)

41. Standard accounts of 1848 include Veit Valentin, *Geschichte der deutschen Revolution, 1848/49*, 2 vols. (Berlin, 1930); and Rudolf Stadelmann, *Soziale und politische Geschichte von 1848* (Munich, 1948). See also the remarks of Michael Stürmer in "1848 in der deutschen Geschichte," in Wehler, *Sozialgeschichte heute*, 228–42.

42. Quoted in Leonard Krieger, *The German Idea of Freedom: History of a Political Tradition* (Chicago, 1957), 353 (all translations quoted from this work are Krieger's own).

43. Quoted in ibid.

44. Quoted in ibid., 354.

45. Ibid., 355.

46. Ibid., 362.

47. Quoted in Stürmer, "1848," 228.

48. Quoted in Theodore S. Hamerow, *The Social Foundations of German Unification, 1858–1871*, 2 vols. (Princeton, N.J., 1969–72), II, 160–61 (Hamerow's translation).

49. Krieger, *German Idea of Freedom*, 337, 348.

50. Stürmer, "1848," 237.

51. Koselleck, *Preussen zwischen Reform und Revolution*, 620–21.

52. Helmut Bleiber, "Die Revolution von 1848/49 in Deutschland in der bürgerlichen Geschichtsschreibung der BRD," in idem, ed., *Bourgeoisie und bürgerliche Umwälzung in Deutschland, 1789–1871* (Berlin, 1977), 193–277, quotation from 193–94: "Die deutsche Revolution 1848/49 scheiterte, weil die Bourgeoisie ab März 1848 an der Orientierung auf ein Bündnis mit dem Adel und der Frontstellung gegen die Volksmassen festhielt."

53. See Stürmer, "1848," 229; and Bleiber, "Die Revolution von 1848/49," 222.
54. Krieger, *German Idea of Freedom,* 292–94.
55. James H. Sheehan, "Partei, Volk, and Staat: Some Reflections on the Relationship between Liberal Thought and Action in Vormärz," in Wehler, *Sozialgeschichte heute,* 162–74, quotation from 166. Sheehan speaks in similar terms in his *German Liberalism in the Nineteenth Century* (Chicago, 1978), 24.
56. Wolfram Fischer, "Staat und Gesellschaft Badens im Vormärz," in idem, *Wirtschaft und Gesellschaft im Zeitalter der Industrialisierung* (Göttingen, 1972), 86–109.
57. Jerry M. Diefendorf, *Businessmen and Politics in the Rhineland, 1789–1834* (Princeton, N.J., 1980); Hansemann is discussed on 342–47.
58. Stürmer, "1848," 236.
59. See Hans-Ulrich Thamer, "Emanzipation und Tradition: Zur Ideen- und Sozialgeschichte von Liberalismus und Handwerk in der ersten Hälfte des 19. Jahrhunderts," in Wolfgang Schieder, ed., *Liberalismus in der Gesellschaft des deutschen Vormärz* (Göttingen, 1983), 55–73.
60. Wolfgang Schieder, "Probleme einer Sozialgeschichte des frühen Liberalismus in Deutschland," in idem, *Liberalismus,* 9–21, quotation from 17: "Es ist kein Zufall, dass in Deutschland im Unterschied zu England und Frankreich bis 1848 der Begriff des 'Mittelstandes' fur die ganze Breite des bürgerlichen Spektrums 'ununterbrochen' geläufig blieb."
61. Koselleck, *Preussen zwischen Reform und Revolution,* 560.
62. Stürmer, "1848"; Sheehan, *German Liberalism,* 7–50.
63. Mack Walker, *German Home Towns: Community, State, and General Estate, 1648–1871* (Ithaca, N.Y., 1971), 354–404.
64. Sheehan, *German Liberalism,* 7–18.
65. John Cameron, "Federalism in Marseilles," and James Hood, "Federalist Mobilization in the Gard," both in Fourteenth Consortium on Revolutionary Europe, *Proceedings,* 99–104, 105–15; W. Edmonds, " 'Federalism' and Urban Revolt in France in 1793," *Journal of Modern History* 55 (1983):22–53; Colin Lucas, *The Structure of the Terror: The Example of Javogues and the Loire* (Oxford, 1973); G. Lewis, *The Second Vendée: The Continuity of Counter-Revolution in the Department of the Gard, 1789–1815* (Oxford, 1978).
66. Wehler, *Das deutsche Kaiserreich,* 122–31; Rosenberg, "Pseudodemokratisierung."
67. Heidi Rosenbaum, *Formen der Familie: Untersuchungen zum Zusammenhang von Familienverhältnissen, Sozialstruktur, und sozialem Wandel in der deutschen Gesellschaft des 19. Jahrhunderts* (Frankfurt, 1982), 324 and notes.
68. Mayer, *Persistence,* 79–127.
69. David Blackbourn, "Wie es eigentlich nicht gewesen," in Blackbourn and Eley, *Mythen deutscher Geschichtsschreibung,* 71–139. (The English version, "The Discrete Charm of the Bourgeoisie," is on pp. 159–92 of Blackbourn and Eley, *Peculiarities of German History.*)
70. See Stürmer, *Das ruhelose Reich,* 25–48; and José Harris and Pat Thane, "British and European Bankers, 1880–1914: An 'Aristocratic Bourgeoisie'?" in Pat Thane, Geoffrey Crossick, and Roderick Floud, eds., *The Power of the Past: Essays for Eric Hobsbawm* (Cambridge, 1984), 215–34. On Krupp, see E. McCreary, "Social Welfare and Business: The Krupp Welfare Program, 1860–1914," *Business History Review* 42 (1968):24–50; and Brandt, Hofmann, and Zilkenat, *Preussen,* 245–48. David F. Crew, *Town in the Ruhr: A Social History of Bochum, 1860–1914* (New York, 1979), 145–56, argues for the modernity and rationality of paternalistic policies, as does Eley, "Deutscher Sonderweg," 43–44.
71. Lawrence Stone discusses status inconsistency in his "The English Revolution," in Robert Forster and Jack P. Greene, eds., *Preconditions of Revolution in Early Modern Europe* (Baltimore, 1970), 55–108, especially 62. Other important reviews of the controversy in-

clude J. H. Hexter, "Storm over the Gentry," in idem, *Reappraisals in History* (London, 1961), 117–62; and Christopher Hill, "Parliament and People in Seventeenth-Century England," *Past and Present*, no. 92 (1981), 100–24. See also Keith Tribe, *Genealogies of Capitalism* (Atlantic Highlands, N.J., 1981).

72. Lawrence Stone, *The Causes of the English Revolution, 1529–1642* (New York, 1972), 75.

73. Conrad Russell, *Parliaments and English Politics, 1621–1629* (Oxford, 1979).

74. Patrice Higonnet, *Class, Ideology, and the Rights of Nobles during the French Revolution* (Oxford, 1981), especially 63–71.

75. E. P. Thompson, *The Making of the English Working Class* (New York, 1963). Thompson discusses this fallacy on 189–94.

76. Compare, for example, E. J. Hobsbawm's *The Age of Revolution, 1789–1848* (New York, 1962), 44–72, with Ashton, *The Industrial Revolution,* or Deane, *The First Industrial Revolution;* significant agreement is evident.

77. An excellent anthology on the standard-of-living debate is Arthur J. Taylor, ed., *The Standard of Living in Britain in the Industrial Revolution* (London, 1975), which includes T. S. Ashton's 1949 essay, the exchanges between E. J. Hobsbawm and R. M. Hartwell of 1957–61, relevant excerpts from Thompson's *The Making,* and postscripts from Hobsbawm and Hartwell. See also Deane, *The First Industrial Revolution,* 255–71.

78. Thompson discusses the Hammonds' efforts of the 1930s to shift the debate onto these grounds in *The Making,* 196–97, 207–08.

79. This is the central thesis in *The Making,* most forcefully stated on 194–95.

80. Problems with Thompson's thesis in the larger context of English history are reviewed by Keith Nield, "A Symptomatic Dispute? Notes on the Relation between Marxian Theory and Historical Practice in Britain," *Social Research* 47 (1980):479–506. See also the very different views of Gareth Stedman Jones in his "The Language of Chartism," in James Epstein and Dorothy Thompson, eds., *The Chartist Experience* (London, 1982), 3–58, reprinted under the title "Rethinking Chartism," in Stedman Jones, *Languages of Class: Studies in English Working-Class History, 1832–1982* (Cambridge, 1983), 90–178. The evaluation of Thompson's thesis revolves around the question whether Chartism was truly a working-class movement and, if so, in what sense it was such and why it died a slow death in the period 1842–60. See also James Epstein, *The Lion of Freedom: Feargus O'Connor and the Chartist Movement, 1832–1842* (London, 1982).

81. See, for example, Craig Calhoun, *The Question of Class Struggle: Social Foundations of Popular Radicalism during the Industrial Revolution* (Oxford, 1982).

82. This statement of the matter may be found in V. I. Lenin, *Imperialism, the Highest Stage of Capitalism: A Popular Outline* (1916), in chap. 8. (In the *Collected Works,* 45 vols. [Moscow, 1963–70], see XXII, 281–84.) A good review of the subject is H. F. Moorhouse, "The Marxist Theory of the Labor Aristocracy," *Social History* 3 (1978):61–82.

83. That is, Lancashire mule spinners, especially those tending self-actors; see Joyce, *Work, Society, and Politics,* 50–89.

84. C. K. Harley, "Skilled Labor and the Choice of Technique in Edwardian Industry," *Explorations in Economic History,* ser. 2, 11 (1974):391–414.

85. Joyce, *Work, Society, and Politics,* 90–133; the quotation is from Robert Q. Gray, *The Labour Aristocracy in Victorian Edinburgh* (Oxford, 1976), 184.

86. Joyce, *Work, Society, and Politics,* 201–39; Joyce states that "there was no inexorable progression to an individualist democracy in which public opinion, separable from influence, achieved its free play some time in the third quarter of the century" (201).

87. Geoffrey Crossick, *An Artisan Elite in Victorian Society: Kentish London, 1840–1880* (London, 1978), especially 253. Crossick finds artisans openly embracing (while reinterpreting) middle-class respectability and Gladstonian liberalism (see 20, 219). But this cannot be called *embourgeoisement,* he concludes.

88. Gareth Stedman Jones, "Working-Class Culture and Working-Class Politics in London, 1870–1900: Notes on the Remaking of a Working Class," in idem, *Languages of Class*, 179, 238.

89. Michelle Perrot, *Les ouvriers en grève: France, 1871–1890*, 2 vols. (Paris, 1974); Maurice Agulhon, *La république au village* (Paris, 1971); Remi Gossez, *Les ouvriers de Paris*, I, *L'organisation, 1848–1851* (La Roche-sur-Yon, 1967); Roland Trempé, *Les mineurs de Carmaux, 1848–1914*, 2 vols. (Paris, 1971).

90. Both Joan Scott and Michael Hanangan have stressed the making and unmaking of such alliances. See Joan W. Scott, *The Glassworkers of Carmaux* (Cambridge, Mass., 1974); and Michael P. Hanagan, *The Logic of Solidarity: Artisans and Industrial Workers in Three French Towns, 1871–1914* (Urbana, Ill., 1980).

91. Royden Harrison, ed., *Independent Collier: The Coal Miner as Archetypal Proletarian Reconsidered* (New York, 1978); William H. Lazonick, "Industrial Relations and Technical Change: The Case of the Self-Acting Mule," *Cambridge Journal of Economics* 3 (1979):231–62; William M. Reddy, *The Rise of Market Culture: The Textile Trade and French Society, 1750–1900* (Cambridge, 1984); Joan W. Scott, "Men and Women in the Parisian Garment Trades: Discussions of Family and Work in the 1830s and 1840s," in Thane, Crossick, and Floud, *The Power of the Past*, 67–93.

92. See, for example, Christopher H. Johnson, "Patterns of Proletarianization: Parisian Tailors and Lodève Woolens Workers," in Merriman, *Consciousness and Class Experience*, 65–84; see also Ronald Aminzade, "Reinterpreting Capitalist Industrialization: A Study of Nineteenth-Century France," in Steven Laurence Kaplan and Cynthia J. Koepp, eds., *Work in France: Representations, Meaning, Organization, and Practice* (Ithaca, N.Y., 1986), 393–417. Wolfgang Renzsch follows a similar method when he includes the "proletaroid" small masters and homeworkers in his working class, reiterating the Thompsonian credo that despite all diversity, one must still hold by the notion of a single class; see his *Handwerker und Lohnarbeiter in der frühen Arbeiterbewegung: Zur sozialen Basis von Gewerkschaften und Sozialdemokratie im Reichsgrundungsjahrzehnt* (Göttingen, 1980), 12. In contrast, Martin Henkel and Rolf Taubert wish to insist on the temporal diversity of forms of protest and argue forcefully against all teleological tendencies in labor history in their *Maschinenstürmer: Ein Kapitel aus der Sozialgeschichte des technischen Fortschritts* (Frankfurt, 1979), 9–30.

93. Jacques Rancière, "The Myth of the Artisan: Critical Reflections on a Category of Social History," *International Labor and Working Class History*, no. 24 (1983), 1–16.

94. This is the thrust of Cobban's insistence on paying attention to contemporary social vocabulary in *Social Interpretation*, 15–24. Roland Mousnier likewise restricts the use of the term "class" to the nineteenth century alone (even the twentieth century he sees as full of societies of orders rather than classes); see his *Les hiérarchies sociales de 1450 à nos jours* (Paris, 1969).

95. Stone, *Causes of the English Revolution*, 33–34.

96. It is worth noting, however, that Jane Caplan, in a recent article, has concluded that "the class subject . . . is being withered away." See her "Myths, Models, and Missing Revolutions: Comments on a Debate in German History," *Radical History Review* 34 (1986):87–99.

97. See Sewell, *Work and Revolution;* Raymond Williams, *Marxism and Literature* (Oxford, 1977); Rainer Wirtz, *"Widersetzlichkeiten, Excesse, Crawalle, Tumulte und Skandale": Soziale Bewegung und gewalthafter sozialer Protest in Baden, 1815–1848* (Frankfurt, 1981); Sean Wilentz, *Chants Democratic: New York City and the Rise of the American Working Class, 1788–1850* (New York, 1984); Jacques Rancière, *La nuit des prolétaires* (Paris, 1981); Eley, "Deutscher Sonderweg"; Ronald Aminzade, *Class, Politics, and Early Industrial Capitalism: A Study of Mid-Nineteenth-Century Toulouse, France* (Albany, N.Y.,

1981); David Abraham, *The Collapse of the Weimar Republic: Political Economy and Crisis* (Princeton, N.J., 1981); Schissler, *Preussische Agrargesellschaft;* E. P. Thompson, "Eighteenth-Century English Society: Class Struggle without Class?" *Social History* 3 (1978):133–65; and Blackbourn, "Wie es eigentlich nicht gewesen."

98. Ralf Dahrendorf, *Class and Class Conflict in Industrial Society* (Stanford, Calif., 1959); Nicos Poulantzas, *Political Power and Social Classes* (London, 1973); Lucio Colletti, *From Rousseau to Lenin: Studies in Ideology and Society* (New York, 1972); Pierre Bourdieu, *La distinction: Critique social du jugement* (Paris, 1979); Erik Olin Wright, *Classes* (London, 1985); Michael Burawoy, *The Politics of Production* (London, 1985).

99. Bourdieu, *La distinction.*

100. Wright, *Classes.*

101. Burawoy, *Politics of Production.*

2. Meaning and its material base

1. Lenard R. Berlanstein raises this question forcefully in the concluding remarks of his *The Barristers of Toulouse in the Eighteenth Century (1740–1793)* (Baltimore, 1975), 183–86. In effect, lawyers who went to the meeting of the Estates General appear to have become far more radical than their counterparts – indistinguishable in every other respect – who stayed at home.

2. Natalie Z. Davis, "The Rites of Violence: Religious Riot in Sixteenth-Century France," *Past and Present,* no. 59 (1973), 51–91. This essay was reprinted in her collection *Society and Culture in Early Modern France* (Stanford, Calif., 1975), 152–87.

3. E. P. Thompson, "The Moral Economy of the English Crowd in the Eighteenth Century," *Past and Present,* no. 50 (1971), 76–136, quotation from 76.

4. Ibid., 78.

5. See especially two works of Michel Foucault: *Les mots et les choses: Une archéologies des sciences humaines* (Paris, 1966); and *Surveiller et punir: Naissance de la prison* (Paris, 1975). They have been translated respectively as *The Order of Things: An Archeology of the Human Sciences* (New York, 1971) and *Discipline and Punish: The Birth of the Prison,* trans. Alan Sheridan (New York, 1977). On Foucault, see the still-useful review by Hayden White, "Foucault Decoded: Notes from Underground," *History and Theory* 12 (1973):23–54; and Hubert L. Dreyfus and Paul Rabinow, *Michel Foucault: Beyond Structuralism and Hermeneutics* (Chicago, 1982).

6. Clifford Geertz, *The Interpretation of Cultures* (New York, 1973); on his influence on historians, see Ronald G. Walters, "Signs of the Times: Clifford Geertz and Historians," *Social Research* 47 (1980):537–56.

7. See, for example, Albert O. Hirschman, *The Passions and the Interests: Political Arguments for Capitalism before Its Triumph* (Princeton, N.J., 1977); Joyce Oldham Appleby, *Economic Thought and Ideology in Seventeenth-Century England* (Princeton, N.J., 1978); Maxine Berg, *The Machinery Question and the Making of Political Economy, 1815–1848* (Cambridge, 1980); Gertrude Himmelfarb, *The Idea of Poverty: England in the Early Industrial Age* (New York, 1984); and Keith Tribe, *Genealogies of Capitalism* (Atlantic Highlands, N.J., 1981).

8. See the exchange between David Selbourne and Raphael Samuel in *History Workshop Journal,* no. 9 (1980):150–76, and the letter from David Selbourne in no. 13 (Spring 1982), 189–90.

9. Thomas W. Laqueur, "The Queen Caroline Affair: Politics as Art in the Reign of George IV," *Journal of Modern History* 54 (1982):417–66; Gareth Stedman Jones, "The Language of Chartism," in James Epstein and Dorothy Thompson, eds., *The Chartist Experience* (London, 1982), 3–58, reprinted under the title "Rethinking Chartism," in Sted-

man Jones, *Languages of Class; Studies in English Working-Class History, 1832–1982* (Cambridge, 1983), 90–178.

10. See, for example, a number of recent anthologies on this theme: Gerhard Huck, ed., *Sozialgeschichte der Freizeit* (Wuppertal, 1980); Jürgen Reulecke and Wolfhard Weber, eds., *Fabrik, Familie, Feierabend: Beiträge zur Sozialgeschichte des Alltags im Industriezeitalter* (Wuppertal, 1978); and Peter Borscheid and Hans J. Teuteberg, eds., *Ehe, Liebe, Tod: Studien zur Geschichte des Alltags* (Munster, 1983). See also Vernon Lidtke, *The Alternative Culture: The Socialist Labor Movement in Imperial Germany* (Oxford, 1985).

11. Alf Lüdtke, *"Gemeinwohl," Polizei, und "Festungspraxis": Staatliche Gewaltsamkeit und innere Verwaltung in Preussen, 1815–1850* (Göttingen, 1982); David Warren Sabean, *Power in the Blood: Popular Culture and Village Discourse in Early Modern Germany* (Cambridge, 1984).

12. It was just in struggling with such limiting phenomena of the age that Lucien Febvre sought to understand its religiosity in his *Le problème de l'incroyance au XVIe siècle: La religion de Rabelais* (Paris, 1942). It is not that there is any fundamental disagreement between Febvre and Davis but that cultural interpretation as she uses it in this essay offers few guides for dealing with limiting phenomena.

13. Robert Forster, *Merchants, Landlords, Magistrates: The Depont Family in Eighteenth-Century France* (Baltimore, 1980), 5–11.

14. Philip D. Curtin used such records in his *The Atlantic Slave Trade: A Census* (Madison, Wis., 1969), 275–86 (cited by Forster, *Merchants*, 11).

15. Forster, *Merchants*, especially 24.

16. The following passage is based on Jacques-Louis Ménétra, *Journal de ma vie: Compagnon vitrier au 18e siècle*, ed. with a commentary by Daniel Roche (Paris, 1982).

17. Studies like Forster's work on the Deponts and Roche's commentary on Ménétra (cited in notes 13 and 16 to this chapter) have been prompted by just this realization. Social historians in recent years have become increasingly concerned with individual biography as a key for understanding cultural forms and influences. Other examples are Robert Darnton's studies in *The Literary Underground of the Old Regime* (Cambridge, Mass., 1982), his *The Business of Enlightenment: A Publishing History of the Encyclopédie, 1775–1800* (Cambridge, Mass., 1979), and his most recent collection of papers, *The Great Cat Massacre and Other Episodes in French Cultural History* (New York, 1984); or Jacques Rancière's *La nuit des prolétaires* (Paris, 1981).

18. See "Debate: The Rites of Violence, Religious Riot in Sixteenth-Century France," in *Past and Present*, no. 67 (1975); "A Comment" by Janine Estèbe, 127–30, and "A Rejoinder" by Natalie Z. Davis, 131–35, quotation from 132.

19. Abbé Prévost, *Histoire du chevalier Des Grieux et de Manon Lescaut* (1731); Restif de la Bretonne, *Le paysan perverti, ou des dangers de la ville: Histoire récente mise au jour d'après les véritables lettres des personnages* (1776). A good example from Bossuet is his short homily "Liberté et indépendance" (1659), reprinted in Jacques Le Brun, *Bossuet* (Paris, 1970), 125–26. Louis-Sébastien Mercier, *Tableau de Paris: Nouvelle édition corrigée et augmentée* (Amsterdam, 1783).

20. François Furet, *Penser la Révolution française* (Paris, 1978), trans. Elborg Forster under the title *Interpreting the French Revolution* (Cambridge, 1981).

21. See Lynn Hunt's review of Furet's book in *History and Theory* 20 (1981):313–23.

22. Furet, *Interpreting the French Revolution*, 51.

23. Ibid., 48.

24. Ibid., 49.

25. Lynn Hunt, *Politics, Culture, and Class in the French Revolution* (Berkeley, Calif., 1984).

26. Ibid., 55.

27. Historical opinion has been generally negative, ranging from A. J. P. Taylor's post–World War II verdict that the German liberals of the 1860s "would have been ashamed of

a liberty that had been fought for" (*The Course of German History: A Survey of the Development of Germany since 1815* [London, n.d.], 100) to James J. Sheehan's observations that German liberals experienced "self doubts" and "practical and theoretical difficulties" vis-à-vis the state (*German Liberalism in the Nineteenth Century*) [Chicago, 1978], 109, 115).

28. Theodores S. Hamerow, *The Social Foundations of German Unification, 1858–1871*, 2 vols. (Princeton, N.J., 1969–72), II, 150–58, argues that the liberals in the Prussian Parliament were anxious for compromise and were maneuvered against their will into a confrontation with the crown in the early 1860s.

29. Ralf Dahrendorf, *Gesellschaft und Demokratie in Deutschland* (Munich, 1965), 415–48, trans. under the title *Society and Democracy in Germany* (Garden City, N.J., 1967), 385–418.

30. William H. Sewell, *Work and Revolution in France: The Language of Labor from the Old Regime to 1848* (Cambridge, 1980).

31. Sewell's method is in fact extremely similar to Raymond Williams's in practice; compare Williams's *The Country and the City* (Oxford, 1973), which likewise shows dominant notions of legitimacy and justice constantly opening opportunities of protest.

32. Rancière, *La nuit des prolétaires*.

33. Ironically, this shift in interest toward cultural interpretation was occurring in French and English social history just as a new generation of German historians, including Hans-Ulrich Wehler and Jürgen Kocka, was seeking to jettison the vagueness of previous interpretive practice there. Tired of characterizations of the German spirit and German traditions, these historians wanted concrete examination of institutions and social structure. See Theodore S. Hamerow, "Guilt, Redemption, and Writing German History," *American Historical Review* 88 (1983):53–72. The absence of a revisionist thrust in German historiography was crucial to this gap. As late as 1972 Hamerow could still make statements like the following, in terms that would have satisfied Lenin perfectly: "The failure of the new era to reconcile the opposing interests of the landed aristocracy and the urban bourgeoisie in Prussia led to a struggle between crown and parliament" (*Social Foundations*, II, 149). This is a way of talking in which no one would dare indulge any more for France.

34. Hayden White, *Metahistory: The Historical Imagination in Nineteenth-Century Europe* (Baltimore, 1973); Foucault, *Les mots et les choses*.

35. On Hector, see James M. Redfield, *Nature and Culture in the Iliad: The Tragedy of Hector* (Chicago, 1977).

36. See, for example, John Keegan, *The Face of Battle* (New York, 1976); or Harold T. Parker, *Three Napoleonic Battles* (Durham, N.C., 1944).

37. Bernard at first hesitated to sanction a religious fraternity dedicated to violence (the Knights Templar); see P. Cousin, "Les débutants de l'order des Templiers et Saint Bernard," in *Mélanges Saint Bernard: XXVᵉ Congrès de l'Association bourguignonne des sociétés savantes* (Dijon, 1953), 41–52.

38. Gavan Daws, *Shoal of Time: A History of the Hawaiian Islands* (New York, 1968), 31.

39. See Ralph S. Kuykendall, *The Hawaiian Kingdom, 1778–1854* (Honolulu, 1947), 29–60.

40. Marshall Sahlins, *Historical Metaphors and Mythical Realities: Structure in the Early History of the Sandwich Island Kingdom* (Ann Arbor, Mich., 1981).

41. Sahlins, in ibid., 22–26, for example, provides an account of the death of Cook in which the cultural logic of his killing is clear but in which, on reflection, it is also clear that at the crucial moment before his death no one knew what to do. Although Sahlins generally underplays the role of uncertainty and blithely treats the impact of European technology as just so much "[mana] in the form of guns, ships, and resident advisers" (26), nonetheless his general theoretical approach to cultural change is highly relevant here and superior on several accounts to that of Furet or Sewell.

42. See accounts of the death of Keoua in Daws, *Shoal of Time*, 36; and Kuykendall, *Hawaiian Kingdom*, 38.

43. Elizabeth Fox-Genovese and Eugene D. Genovese, *Fruits of Merchant Capital: Slavery and Bourgeois Property in the Rise and Expansion of Capitalism* (Oxford, 1983), quotations from 200, 208.

44. See two well-known examples: Marcel Mauss, "Essai sur le don: Forme et raison de l'échange dans les sociétés archaïques," *Année sociologique* 1, n.s. (1925):30–186, trans. Ian Cunnison under the title *The Gift: Forms and Functions of Exchange in Archaic Societies* (New York, 1967); and Karl Polanyi, *The Great Transformation* (Boston, 1967), 43–55.

45. Bronislaw Malinowski, *Argonauts of the Western Pacific* (London, 1922). An extensive bibliography of studies of kula trade and references to it in theoretical discussions has been compiled by Martha Macintyre: *The Kula: A Bibliography* (Cambridge, 1983), especially 21–66. See also the recent anthology *The Kula: New Perspectives on Massim Exchange*, ed. Jerry W. Leach and Edmund Leach (Cambridge, 1983).

46. Especially in the practice of invoking magical powers to induce others to give oneself coveted gifts. See Malinowski, *Argonauts*, especially 392–427.

47. Lester C. Thurow, *Dangerous Currents: The State of Economics* (New York, 1983), 219.

48. See the appendix by John Liep in Macintyre, *The Kula*, 85–86; Liep concludes that "for two of the three sources of kula necklaces we can therefore establish that Malinowski was wrong."

49. An excellent review of this matter is Theodore K. Rabb, *The Struggle for Stability in Early Modern Europe* (Oxford, 1975), especially 83–99. See also Heiner Haan, "Prosperität und Dreissig jähriger Krieg," *Geschichte und Gesellschaft* 7 (1981):91–118; Peter Burke, ed., *Economy and Society in Early Modern Europe: Essays from Annales* (London, 1972); Carlo M. Cipolla, *Before the Industrial Revolution: European Economy and Society, 1000–1700*, 2d ed. (New York, 1980), 225–33; and Dennis O. Flynn, "Sixteenth-Century Inflation from a Production Point of View," in Nathan Schmukler and Edward Marcus, eds., *Inflation through the Ages: Economic, Social, Psychological, and Historical Aspects* (New York, 1983), 157–69.

50. See Jack H. Hexter, "Storm over the Gentry," in idem, *Reappraisals in History* (London, 1961), 117–62; and Lawrence Stone, *The Causes of the English Revolution, 1529–1642* (New York, 1972), 74.

51. See H. R. Ghosal, *Economic Transition in the Bengal Presidency (1793–1833)* (Calcutta, 1966), 1–39; and Michael Edwardes, *British India, 1772–1947: A Survey of the Nature and Effects of Alien Rule* (New York: 1967), 86–93.

52. Edwardes, *British India*, 89.

53. Ghosal, *Economic Transition*, 32.

54. Quoted in ibid., 286–87 (Ghosal's translation).

55. See William M. Reddy, *The Rise of Market Culture: The Textile Trade and French Society, 1750–1900* (Cambridge, 1984), chap. 2.

56. See Ronald B. Inden, *Marriage and Rank in Bengali Culture: A History of Caste and Clan in Middle Period Bengal* (Berkeley, 1976); E. P. Thompson, *The Making of the English Working Class* (New York, 1963), 269–313; and Duncan Bythell, *The Handloom Weavers: A Study in the English Cotton Industry during the Industrial Revolution* (Cambridge, 1969).

3. Growth of the liberal illusion

1. See Joyce Oldham Appleby, *Economic Thought and Ideology in Seventeenth-Century England* (Princeton, N.J., 1978), especially 52–72.

2. Quoted in Appleby, *Economic Thought,* 45; see also Albert O. Hirschman, *The Passions and the Interests: Political Arguments for Capitalism before Its Triumph* (Princeton, N.J., 1977).

3. Quoted in Appleby, *Economic Thought,* 71.

4. This line of reasoning is discussed by Hirschman, *The Passions and the Interests.*

5. Taken from the 1769 edition, as excerpted in Peter Gay, ed., *The Enlightenment: A Comprehensive Anthology* (New York, 1973), 253 (Gay's translation). The original French reads: "Un missionnaire voyageant dans l'Inde rencontra un fakir chargé de chaines, nu comme un singe, couché sur le ventre, et se faisant fouetter pour les péchés de ses compatriotes, les Indiens, qui lui donnaient quelques liards du pays. 'Quel renoncement à soi-même!' disait un des spectateurs. 'Renoncement à moi-même!' reprit le fakir; 'apprenez que je ne me fais fesser dans ce monde que pour vous le rendre dans l'autre, quand vous serez chevaux et moi cavalier.' "

6. Richard S. Dunn, *Sugar and Slaves: The Rise of the Planter Class in the English West Indies, 1624–1713* (Chapel Hill, N.C., 1972).

7. Voltaire, in his famous *Lettres anglaises* of 1734, used just such an image in the sixth letter: "Entrez dans la Bourse de Londres, cette Place plus respectable que bien des Cours; vous y voyez rassemblés les députés de toutes les Nations pour l'utilité des hommes. La, le Juif, le Mahometan, et le Chrétien traitent l'un avec l'autre comme s'ils étaient de la même Religion, et ne donnent le nom d'infidèles qu'à ceux qui font banqueroute; là, le Presbytérien se fie à l'Anabaptiste, et l'Anglican reçoit la promesse du Quaker. Au sortir de ces pacifiques et libres assemblées, les uns vont à la Synagogue, les autres vont boire; celui-ci va se faire baptiser dans une grande cuve au nom du Père par le Fils au Saint Esprit; celui-là fait couper la prépuce de son fils et fait marmotter sur l'enfant des paroles hébraïque qu'il n'entend point; ces autres vont dans leur Eglise attendre l'inspiration de Dieu, leur chapeau sur la tête, et tous sont contents."

8. On the life of the rich at the beginning of the eighteenth century, see Raymond Williams, *The Country and the City* (Oxford, 1973), 55–107; E. P. Thompson, *Whigs and Hunters: The Origin of the Black Act* (New York, 1975); Pierre Goubert, *Beauvais et le Beauvaisis de 1600 à 1730* (Paris, 1960), 197–222; Jean Meyer, *La vie quotidienne en France au temps de la Régence* (Paris, 1979); and G. E. Mingay, *The Gentry: The Rise and Fall of a Ruling Class* (London, 1976), 80–164.

9. On the life of the poor at this time, see Thompson, *Whigs;* Peter Laslett, *The World We Have Lost* (New York, 1966); Daniel Roche, *Le peuple de Paris: Essai sur la culture populaire au XVIIIᵉ siècle* (Paris, 1981); and Michael Sonenscher, "Work and Wages in Paris in the Eighteenth Century," in Maxine Berg, Pat Hudson, and Michael Sonenscher, eds., *Manufacture in Town and Country before the Factory* (Cambridge, 1983), 147–72.

10. See especially Steven L. Kaplan, *The Famine Plot Persuasion in Eighteenth-Century France* (Philadelphia, 1982); and Richard Cobb, *The Police and the People: French Popular Protest, 1789–1820* (Oxford, 1970), 215–324.

11. For rural areas, see notes 15 and 16 to this chapter; for urban workshops, see Sonenscher, "Work and Wages in Paris."

12. G. E. Mingay, *English Landed Society in the Eighteenth Century* (London, 1963), 169.

13. The passage cited from Mingay may be paired with Raymond Williams's discussion of a passage from George Eliot's *Adam Bede* on the helplessness of tenant farmers before the landlord's caprices; see *The Country and the City,* 166–68. The point being made here echoes the incisive discussion of Charles E. Lindblom, *Politics and Markets: The World's Political-Economic Systems* (New York, 1977), 33–51.

14. Marcel Mauss, *The Gift: Forms and Functions of Exchange in Archaic Societies,* trans. Ian Cunnison (New York, 1967), 40–41.

15. On sharecroppers' being subjected to direct and detailed surveillance, see the remarks of G. E. M. de Ste. Croix, *Class Struggle in the Ancient Greek World from the Archaic Age to the Arab Conquests* (Ithaca, N.Y., 1981), 257; see also the excellent study on the Emilia Romagna by David I. Kertzer, *Family Life in Central Italy, 1880–1910: Sharecropping, Wage Labor, and Coresidence* (New Brunswick, N.J., 1984). To reduce the need for direct surveillance, landowners sometimes had recourse to sharecropping agreements in which the half share due as rent was simultaneously specified in the contract by exact amounts of grain or other produce. This "half" was due even if it was more than half; see Louis Merle's brilliant discussion of sharecropping in *La métairie et l'évolution agraire de la Gâtine poitevine de la fin du Moyen Age à la Révolution* (Paris, 1958), especially 161–85.

16. Leaseholds for money rent were apparently most common in England by 1700; they were also widespread (and on the increase) in France and less common though spreading in Germany. See, in general, Mingay, *Landed Society,* 163–88; Paul Bois, *Les paysans de l'ouest: Des structures économiques et sociales aux opinions politiques depuis l'époque révolutionnaire dans la Sarthe* (Le Mans, 1960), 423–69; Goubert, *Beauvais et le Beauvaisis,* 151–96; Wilhelm Abel, *Geschichte der deutschen Landwirtschaft vom frühen Mittelalter bis zum 19. Jahrhundert* (Stuttgart, 1962), 91–93; Hanna Schissler, *Preussische Agrargesellschaft im Wandel: Wirtschaftliche, gesellschaftliche, und politische Transformationsprozesse von 1763 bis 1847* (Göttingen, 1978), 87–89; and Eberhard Weiss, "Ergebnisse eines Vergleichs der grundherrschaftlichen Strukturen Deutschlands und Frankreichs vom 13. bis zum Ausgang des 18. Jahrhunderts," *Vierteljahrschrift fur Sozial- und Wirtschaftsgeschichte* 57 (1970):1–14. On the special nature of heritable leaseholds, see Merle, *La métairie,* 166; Friedrich Mager, *Geschichte des Bauerntums und der Bodkenkulture im Lande Mecklenburg* (Berlin, 1955), 359–62; and T. J. A. Le Goff and D. M. G. Sutherland, "The Social Origins of Counter-Revolution in Western France," *Past and Present,* no. 99 (1983), 65–87. Forms of tenure in France are discussed in more detail in Chapter 4.

17. See de Ste. Croix, *Class Struggle,* 278–326; and M. I. Finley, *Ancient Slavery and Modern Ideology* (Harmondsworth, 1983), 67–92.

18. See the works cited in the preceding note; see also the pertinent summary of recent research in John V. A. Fine, *The Ancient Greeks: A Critical History* (Cambridge, Mass., 1983), 383–441.

19. See P. A. Brunt, *Social Conflicts in the Roman Republic* (London, 1971); see also de Ste. Croix, *Class Struggle,* 332–44, 453–503; Finley, *Ancient Slavery,* 123–49; and Walter A. Goffart, *Caput and Colonate: Towards a History of Late Roman Taxation* (Toronto, 1974).

20. De Ste. Croix remarks that "the disagreement about the best way of using the expression 'class' has been so great that anyone who attempts an analysis of any society in terms of class is entitled to establish his own criteria, within very wide limits, and that our verdict on the definition he adopts ought to depend solely on its clarity and consistency, the extent to which it corresponds with the historical realities to which it is applied, and its fruitfulness as a tool of historical and sociological analysis" (*Class Struggle,* 43).

21. Use of the term "serf" here follows de Ste. Croix, *Class Struggle,* 226–59. See also Goffart, *Caput and Colonate;* and A. H. M. Jones, *The Roman Economy* (Oxford, 1974) – the latter reference thanks to Dennis Trout.

22. See Marc Bloch, *French Rural History: An Essay on Its Basic Characteristics,* trans. Janet Sondheimer (Berkeley, Calif., 1966), 64–118; Guy Bois, *Crise du féodalisme* (Paris, 1981), especially 160–214, 280–83, 318–28; Robert Brenner, "Agrarian Class Structure and Economic Development in Pre-Industrial Europe," *Past and Present,* no. 70 (1976), 30–75; and Peter Blickle, *Die Revolution von 1525* (Munich, 1975).

23. Bloch, *French Rural History,* 118–49; Emmanuel Le Roy Ladurie, *Les paysans de*

Languedoc, 2 vols. (Paris, 1966), especially I, 415–508; Goubert, *Beauvais et le Beauvaisis,* 151–222.

24. C. B. Macpherson, *The Political Theory of Possessive Individualism: Hobbes to Locke* (Oxford, 1962), 107–59.
25. Ibid., 123.
26. Ibid., 124.
27. Quoted in ibid., 208–09, emphasis in original.
28. Quoted in ibid., 223.
29. Charles de Secondat, Baron de la Brède et de Montesquieu, *De l'esprit des lois,* 2 vols. (1748; Paris: Editions Garnier frères, 1973), quotation from XI, 6, vol. I, p. 172 (citations are by book [roman] and chapter [arabic], with volume and page references to the Garnier edition). The whole original sentence reads: "Tous les citoyens, dans les divers districts, doivent avoir droit de donner leur voix pour choisir le représentant; excepté ceux qui sont dans un tel état de bassesse, qu'ils sont réputés n'avoir point de volonté propre."
30. Ibid., XI, 6, vol. I, pp. 172–73: "Il y a toujours dans un Etat des gens distingués par la naissance, les richesses ou les honneurs; mail s'ils étoient confondus parmi le peuple, et s'ils n'y avoient qu'une voix comme les autre, la liberté commune seroit leur esclavage, et ils n'auroient aucun intérêt à la défendre, parce que la plupart des résolutions seroient contre eux."
31. Ibid., XI, 8, vol. I, pp. 180–81: "Violà l'origine du gouvernement gothique parmi nous. Il fut d'abord mêlé de l'aristocratie et de la monarchie. Il avoit cet inconvénient que le bas peuple y étoit esclave. C'étoit un bon gouvernement qui avoit en soi la capacité de devenir meilleur. La coutume vint d'accorder des lettres d'affranchissement; et bientôt la liberté civile du peuple, les prérogatives de la noblesse et du clergé, la puissance des rois, se trouvèrent dans un tel concert, que je ne crois pas qu'il y ait eu sur la terre de gouvernement si bien tempéré que le fut celui de chaque partie de l'Europe dans le temps qu'il y subsista."
32. Ibid., XXVI, 15, vol. II, p. 185; XI, 18, vol. I, p. 197; XIII, I, vol. I, p. 229: ". . . le bien public est toujours que chacun conserve invariablement la propriété que lui donnent les lois civiles"; "La constitution de Rome étoit fondée sur ce principe, que ceux-là devoient être soldats, qui avoient assez de bien pour répondre de leur conduite à la république. Les chevaliers, comme les plus riches, formoient la cavalerie des legions. Lorsque leur dignité fut augmentée, ils ne voulurent plus servir dans cette milice; il fallut lever une autre cavalerie: Marius prit toute sorte de gens dans les légions, et la république fut perdue"; "Les revenus de l'Etat sont une portion que chaque citoyen donne de son bien pour avoir la sureté de l'autre. . . . Il n'y a rien que la sagesse et la prudence doivent plus regler que cette portion qu'on ôte et cette portion qu'on laisse aux sujets."
33. See the articles on *propriété, liberté naturelle,* and *liberté civile* in the *Encyclopédie ou dictionnaire raisonné des sciences, des arts et des métiers,* 35 vols. (various places of publication, 1751–70).
34. A convenient translation appears in an appendix to Georges Lefebvre, *The Coming of the French Revolution,* trans. R. R. Palmer (Princeton, N.J., 1947; New York, [1960]).
35. See the remarks of John B. Noone, Jr., *Rousseau's Social Contract: A Conceptual Analysis* (Athens, Ga., 1980), 88–109.
36. Montesquieu, *De l'esprit des lois,* XX, 2, vol. II, p. 3.
37. Ibid.
38. Adam Ferguson, *An Essay on the History of Civil Society,* ed. with an introduction by Duncan Forbes (Edinburgh, 1966), 184–85.

39. Ibid., 186.
40. Adam Smith, *An Inquiry into the Nature and Causes of the Wealth of Nations* (1776): see bk. I, chaps. 1 and 2.
41. Ibid., bk. I, chap. 10. This is the first paragraph of that chapter, entitled, "Of Wages and Profits in the Different Employments of Labor and Stock."
42. François Quesnay, *Tableau économique* (1758).
43. Nassau W. Senior, *An Outline of the Science of Political Economy* (London, 1836; London: Allen & Unwin, 1938), 205–06.
44. John Stuart Mill, *Principles of Political Economy with Some of Their Applications to Social Philosophy* (London, 1848; London: Longmans, Green, 1904), bk. II, chap. 14, p. 386.
45. See, for example, the exchange on this point between Rottenberg and Lampmann: Simon Rottenberg, "On Choice in Labor Markets," and Robert J. Lampmann, "On Choice in Labor Markets: Comment," in John F. Burton, Jr., Lee K. Benham, William M. Vaughn, III, and Robert J. Flanagan, eds., *Readings in Labor Market Analysis* (New York, 1971), 37–52, 53–60; see also Lester C. Thurow, *Generating Inequality: Mechanisms of Distribution in the U.S. Economy* (New York, 1975), 211–30.
46. Senior, *Outline*, 202.
47. For some interesting remarks on this point, see Max Weber, *Economy and Society: An Outline of Interpretive Sociology*, ed. Guenther Roth and Claus Wittich, 3 vols. (New York, 1968), I, 108; and David Harvey, *The Limits to Capital* (Chicago, 1982), 239–82.
48. Marie E. Vopelius, *Die altliberalen Oekonomen und die Reformzeit* (Stuttgart, 1968).
49. See ibid., especially 16–23, 48–51, for her discussions of Christian Garve, Friedrich Benedikt Weber, and Michael Alexander Lips. A notable exception, who felt that Smith's theory was an inappropriate tool for understanding land distribution, was Georg Sartorius (discussed in ibid., 36–42).
50. Ibid., 26.
51. Ibid., 26–28.
52. Quoted in ibid., 27.
53. In contrast, Sartorius, in an 1820 essay, worried that personal freedom would be of little use to the peasant, who would be ruined by the "unwiderstehliche 'Gewalt des Geldes' " ("irresistible power of money") (quoted in ibid., 40).
54. Ibid., 31.
55. Reinhart Koselleck, *Preussen zwischen Reform und Revolution: Algemeines Landrecht, Verwaltung, und soziale Bewegung von 1791 bis 1848*, 2d ed. (Stuttgart, 1975), 487.
56. Schissler, *Preussische Agrargesellschaft*, 115–30; Koselleck, *Preussen zwischen Reform und Revolution*, 489–91.
57. Schissler, *Preussische Agragesellschaft*, 92, 107. This explanation oversimplifies; Schissler reports that "die Bauern, die ihren Hof zu lassitischem Recht besassen, und die Zeitpachtbauern mussten ein Drittel bis die Hälfte, nach speziellen Ermittlungen auch mehr von ihrem Land als Entschädigung an die Gutzbesitzer abtreten" (107).
58. Koselleck, *Preussen zwischen Reform und Revolution*, 491.
59. Schissler, *Preussische Agrargesellschaft*, 107.
60. Schissler reviews the development of this opposition in ibid., 123–30.
61. Quoted in Peter Brandt, Thomas Hofmann, and Reiner Zilkenat, *Preussen, zur Sozialgeschichte eines Staates: Eine Darstellung in Quellen* (Reinbek bei Hamburg, 1981), 102: "Diese durch heilig gehaltene Verträge begrundete Ständische Verfassung war das schönste Band zwischen dem Landesherrn und der Nation, sie begründete die unerschütterliche Anhänglichkeit derselben, die unsern Staat früherhin in den gefährlichsten Krisen aufrecht erhielt, sie wird, gehörig benutzt, auch itzt ihren Nützen bewähren, geachtet und unverletzt den Staatskredit sichern, den neuen Gesetzen zur Garantie ihrer Dauer und Würkung dienen und den gefährlichen Wechsel gesetzlicher

Bestimmungen verhindern, der so oft den Umsturz aller Staatsverfassungen herbeigeführt hat."

62. Koselleck, *Preussen zwischen Reform und Revolution,* 491.
63. Schissler, *Preussische Agrargesellschaft,* 92, 108.
64. Koselleck, *Preussen zwischen Reform und Revolution,* 493–98.
65. Ibid., 492.
66. Vopelius, *Die altliberalen Oekonomen,* 32–36, 43–47.
67. Koselleck, *Preussen zwischen Reform und Revolution,* 499.
68. Ibid., 501–06; Schissler, *Preussische Agragesellschaft,* 109–13, 159–85.
69. Koselleck, *Preussen zwischen Reform und Revolution,* 499.
70. Quoted in ibid., 490.
71. Ibid., 500, 503.
72. On punishment for flight as well as Junker control of the number of serf plots, see Otto Büsch, *Militärsystem und Sozialleben im alten Preussen, 1713–1807: Die Anfänge der sozialen Militarisierung der preussisch-deutschen Gesellschaft* (Frankfurt, 1981), 27–29, 156–58.
73. Vopelius, *Die altliberalen Oekonomen,* 36–39.
74. R. S. Neale, *Class in English History, 1680–1850* (Totowa, N.J., 1981), 154–92, is an excellent overview of these theorists and of what historians have had to say about them. See also Noel W. Thompson, *The People's Science: The Popular Political Economy of Exploitation and Crisis, 1816–34* (Cambridge, 1984); E. P. Thompson, *The Making of the English Working Class* (New York, 1963), 711–832; Gareth Stedman Jones, "The Language of Chartism," in James Epstein and Dorothy Thompson, eds., *The Chartist Experience* (London, 1982), 3–58, reprinted under the title "Rethinking Chartism," in Stedman Jones, *Languages of Class: Studies in English Working-Class History, 1832–1982* (Cambridge, 1983), 90–178; and Barbara Taylor, *Eve and the New Jerusalem: Socialism and Feminism in the Nineteenth Century* (New York, 1983).
75. This point is emphasized in Stedman Jones, "Rethinking Chartism."
76. Karl Marx, *Capital: A Critique of Political Economy,* vol. I, trans. Ben Fowkes (New York, 1977), chap. 27, pp. 880–81.
77. Ibid., chap. 6, pp. 271–73.
78. Harvey, *Limits,* 1–2; for further, penetrating discussion of this aspect of Marx's thought, see Lucien Goldmann, *Lukacs et Heidegger* (Paris, 1973), especially 74–87.
79. This passage follows Harvey, *Limits,* 1–2, 61–68.
80. Ibid., 36–37.
81. Ibid., 190–203, 324–29, 424–45.
82. An example: If competition does not enforce uniform wage levels, then prices for other commodities may not enforce uniform production methods on all enterprises; the rate of accumulation may be more closely related to exploitation of disciplinary potentials than to reinvestment in productivity-enhancing equipment. The concept of relative surplus value, therefore, might have to be split up into a variety of new subtypes, depending on the degree of discipline enhancement vs. productive machinery used in creating it. (The assembly line could be regarded as a hybrid.) None of this, of course, represents a crucial threat to the edifice of Marxist theory, but consequences for practical application would be manifold.
83. See the description of Lancashire in Friedrich Engels, *The Condition of the Working Class in England in 1844,* first published in German in 1845. In the translation by W. O. Henderson and W. H. Chaloner (New York, 1958), see 30–87. On this work, see Steven Marcus, *Engels, Manchester, and the Working Class* (New York, 1974).
84. Quoted in Thompson, *The Making,* 200.
85. Quoted in ibid., 202.

86. H. I. Dutton and J. E. King, *"Ten Percent and No Surrender": The Preston Strike, 1853–1854* (Cambridge, 1981), 86–93.
87. Harvey, *Limits*, 34.
88. Neale, *Class in English History*, 17–46, attempts a thorough review of Marx's scattered utterances on the subject; see also Erik Olin Wright, *Classes* (London, 1985), 6–63.
89. Karl Marx, *Critique of the Gotha Program* (1875), reprinted in Karl Marx and Friedrich Engels, *Selected Works* (New York, 1968), 319–35, quotations from 326.
90. Ibid., 328–29.
91. Gareth Stedman Jones, "Engels and the History of Marxism," in Eric Hobsbawm, ed., *The History of Marxism, I, Marxism in Marx's Day* (Bloomington, Ind., 1982), 290–326, quotation from 293.
92. Friedrich Engels, *Socialism: Utopian and Scientific,* reprinted in Marx and Engels, *Selected Works,* 399–434, quotations from 420–21.
93. See Neale, *Class in English History,* 34–36.
94. See Taylor, *Eve and the New Jerusalem,* 83–117, for some telling, and still-relevant, evidence on self-supporting women workers.
95. The pioneer work on this issue was Thompson, *The Making.* On Russia, see Victoria Bonnell, *Roots of Rebellion: Workers' Politics and Organizations in St. Petersburg and Moscow, 1900–1914* (Berkeley, Calif., 1983). On the 1920s, see the collection of essays edited by James E. Cronin and Carmen Sirianni, *Work, Community, and Power: The Experience of Labor in Europe and America, 1900–1925* (Philadelphia, 1983).
96. A full statement of this view may be found in Craig Calhoun, *The Question of Class Struggle: Social Foundations of Popular Radicalism during the Industrial Revolution* (Oxford, 1982).
97. Building trades in both England and Germany in the nineteenth century have been subject to recent, illuminating attention; see Richard Price, *Masters, Unions, and Men: Work Control in Building and the Rise of Labor, 1830–1914* (Cambridge, 1980); and Wolfgang Renzsch, *Handwerker und Lohnarbeiter in der frühen Arbeiterbewegung: Zur sozialen Basis von Gewerkschaften und Sozialdemokratie im Reichsgrundungsjahrzehnt* (Göttingen, 1980), 35–69.
98. Martin Nadaud, *Mémoires de Leonard, ancien garçon maçon,* ed. with an introduction by Maurice Agulhon (Paris, 1976), 265–72.
99. Ibid., 267.
100. Ibid., 268.
101. Ibid., 271.
102. See Carol A. Smith, "Labor and International Capital in the Making of a Peripheral Social Formation: Economic Transformations in Guatemala, 1850–1980," in Charles Bergquist, ed., *Labor in the Capitalist World Economy* (Beverly Hills, Calif., 1984), 135–56; Peter Lloyd, *A Third World Proletariat?* (London, 1982).
103. Harvey, *Limits,* 67.
104. The basics of marginal utility theory can be found in any elementary economics textbook. The pioneers of this approach were W. S. Jevons, Leon Walras, and other economists of the second half of the nineteenth century; see Mark Blaug, *Economic Theory in Retrospect,* 3d ed. (Cambridge, 1978), 309–34. Maurice Godelier offers a penetrating Marxist critique of marginal utility in *Rationality and Irrationality in Economics* (New York, 1972), 3–104. More significant still is Thurow's critique of the theory as it concerns labor in *Generating Inequality.*
105. Joseph A. Schumpeter, *Capitalism, Socialism, and Democracy,* 3d ed. (New York, 1950), uses the concept of imperfect markets in a highly revealing manner. Recent challenges to economic orthodoxy include Thurow, *Generating Inequality;* and Lindblom, *Politics and Markets.* See also the recent review essay by Steven E. Rhoads, *The Economist's View of the World: Government, Markets, and Public Policy* (Cambridge, 1985), 143–98.

106. See, for example, Gary Becker, *The Economic Approach to Human Behavior* (Chicago, 1976); or Milton Friedman, *Price Theory* (Chicago, 1976), especially 201–50.

107. Georges Dupré and Pierre-Philippe Rey, "Reflections on the Pertinence of a Theory of the History of Exchange," *Economy and Society* 2 (1973):131–63, quoted in de Ste. Croix, *Class Struggle*, 37.

108. See the discussions in Chapter 1, in the sections called "Standard of living and way of life in England" and "Class by another name," as well as the references in notes 85–93 and 97 to that chapter.

109. Nicos Poulantzas, *Political Power and Social Classes* (London, 1973); Wright, *Classes;* John Roehmer, *A General Theory of Exploitation and Class* (Cambridge, Mass., 1982); Michael Burawoy, *The Politics of Production* (London, 1985).

110. See note 20 to this chapter.

111. Arno J. Mayer, *The Persistence of the Old Regime: Europe to the Great War* (New York, 1981), especially 129–35; Patrice Higonnet, *Class, Ideology, and the Rights of Nobles during the French Revolution* (Oxford, 1981); Sean Wilentz, *Chants Democratic: New York City and the Rise of the American Working Class, 1788–1850* (New York, 1984); William Doyle, *Origins of the French Revolution* (Oxford, 1980), especially 128–38; R. S. Neale, *Class in English History*, 120–53; Charles Maier, *Recasting Bourgeois Europe: Stabilization in France, Germany, and Italy in the Decade after World War I* (Princeton, N.J., 1975), especially 19–21.

112. E. P. Thompson, "Eighteenth-Century English Society: Class Struggle without Class?" *Social History* 3 (1978):133–65, quotation from 151.

4. Money and the rights of man in 1789

1. On marginal utility, see references in Chapter 3, note 104.

2. See references in Chapter 3, note 45.

3. Excellent discussion and documentation on use of wet nurses may be found in Maurice Garden, *Lyons et les lyonnais au XVIIIᵉ siècle* (Paris, 1970), 107–40. For a general history of the phenomenon, see George D. Sussman, *Selling Mother's Milk: The Wetnursing Business in France, 1715–1914* (Urbana, Ill., 1982).

4. See, for example, Peter N. Stearns, *Lives of Labor: Work in Maturing Industrial Society* (New York, 1975), 45–84; Louise A. Tilly and Joan W. Scott, *Women, Work, and Family* (New York, 1978), 209–10; and Lenard R. Berlanstein, *The Working People of Paris, 1871–1914* (Baltimore, 1984), 61–62, 74–79, 141–42.

5. See the discussion of Marx in Chapter 3; see also, for the precise point being made here, David Harvey, *The Limits to Capital* (Chicago, 1982), 13.

6. A fascinating recent exploration of how rich–poor exchange relations can be structured by established practices building on the basic imbalance of power is Sarah C. Maza, *Servants and Masters in Eighteenth-Century France: The Uses of Loyalty* (Princeton, N.J., 1983).

7. The notion of conspicuous consumption was originated by Thorstein Veblen in his *The Theory of the Leisure Class: An Economic Study in the Evolution of Institutions* (New York, 1908). Kenneth Burke's dissatisfaction with Veblen's idea is highly relevant to the present discussion; see his *A Rhetoric of Motives* (New York, 1950), 127–32.

8. On such shifts in fashion, see especially Claude Perrot, *Les dessus et les dessous de la bourgeoisie: Une historie du vêtement au XIXᵉ siècle* (Paris, 1981).

9. R. H. Tawney's *Religion and the Rise of Capitalism* (1926; New York, 1947) was first given as a series of lectures in 1922.

10. Most subsequent discussion of Tawney's thesis has revolved around the causes and significance of the Puritan Revolution; see J. H. Hexter, *Reappraisals in History* (London,

1961); and the writings of Christopher Hill, e.g., *Society and Puritanism in Pre-Revolutionary England* (New York, 1964); or Lawrence Stone, e.g., *The Causes of the English Revolution, 1529-1642* (New York, 1972).

11. For treatment of religion as a service, see R. M. Hartwell, "The Service Revolution: The Growth of Services in Modern Economy, 1700-1914," in *The Fontana Economic History of Europe*, III, *The Industrial Revolution*, ed. Carlo M. Cipolla (London, 1973), 358-96, especially 364.

12. Emile Durkheim, *The Elementary Forms of the Religious Life* (New York, 1965); Carl E. Schorske, "Politics and Patricide in Freud's *Interpretation of Dreams*," in idem, *Fin-de-Siècle Vienna: Politics and Culture* (New York, 1980), 181-207; Gary Becker, *The Economic Approach to Human Behavior* (Chicago, 1976); Robert William Fogel and Stanley L. Engerman, *Time on the Cross* (Boston, 1974); Charles E. Lindblom, *Politics and Markets: The World's Political-Economic Systems* (New York, 1977).

13. See Brian Tierney, *The Crisis of Church and State, 1050-1300* (Englewood Cliffs, N.J., 1964), 33-95; or the interesting treatment of the same period—quite relevant to the present discussion—in R. R. Palmer and Joel Colton, *A History of the Modern World*, 5th ed. (New York, 1978), 32-35.

14. A classic treatment of undue influence on clergy is Liston Pope, *Millhands and Preachers: A Study of Gastonia* (New Haven, Conn., 1942).

15. John Locke, *A Letter concerning Toleration* (1689).

16. It is widely recognized that for a competitive system to be fair, even on its own terms, it must have a fair starting point; see Lester C. Thurow, *Generating Inequality: Mechanisms of Distribution in the U.S. Economy* (New York, 1975), 27-32; and John Rawls, *A Theory of Justice* (Cambridge, Mass., 1971).

17. Medievalists are sometimes uncomfortable with use of the terms "feudal" and "feudalism" to apply to all aspects of early medieval social and political institutions. Manorial institutions, in particular, are often thought to be an entirely separate phenomenon from feudalism proper—the exchange of fiefs for military service. It was, however, early modern French legal experts who first took to calling manorial law "feudal." The practice continued into the nineteenth century, was picked up by Marx, and passed from him to his disciples. Its usage in this tradition is perfectly unambiguous and presents few problems in a work on modern history. Part of the problem of modern society, after all, is to understand what the revolutionaries meant in 1789 when they said they were abolishing "feudalism." It will be argued in this chapter that they meant a certain set of impediments to the free substitutability of money for things. In both this chapter and the next the terms "feudal" and "feudalism" will therefore be used in the same way, in order to simplify the exposition.

18. Almost any study of the society or economy of this period brings out the important advances in production and distribution. See, for example, Neil McKendrick, John Brewer, and J. H. Plumb, *The Birth of a Consumer Society: The Commercialization of Eighteenth-Century England* (Bloomington, Ind., 1982); Philippe Guignet, *Mines, manufactures, et ouvriers du Valenciennois au XVIIIe siècle* (New York, 1977); Pierre Goubert, *Beauvais et le Beauvaisis de 1600 à 1730* (Paris, 1960); Herbert Kisch, *Die hausindustriellen Textilgewerbe am Niederrhein vor der industriellen Revolution* (Göttingen, 1981); and Peter Kriedte, *Spätfeudalismus und Handelskapital: Grundlinien der europäischen Wirtschaftsgeschichte vom 16. bis zum Ausgang des 18. Jahrhunderts* (Göttingen, 1980). On small metal wares, see J. R. Harris, "Attempts to Transfer English Steel Techniques to France in the Eighteenth Century," in Sheila Marriner, ed., *Business and Businessmen: Studies in Business, Economic, and Accounting History* (Liverpool, 1978), 199-233. On the book trade, see Robert Darnton, "A Clandestine Bookseller in the Provinces," in idem, *The Literary Underground of the Old Regime* (Cambridge, Mass., 1982), 122-47; and Rob-

ert Mandrou, *De la culture populaire aux XVIIe et XVIIIe siècles: La bibliothèque bleue de Troyes,* 2d ed. (Paris, 1975).

19. Small Flemish farmers were among the pioneers of the agricultural revolution later advanced by large English tenant farmers; see Paul Bairoch, "Agriculture and the Industrial Revolution, 1700–1914," in Cipolla, *The Industrial Revolution,* 452–506.

20. The classic study of this phenomenon is Rudolf Braun, *Industrialisierung und Volksleben: Veränderungen der Lebensformen unter Einwirkung der verlugsindustriellen Heimarbeit in einem landlichen Industriegebiet (Zurcher Oberland),* 2d ed. (Göttingen, 1979). See also Franklin Mendels, "Les temps de l'industrie et les temps de l'agriculture: Logique d'une analyse régionale de la proto-industrialisation," *Revue du Nord* 63 (1981):21–34; and Peter Kriedte, Hans Medick, and Jürgen Schlumbohm, *Industrialisierung vor der Industrialisierung: Gewerbliche Warenproduktion auf dem Land in der Formationsperiode des Kapitalismus* (Göttingen, 1978).

21. On expectancy and disappointment, see Robert Darnton, "The High Enlightenment and the Low-life of Literature," in idem, *Literary Underground,* 1–40. Darnton's work is discussed in greater detail later in this chapter.

22. See William M. Reddy, *The Rise of Market Culture: The Textile Trade and French Society, 1750–1900* (Cambridge, 1984), 19–47; and Hans Medick, 'Freihandel fur die Zunft': Ein Kapitel aus der Geschichte der Preiskämpfe in Württembergischen Leinengewerbe des 18. Jahrhunderts," in *Mentalitäten und Lebensverhältnisse: Beispiele aus der Sozialgeschichte der Neuzeit,* ed. by colleagues and students of Rudolf Vierhaus (Göttingen, 1982), 277–94.

23. See Otto Büsch, *Militärsystem und Sozialleben im alten Preussen, 1713–1807: Die Anfänge der sozialen Militarisierung der preussisch-deutschen Gesellschaft* (Frankfurt, 1981), 42–43.

24. See E. P. Thompson, *Whigs and Hunters: The Origin of the Black Act* (New York, 1975); G. E. Mingay, *The Gentry: The Rise and Fall of a Ruling Class* (London, 1976); and Lawrence Stone, "The New Eighteenth Century," *New York Review of Books,* 29 March 1984, pp. 42–48.

25. The following passage draws on a number of classic studies, including Georges Lefebvre, *Les paysans du Nord pendant la Révolution française* (1924; Paris, 1972), 117–63; Goubert, *Beauvais et le Beauvaisis,* 151–96; and Paul Bois, *Les paysans de l'ouest: Des structures économique et sociales aux opinions politiques depuis l'époque révolutionnaire dans la Sarthe* (Le Mans, 1960), 375–407. For two excellent overviews of the subject, see Pierre Goubert, *The Ancien Régime: French Society, 1600–1750,* trans. Steve Cox (New York, 1973), 82–7; and Albert Soboul, "Sur le prélèvement féodal," in idem, *Problèmes paysans de la Révolution, 1789–1848: Etudes d'histoire révolutionnaire* (Paris, 1983), 89–115.

26. On tenant turnover rates and local resistance to evictions, see especially Lefebvre, *Paysans du Nord,* 93–97, 261–68; and Louis Merle, *La métairie et l'évolution agraire de la Gâtine poitevine de la fin du Moyen Age à la Révolution* (Paris, 1958), 167, 184. On estate agents, see Goubert, *Beauvais et le Beauvaisis,* 175–78.

27. See Lefebvre, *Paysans du Nord,* 261–68; Merle, *La métairie,* 161–84; Goubert, *Beauvais et le Beauvaisis,* 164–70; Bois, *Paysans de l'ouest,* 423–69; and T. J. A. Le Goff and D. M. G. Sutherland, "The Social Origins of Counter-Revolution in Western France," *Past and Present,* no. 99 (1983), 65–87.

28. Lefebvre, *Paysans du Nord,* 261.

29. On the word *métayage,* see Merle, *La métairie,* 161; and Bois, *Paysans de l'ouest,* 431–35.

30. Bois, *Paysans de l'ouest,* 433.

31. Goubert, *Beauvais et le Beauvaisis,* 168.

32. See Jean-Claude Perrot, *Génèse d'une ville moderne: Caen au XVIIIe siècle,* 2 vols. (Lille, 1974), II; 712–80; Olwen Hufton, *Bayeux in the Late Eighteenth Century: A Social Study* (Oxford, 1967), 113–30; Alain Lottin, *Chavatte, ouvrier lillois: Un contemporain de Louis*

XIV (Paris, 1979); and Guignet, *Mines, manufactures, et ouvriers du Valenciennois*, 68–125.

33. Goubert, *The Ancien Régime*, 85–86; Emmanuel Le Roy Ladurie, "Révoltes et contestations rurales en France de 1675 à 1788," *Annales: Economies, sociétés, civilisations* 29 (1974):6–22.

34. On Voltaire, see Gita May, *Madame Roland and the Age of Revolution* (New York, 1970), 118; on Duplain, see Robert Darnton, *The Business of Enlightenment: A Publishing History of the Encyclopédie, 1775–1800* (Cambridge, Mass., 1979); on Depont, see Robert Forster, *Merchants, Landlords, Magistrates: The Depont Family in Eighteenth-Century France* (Baltimore, 1980), 14–19.

35. See Alfred Cobban, *The Social Interpretation of the French Revolution* (Cambridge, 1964), 44–45.

36. See Goubert, *The Ancien Régime*, 153–202; and David Bien, "The Army in the French Enlightenment," *Past and Present*, no. 85 (November 1979), 68–98.

37. See Kristen Brooke Neuschel, "The Prince of Condé and the Nobility of Picardy: A Study of the Structure of Noble Relationships in Sixteenth-Century France" (Ph.D. thesis, Brown University, 1982).

38. Robert Mandrou, *Louis XIV et son temps, 1661–1715*, 2d ed. (Paris, 1973).

39. May, *Madame Roland*, 118–27; Robert Forster, *The Nobility of Toulouse in the Eighteenth Century: A Social and Economic Study* (Baltimore, 1960); idem, "*Seigneurs* and Their Agents," in Ernst Hinrichs, Eberhard Schmitt, and Rudolf Vierhaus, eds., *Vom ancien Régime zur Französischen Revolution: Forschungen und Perspektiven* (Göttingen, 1978), 169–87.

40. Compare Mandrou, *Louis XIV*, 117–21, with Maza, *Servants and Masters*.

41. On royal encouragement of manufactures, see André Rémond, *John Holker, manufacturier et grand fonctionnaire en France au XVIIIe siècle, 1719–1786* (Paris, 1946); and Harold Parker, *The Bureau of Commerce in 1781 and Its Policies with Respect to French Industry* (Durham, N.C., 1979).

42. François Bluche, *Les magistrats du Parlement de Paris au XVIIIe siècle, 1715–1771* (Paris, 1960), especially 47–120, 242–302; Jean Egret, *La pré-révolution française, 1787–1788* (Paris, 1962), 204–65, trans. Wesley D. Camp under the title *The French Pre-revolution, 1787–1788* (Chicago, 1977), 119–69; Bailey Stone, *The Parlement of Paris, 1774–1789* (Chapel Hill, N.C., 1981), 14–33.

43. Jean Quéniart, *Les hommes, l'église, et Dieu dans la France du XVIIIe siècle* (Paris, 1978), 15–34, 77–85; John McManners, *The French Revolution and the Church* (New York, 1970), 5–19, 31–35.

44. Barrington Moore, *Social Origins of Dictatorship and Democracy: Lord and Peasant in the Making of the Modern World* (Boston, 1966), 55.

45. Robert Darnton, "A Bourgeois Puts His World in Order: The City as a Text," in idem, *The Great Cat Massacre and Other Episodes in French Cultural History* (New York, 1984), 107–43, quotation from 128.

46. Moore, *Social Origins*, 69, 65, 61.

47. George V. Taylor, "Noncapitalist Wealth and the Origins of the French Revolution," *American Historical Review* 72 (1967):469–96.

48. Le Roy Ladurie, "Révoltes et contestation rurales," discusses the "physiocratic" management of seigneurial incomes.

49. For a view that parallels Moore's see William H. Sewell, *Work and Revolution in France: The Language of Labor from the Old Regime to 1848* (Cambridge, 1980), 114–42.

50. Moore, *Social Origins*, 60, 59. Moore's reference to venal office as "mana" is taken from Ernest Lavisse, *Histoire de France depuis les origines jusqu'à la Révolution*, 9 vols. (Paris, 1900–11), VII, pt. 1, 368; Lavisse attributes it to Loyseau.

51. On parcelization and protoindustrialization, see Lefebvre, *Paysans du Nord*, 31–44; Ol-

wen Hufton, *The Poor of Eighteenth-Century France, 1750–1789* (Oxford, 1974), 11–24; Franklin F. Mendels, "Protoindustrialization: The First Phase of the Industrialization Process," *Journal of Economic History* 32 (1972):241–61; Le Roy Ladurie, "Révoltes et contestations rurales"; and Kriedte, Medick, and Schlumbohm, *Industrialiserung vor der Industrialisierung.* See also two special issues on protoindustrialization of the *Revue du Nord:* vol. 61, no. 240 (January–March 1979), and vol. 63, no. 248 (January–March 1981). An especially useful critical review of the concept of protoindustrialization may be found in the editors' introduction to Maxine Berg, Pat Hudson, and Michael Sonenscher, eds., *Manufacture in Town and Country before the Factory* (Cambridge, 1983), 1–32.

52. Hanna Schissler, *Preussische Agrargesellschaft im Wandel: Wirtschaftliche, gesellschaftliche, und politische Transformationsprozesse von 1763 bis 1847* (Göttingen, 1978), 94. See also Chapter 3 herein, note 68.

53. See references in note 27 to this chapter. That sharecroppers could be subject to serflike duties and restrictions is clear from David I Kertzer's study of the Emilia Romagna, *Family Life in Central Italy, 1880–1910: Sharecropping, Wage Labor, and Coresidence* (New Brunswick, N.J., 1984).

54. Hufton, *The Poor,* 12–24; William Doyle, *Origins of the French Revolution* (Oxford, 1980), 158–62.

55. Egret, *La pré-révolution,* 311–19; Doyle, *Origins,* 49–50.

56. See the discussion of Furet's work in Chapter 2, in the section entitled "Crises of meaning." For a general introduction to the problem of public opinion, see Doyle, *Origins,* 78–95.

57. Robert Darnton's work has now been gathered into three readily available books: *Literary Underground, The Business of Enlightenment,* and *The Great Cat Massacre.*

58. Jack R. Censer, "Eighteenth-Century Journalism in France and Its Recruits: A Selective Survey," in Fourteenth Consortium on Revolutionary Europe, *Proceedings,* ed. Harold T. Parker, Louise S. Parker, and William M. Reddy (Athens, Ga., 1986), 165–79; idem, *Prelude to Power: The Parisian Radical Press, 1789–1791* (Baltimore, 1976). See also Daniel Roche, *La siècle des lumières en province: Académies et académiciens provinciaux, 1680–1789,* 2 vols. (Paris, 1978).

59. Reinhart Koselleck, *Kritik und Krise: Ein Beitrag zur Pathogenese der bürgerlichen Welt* (Freibug, 1959).

60. Robert Darnton, "A Police Inspector Sorts His Files: The Anatomy of the Republic of Letters," in idem, *The Great Cat Massacre,* 145–89; Censer, "Eighteenth-Century Journalism."

61. Darnton, "Police Inspector," 153; Censer, "Eighteenth-Century Journalism."

62. Darnton, "Police Inspector," 164–65: Mme de Pompadour extended protection to the poet Bernis; Bernis found Duclos a position as historiographe de France. Voltaire found jobs for Gaillard (ibid., 168). Condorcet was accepted early on thanks to d'Alembert's favor; see Keith Michael Baker, *Condorcet: From Natural Philosophy to Social Mathematics* (Chicago, 1975). Marmontel recommended Boissy to Pompadour for the post of editor of the *Mercure de France* (Censer, "Eighteenth-Century Journalism," 169–70).

63. Robert Darnton, "A Pamphleteer on the Run," in idem, *Literary Underground,* 71–121.

64. D'Alembert's early acceptance into the Académie des Sciences gave him a certain independence; he lived in an extremely modest fashion, refused repeated offers of posts from Frederick II, but was also admitted into the Académie française thanks to the intervention of Madame du Deffand. Diderot lived from his earnings as author and editor, but his great project, the *Encyclopédie,* could not have survived without the powerful protection of Choiseul, Malesherbes, and Pompadour. On Condorcet, see note 62 to this chapter. Rousseau's love-hate relationships with his protectors are chronicled at length in his *Confessions.*

65. It was already an explicit theme, if not a central one, thanks to the publication in 1752 of d'Alembert's *Essai sur la société des gens de lettres et des grands;* see Darnton, "Police Inspector," 170n.

66. Robert Darnton, "Readers Respond to Rousseau: The Fabrication of Romantic Sensitivity," in idem, *The Great Cat Massacre,* 215–56; see also Koselleck, *Kritik und Krise,* for important observations on the same theme.

67. Sewell, *Work and Revolution,* 64–72.

68. Abbé André Morellet, *Mémoires,* 2 vols. (Paris, 1821). (Robert Darnton first brought this work to the author's attention.)

69. Archives nationales, dossier F^{12}560.

70. On Roland's life, see especially Marie-Jeanne Phlipon Roland de la Platière, *Lettres de Madame Roland,* 2 vols., ed. Claude Perroud (Paris, 1900–02); and May, *Madame Roland.*

71. Robert Darnton, "A Spy in Grub Street," in idem, *Literary Underground,* 41–70, quotation from 42.

72. See Norman Hampson, *The Life and Opinions of Maximilien Robespierre* (London, 1974).

73. Ibid., 23.

74. Robespierre was elected to represent the Third for Arras after a vigorous campaign of publishing and speaking. Brissot just missed being elected for Paris in the final round of voting after the success of his new newspaper *Le Patriot Français;* as a Paris elector he became a member of the new municipal council.

75. Even the efforts to rally popular votes for monarchists in the late 1790s did not really establish the pattern, which emerged only after 1848. Compare Edward Berenson, *Populist Religion and Left-Wing Politics in France, 1830–1852* (Princeton, N.J., 1984), with Theodore Zeldin, *The Political System of Napoleon III* (New York, 1971).

76. Lenard R. Berlanstein, *The Barristers of Toulouse in the Eighteenth Century (1740–1793)* (Baltimore, 1975), 184–85.

77. On the food riots, see R. B. Rose, "The French Revolution and the Grain Supply," *Bulletin of the John Rylands Library* 39 (1956–57):171–87; and Georges Lefebvre, *The Great Fear of 1789,* trans. Joan White (New York, 1973), 7–33.

78. Theda Skocpol, *States and Social Revolutions: A Comparative Analysis of France, Russia, and China* (Cambridge, 1979), 118–28.

79. Lefebvre, *The Great Fear,* especially 34–46, 100–21; see also Albert Soboul, "Problèmes de la communauté rurale (XVIIIe–XIXe siècles)," in idem, *Problèmes paysans,* 183–214.

80. Lefebvre, *Paysans du Nord,* 98–103, 262; Le Goff and Sutherland, "The Social Origins of Counter-Revolution."

81. Soboul quotes at length with evident approval in "Sur le prélèvement féodal," 114–15, from Tocqueville's *L'ancien régime et la Révolution,* bk. II, chapt. 1. Tocqueville notes in particular the grievance that feudal dues were "imprescriptible et irrachetable"–that is, they could not be evaded or bought out–in a time of land hunger and frequent land sales. François Furet notes Soboul's use of Tocqueville with evident dissatisfaction in "The Revolutionary Catechism," in idem, *Interpreting the French Revolution,* trans. Elborg Forster (1978; Cambridge, 1981), 81–131, especially 92–100.

82. Lefebvre, *Paysans du Nord,* 358–74; idem, *The Great Fear,* 34–46.

83. Cobban, *Social Interpretation,* 39; Doyle, *Origins,* 205–06; Skocpol, *States and Social Revolutions,* 183–84.

84. Sewell has categorized property forms in a most useful way in *Work and Revolution,* 114–42.

85. The following discussion is based on Georges Lefebvre, *The Coming of the French Revolution,* trans. R. R. Palmer (Princeton, N.J., 1947; New York, [1960]), 133–56; and Philippe Sagnac, *La législation civile de la Révolution française (1789–1804)* (Paris, 1898), 85–137.

86. Cobban, *Social Interpretation*, 132–44; Moore, *Social Origins;* Sewell, *Work and Revolution*, 114–42.
87. Le Goff and Sutherland, "The Social Origins of Counter-Revolution," 75.
88. See references in note 85; a good summary of the reform of the judiciary is in Charles Downer Hazen, *The French Revolution*, 2 vols. (New York, 1932), I, 371–85.
89. Le Goff and Sutherland, "The Social Origins of Counter-Revolution," 76. See also, on this whole matter, McManners, *The French Revolution and the Church;* and Hazen, *The French Revolution*, I, 339–70.
90. *Lettres de Madame Roland*, II, 59–60: "Nos provinces retentissent bien autrement que la capitale des clameurs des aristocrates, non qu'il y ait plus de nobles, mais l'inégalité des conditions y est plus marquée, plus durement ressentie, plus fanatiquement défendue. . . . Vous ne voyez partout que petits conseillers, petits financiers, que fils de boulanger, de cabaretier, qui sont furieux aujourd'hui de se voir rapprochés de leurs parents. . . . La religion est perdue, L'Etat est dissous, on est dans l'anarchie, il n'y a plus de subordination: ce sont là leurs expressions favorites. . . . Les officiers d'une petite sénéchaussée, les chanoines d'une collégiale, ignorés partout ailleurs que là ou elle existe, s'élèvent au dessus des autres particuliers bien plus que vos conseillers au Parlement ou vos gros abbés sur un marchand de la rue Saint-Denis."
91. Quoted in Hampson, *Robespierre*, 60 (Hampson's translation).
92. Albert Soboul, *The Sans-Culottes*, trans. Rémy Inglis Hall (Princeton, N.J., 1980), 20.
93. Quoted in ibid., 25 (Hall's translation).
94. Quoted in ibid., 18 (Hall's translation).
95. Quoted in ibid., 21 (Hall's translation).
96. Quoted in May, *Madame Roland*, 205 (May's translation).
97. Ibid.
98. See the discussion of his views in Chapter 2.
99. This is why covert opposition to the regime by, for example, nonjuring priests was so easily associated with speculative grain deals or bribery of representatives. All such activities were condemned equally as aristocratic even though some represented free self-expression and others submission to the power of money.
100. See Richard M. Andrews, "Social Structures and Political Elites in Revolutionary Paris, 1792–94: A Critical Appraisal of Soboul's *Sans-culottes parisiens*," in Fourteenth Consortium on Revolutionary Europe, *Proceedings*, 329–69; this paper has also appeared in the *Journal of Social History* 19 (1985):71–112.
101. Michael Sonenscher, "The Sans-culottes of the Year II: Rethinking the Language of Labor in Revolutionary France," *Social History* 9 (1984):301–28.
102. Jacques-Louis Ménétra, a window maker, lived through the Terror; he obviously supported the Revolution but equally obviously was forced into a life of hypocrisy to ensure his own survival; see his revealing account in *Journal de ma vie: Compagnon vitrier au 18ᵉ siècle*, ed. with a commentary by Daniel Roche (Paris, 1982), 259–81.
103. See Patrice Higonnet, *Class, Ideology, and the Rights of Nobles during the French Revolution* (Oxford, 1981); and idem, "The Social and Cultural Antecedents of Revolutionary Discontinuity: Montagnards and Girondins," *English Historical Review* 100 (1985):513–44.
104. Furet, "The Revolutionary Catechism."

5. Challenging one's master in the nineteenth century

1. See the discussion of Moore's views in Chapter 4, in the section entitled "The perfectly sensible ancien régime."
2. Quoted in Robert L. Heilbroner, *The Worldly Philosophers: The Lives, Times, and Ideas of the Great Economic Thinkers*, rev. ed. (New York, 1961), 52.

3. See, for example, Milton Friedman, *Price Theory* (Chicago, 1976), 201–12.
4. Lester C. Thurow, *Dangerous Currents: The State of Economics* (New York, 1983), 174, 176–77.
5. An example of treating families like enterprises that is directly relevant to the current context is Nancy Folbre, "Of Patriarchy Born: The Political Economy of Fertility Decisions," *Feminist Studies* 9 (1983):261–84. But such analyses are also common among Marxists who seek to understand societies in which commerce is nonexistent or marginal. A study that explains the position of the household in capitalist production as a consequence of patriarchy is Heidi I. Hartmann, "The Family as the Locus of Gender, Class, and Political Struggle: The Example of Housework," *Signs* 6 (1981):366–94. On the difficulties of this concept, see the exchange among Sheila Rowbotham, Sally Alexander, and Barbara Taylor in *People's History and Socialist Theory*, ed. Raphael Samuel (London, 1981), 363–73. Jane Humphries gives a critique of Marxist treatments of the family in "Class Struggle and the Persistence of the Working Class Family," *Cambridge Journal of Economics* I (1977):241–58. The argument being made here closely follows Eli Zaretsky, *Capitalism, the Family, and Personal Life* (New York, 1976), 23–35. See also the review by Joan Scott, "Women in History: The Modern Period," *Past and Present*, no. 101 (1983), 141–57.
6. See the passionate study by Jill Liddington and Jill Norris, *One Hand Tied behind Us: The Rise of the Women's Suffrage Movement* (London, 1978), 30–46; Louise A. Tilly and Joan W. Scott, *Women, Work, and Family* (New York, 1978), 104–45, 176–213; Heidi Rosenbaum, *Formen der Familie: Untersuchungen zum Zusammenhang von Familienverhältnissen, Sozialstruktur, und sozialem Wandel in der deutschen Gesellschaft des 19. Jahrhunderts* (Frankfurt, 1982), 381–476; and Klaus Saul et al., eds., *Arbeiterfamilien im Kaiserreich: Materialien zur Sozialgeschichte in Deutschland, 1871–1914* (Dusseldorf, 1982), especially 161–200.
7. See, for example, Albie Sachs and Joan Hoff Wilson, *Sexism and the Law: A Study of Male Beliefs and Legal Bias in Britain and the United States* (New York, 1978).
8. Mary Wollstonecraft had made this argument by 1792; on her thought and her milieu, see Barbara Taylor, *Eve and the New Jerusalem: Socialism and Feminism in the Nineteenth Century* (New York, 1983), 1–18.
9. Taylor, *Eve and the New Jerusalem*, 83–117; Sally Alexander, "Women, Class, and Sexual Differences in the 1830s and 1840s: Some Reflections on the Writing of a Feminist History," *History Workshop Journal*, no. 17 (1984), 125–49; Madeleine Guilbert, *Les femmes et l'organisation syndicale avant 1914* (Paris, 1966).
10. On the changing nature of female and child wage work, see Tilly and Scott, *Women, Work, and Family*, 63–88; Duncan Bythell, *The Sweated Trades: Outwork in Nineteenth-Century Britain* (New York, 1978); William M. Reddy, *The Rise of Market Culture: The Textile Trade and French Society, 1750–1900* (Cambridge, 1984), 1–18, 138–84; and Joan W. Scott, "Men and Women in the Parisian Garment Trades: Discussions of Family and Work in the 1830s and 1840s," in Pat Thane, Geoffrey Crossick, and Roderick Floud, eds., *The Power of the Past: Essays for Eric Hobsbawm* (Cambridge, 1984), 67–93. On women in protest movements, see references in the preceding note and also Louise A. Tilly, "Paths of Proletarianization: Organization of Production, Sexual Division of Labor, and Women's Collective Action," *Signs* 7 (1981):400–17; and Dorothy Thompson, *The Chartists: Popular Politics in the Industrial Revolution* (New York, 1984), 120–51.
11. Reddy, *Rise of Market Culture*, 62–74, 114–27, 187–99, 246–52, 295–96; Daphne Simon, "Master and Servant," in John Saville, ed., *Democracy and the Labor Movement* (London, 1954), 160–200.
12. See references in note 10 to this chapter and also Neil Smelser, *Social Change and the In-*

dustrial Revolution (Chicago, 1959); and Patrick Joyce, *Work, Society, and Politics: The Culture of the Factory in Later Victorian England* (New Brunswick, N.J., 1980), 50–64.

13. Fuel and machinery markets were often broken up by high transport costs and protective tariffs; raw materials were more often competitively traded on an international basis. See, in general, David Landes, *The Unbound Prometheus: Technological Change and Industrial Development in Western Europe from 1750 to the Present* (Cambridge, 1969), especially 124–92; and Maurice Lévy-Leboyer, *Les banques européennes et l'industrialisation internationale* (Paris, 1964).

14. See Landes, *Unbound Prometheus*, 131–32; Reddy, *Rise of Market Culture*, 289–325; Jean Lambert-Dansette, *Quelques familles du patronat textile de Lille-Armentières, 1789–1914* (Lille, 1954); Bonnie G. Smith, *Ladies of the Leisure Class: The "Bourgeoises" of Northern France in the Nineteenth Century* (Princeton, N.J., 1981); and Joyce, *Work, Society, and Politics*, 1–49, 168–91.

15. See references in note 11 to this chapter and Klaus Saul, "Zwischen Repression und Integration: Staat, Gewerkschaften, und Arbeitskampf in kaiserlichen Deutschland, 1884–1914," in K. Tenfelde and H. Volkmann, eds., *Streik: Zur Geschichte des Arbeitskampfes in Deutschland während der Industrialisierung* (Munich, 1981), 209–36. See also, in the same volume, Jürgen Reulecke, "Sozialer Konflikt und bürgerliche Sozialreform in der Frühindustrialisierung," 237–52.

16. Some data on accident rates may be found in, e.g., Peter Borscheid, *Textilarbeiterschaft in der Industrialisierung: Sozial Lage und Mobilität in Württemberg (19. Jahrhundert)* (Stuttgart, 1978), 367–69; or Pierre Pierrard, *La vie ouvrière à Lille sous le Seconde Empire* (Paris, 1965), 150–61.

17. See Thompson, *The Chartists;* James Epstein, *The Lion of Freedom: Feargus O' Connor and the Chartist Movement, 1832–1842* (London, 1982); Noel W. Thompson, *The People's Science: The Popular Political Economy of Exploitation and Crisis, 1816–34* (Cambridge, 1984); Bernard H. Moss, *The Origins of the French Labor Movement: The Socialism of Skilled Workers, 1830–1914* (Berkeley, Calif., 1976); William H. Sewell, *Work and Revolution in France: The Language of Labor from the Old Regime to 1848* (Cambridge, 1980); K. Steven Vincent, *Pierre-Joseph Proudhon and the Rise of French Republican Socialism* (Oxford, 1984); Helga Grebing, *Geschichte der deutschen Arbeiterbewegung* (Munich, 1966), especially 25–93; and Wolfgang Renzsch, *Handwerker und Lohnarbeiter in der frühen Arbeiterbewegung: Zur sozialen Basis von Gewerkschaften und Sozialdemokratie im Reichsgrundungsjahrzehnt* (Gottingen, 1980).

18. See Reddy, *Rise of Market Culture*, 302–25; Joyce, *Work, Society, and Politics*, 282–330; and Carl E. Schorske, *German Social Democracy, 1905–1917: The Development of the Great Schism* (Cambridge, Mass., 1955; New York, 1972), 122–27.

19. See references in note 9 to this chapter. Needless to say, there is plenty of evidence that not all women felt this way, and the importance of those who broke with feminine role expectations cannot be understated. See especially Liddington and Norris, *One Hand Tied behind Us;* and Scott, "Men and Women in the Parisian Garment Trades."

20. H. I. Dutton and J. E. King, *"Ten Percent and No Surrender": The Preston Strike, 1853–1854* (Cambridge, 1981), 59.

21. Ibid., 64–65, 98, 191.

22. Ibid., 152–54.

23. Ibid., 163–76, 198, 203.

24. The standard account of the weaver uprising is still Alfred Zimmermann, *Blüthe und Verfall des Leinengewerbes in Schlesien* (Breslau, 1885); see also the forceful contemporary account by Wilhelm Wolff, "Das Elend und der Aufruhr in Schlesien," in H. Puttman, ed., *Deutsches Bürgerbuch für 1845* (Darmstadt, 1845). Wolff's piece has been fre-

quently reprinted, most conveniently in Hans Schwab-Felisch, *Gerhart Hauptmann, Die Weber: Vollständiger Text des Schauspiels, Dokumentation* (Frankfurt, 1981), 133–52.

25. *Kölnische Zeitung,* 23 June 1844, reprinted in Schwab-Felisch, *Die Weber,* 128–29: "Es ist dieser Tumult eine Manifestation des Proletariats, der im kleinern Masstabe wiederholt, wie wir dieselben längst in anderen Ländern kannten."

26. *Kölnische Zeitung,* 18 June 1844, reprinted in Schwab-Felish, *Die Weber,* 122–24: "die nothwendigen Anstrengungen gegen das wachsende Proletariat."

27. Werner Conze, "Vom 'Pöbel' zum 'Proletariat': Sozialgeschichtliche Voraussetzungen für den Sozialismus in Deutschland," in Hans-Ulrich Wehler, ed., *Moderne deutsche Sozialgeschichte* (Cologne, 1966), 111–36.

28. Ibid., 119–21.

29. *Kölnische Zeitung,* 18 June 1844, reprinted in Schwab-Felisch, *Die Weber,* 122–23: "dass Hunger mittels blosser Worte sich weder hervorrufen noch stillen lässt."

30. Wolff, "Das Elend," reprinted in Schwab-Felisch, *Die Weber,* quotation from 145: "Ein Stück Brod und 1 Viergroschen Stück reichten hin, die Wuth der von Hunger und Rache Getriebenen, im Zaum zu halten!"

31. Alexander Schneer, *Ueber die Noth der Leinen-Arbeiter in Schlesien und die Mittel ihr abzuhilfen* (Berlin, 1844), 31: "es ein Minimum der Bedürfnisse für jeden Menschen in einem civilisierten Land und unter unserem Himmelstrich giebt, und dass, wenn auch nicht einmal dies befriedigt wird, die wirkliche Noth und das Elend vorhanden ist."

32. Ibid., 32: "nicht eine kleine Zahl der Bewohner der Provinz, die man die Perle in Preussens Krone nennt, lebt materiell bei Weitem schlechter als die Sträflinge in den Zuchthäusen."

33. Ibid., 30.

34. On Villermé, see William Coleman, *Death Is a Social Disease: Public Health and Political Economy in Early Industrial France* (Madison, Wis., 1982); and Reddy, *Rise of Market Culture,* 138–84.

35. Schneer, *Die Noth der Leinen-Arbeiter,* 42–54.

36. Ibid., 72: "Es ist der tiefe Grund des Wehes, an welchem unsere Gesellschaft leidet, es ist der arge Krebschaden, an welchem sie erkrankt ist, es ist zugleich des gefahrdrohendste Element in unserer Zeit."

37. See Steven Marcus, *Engels, Manchester, and the Working Class* (New York, 1974).

38. Schneer, *Die Noth der Leinen-Arbeiter,* 28–30.

39. Helmut Bleiber, *Zwischen Reform und Revolution: Lage und Kämpfe der schlesischen Bauern und Landarbeiter im Vormärz, 1840–1847* (Berlin, 1966), 54, 201–18. As explained in Chapter 4, note 17, the words "feudal" and "feudalism" are being used as acceptable labels for early modern manorial institutions.

40. Hanna Schissler, *Preussische Agrargesellschaft im Wandel: Wirtschaftliche, gesellschaftliche, und politische Transformationsprozesse von 1763 bis 1847* (Göttingen, 1978), 123–26; Bleiber, *Zwischen Reform und Revolution,* 32–45.

41. Bleiber, *Zwischen Reform und Revolution,* 20–21.

42. Ibid., 59–68.

43. Ibid., 37–88, 45–46, 59–60.

44. A typical budget, drawn up by Eduard Pelz, is reproduced by Wolff in "Das Elend," reprinted in Schwab-Felisch, *Die Weber,* 140.

45. On the limited horizons of the weaver, see Ernst Klein, "Die Noth der Weber in der Grafschaft Glatz," reprinted in Helmut Praschek, ed., *Gerhard Hauptmanns "Die Weber": Eine Dokumentation* (Berlin, 1981), 82–87. On debts and immobility, see Schneer, *Die Noth der Leinen-Arbeiter,* 39; and Wolff, "Das Elend," reprinted in Schwab-Felisch, *Die Weber,* 138–40. On certificates of morality, see Bleiber, *Zwischen Reform und Revolution,* 65–66.

46. Bleiber, *Zwischen Reform und Revolution*, 201–18; Bleiber provides a review of the East German discussion up to 1965.
47. This is thanks to work like that of E. P. Thompson (see *The Making of the English Working Class* [New York, 1963]) or of Natalie Z. Davis (see, for example, her essay discussed in Chapter 2, "The Rites of Violence: Religious Riot in Sixteenth-Century France," *Past and Present*, no. 59 [1973], 51–91, reprinted in her *Society and Culture in Early Modern France* [Stanford, Calif., 1975], 152–87). German social historians have been quick to apply these lessons; see, for example, Rainer Wirtz, *"Widersetzlichkeiten, Excesse, Crawalle, Tumulte, und Skandale": Soziale Bewegung und gewalthafter sozialer Protest in Baden, 1815–1848* (Frankfurt, 1981).
48. See, for example, E. P. Thompson, "Time, Work Discipline, and Industrial Capitalism," *Past and Present*, no. 38 (1967), 59–97; Edward Shorter and Charles Tilly, *Strikes in France, 1830–1968* (Cambridge, 1974); Ted W. Margadant, *French Peasants in Revolt: The Insurrection of 1851* (Princeton, N.J., 1979); and K. Tenfelde and H. Volkmann, "Zur Geschichte des Streiks in Deutschland," in Tenfelde and Volkmann, *Streik*, 9–30. For some critical reflections on this approach to the history of protest, see Martin Henkel and Rolf Taubert, *Maschinenstürmer: Ein Kapitel aus der Sozialgeschichte des technischen Fortschritts* (Frankfurt, 1979), 9–30; and Charles Tilly, "Did the Cake of Custom Break?" in John M. Merriman, ed., *Consciousness and Class Experience in Nineteenth-Century Europe* (New York, 1979), 17–44.
49. Veit Valentin, *Geschichte der deutschen Revolution, 1848/49*, 2 vols. (Berlin, 1930), I, 52–55; Rudolf Stadelmann, *Soziale und politische Geschichte von 1848* (Munich, 1948), 18–19. See also, for example, Reinhart Koselleck, "Staat und Gesellschaft in Preussen, 1815–1848," in Wehler, *Moderne deutsche Sozialgeschichte*, 55–84, especially 75; or Reulecke, "Sozialer Konflikt," 239–43.
50. Dutton and King, *"Ten Percent,"* 198–99.
51. Schwab-Felisch, *Die Weber*, is a West German collection; Praschek, *Hauptmanns "Die Weber,"* is from the DDR.
52. A review in *Die Gegenwart*, 11 March 1893, reprinted in Praschek, *Hauptmanns "Die Weber,"* 160–65, quotation from 162: "Der Dichter behauptet zwar, sein Drama spiele in den vierziger Jahren, in den Ortschaften des Eulengebirges. Er irrt sich. Es spielt, übersieht man nebensächliche Einzelheiten, im Jahre 1890."
53. Dutton and King, *"Ten Percent,"* 31.
54. Ibid., 10.
55. Ibid., 21. Challenger is quoted on the same page.
56. Quoted in ibid., 28.
57. Quoted in ibid., 42.
58. See Michael Anderson, *Family Structure in Nineteenth-Century Lancashire* (Cambridge, 1971), 34–39.
59. Dutton and King, *"Ten Percent,"* 83.
60. See William H. Lazonick, "Industrial Relations and Technical Change: The Case of the Self-Acting Mule," *Cambridge Journal of Economics* 3 (1979):231–62; H. Catling, "The Development of the Spinning Mule," *Textile History* 9 (1978):35–37; and Reddy, *Rise of Market Culture*, 89–112, 157–68.
61. Dutton and King, *"Ten Percent,"* 45, 55, 110, 114.
62. Ibid., 55.
63. Quoted in ibid., 178.
64. Ibid., 181.
65. Quoted in ibid., 40.
66. Quoted in ibid., 41.
67. Quoted in ibid., 4.

68. Quoted in ibid., e.g., 47, 55, 110, 174.
69. Quoted in ibid., 81.
70. Ibid., 87, 122, 137.
71. Ibid., 78.
72. Ibid., 193.
73. Ibid., 26.
74. Ibid., 37, 53, 103, 191.
75. Ibid., 193.
76. Quoted in ibid., 51–52, 94.
77. Bleiber, *Zwischen Reform und Revolution* 45–46, 58–59, 69–71, 75, 83–91.
78. On nonnoble purchases of estates in the east, see Reinhart Koselleck, *Preussen zwischen Reform und Revolution: Allgemeines Landrecht, Verwaltung, und soziale Bewegung von 1791 bis 1848,* 2d ed. (Stuttgart, 1975), 512–16.
79. Hans Rosenberg, "Die Pseudodemokratisierung der Rittergutsbesitzerklasse," in Wehler, *Moderne deutsche Sozialgeschichte,* 287–308.
80. Schissler, *Preussische Agrargesellschaft,* 103; Peter Kriedte, *Spätfeudalismus und Handelskapital: Grundlinien der europäischen Wirtschaftsgeschichte vom 16. bis zum Ausgang des 18. Jahrhunderts* (Göttingen, 1980).
81. Koselleck, *Preussen zwischen Reform und Revolution,* 544–47; Bleiber, *Zwischen Reform und Revolution,* 96–105.
82. Quoted in Bleiber, *Zwischen Reform und Revolution,* 75: "Kommt nicht hier; Leute kriegen wir genug! Was will der arme Mann machen? Entweder er muss sich eine solch Behandlung gefallen lassen oder, wenn er aus dem Dienst geht, riskieren, auf der Strasse liegen zu mussen."
83. Koselleck, *Preussen zwischen Reform und Revolution,* 490; Bleiber, *Zwischen Reform und Revolution,* 37.
84. Bleiber, *Zwischen Reform und Revolution,* 106–07.
85. Ibid., 184–90.
86. Ibid., 73, 143–44.
87. Ibid., 184–87.
88. Ibid., 155–56. The quotation in the original reads: "dass jeder, der lesen kann, mit dem Herrn unter eine Decke steckt und ihnen die Wahrheit des Gesetzes vorenthält."
89. Reddy, *Rise of Market Culture,* 19–86; Sydney Pollard, *The Genesis of Modern Management* (Cambridge, Mass., 1965), 14–37, 48–51, 214; Hans Medick, " 'Freihandel fur die Zunft': Ein Kapitel aus der Geschichte der Preiskämpfe in Württembergischen Leinengewerbe des 18. Jahrhunderts," in *Mentalitäten und Lebensverhältnisse: Beispiele aus der Sozialgeschichte der Neuzeit,* ed. by colleagues and friends of Rudolf Vierhaus (Göttingen, 1982), 277–94.
90. On merchant-manufacturers' methods, see Schneer, *Die Noth der Leinen-Arbeiter,* 60–73; *Leipziger Zeitung,* 10 June 1844, article reprinted in Schwab-Felisch, *Die Weber,* 119; and Wolff, "Das Elend," reprinted in Schwab-Felisch, *Die Weber,* especially 139.
91. On Zwanziger's and other merchant-manufacturers' style of life, see Wolff, "Das Elend," reprinted in Schwab-Felisch, *Die Weber,* 140–45; Zimmerman, *Blüthe und Verfall,* excerpted in Praschek, *Hauptmanns "Die Weber,"* 56–57; and *Kölnische Zeitung,* 13 June 1844, reprinted in Schwab-Felisch, *Die Weber,* 122–24.
92. The song is reprinted in Schwab-Felisch, *Die Weber,* 115–18.
93. *Algemeine Zeitung* (Augsburg), 16 June 1844, reprinted in Schwab-Felisch, *Die Weber,* 120–21: "So eben hier eingetroffen, finde ich Bielau in einem Zustand welchen ich nie zu sehen gefürchtet habe. Ist noch ein Funke Eurer alten Liebe und Anhänglichkeit an Eure Grundherrschaft in Eurem Herzen, lebt noch ein Gefühl für Ordnung und Recht in Euch, so bitte, so beschwöre ich Euch, entsagt allem sträflichen Unternehem und kehrt

in den Zustand zurück welchen so lange zu bewahren Euer Ruhm war. Glaubt nich, dass ein anderes Interesse also das für Euer Wohl, für den Ruf Eures Ortes mich diese Bitte an Euch thun lässt. Ich hege noch die Überzeugung, dass, wenn nicht ein gluckliches Ungefähr mich in diesen Tagen von Euch fern gehalten hätte, Auftritte die – ich kann es nicht verhehlen – Euch schänden, vielleicht unterblieben wären. Nun zu Euch zurückgekehrt, will ich es versuchen, in Eurer Mitte und unter Euch in Güte die Ordnung wiederherzustellen, welche sonst unausbleiblich und durch die Gewalt der Waffen wieder aufrecht erhalten würde. Gott und Eure Liebe mögen mich daran unterstützen! Gez. Graf v. Sandreczky-Sandraschütz."

94. See, for example, references cited in note 49 to this chapter and, in addition, Roland Mousnier, *Fureurs paysannes: Les paysans dans les révoltes du XVIIe siècle (France, Russie, Chine)* (Paris, 1967); George Rudé, *The Crowd in History: A Study of Popular Disturbances in France and England, 1730–1848* (New York, 1964); Georges Lefebvre, *La grande peur de 1789* (Paris, 1932); and Reddy, *Rise of Market Culture*, 31–34, 59–60, 114–37.

95. This is especially evident in Acts 2 and 3.

96. "Die meisten der harrenden Webersleute gleichen Menschen, die vor die Schranken des Gerichts gestellt sind, wo sie in peinigender Gespanntheit eine Entscheidung über Tod und Leben zu erwarten haben. Hinwiederum haftet allen etwas Gedrücktes, dem Almosenempfänger Eigentümliches an, der, von Demütigung zu Demütigung schreitend, im Bewussstsein, nur geduldet zu sein, sich so klein als möglich zu machen gewohnt ist."

97. "Da hätte Herr Dreissiger weess Gott viel zu tun, wenn er sich um jede Kleenigkeit selber bekimmern sollte."

98. See the discussions of this issue in Chapters 1 and 3. On Paris, Berlin, and London, see Gareth Stedman Jones, *Outcast London: A Study in the Relationship between Classes in Victorian Society* (Oxford, 1971; Harmondsworth, 1976); Lenard R. Berlanstein, *The Working People of Paris, 1871–1914* (Baltimore, 1984); and Renzsch, *Handwerker und Lohnarbeiter*.

99. Jacques Rancière, "The Myth of the Artisan: Critical Reflections on a Category of Social History," *International Labor and Working Class History*, no. 24 (1983), 1–16; Reddy, *Rise of Market Culture*, 24–31, 134–37.

100. See Erik Olin Wright, *Classes* (London, 1985), 19–63; and idem, *Class, Crisis, and the State* (London, 1978). R. S. Neale, in his *Class in English History, 1680–1850* (Totowa, N.J., 1981), has argued that Marx never intended strict accounting of relation to the means of production to decide all questions of class identity; instead, the long-term vector of capitalist development should allow one to cut through the complexity of the present and identify those who are tending to be incorporated into the exploited sector. But this transforms the historian into a prophet; and prophesying about impending proletarianization has proved to be a difficult business, as discussed in the last two sections of Chapter 3.

101. See Asa Briggs, "The Language of 'Class' in Early Nineteenth-Century England," in Asa Briggs and John Saville, eds., *Essays in Labor History* (London, 1960), 43–73; Raymond Williams, *Keywords: A Vocabulary of Culture and Society* (New York, 1976), 51–59; and Sewell, *Work*, 78–86, 282–83.

102. Gareth Stedman Jones, "The Language of Chartism," in James Epstein and Dorothy Thompson, eds., *The Chartist Experience* (London, 1982), 3–58, reprinted under the title "Rethinking Chartism," in Stedman Jones, *Languages of Class: Studies in English Working-Class History, 1832–1982* (Cambridge, 1983), 90–178. Other essays in this collection are relevant as well, including the Introduction (1–24) and "Why Is the Labor Party in a Mess?" (239–56).

103. Reddy, *Rise of Market Culture*, 204–52.

104. Asa Briggs, ed., *Chartist Studies* (London, 1959); Epstein and Thompson, *The Chartist Experience;* Epstein, *The Lion of Freedom;* Thompson, *The Chartists.*
105. See the reference to this metaphor in Chapter 3, in the section entitled "Prices and classes"; it is taken from E. P. Thompson, "Eighteenth-Century English Society: Class Struggle without Class?" *Social History* 3 (1978): 133–65.

6. Conclusion

1. Alfred Cobban, *The Social Interpretation of the French Revolution* (Cambridge, 1964), 8–11.
2. E. P. Thompson, *The Making of the English Working Class* (New York, 1963).
3. It is worth noting, in passing at least, the resemblance between this conception of established practice and Pierre Bourdieu's notion of *habitus;* see his *Esquisse d'une théorie de la pratique* (Geneva, 1972), especially 157–200. The whole problem of liberating conceptions of action from the theoretical tyranny of structures, norms, functions, and roles is attracting increasing attention in recent years. See, for example, Renato Rosaldo, *Ilongot Headhunting, 1883–1974: A Study in Society and History* (Stanford, Calif., 1980); or Anthony Giddens, *Central Problems in Social Theory: Action, Structure, and Contradiction in Social Analysis* (Berkeley, Calif., 1979).
4. On the dissemination of simplified Marxism, see Claude Willard, *Le mouvement socialiste en France (1893–1905): Les guesdistes* (Paris, 1965), 159–221, 237–42; William M. Reddy, *The Rise of Market Culture: The Textile Trade and French Society, 1750–1900* (Cambridge, 1984), 289–325; Gareth Stedman Jones, "Engels and the History of Marxism," in Eric Hobsbawm, ed., *The History of Marxism,* I, *Marxism in Marx's Day* (Bloomington, Ind., 1982), 290–326; Raymond Williams, *Marxism and Literature* (Oxford, 1977); Lucien Goldmann, *Lukacs et Heidigger* (Paris, 1973); and Lucio Colletti, "Bernstein and the Marxism of the Second International," in idem, *From Rousseau to Lenin: Studies in Ideology and Society* (New York, 1972), 45–108. On small farmers, see Geoff Eley, *Reshaping the German Right: Radical Nationalism and Political Change after Bismarck* (New Haven, Conn., 1980); Aaron Noland, *The Founding of the French Socialist Party (1893–1905)* (Cambridge, Mass., 1956), 28–30; and Tony Judt, *Socialism in Provence (1871–1914): A Study of the Origins of the Modern French Left* (Cambridge, 1979).
5. For this whole section on the history of the Second International and its period, see works cited in the previous note; George Lefranc, *Le mouvement socialiste sous la Troisième République,* 2 vols. (Paris, 1977); Leslie Derfler, "Reformism and Jules Guesde," *International Review of Social History* 12 (1967):66–80; and Carl E. Schorske, *German Social Democracy, 1905–1917: The Development of the Great Schism* (Cambridge, Mass., 1955; New York, 1972).
6. On these incidents, see Reddy, *Rise of Market Culture,* 289–325; Gareth Stedman Jones, *Outcast London: A Study in the Relationship between Classes in Victorian Society* (Oxford, 1971; Harmondsworth, 1976), 315–21; Klaus Tenfelde, *Sozialgeschichte der Bergarbeiterschaft an der Ruhr im 19. Jahrhundert* (Bonn, 1981), 573–97; and Barrington Moore, *Injustice: The Social Bases of Obedience and Revolt* (New York, 1978), 227–74. See also Michelle Perrot, *Les ouvriers en grève: France, 1871–1890,* 2 vols. (Paris, 1974), II; 411–49, especially 431, where Perrot remarks that 72 percent of strikes in France involved no unions in the period 1871–90.
7. Rosa Luxemburg, *The Mass Strike: The Political Party and the Trade Unions,* trans. Patrick Lavin (1906; New York, 1971); 58–59.
8. *Vorwärts,* 25 January 1905.
9. Examples of studies that have come to such conclusions include, for France, Joan W. Scott, *The Glassworkers of Carmaux* (Cambridge, Mass., 1974); Michael P. Hanagan, *The Logic of Solidarity: Artisans and Industrial Workers in Three French Towns, 1871–1914* (Ur-

bana, Ill., 1980); Perrot, *Les ouvriers en grève;* and Edward Shorter and Charles Tilly, *Strikes in France, 1830—1968* (Cambridge, 1974). On Germany, see Alf Lüdtke, "Cash, Coffee-Breaks, Horse-Play: *'Eigensinn'* and Politics among Factory Workers in Late Nineteenth- and Early Twentieth-Century Germany," paper delivered to the Davis Center Seminar, Princeton University, April 1982; Tenfelde, *Sozialgeschichte der Bergarbeiterschaft;* David F. Crew, *Town in the Ruhr: A Social History of Bochum, 1860—1914* (New York, 1979); and Mary Nolan, *Social Democracy and Society: Working-Class Radicalism in Düsseldorf, 1890—1920* (Cambridge, 1981). On England, see Keith Nield, "A Symptomatic Dispute? Notes on the Relation between Marxian Theory and Historical Practice in Britain," *Social Research* 47 (1980):479—506; Stedman Jones, *Outcast London;* and idem, "Working-Class Culture and Working-Class Politics in London, 1870—1900: Notes on the Remaking of a Working Class," in idem, *Languages of Class: Studies in English Working-Class History, 1832—1982* (Cambridge, 1983), 179—238. See also, in Chapter 1, the section entitled "Standard of Living and Way of Life in England" and the references cited there. Of course, these works are merely representative of a much more general trend of research.

10. Tenfelde, *Sozialgeschichte der Bergarbeiterschaft,* 575. Tenfelde argues that the miners needed "Gewinnorientierung und Dispositionsallmacht ihrerseits in Frage stellende Machtmittel."

11. Ibid., 574; he comments that "nach der rechtlichen und materiellen Auslieferung der Arbeiterschaft an die Gesetzlichkeit und Dynamik der industriellen Markte," a formative opposition between capital and labor resulted.

12. Moore, *Injustice,* 227—74.

13. Ibid., 254.

14. Ibid., 253.

15. Ibid., 241.

16. See works on Germany cited in note 9 to this chapter, as well as Hans-Ulrich Wehler, *Das deutsche Kaiserreich, 1871—1918,* 4th ed. (Göttingen, 1980), 131—40.

17. Klaus Saul, "Zwischen Repression und Integration: Staat, Gewerkschaften, und Arbeitskampf in kaiserlichen Deutschland, 1884—1914," in K. Tenfelde and H. Volkmann, eds., *Streik: Zur Geschichte des Arbeitskampfes in Deutschland während der Industrialisierung* (Munich, 1981), 220.

18. Crew, *Town in the Ruhr,* 223.

19. Ibid.

20. Reddy, *Rise of Market Culture,* 289—336.

21. Donald Reid, "Decazeville: Company Town and Working-Class Community, 1826—1914," in John M. Merriman, ed., *French Cities in the Nineteenth Century* (New York, 1981), 193—203; see also Donald Reid, *The Miners of Decazeville: A Genealogy of Deindustrialization* (Cambridge, Mass., 1985), 72—113.

22. E. P. Thompson, "The Peculiarities of the English," in idem, *The Poverty of Theory and Other Essays* (New York, 1978), 245—303; Nield, "A Symptomatic Dispute?"

23. David Blackbourn and Geoff Eley, *Mythen deutscher Geschichtsschreibung: Die gescheiterte bürgerliche Revolution von 1848* (Frankfurt, 1980).

24. David Blackbourn and Geoff Eley, *The Peculiarities of German History: Bourgeois Society and Politics in the Nineteenth Century* (Oxford, 1984), 2.

, 25. See James Joll, *The Second International, 1889—1914* (New York, 1966); Michelle Perrot and Annie Kriegel, *Le socialisme français et le pouvoir* (Paris, 1966); Annie Kriegel, *Les communistes français* (Paris, 1968); Peter N. Stearns, *Revolutionary Syndicalism and French Labor: A Cause without Rebels* (New Brunswick, N.J., 1971); Shorter and Tilly, *Strikes in France;* Bernard H. Moss, *The Origins of the French Labor Movement: The Socialism of Skilled Workers, 1830—1914* (Berkeley, Calif., 1976); and Jean-Paul Brunet, *Saint-Denis, la ville rouge, 1890–1939* (Paris, 1980). On Laval, see Robert Aron, *The Vichy Regime, 1940–44* (New York, 1958).

26. Sean Wilentz, "Against Exceptionalism: Class Consciousness and the American Labor Movement," *International Labor and Working Class History*, no. 26 (1984), 1–24.

27. Wehler, *Das deutsche Kaiserreich*, 87–90; Moore, *Injustice*, 173–96.

28. Crew, *Town in the Ruhr;* Tenfelde, *Sozialgeschichte der Bergarbeiterschaft;* Nolan, *Social Democracy and Society;* Rolande Trempé, *Les mineurs de Carmaux, 1848–1914*, 2 vols. (Paris, 1971); Scott, *Glassworkers;* Hanagan, *Logic of Solidarity;* Robert Q. Gray, *The Labour Aristocracy in Victorian Edinburgh* (Oxford, 1976); Geoffrey Crossick, *An Artisan Elite in Victorian Society: Kentish London, 1840–1880* (London, 1978); Patrick Joyce, *Work, Society, and Politics: The Culture of the Factory in Later Victorian England* (New Brunswick, N.J., 1980).

29. Joyce, *Work, Society, and Politics;* Moore, *Injustice*, 223–24; see also Alf Lüdtke, "Erfahrung von Industriearbeitern: Thesen zu einer vernachlässigten Dimension der Arbeitergeschichte," in Werner Conze and Ulrich Engelhardt, eds., *Arbeiter im Industrialisierungsprozess: Herkunft, Lage, und Verhalten* (Stuttgart, 1979), 494–512.

30. On Krupp, see references in Chapter 1, note 70. See also Lion Murard and Patrick Zylberman, *Le petit travailleur infatigable ou le prolétaire régénéré: Villes-usines, habitat, et intimités au XIXe siècle* (Fontenay-sous-Bois, 1976); and the special number of *Le mouvement social*, no. 99 (1977), "Au pays de Schneider."

31. Stedman Jones, "Working-Class Culture"; Lenard R. Berlanstein, *The Working People of Paris, 1871–1914* (Baltimore, 1984), 39–73, 122–50; David Smith, "Tonypandy, 1910: Definitions of Community," *Past and Present*, no. 87 (1980), 158–84.

32. Lüdtke, " 'Eigensinn.' " See also Peter Linebaugh, "Labor History without the Labor Process: A Note on John Gast and His Times," *Social History* 7 (1982):319–28; and Richard Price, "The Labor Process and Labor History," *Social History* 8 (1983):57–75.

33. Antoine-Quentin Fouquier-Tinville has found a special place in the thought of Richard Cobb; see his *The Police and the People: French Popular Protest, 1789–1820* (Oxford, 1970). On Germans joining the NSDAP in 1933, see William S. Allen, *The Nazi Seizure of Power: The Experience of a Single German Town, 1922–1945*, 2d ed. (New York, 1984), 240–42.

34. A. J. P. Taylor, *The Course of German History: A Survey of the Development of Germany since 1815* (London, n.d.; New York, 1961); idem, *Bismarck, the Man and the Statesman* (New York, 1955).

35. Wehler, *Das deutsche Kaiserreich*, 60–69.

36. Barrington Moore, *Social Origins of Dictatorship and Democracy: Lord and Peasant in the Making of the Modern World* (Boston, 1966), 3–39.

37. *Washington Post*, 28 July 1985.

38. John Rawls, *A Theory of Justice* (Cambridge, Mass., 1971).

39. Jürgen Habermas, *Theorie des kommunikativen Handels*, I, *Handlungsrationalität und gesellschaftliche Rationalisierung* (Frankfurt, 1981); trans. Thomas McCarthy under the title *The Theory of Communicative Action*, I, *Reason and the Rationalization of Society* (Boston, 1984).

40. M. I. Finley, *The Ancient Economy* (Berkeley, Calif., 1973), 25.

Index

An italicized number in this index refers to a note at the end of the text and follows the number of the page on which the note appears. All authors cited more than once in the notes have been indexed.

257

Index